New Medieval Literatures

New Medieval Literatures is an annual journal of work on medieval textual cultures. Its scope is inclusive of work across the theoretical, archival, philological, and historicist methodologies associated with medieval literary studies. The title announces an interest both in new writing about medieval culture and in new academic writing. As well as featuring challenging new articles, each issue includes an analytical survey by a leading international medievalist of recent work in an emerging or established field. The editors aim to engage with intellectual and cultural pluralism in the Middle Ages and now. Within this generous brief, they recognize only two criteria: excellence and originality.

Editors

Rita Copeland *University of Pennsylvania*
David Lawton *Washington University in St. Louis*
Wendy Scase *University of Birmingham*

Advisory Board

Jocelyn Wogan-Browne *University of York*
Hans Ulrich Gumbrecht *Stanford University*
Jeffrey Hamburger *Harvard University*
Sarah Kay *Princeton University*
Alastair Minnis *Yale University*
Margaret Clunies Ross *University of Sydney*
Miri Rubin *Queen Mary, University of London*
Paul Strohm *Columbia University*
Christiane Klapisch-Zuber *École des Hautes Études en Sciences Sociales, Paris*

Submissions are invited for future issues. Please write to any of the editors:

Rita Copeland
Department of Classical Studies
University of Pennsylvania
201 Logan Hall
Philadelphia, Pennsylvania 19104, USA
rcopelan@sas.upenn.edu

David Lawton
Department of English
Washington University
Campus Box 1122, 1 Brookings Drive
St. Louis, Missouri 63130-4899, USA
dalawton@artsci.wustl.edu

Wendy Scase
Department of English
University of Birmingham
Edgbaston
Birmingham, B15 2TT, UK
W.L.Scase@bham.ac.uk

For information about subscriptions and orders, guidelines for contributors, and contents of previous issues, please visit the NML Web site: http://artsci.wustl.edu/~nml/

NEW MEDIEVAL LITERATURES

9 (2007)

Edited by

David Lawton, Wendy Scase, and Rita Copeland

BREPOLS

D/2008/0095/27
ISBN 978-2-503-52331-6
ISSN 1465-3737

Printed in the E.U. on acid-free paper

CONTENTS

FOREWORD

The essays in volume 9 of *New Medieval Literatures* range, as usual, across disciplines, languages, and historical periods. They concern themselves with rhetoric and ethics, with the pleasure and labour of writing and book production — including the professional pleasure and labour of medieval and early-modern studies. A frankly experimental innovation in the current volume is the inclusion of two, often polemical, symposia which raise fundamental issues about our modern scholarly practice. Both arise from conference presentations: the first a panel from MLA in Philadelphia in December 2006 on the topic 'Can You be a Comparatist in Translation?' convened by Jeanette Beer; the second from the New Chaucer Society congress in New York in July 2006 on the topic 'What Is Happening to the Middle Ages?' proposed by Stephanie Trigg. I am grateful to Jeanette Beer for guiding her panel's work into print. We have not sought to erase traces of the original occasion: oral performance is a feature of the volume, as in Martin Camargo's contribution, 'Medieval Rhetoric Delivers'. It is balanced by the material work and circumstances of the writer in several contributions, culminating in Alexandra Gillespie's analytical survey on the history of the book. We hope that the professional reflection and polemic in the volume will stimulate thought and creative disagreement, some of which may reach future pages of *New Medieval Literatures*.

My thanks on behalf of the editors, as ever, go to the contributors, for work that sets the highest standards; to the readers of individual submissions, whose advice has proved so helpful; to Brepols, especially Simon Forde; to Heather Padgen; and to Sarah Noonan, for her invaluable assistance in compiling the completed volume.

David Lawton

NARCISSUS AFTER ARISTOTLE:
LOVE AND ETHICS IN *LE ROMAN DE LA ROSE*

Jessica Rosenfeld

A
ristotle is rarely considered a philosopher of love. That title is not uncommonly attached to his teacher Plato, who gave philosophy fables of human incompleteness and erotic desire, and ideals of mystical union and ascent. Plato's narrative of physical lack translated into both physical and spiritual longing, as well as his suspicion of actions rooted in this longing, resonates nicely with our post-Freudian understanding of ourselves as desiring subjects, condemned to acting out fantasies of which we are at most partially aware. Aristotle's refusal of transcendence, and an insistence on a rational understanding of the self that includes one's physical surroundings, one's emotions, and one's relationships to others, does not seem to take into account the unconscious sexual drives that many now assume to be constitutive of our desires and our identities. For the psychoanalyst Jacques Lacan, Aristotle's neglect of sexual desire, placing it outside the field of morality, renders the philosopher's ethics 'surprising, primitive, paradoxical and, in truth, incomprehensible'.[1] This

I am grateful to several people who generously gave feedback on various versions of this essay and who have contributed in many ways to my thinking on the topic: Kevin Brownlee, Rita Copeland, Emily Steiner, David Wallace, Simon Gaunt, Bruce Holsinger, and Mark Miller.

[1] Jacques Lacan, *The Ethics of Psychoanalysis, 1959–1960*, trans. by Dennis Porter (New York, 1997), p. 5. For a different take on the role of sexuality in ancient Greek culture, see David Halperin, *One Hundred Years of Homosexuality and Other Essays on Greek Love* (New York, 1990). Halperin's extension of Foucault's theory that sexuality is culturally constructed does not give us an Aristotle who is blind to the centrality of the sexual drives to human behaviour and ethics, but rather an Aristotle who includes a range of amorous, familial, companionable, and charitable behaviour under his discussion of 'Friendship' — a category that for him is as wide-ranging and

essay argues, nevertheless, that the development of medieval Aristotelian ethics is an essential part of the development of that famous and much-debated medieval phenomenon 'courtly love' — the phenomenon that Lacan and others have determined to be foundational for our own modern experience of erotic desire.

The synthesis of the discourses of courtly poetry and philosophy was not coincident with the birth of Western vernacular love poetry. Historian of philosophy William Courtenay expresses surprise that, given twelfth-century poetry's preoccupations with love and loss, theories of desire, longing, despair, and pleasure did not enter into the concerns of twelfth-century scholastic writers, especially given that theologians during this period developed the concept of pure, self-sacrificial love of God (*castus amor*).[2] Courtenay notes that Peter Lombard's *Sentences* is unusual for the twelfth century in that he chose the topic of enjoyment — inhering with love in an object for its own sake — for his opening theme.[3] Yet when the Lombard's book later became central to the university curriculum, the nature of enjoyment came to the forefront of theological concerns.[4] Commentaries on the *Sentences* defined love, addressed the relationship between use and enjoyment, and discussed love's relationship to both pleasure and pain. In a sense, scholastic philosophy followed the lead of poetry, which had addressed issues of love, pleasure, and despair from the beginning of its entrée into romantic love. The ethical stakes of vernacular love poetry had always far exceeded the dutiful *ethica supponitur* with which medieval commentators tagged classical poetry, from Virgil to Ovid to Boethius.[5] The logic that placed poetry 'under' ethics not only allowed for the freedom to read subversive classical poets such as Ovid, and often to recuperate them in Christian or simply practical moral contexts, but also allowed vernacular poets to explore the ethics of speech and silence, passionate love, friendship, social networks, and the conflict between

encompassing as sex was for Freud and continues to be (arguably) for us. For an argument that Aristotle's *philia* should be translated as 'love', see Gregory Vlastos, 'The Individual as Object of Love in Plato', in *Platonic Studies* (Princeton, 1973), p. 4.

[2] William Courtenay, 'Between Despair and Love: Some Late Medieval Modifications of Augustine's Teaching on Fruition and Psychic States', in *Augustine, the Harvest, and Theology (1300–1650): Essays Dedicated to Heiko Augustinus Oberman in Honor of His Sixtieth Birthday*, ed. by Kenneth Hagen (New York, 1990), pp. 5–20 (p. 14).

[3] Augustine gives this definition of 'enjoyment' (*fruitio*) in *De doctrina Christiana*, I. 4.

[4] Courtenay, 'Between Despair and Love', p. 15.

[5] Judson Boyce Allen, *The Ethical Poetic of the Later Middle Ages: A Decorum of Convenient Distinction* (Toronto, 1982), p. 6 and passim.

the secular and the spiritual.[6] By the time enjoyment became a main topic in philosophy, its terms and questions had been contemplated in poetry for quite some time. In the thirteenth century, both philosophy and poetry grappled with shifting understandings of earthly and divine love, physical and intellectual pleasure, and human happiness. The Aristotelianism that came to dominate this period with the full translation and dissemination of many of the philosopher's works into Latin did not leave medieval understandings of love untouched. Narcissus was always 'after Aristotle', as my title seems unnecessarily to remind us, but the succession was reversed for the Latin Middle Ages, where Ovid preceded the Philosopher by centuries, at least in terms of textual reception.[7] My concern here is to address what happens to Narcissus — Ovid's Narcissus along with his avatars, the self-reflexive, self-sacrificing protagonists of much love poetry — after Aristotle is fully returned to medieval discourse.

I concentrate below on the way that Aristotle's ethical works transformed both poetic and philosophical understandings of love, taking as my focus the *Roman de la Rose* of Guillaume de Lorris and Jean de Meun. An examination of thirteenth-century Aristotelianism in this light will allow us to add another facet to our reading of Jean's transformation of Guillaume's *Rose*, to the poetic legacy of the conjoined text, and also to our understanding of courtly love's legacy in the psychoanalytic ethics of Lacan. Understanding Aristotle's evolution from 'incomprehensible' in Lacan's Seminar VII, *The Ethics of Psychoanalysis*, to a philosopher whose seeking after the 'jouissance of being' paved the way for a medieval 'physical theory of love'[8] by the time of his Seminar XX, *Encore*, is essential to the ongoing project of parsing the difficult but mutually illuminating relationship between contemporary 'theory' and the medieval.[9] Aristotle's

---

[6] See Simon Gaunt, *Love and Death in Medieval French and Occitan Courtly Literature: Martyrs to Love* (Oxford, 2006), for an exploration of the way that twelfth-century lyric and romance created a space for ethical debate through their mixing of the sacred and the profane, and especially through the motif of sacrifice and death for passionate love.

[7] Boethius performed the earliest surviving Latin translations of Aristotle's philosophy but completed only the *Categories*, *De interpretatione*, *Prior Analytics*, *Topics*, and *Sophistici elenchi*. For a narrative of translations of the Aristotelian corpus into Latin, see 'Aristoteles Latinus' in *The Cambridge History of Later Medieval Philosophy: From the Rediscovery of Aristotle to the Disintegration of Scholasticism, 1100–1600*, ed. by Norman Kretzmann, Anthony Kenny, Jan Pinborg, and assoc. ed. Eleonore Stump (Cambridge, 1982), pp. 45–79.

[8] Lacan, *On Feminine Sexuality: The Limits of Love and Knowledge (Encore), 1972–1973*, trans. by Bruce Fink (New York, 1999), p. 70.

[9] For readings of Lacan's medievalism, see Bruce Holsinger, *The Premodern Condition: Medievalism and the Making of Theory* (Chicago, 2005), and Erin Labbie, *Lacan's Medievalism*

transformation from incomprehensibly asexual to a philosopher of love and pleasure is not confined to Lacan's seminars, but is a way of understanding a medieval historical phenomenon, embedded in the reception of Aristotelian ethics in the thirteenth century. I am interested here not in a Lacanian reading of Aristotle, nor even an Aristotelian reading of the *Rose*, but in the way that Lacan's evolving readings of Aristotle and medieval poetry in the context of psychoanalytic ethics allow us to see that Aristotle was crucial not only for a late-medieval systematizing of knowledge and for a transformed relationship to the sensory world, but for new ways of thinking about human desire that touched both moral philosophy and poetry. The *Roman de la Rose* — as a poem at the centre of the intellectual universe of the thirteenth century, and a poem that would immediately become and remain central to the traditions of love poetry, dream vision, encyclopedic narrative, personification allegory, and penitential and confessional narratives — is thus at the centre of this story.

The modern recontextualization of the *Rose* within its full intellectual environment at the end of the thirteenth century is a project that began with Gérard Paré more than fifty years ago, and which remains uncompleted, though other critics besides Paré have located Jean de Meun at the centre of intellectual discourse and controversies.[10] Alastair Minnis argues for the similarity of Jean's 'texts and intellectual pursuits' with those of the thirteenth-century Parisian arts faculty, lightly noting that Jean was writing his *Rose* at the same time that Boethius of Dacia, the 'radical Aristotelian', was active at the University of Paris.[11]

(Minneapolis, 2006). For an extended bidirectional engagement with the relationship between Lacan and the medieval, see the scholarship of L. O. Aranye Fradenburg, especially *Sacrifice Your Love: Psychoanalysis, Historicism, Chaucer* (Minneapolis, 2002).

[10] Daniel Heller-Roazen makes this observation in *Fortune's Faces: The 'Roman de la Rose' and the Poetics of Contingency* (Baltimore, 2003), p. 78, as a prelude to his own consideration of the poem's depiction of Fortune in the context of Aristotelian philosophy (pp. 79–99). See Gérard Paré, *Les Idées et les lettres au XIIIᵉ siècle: 'Le Roman de la Rose'* (Montréal, 1947) and *Le 'Roman de la Rose' et la scholastique courtoise* (Paris, 1941). Giorgio Agamben situates the *Rose* in the context of thirteenth-century theories of imagination, lovesickness, and language in *Stanzas: Word and Phantasm in Western Culture*, trans. by Ronald L. Martinez (Minneapolis, 1993), pp. 63–89. Suzanne Akbari places both Guillaume and Jean, along with Dante and Chaucer, in the context of scholastic interest in optics in *Seeing through the Veil: Optical Theory and Medieval Allegory* (Toronto, 2004). The *Rose* has more often been read in the context of twelfth-century neoplatonism, as in Winthrop Wetherbee, *Platonism and Poetry in the Twelfth Century* (Princeton, 1972).

[11] Alastair Minnis, *Magister Amoris: 'The Roman de la Rose' and Vernacular Hermeneutics* (Oxford, 2001), pp. 4–6.

Jean seems to be patently interested in the new learning of the schools, an interest that invites speculation that Jean was motivated for this reason to work with the commentary of William of Aragon — to him a very recent, very Aristotelian text — when writing his translation of the sixth-century Boethius's *Consolation of Philosophy*.[12] There is also evidence for an educated medieval audience for the poem: it was listed (as missing) in the 1338 inventory of the Sorbonne Library and manuscript evidence points to readers who approached the poem with a wide range of perspectives and concerns.[13] A mid-fourteenth-century manuscript (MS Bibl. Nat. fr. 1560) demonstrates that at least one of its readers engaged with the poem as a part of philosophical discourse. This reader glosses the poem with references to Aristotle, among other learned writers, and specifically quotes the first book of the *Ethics* in reference to the personification of Reason: 'Primo ethicorum. Semper ratio deprecatur ad optimam' (The first book of the *Ethics*. Reason always urges to the best; fol. 29ʳ, v. 4198).[14] Sylvia Huot reminds us that 'for a fourteenth-century reader, there was nothing strange about seeking points of contact between poetry, philosophy, theology, law'.[15]

I will begin my exploration of the Aristotelian aspects of the *Rose* with Guillaume de Lorris, in order to investigate why his poem might have provided such an attractive text for Jean's later experimentation with new ethical ideas. Below, I explore the way in which the 'new Aristotle', that flood of translation into Latin from Greek and Arabic in the twelfth and thirteenth centuries, affected courtly poetry by examining this famously bifurcated poem as a work divided not only by a temporal gap and a shift in authorship, but by the impact of the full translation of Aristotle's *Nicomachean Ethics* which takes place during that gap. Most importantly, this translation brought with it Aristotle's definition of contemplative activity as the highest human happiness, accessible in this life. This understanding of ethics as bound to the human sphere, and as oriented toward a good achievable in this life, would be particularly difficult for medieval philosophy to absorb. In this context of debate, Jean de Meun takes a poem already steeped in ethical categories of self-knowledge, desire, and free will and exploits its fissures in order to explore the erotic assumptions of both courtly poetry and scholastic

---

[12] Alastair Minnis, 'Aspects of the Medieval French and English Traditions of the *De Consolatione Philosophiae*', in *Boethius: His Life, Thought, and Influence*, ed. by Margaret Gibson (Oxford, 1981), pp. 312–61 (pp. 323–24).

[13] Sylvia Huot, *'The Romance of the Rose' and Its Medieval Readers* (Cambridge, 1993), p. 84.

[14] Described in Huot, *'The Romance of the Rose'*, p. 50.

[15] Huot, *'The Romance of the Rose'*, p. 74.

philosophy. For Jean, this is still a poem about love, but it is a poem about how the poetic expression of erotic desire must always also be about intellectual and spiritual desire. His renamed *Rose*, now the *Miroër aus Amoreus*, will ideally include all of the conflicting contemporary sciences of love in its polished surface.

Guillaume de Lorris: Narcissus and the 'Vita Activa'

Jean de Meun does not choose to work upon what he sees as a naive, earlier poem, but is interested in the 'first *Rose*' precisely because Guillaume de Lorris in certain ways seems to address Aristotelian ethical controversies even before the full translation of the *Nicomachean Ethics* into Latin. Operating within a framework prior to the dissemination of Aristotle's contemplative definition of human happiness, Guillaume's poem explores the ethical implications of an erotic quest that remains firmly in a circular structure of desire and poetic activity, a structure that on its face does not seem to trouble the distinctions that medieval philosophy maintains between imperfect earthly goods and the perfect good reserved for divine illumination.[16] Instead the poem appears to adhere to conventional, ironic parallels between the unattainable love object and the *summum bonum* of the heavenly realm; in his dream vision Amant courts his inaccessible rose by maintaining the 'commandments' given to him by Amor, the God of Love. It is Guillaume's exploration of erotic desire as expressed in a variety of activities associated with contemplation that make his poem so relevant to thirteenth-century ethics. Despite the poem's narrative form, Guillaume maintains the lyric stasis of Amant's quest through a collapsing of the distinction between productive and unproductive labour, especially with respect to the labours of self-reflection and writing love poetry. These terms will become key to medieval understandings of Aristotelian contemplation as a pleasurable activity, esteemed in itself; Guillaume's linking of the Narcissus myth, poetic activity, intellectual self-reflection, and physical labour will prove a fruitful nexus for his successor.

The protagonist-narrator Amant's entry into the garden of delight appears to be an entry into the perils not only of irrational desire, but irrational poetic activity. He is first welcomed by a figure named Oiseuse who allows him entry into the garden. Earl Jeffrey Richards has argued convincingly that we should understand Guillaume's use of *oiseuse* as continuous with the twelfth-century use

---

[16] On the circularity of Amant's quest in Guillaume's *Rose*, see David Hult, *Self-fulfilling Prophecies: Readership and Authority in the First Roman de la Rose* (Cambridge, 1986), p. 183.

of the word to connote verbal folly or frivolity, a definition more encompassing than 'Idleness', given in Charles Dahlberg's translation.[17] Richards argues that in the twelfth and early thirteenth centuries the term shifted away from its Latin etymology (though he notes that the word *otium* is itself polyvalent) and did not carry strong associations of either sinful idleness or the leisure necessary for study. Amant recounts his first impressions of Oiseuse's paradise, full of birds and their songs. In the midst of describing his past gratitude to the figure who offered him entry, the speaker shifts persona to become external narrator again, breaking into the present and future tense to remark to his reader that he will describe the appearance of the garden:

> fui plains de grant joliveté
> et lores soi ge bien et vi
> qu'Oiseuse m'avoit bien servi,
> qui m'avoit en ce deduit mis.
> Bien deüsse estre ses amis,
> quant ele m'avoit desfermé
> le guichet dou vergier ramé.
> Des or mes, si con je savrai,
> tot l'afeire vos conterai.
>
> (ll. 682–90)

(I was filled with great joy and I saw that Oiseuse, who had placed me in the midst of this delight, had served me well. My love was due to her when she unlocked the wicket gate of the branching garden. From now on, I shall recount to you, as well as I know, how I went to work.)[18]

[17] Earl Jeffrey Richards, 'Reflections on Oiseuse's Mirror: Iconographic Tradition, Luxuria, and the *Roman de la Rose*', *Zeitschrift für romanische Philologie*, 98.3–4 (1982), 296–311 (p. 309). Richards distinguishes his approach to *Oiseuse* from D. W. Robertson and John Fleming, who both caution against reading this figure as anything but idleness and the gateway to cupidity. See Fleming, *The 'Roman de la Rose': A Study in Allegory and Iconography* (Princeton, 1969), pp. 73–81, and D. W. Robertson, *A Preface to Chaucer* (Princeton, 1962), pp. 92–93. Agamben resolves the binary question as to whether Oiseuse means lechery or leisure by interpreting her mirror — and thus Oiseuse — as imagination itself, encompassing spiritual contemplation and false fantasy (*Stanzas*, p. 88, n. 16). Frédéric Godefroy gives a variety of definitions for *oiseuse*: oisiveté, lâcheté, paresse, chose oiseuse, inutile, parole vaine, futilité; see *Dictionnaire de l'ancienne langue française* (Paris, 1881–1902).

[18] All internal references to *Le Roman de la Rose* are to Félix Lecoy's standard edition of the poem (Paris, 1965–70), though I will occasionally refer to Ernest Langlois's edition (Paris, 1914–24). The translations are from Charles Dahlberg, *The Romance of the Rose* (Princeton, 1971),

In Lecoy's edition of the poem (based on MS Bibl. Nat. fr. 1573), the narrator promises to tell us about the 'afeire' or disposition of the garden, while Langlois's edition has the narrator promising to tell us 'coment j'ovrai' (how I went to work; l. 690). In either case, the status of work, loving, and writing is immediately raised at this moment of entry and introduction; allegorically, Amant is allowed to enter the *locus amoenus* through his engagement with 'oiseuse', and this engagement is linked to the work of narrative, now associated with verbal frivolity.[19] Dreaming placed Amant in this position, we understand, but the narrator's poetic activity places him there again so that we may witness his experience. The personified Oiseuse suggests that Amant's primary activity will be a verbal activity, a learning about love *par parole* that will be the subject of critique by Amor himself.[20] The verb *ouvrer* as an intransitive verb means simply 'to work', but as a transitive verb *ouvrer* can mean 'to work materials', the material of language in this context. Amant's work and the affairs of the garden are the work of falling in love, of pursuing the rose, and ultimately of continuing this pursuit in the very writing of the *Rose* itself. We will hear not only about Amant's dream-work, but the art of the narrator. Just farther on, the poem reveals the narrator's work to be narrative itself, for as he explains his task, he cannot convey the simultaneity of his experience upon entering the garden, but must 'tot vos conteré par ordre' (tell you everything in order; l. 697), creating narrative out of a single moment of experience. Claire Nouvet has read the poem's conception of allegory as a split between an ideal vision that encompasses everything at once and the fallen, allegorical speculum that requires that we see things in a discrete, temporal succession.[21] Here the fate of fallen vision is coextensive with the experience of both reading and writing love poetry. Amant has a simultaneous, comprehensive experience, but transferring that experience into verse requires a fall into

though I have silently amended this translation in limited places and have left the word *oiseuse* untranslated.

[19] Hult suggests that the birdsong (the songs of the 'oisiaus') directly before this narrative intrusion calls up associations with poetic activity and thus in effect calls the narrator/poet into being at this moment (*Self-fulfilling Prophecies*, p. 162).

[20] Richards, 'Reflections on Oiseuse's Mirror', p. 311.

[21] Claire Nouvet, 'An Allegorical Mirror: The Pool of Narcissus in Guillaume de Lorris' *Romance of the Rose*', *Romanic Review*, 91.4 (2000), 353–74 (p. 367). Nouvet cites Augustine's *Confessions* on 'intellectual heaven' (*caelum intellectuale*) as the place where the intellect is privileged to 'know all at once' (*nosse simul*) (XII. 13).

temporality and thus into 'oiseuse' — the verbal frivolity associated with courtly delights and romance writing.

Given that the key emblem associated with this strangely active Oiseuse is the mirror in her hand, it is tempting to take her as an ironic figure for the contemplative life. In the appendix to his book *The Roman de la Rose*, John Fleming suggestively places a manuscript illustration of Oiseuse with her comb and mirror next to an illustration from another *Rose* manuscript of Christ with his mirror of wisdom — both figures holding their reflected faces in the same manner.[22] Yet Fleming also states firmly that while mirrors in general in the late Middle Ages mean many things, including *luxuria*, self-knowledge, and the contemplative life, Oiseuse *is luxuria,* and her mirror has nothing whatsoever to do with the *vita contemplativa.*[23] While it seems unlikely that Guillaume is satirizing the contemplative life as idle or cupidinous, it is possible to imagine Oiseuse as a gently parodic figure of contemplation gone awry — turning herself to the vanity of her toilette and inviting Amant to engage in the irrational activity of writing romance narratives rather than rational pleasures.[24] Within the ethical landscape of the garden, she contrasts strikingly with Amor, whose commandments, and especially his proclamation that 'covient vivre | les amanz, qu'il lor est mestiers' (lovers must live, for life is their occupation; ll. 2594–95) add up to a recommendation that Amant should choose the active life of loving rather than writing books about love — an irrational, unending project. For while up to this point the narrator's work has appeared to be the work of narrative, at other moments the work of romance writing is revealed to be definitively antinarrative; indeed it appears to condemn one to continual stasis. Just before his recommendation of 'living' as an occupation, Amor tells Amant that

> Nes qu'em puet espuisier la mer,
> ne poroit nus les maus d'amer
> conter en romanz ne en livre.
> (ll. 2591–93)

---

[22] Fleming, *The Roman de la Rose*, appendix images 17 and 18: Pierpont Morgan MSS M. 0324, fol. 5ᵛ, and MSS M. 0132, fol. 130ᵛ.

[23] Fleming, *The Roman de la Rose*, pp. 76–78; Richards notes in opposition that the vice of *luxuria* was not typically depicted with mirror iconography in the thirteenth century, but more often with an image of a woman whose abdomen has been set upon by toads or snakes ('Reflections', pp. 296–304).

[24] For a reading of Guillaume's *Rose* as addressing the difficulty of attaining self-knowledge through figures of deceptive vision and mirrors, see Akbari, *Seeing through the Veil*, pp. 19–20 and chap. 3.

(No more than one can empty the sea could any man recount in a romance or a book the woes of love.)

Considering that the *Rose* itself is largely constituted by the woes and joys of Amant, it appears that the poem is exactly the hopeless task that Amor warns against undertaking. The endless nature of romance writing is perhaps one more reason for the seemingly unfinished nature of the poem.[25] Rather than writing a romance for his beloved lady, the poet should be 'living', according to Amor. At this moment the multiple subject positions of the narrator come to the fore again: as the character of Amant, he follows Amor's precepts, but as narrator and author figure he is engaged in pointless labour. Whereas the personified figure of Oiseuse had melded the notions of productive and unproductive activity by locating both loving and writing in the garden of delight, Amor disentangles the two kinds of activities.[26] Writing love poetry becomes an idle task in a negative sense, while loving itself is valorized, distinguished from merely participating in a scene of courtly flirtations and pleasures. Amor ethicizes this scene, makes distinctions, and demands a particular kind of productive activity. With this contrast between Oiseuse and Amor, it appears that unfocused desire allows for the free play of both physical and intellectual pleasure, while focused desire brings with it a series of commandments and rules, prescribing activity oriented toward a particular end; in this way the recipe for the good, active (courtly) life comes into being. Guillaume's *Rose* seems interested in illustrating how love poetry depends upon a tension between deferred, specific desire that brings with it an elaborate code of conduct and a diffuse desire that remains objectless. He might agree with many modern readers of troubadour poetry who have understood the poets to be less in love with a particular person than interested in perpetuating desire itself.

The poem's unstable oppositions between productive and unproductive labour, writing and loving, are most poignantly expressed in the episode of Amant at the fountain of love. In recounting Amant's gaze into the perilous mirror of Narcissus, Guillaume sets up a parallel between the experience of encountering an exemplum as mirror, and the physical, immediate experience of self-reflection.

---

[25] On the 'finishedness' of Guillaume's poem, see Hult, *Self-Fulfilling Prophecies*, p. 174, and Kevin Brownlee, 'Pygmalion, Mimesis, and the Multiple Endings of the *Roman de la Rose*', *Yale French Studies*, 95 (1999), 193–211 (p. 195).

[26] Here my reading of Oiseuse has some affinities with Gregory Sadlek's interpretation; he argues that even more than leisure, 'nonproductivity is the hallmark of [Oiseuse's] character'. See *Idleness Working: The Discourse of Love's Labor from Ovid through Chaucer and Gower* (Washington, DC, 2004), p. 123.

Suzanne Akbari has explored the way that both Guillaume and Jean were deeply interested in the science of optics, both writing in the midst of new translations of philosophical and scientific texts from the Greek and Arabic.[27] She argues that Guillaume holds out the possibility that seeing might allow for self-knowledge, though this knowledge remains inaccessible to Amant.[28] Akbari usefully traces the optical theories that both poets of the *Rose* may have put to both poetic and ethical purposes; these optical metaphors are also inherent in ethical discourse, with its emphasis on reflection and self-knowledge. When Amant comes upon the fountain, he does not immediately look in, but instead reads the inscription on the encompassing stone, an inscription written by Nature herself, which reveals that the fountain was the site of Narcissus's death. The narrator then shifts to an extra-diegetic telling of the Narcissus myth. In Guillaume's version of the tale, Narcissus does not recognize himself (as he does in Ovid's *Metamorphoses*), but rather mistakes his reflection for that of a beautiful child. Overcome by the fruitlessness of his desire, Narcissus loses his sense and dies. The narrator then offers a gloss on this exemplum, stating that Narcissus received just punishment for having scorned Echo and that all ladies should therefore take care not to neglect their lovers. The narrator refuses to find his own image (of himself as the young Lover) in the exemplum — the moral is instead thrust upon his beloved, in what is often read as a humorous and ironic attempt to reinforce his plea that she should return his love.

Yet while the gloss may offer a moment of ironic humour, it is also a trenchant illustration of the way that Amant takes on the roles of both Echo and Narcissus. He is both Echo, the pursuer of the distant love object, the rose/lady, and the lover Narcissus gazing at his own reflection; he is Amant at the fountain and the narrator gazing upon his prior self. Not only does this version of Narcissus fail to recognize his own reflection, but with the ill-fitting gloss the narrator creates a textual precedent that implicitly endorses Amant's decision to gaze into the fountain and find his impossible object of desire. At the same time, he endorses his own position as the subject of desire for the lady 'who deserves to be called Rose' outside the dream vision. His identification with both doomed lovers renders Amant's quest both super-determinedly unsuccessful and universalized. As other scholars have argued, the 'narcissism' exhibited by Amant is not depicted

---

[27] Akbari, *Seeing through the Veil*, p. 19.

[28] Akbari, *Seeing through the Veil*, p. 76.

as an avoidable pathology, but as a constitutive aspect of human desire.[29] Amant encounters the fountain of Narcissus, the Narrator encounters the myth of Narcissus, but each fails to see the reflection of his desire. The Narcissus tale as recounted in the *Rose* is an illustration of the failure of a variety of modes of self-reflection — visual art, narrative, contemplation — to bring about self-recognition; the gloss recapitulates this failure.

At other points in the poem, the theme of failed self-reflection is clarified as unproductive labour. In her first words to Amant, the figure Raison assimilates the 'perilousness' of Narcissus's mirror to the dangers of *oiseuse*, especially when *oiseuse* is understood as improper contemplation. Raison creates an equation between Oiseuse herself and the perilous mirror of Narcissus, telling Amant that 'Fox est qui s'acointe d'Oiseuse; | S'acointance est trop perilleuse (He who acquaints himself with Oiseuse is a fool; acquaintance with her is very dangerous; ll. 2989–90). In this context, the entry of Amant into the garden of delight and into the hopeless task of recounting his narrative in romance is a peril that prefigures his gaze into the perilous fountain of Narcissus. Amant's acquaintance with Oiseuse has caused him to have 'folement ovré' (worked foolishly; l. 2995) according to Raison, who would rather have him engaged in rational contemplation. Raison thus associates the 'madness' of love with a loss of productivity:

> Hons qui aime ne puet bien fere
> ne a nul preu dou monde entendre:
> s'il est clers, i piart son aprendre;
> et se il fet autre mestier,
> il n'em puet gaires esploitier.
>
>   (ll. 3028–32)

(A man who loves can do nothing well nor attend to any worldly gain: if he is a clerk, he loses his learning, and if he follows some other trade, he can hardly accomplish it.)

Guillaume's Raison does not attempt to seduce Amant, as she does in Jean's *Rose*, nor does she advocate fruitful procreation, but her emphasis on work and productivity clearly points toward such later transformations. Amant responds to her critique, claiming that love itself is the only worthy activity, and that Raison herself 'poriez bien gaster | en oiseuse vostre françois' (could waste her French in oiseuse; ll. 3072–73) arguing with him. Having rejected Raison, Amant continues

---

[29] See most recently, Mark Miller, *Philosophical Chaucer: Love, Sex, and Agency in the 'Canterbury Tales'* (Cambridge, 2004), p. 152; also Sarah Kay, *The Romance of the Rose* (London, 1995), p. 79; and Hult, *Self-fulfilling Prophecies*, pp. 285–87.

in his pursuit of the rose, which, despite the narrator's assurances to the contrary, he will not achieve.

In fact, immediately after gaining an apparent triumph in kissing the rose, the narrator swears that he will pursue 'tote l'estoire', implying both that there is a 'whole' history that might be completed, and yet that it might be possible to write this history perpetually. He breaks into the narrative and swears:

> Tote l'estoire veil parsuivre,
> ja ne m'est parece d'escrivre,
> por quoi je cuit qu'il abelise
> a la bele, que Dex guerisse.
> (ll. 3487–90)

(I want to pursue the whole history, and I shall never be idle in writing it down as long as I believe that it may please the beautiful lady — may God be her cure.)

For while Amor urges Amant to 'live' rather than write, the narrator seems to hold himself to an ethic of continuous writing. Here it seems that the 'oiseuse' of literary production will in fact defend him from the more serious 'parece'. Though Guillaume's poem contains a promise to continue writing so long as it is pleasurable for the narrator's lady, the poem remains unfinished, breaking off about five hundred lines later. Ending with a plea to Bel Acueil (Fair Welcome), expressing the woe and agitated desire of Amant, the poem is caught in just the position that Amor warned against — that of attempting to recount love's woes in a romance. Perhaps the narrator believes that his lady has ceased to be pleased by Amant's history, or perhaps his desire has been accomplished, thus rendering the writing of the poem both superfluous and obscene.[30] These possibilities remain unaddressed, and we are left with a poem about the relationship between unproductive and productive labour, overlaid upon physical and intellectual labour, explored through an erotic love that encompasses all forms of work. The ethical precepts of Amor are an alternative to the pleasurable but unproductive *oiseuse* of the garden and the nonamorous labour prescribed by Raison. Yet this version of the ethical, active life proves inextricable from Amant's narcissistic self-reflection on the one hand, and his inexhaustible writerly engagements on the other. The difficulty in disentangling productive from unproductive labour and the association of labour with both objectless desire and desire for a loved object

---

[30] In Hult's reading, the 'translation' of the allegory of Amant taking the castle would not be physical consummation, but the winning of the lady's good graces (*Self-fulfilling Prophecies*, p. 172).

is one of the key subjects of Guillaume's *Rose*. That ethicizing this desire and labour makes these distinctions no easier to maintain is one of its keener insights. This thinking through of intellectual and physical work by means of thinking about love, both passionate and divine, will become central for the reception of Aristotle's ethical writings, especially those that make clear that the philosopher's investment in earthly happiness is constituted by a version of contemplation that seems to have nothing at all to do with love. Guillaume thus leaves Jean with a poem containing a set of meditations on productive and unproductive activity, lyric stasis and narrative work, writing and reflection that will prove ripe for development in a world seeking to come to terms with growing conflicts over the nature of human happiness and the sovereign good.

Aristotle's 'Ethics' in the Thirteenth Century

Where Guillaume de Lorris writes within an ideological framework in which neither the *vita activa* nor the *vita contemplativa* offer any hope of earthly perfection, Jean de Meun writes within a new, controversial context of Aristotelian contemplation, where contemplation is the best life for man on earth and therefore confers human happiness. Suddenly, the earthly, bodily ethics offered within courtly poetry has a philosophical counterpart. With the full translation of the *Nicomachean Ethics* by Robert Grosseteste around 1245, it became impossible to sustain medieval understandings of Aristotelian *felicitas* as confined either to political happiness or to union with God. The *Ethics* in its full form introduced a definition of the sovereign good that would prove difficult to assimilate to a Christian worldview, for in the final book, previously unavailable in Latin, the philosopher defines happiness as a life of contemplation — a life of perfect happiness that is theoretically attainable in the mundane world. Early Christian theologians had certainly treated happiness as a spiritual goal, but this happiness was typically only accessible in the afterlife or through experiences bestowed by God's intervention. Happiness achieved through self-reflection and intellectual contemplation as the highest *human* happiness would require a re-examination of the core concepts in medieval ethics: action, love, pleasure, felicity, the good.[31]

---

[31] Glending Olson discusses the relationship between reception of Aristotelian theories of 'refreshment' (via music, storytelling, or conversation) and poetry in *Literature as Recreation in the Later Middle Ages* (Ithaca, 1982).

Prior to the complete translation of the *Ethics*, medieval commentators on the incomplete versions largely agreed that Aristotle spoke only of political happiness, and not a final 'true' happiness, and read his ethical writings as strictly practical guides for the virtuous life. This version of the 'ethical life' as the active life harmonizes with the commentaries on the twelfth-century versions of Aristotle's *Ethics*, the so-called *Ethica vetus* and *Ethica nova*. These texts, comprising only the first three books of the *Nicomachean Ethics*, where Aristotle defines happiness and the good, *habitus*, the virtue of the mean, and voluntary action, were read as immediately practical guides for virtuous living.[32] On its face, contemplation as constituting happiness seems to be quite compatible with Christianity's emphasis on turning one's intellect toward God; other writers had explored the continuities between self-reflection, contemplation, and the beatific vision.[33] And, indeed, where commentators did address Aristotle's theory of happiness, they almost invariably defined perfect happiness as a state of union with God, not the activity of contemplation.[34] Philosophical *felicitas* was equated with Christian *beatitudo*, and earthly happiness was always held to be flawed — a judgement sustained by Aristotle's own discussions of fortune.[35] Robert Kilwardby alone of the early commentators recognized that Aristotle's philosophy restricts itself to earthly goods, and that his happiness is not to be equated with beatitude.[36] It is this movement from a definition of the good that takes God as its starting point to one that takes the perfection of human activity as its starting point that would be demanded of subsequent commentators once they had access to the explicit definition of contemplative happiness on earth as the sovereign good in Book X of the *Ethics*.[37] The choice that Kilwardby presciently makes to focus on a

---

[32] Georg Wieland, 'Aristotle's Ethics: Reception and Interpretation', in *The Cambridge History of Later Medieval Philosophy* (see n. 7, above), p. 661.

[33] See, for example, Aelred of Rievaulx, *De speculo caritatis*, ed. by Charles H. Talbot, in *Opera Omnia I*, ed. by Anselm Hoste, Charles H. Talbot, and Rolandus Vander Plaetse, Corpus Christianorum Continuatio Mediaevelis, 1 (Turnhout, 1971).

[34] Anthony J. Celano, 'The Understanding of the Concept of *felicitas* in the Pre-1250 Commentaries on the *Ethica Nicomachea*', *Medioevo*, 12 (1986), 29–53.

[35] Celano, 'The Understanding of the Concept of *felicitas*', p. 38.

[36] Celano, 'The Understanding of the Concept of *felicitas*', p. 43.

[37] See Georg Wieland, 'Aristotle's Ethics' and 'Happiness: the Perfection of Man', in *The Cambridge History of Later Medieval Philosophy* (see n. 7, above), pp. 657–72, 673–86; also, Don Adams, 'Aquinas on Aristotle on Happiness', in *Medieval Philosophy and Theology*, 1 (Notre Dame, 1991), pp. 98–118, on the difference between Aristotle's definition of contemplative happiness in Book X and the definitions of happiness in the preceding books.

separate, human happiness becomes necessary with the reception of the complete *Ethics*.

Beyond the difficulty of assimilating Aristotle's notion of happiness as an earthly activity lay the problem that this theory did not appear to include love. Aristotle's theory of happiness as the most excellent activity of the most virtuous person upon the noblest object recognizes pleasure as an integral aspect of this activity, but this pleasure accompanies, 'supervenes upon', the activity of contemplation, not joy in the beloved object.[38] Medieval readers were left to account for and justify this omission. Albert the Great wrote the first complete commentary on the full *Nicomachean Ethics* in the years almost immediately after Grosseteste completed his translation (1248–52).[39] In his commentary on the tenth book of the *Ethics*, Albert must come to terms with Aristotle's definition of contemplation as the highest good for man, and the contemplative life as the happiest. In this section he addresses together the problems that Aristotelian contemplation appears to be an end in itself and that it does not appear to involve love for the object contemplated. He introduces the objection that contemplation of wisdom is not estimable in itself, explaining that contemplation should be considered vain if it were sought on account of nothing else. Further, Albert notes that enjoyment is completed in love ('fruitio completur in amore'), and that therefore contemplation must be ordered further toward love ('ergo contemplatio ipsa ordinatur ulterius ad amorem').[40] Albert resolves that 'the contemplation of happiness is esteemed for its own sake, because it is principal, that is to say it is the contemplation of God, which is according to the Theologian [Augustine] the end of human life' (contemplatio felicitatis diligitur propter se, quia ipsa praecipua est, scilicet contemplatio dei, quae est secundum THEOLOGUM finis humanae vitae).[41]

---

[38] Aristotle, *Ethica Nicomachea*, ed. by René Gauthier, ser. ed. by Lorenzo Minio-Paluello, Aristoteles Latinus, 26. 4 (Leiden, 1973), X. 5, ll. 27–28; 1174b31–33: 'Perficit autem operacionem delectacio non sicut habitus que inest, set ut superveniens quidam finis velud iuvenibus pulcritudo.' References are to the revised version (*c.* 1250–60), perhaps by William of Moerbeke, of Grosseteste's translation of the *Ethics*. Translations, with some emendations, are from C. I. Litzinger's translation of Thomas Aquinas's *Commentary on Aristotle's 'Nicomachean Ethics'* (Notre Dame, 1993).

[39] Wieland, 'Aristotle's Ethics', p. 660.

[40] Albertus Magnus, *Super Ethica*, in *Opera Omnia*, XIV, 1–2, ed. by William Kübel (Monasterii Westfalorum, 1968–72), L. X, lectio XI, section 899, p. 754.

[41] Albertus Magnus, *Super Ethica*, L. X, lectio XI, section 899, p. 754.

Albert leaves the question of love unresolved, although God is reinstated as the object of contemplation.

Albert acknowledges, however, that Aristotelian contemplation is different from theological contemplation. Where many of the earlier commentators on the *Ethics* had conflated Aristotle's definition of happiness with Christian beatitude, Albert is careful to separate the two, making a strict distinction between happiness in this life and the beatitude of heaven.[42] The theologian contemplates through light infused by God ('per lumen infusum a deo') while the philosopher contemplates through acquired disposition of wisdom ('per habitum sapientiae acquisitum').[43] Where philosophy relies upon rational demonstration of certainty, theology rests upon truth without need of reason.[44] Thus, Albert explains, wonder is an indispensable aspect of theology, but not of contemplative philosophy. He ultimately avoids, however, confronting Aristotle's elevation of contemplative philosophy to the best life for man and the accompanying orientation of moral philosophy toward knowledge rather than practised virtue. For Albert, Aristotelian ethics is still understood as having its scientific nature oriented practically toward 'making us good'.[45]

Albert's student Aquinas, however, is the first of the commentators on the *Ethics* neither to relegate Aristotle's philosophy to the purely practical nor subsume it to the theological. Other philosophers in the late thirteenth century have even fewer reservations in embracing Aristotle's definition of the good and even go beyond Aristotle himself by disregarding practical, political considerations altogether, focusing on philosophical contemplation as the only way to happiness. Boethius of Dacia and Siger of Brabant both courted censure by arguing that the supreme good is only accessible to philosophers.[46] A rational, rather than divine,

---

[42] On earlier commentators, see Wieland, 'Aristotle's Ethics', pp. 658–59, as well as Fernand Van Steenbergen, *Aristotle in the West: The Origins of Latin Aristotelianism*, trans. by Leonard Johnston (Louvain, 1955), pp. 95–105.

[43] Albertus Magnus, *Super Ethica*, L. X, lectio XVI, section 927, p. 774.

[44] Albertus Magnus, *Super Ethica*, L. X, lectio XVI, section 928, p. 775.

[45] Albertus Magnus, *Super Ethica*, Prologus, section 5, p. 4; Wieland, 'Aristotle's Ethics', p. 661.

[46] Boethius of Dacia, *De summa bono*, in *Boethii Daci Opera* (Hauniae, 1969–79), translated by John F. Wippel in *On the Supreme Good; On the Eternity of the World; On Dreams* (Toronto, 1987); Siger of Brabant, *Quaestiones morales*, in *Écrits de logique, de morale et de physique*, ed. by Bernardo Bazán (Louvain, 1974). Boethius is careful to define a 'philosopher' as any man who lives according to the right order of nature and who has acquired the best and ultimate end of human life, a slightly tautological saving definition.

authority for Aristotle was espoused by certain members of the Paris arts faculty, and it was this type of authority that led the Bishop of Paris to cite several 'Aristotelian' doctrines among the 219 theses condemned in 1277.[47] The source for these propositions is unclear, though they appear to correspond to the ideas of some contemporary Aristotelians: 'No station in life is to be preferred to the study of philosophy', and 'Happiness is to be had in this life and not in another.'[48] Although Aquinas's writings are occasionally grouped with those of the 'radical Aristotelians' by both medieval and modern critics, his commentary on the *Ethics* and the second section of his *Summa theologiae* (on ethics) are both more interested in harmonizing Aristotle's philosophy with Christian doctrine, while being true to the Philosopher. Despite his assurance to his reader that Aristotle is speaking of imperfect, earthly happiness (*beatitudo imperfecta*), and that perfect happiness is only possible in the afterlife, he clearly accepts, with Aristotle, that ethics should take earthly happiness as its subject. Aquinas agrees with Aristotle unreservedly that contemplation of the truth is the highest good for man, the most virtuous of activities, and that contemplation of a truth already known is more perfect than investigation, because possession is more perfect (complete) than pursuit.[49] He states positively, 'Thus it is clear that the person who gives himself to the contemplation of truth is the happiest a man can be in this life.'[50] Because God himself exercises all his activity in the contemplation of wisdom, the philosopher is accordingly the happiest, and the dearest to God. Yet, as in Guillaume's *Rose,* there is no easy demarcation here between the active and contemplative lives, between the quietude of contemplation and earthly labour; with an Aristotelian understanding of happiness, both striving for the good and

---

[47] In the introduction to this condemnation the only explicitly named text is the *De amore* of Andreas Capellanus, a work condemned along with books on witchcraft, necromancy, etc. The full text of the condemnation is found in the *Chartularium Universitatis Parisiensis*, ed. by Emile Chatelain and Heinrich Denifle, 4 vols (Paris, 1889–97), I, 543–61, and translated by Ernest L. Fortin and Peter D. O'Neill in *Medieval Political Philosophy: A Sourcebook*, ed. by Ralph Lerner and Muhsin Mahdi (New York, 1963), pp. 335–54.

[48] Qtd in Wieland 'Aristotle's Ethics', p. 663; 'quod non est excellentior status quam vacare philosophiae'; 'quod felicitas habetur in ista vita et non in alia': *Chartularium Universitatis Parisiensis*, vol. I, n. 473, sent. 40, sent. 176.

[49] Thomas Aquinas, *In Decem Libros Ethicorum Aristotelis ad Nicomachum Expositio*, ed. by Raymund Spiazzi (Turin, 1949) L. X, l. x, 2092. Translations are from C. I Litzinger, *Commentary on Aristotle's Nicomachean Ethics*.

[50] Aquinas, *Ethicorum Aristotelis Expositio*, L. X, l. x, 2110: 'Sic ergo patet, quod ille qui vacat speculationi veritatis, est maxime felix, quantum homo in hac vita felix esse potest.'

experiencing the good itself are spoken of in the language of action. In Aristotle's discussion of the possibilities of earthly happiness, he states that we 'must, so far as we can, make ourselves immortal, and strain every nerve to live in accordance with the best thing in us', for 'the life of the intellect is best and most pleasant since the intellect more than anything else is man.'[51] It is telling that rather than simply tending toward a life of reason as the life that is most in accordance with the basic definition of humanity, we must stretch and do everything possible (*omnia facere*) to live according to our optimal potential. For humankind, teleology is not a simple gravitational pull or tendency, but a terribly challenging ethical imperative. The oscillation or tension between tendency and strain, teleology and desire, is a defining feature of the Latin reception of Aristotle. For where in the Greek, the *Ethics* begins by stating that 'all things aim at [*ephiesthai*] the good', Grosseteste's Latin translation has it that the 'all things desire [*appetunt*] the good'.[52] Aquinas comments that 'this very tendency to good is the desiring of good', rendering desire both rational and teleological.[53] The very attainability of Aristotle's felicity is ironically what makes it compatible with Christianity, which has no virtuous place for the desire of unattainable objects. Aquinas and Aristotle share the same notion of ethical desire: it is finite, rational, and teleological. Infinite and shifting desire for Aristotle is irrational, and for Aquinas is also cupidinous.

This emphasis on telos, and the striving for an end, makes it necessary that desire for the unattainable, even spiritual desire, be rendered ethically problematic. Aquinas states that 'a natural desire is nothing else but an inclination belonging to things by the disposition of the First Mover, and this cannot be frustrated [...] it is impossible that we should proceed to an infinity of ends'.[54] Aquinas's idea of 'natural desire' is the 'inclinatio' discussed in this case — desire is constantly being

---

[51] Aristotle, *Ethica Nicomachea*, X. 9, ll. 14–24; 1177b31–1178a8: 'Oportet [...] in quantum contingit immortalem facere, et omnia facere ad vivere secundum optimum eorum que in ipso [...] homini utique, quae secundum intellectum vita, si quid maxime hoc homo, iste ergo felicissimus.'

[52] This aspect of the translation is noted in Thomas Aquinas, *Summa theologiae*, ed. by E. D'Arcy, XIX (*The Emotions*, Ia IIae 22–30), pp. 76–77, n. c, in reference to Aquinas's understanding of the term *appetitus* (New York, 1967).

[53] Aquinas, *Ethicorum Aristotelis Expositio*, L. I, l. i, 11: 'Ipsum autem tendere in bonum, est appetere bonum.'

[54] Aquinas, *Ethicorum Aristotelis Expositio*, L. I, l. ii, 21: 'naturale desiderium nihil est aliud quam inclinatio inhaerens rebus ex ordinatione primi moventis, quae non potest frustrari. Ergo impossibile est, quod in finibus procedatur in infinitum.'

redefined as divinely implanted rational telos. Both joy (*gaudium*) and hope (*spes*) are differentiated from desire, which actually prevents one from attaining pleasure and doing the good. Desire is defined by the unattainability of its object, while hope implies that its object may be attained. In addressing Aristotle's discussion of the problems of fortune, and thus whether one can truly call a man 'happy' in this life, Aquinas concludes '[s]ince a natural desire is not in vain, we can correctly judge that perfect beatitude is reserved for man after this life'.[55] A Christian rational understanding of desire may demand that perfect happiness be reserved for the afterlife, but it also simultaneously requires that imperfect human happiness be rendered a natural object of desire. Aristotle's discussion of rational contemplation and seeking after knowledge as the best life there is actually allows the field of moral philosophy to take a more optimistic view of life on earth. Virtuous pleasure is not reserved for either the afterlife or mystical experience, but is attainable, however imperfectly, in mundane existence.

Thus in order for Aristotle's emphasis on earthly ethics to be maintained in a Christian context, perfection must be exchanged for imperfection. Aquinas reconciles Aristotelian rational desire for attainable objects with Christian refusal to valorize desire for temporal goods. For Aquinas, Aristotle's happiness is 'imperfect', but also continuous with the perfect happiness reserved for the afterlife. Aquinas's development of the concept of imperfect mundane happiness is crucial to the reception of the complete *Ethics*; in both his commentary proper and in the sections of the *Summa* that treat ethics, imperfect happiness is rendered a proper starting point for moral philosophy — replacing the ethical model which begins with the perfect happiness that one experiences after death in the contemplation of God. A teleological, earthly narrative begins to replace meditative lyricism as the way to approach the good, lending a new shape to morality itself.[56] Indeed in Aquinas's commentary on the *Ethics*, he states that 'we are looking for the happiness that is the end of human acts',[57] therefore cautioning

---

[55] Aquinas, *Ethicorum Aristotelis Expositio*, L. I, l. xvi, 202: 'Et quia non est inane naturae desiderium, recte existimari potest, quod reservatur homini perfecta beatitudo post hanc vitam.'

[56] Vivian Boland reconciles Aristotle's notion of the 'good as attractive' with the neoplatonist (pseudo-Dionysian) notion of the 'good as ecstatic' by suggesting that Aristotle's ethical vision is of a human being searching for what he has already received from the First Mover; see 'Thinking about Good: Thomas Aquinas on *Nicomachean Ethics* I, *Divine Names* IV–V and *De Ebdomadibus*', *New Blackfriars*, 83.979 (2002), 384–400 (p. 391).

[57] Aquinas, *Ethicorum Aristotelis Expositio*, L. I, l. 8, 98: 'Quaerimus enim felicitatem, quae est finis humanorum actuum.'

that '[i]n this work the Philosopher speaks of happiness as it is attainable in this life, for happiness in a future life is entirely beyond the investigation of reason'.[58] Thus while true, infinite happiness is still reserved for the afterlife, it has been neatly removed from the purview of ethical knowledge. The pure, perfect good is neatly bracketed so that Aquinas may continue his investigation of an earthly ethics without danger of heterodoxy. The ethical good is now active, pleasurable, and achieved through a desire less assimilable to traditional ways of thinking about either spiritual or physical love.

Like courtly poetry, the new Aristotle gave the Middle Ages a challenge in thinking through the relationship between earthly desire and pursuits of the divine. As Lacan puts it, Aristotle's philosophy allowed Aquinas to invent a 'physical theory of love [...] namely that the first being we have a sense of is our being, and everything that is for the good of our being must, by dint of this very fact, be the Supreme Being's jouissance, that is, God's'.[59] For Lacan, this narcissistic projection, or 'well-ordered charity', as he jokes (for it 'begins at home'), tells us something about the very jouissance of being itself. The ethical subject of contemplation imitates the divine and the divine imitates narcissistic man. Although Lacan is not as steeped in the nuances of thirteenth-century philosophy as we might like him to be, his linking of Aristotelian metaphysics and ethics with a medieval ethics of self-knowledge and pleasure, and his reading of the projection involved in medieval theories of contemplation are hard to dismiss. For Aristotle, and for his commentators, contemplation is the best activity for man because it is closest to God, and therefore the most loved by God. God loves what is most like him, so the philosopher affirms the medieval notion of a contemplative, active God, taking pleasure in reflecting upon his own image. Narcissus is clearly not very far from Lacan's mind, nor, arguably, from the minds of medieval philosophers and poets. At the very end of Seminar XX, Lacan refers to the 'mirage-like apprehension' (appréhension de mirage) that emerges when one imagines that the relation of being to being is the harmony of either

---

[58] Aquinas, *Ethicorum Aristotelis Expositio*, L. I, l. 9, 113: 'Loquitur enim in hoc libro Philosophus de felicitate, qualis in hac vita potest haberi. Nam felicitas alterius vitae omnem investigationem rationis excedit.'

[59] Lacan, *Encore*, p. 70; Lacan derives the terminology of 'physical' and 'ecstatic' love from Pierre Rousselot, *Pour l'histoire du problème de l'amour au moyen âge* (Münster, 1907), translated by Alan Vincelette as *The Problem of Love in the Middle Ages* (Milwaukee, 2001). For Rousselot, physical love is continuous with self-love while ecstatic love demands that the subject stand outside him or herself.

Aristotelian supreme jouissance or Christian beatitude.[60] This apprehension, in French as in English, is both a feeling of fear and a perception; when one approaches an 'other', one perceives and fears a deluding 'mirage'. Both dread and understanding are generated as 'true love' approaches being itself, giving way to hatred. Lacan's punning model for such an encounter is a concierge and a rat — the concierge fully appreciated the rat's being in his desire to erase (*raturer*) it. Such apprehension might well be felt by Narcissus gazing at the mirage inside the perilous fountain, experiencing feelings of both love and destruction for his love object and for himself. The writings of Aquinas that cause Lacan to 'roll on the floor laughing' at how well Aristotle and Christianity are 'put together' created a similar occasion for productive merriment in Jean de Meun, and the mirage he creates is no less generative of occasionally fearful perception.[61] For Lacan, Aristotle was instrumental in bequeathing the Middle Ages a God who enjoys the same way that we do, and thus allows us to sacrifice our jouissance for his. What Jean's *Rose* makes clear is that Aristotelian philosophy and the controversies it created were not so uniformly assimilated, even within the composition of one poem. The second *Rose* experiments with the ramifications of love and happiness defined through activity, with a love story that includes desire for an attainable object, with this-worldly and other-worldly locations of felicity, and a poetic practice that investigates the potential of self-reflection through art to bring happiness, madness, love, and hate.

The New Narcissus

Jean de Meun asks what Narcissus might look like in this new Aristotelian context, a context where self-reflection might inhabit a continuum including erotic love, intellectual contemplation, and the beatific vision. Jean asks, with Lacan, and with no less irony, play, and resistance to easy categorization, how a lover might experience 'well-ordered charity', and suggests that charity might range from the narcissistic to the social, from distance to possession, from mutuality to destruction. In Jean's *Rose*, questions of self-reflection, labour, and the good are taken up most extensively in the sections of the poem devoted to the discourses of Nature and Genius. These sections are overwhelmingly scholastic in

---

[60] Lacan, *Encore*, p. 145; *Le séminaire, Livre XX, Encore*, ed. by Jacques-Alain Miller (Paris, 1975), p. 133.

[61] Lacan, *Encore*, p. 114.

content and address issues such as the conception of pleasure as the ultimate ethical goal, the dangers of contemplation, and the relationship between labour, writing, and self-knowledge. Jean de Meun does not take up these issues in a strictly Aristotelian context but addresses them in a way that is clearly influenced by and engages in contemporary controversies surrounding the definition of the good.[62] The second part of the *Rose* experiments with the assumption of an Aristotelian ethical system, where rational activity precedes love, self-knowledge determines love, and happiness consists in labour rather than rest.[63]

The exploration of the sovereign good in Jean's poem begins with the confession of Nature, where self-knowledge is rendered a condition of free will.[64] In this section of the poem, Amant absents himself as an interlocutor, as love itself is thus pushed aside, only to return in the content of the dialogue. In confessing to Genius, Nature recounts the story of Genesis and describes the earth and other planets, going on to complain of the sins of men, especially those who kill themselves or refuse to procreate.[65] Her 'confession' is not a catalogue of sins, but the very narrative of the earth's creation and existence.[66] The only sins recounted are in fact the sins of mankind; Nature's interest is the harmonious perpetuation of the species, and man's refusal to cooperate in this goal is Nature's greatest sorrow. Human shortcomings lead to her long discussion of free will, where she

[62] Paré, on the other hand, contends that Jean de Meun was in harmony with the contemporary Aristotelianism of the Arts Faculty at the University of Paris, especially with reference to the doctrine of carnal love espoused by Nature and Genius (which he attributes unironically to Jean); see *Les Idées et les lettres*, p. 322 and passim.

[63] Sadlek finds a 'strong, coherent work ideology' in Jean's *Rose*, manifested in the discourses of Reason, Nature, and Genius (*Idleness Working*, p. 129; pp. 114–66, passim). While Sadlek reads this ideology as a valuing of primarily manual work and a critique of the mendicant orders, I see Jean's largely positive attitude toward labour as a way of experimenting with theorizations of erotic desire, intellectual work, and art.

[64] Daniel Heller-Roazen marks this section of the poem as 'perhaps the most extended chapter of the *Roman de la Rose* in which Jean de Meun invokes and develops a subject drawn from the faculties of theology and philosophy of his time' (*Fortune's Faces*, p. 105).

[65] Alain de Lille's *De planctu naturae*, trans. by James J. Sheridan (Toronto, 1980), the main source for Jean's description of Nature and Genius, also manipulates the binary of idleness and labour. Alain begins the work by complaining of his grief in terms of the labour of childbirth, and he later (Prose 5) describes the ruinous relationship between Venus and Antigenius as being the result of Venus falling prey to Idleness itself.

[66] Hugh White argues that Nature's engagement in the act of confession itself undercuts her moral authority in *Nature, Sex, and Goodness in a Medieval Literary Tradition* (Oxford, 2000), p. 124.

acknowledges that some men believe that their premature deaths and failures to procreate are destined. However, Nature argues that through education and virtuous behaviour, humans may exercise their free will and 'obtain another result'. Nature rehearses and rejects an argument in favour of free will that holds that God's foreknowledge confers necessity on human action, but rather that human actions and their results are the cause of God's foreknowledge.[67] She rebels against the claim that God's foreknowledge would be subordinated to the actions of humankind in such a manner. Instead, she argues that God's foreknowledge is free, complete, and self-sufficient, while also not constraining human action. Rather than using the traditional Boethian explanation for the coexistence of free will and divine omniscience, Nature focuses on the freedom conferred by self-knowledge. Just as God's foreknowledge is represented by an 'eternal mirror' in which he sees all, so human beings seem to be granted the potential to reflect on their own conditions and to predict their own destinies. According to Nature, if a man knows himself well ('s'il est de soi bien connoissanz'; l. 17544), and realizes that sin always struggles for mastery over his heart, then he will be able to maintain his free will ('frans voloirs'; l. 17543) and control his destiny. It is knowledge of self that here trumps destiny and that allows for the expression of free will in action.

She somewhat unexpectedly goes on to discuss the benefits that could fall to mankind if he were granted foreknowledge of events such as storms or famine. According to Nature's logic, it appears that the maintenance of free will in the face of God's providence might actually replace destiny. Nature suggests, for instance, that if men could know that a harsh winter lay ahead, they could provide for themselves ahead of time. Yet she finally admits that only God could bestow such visions and that free will, along with the exercise of good understanding, is the key to controlling one's destiny and living well. She states,

> mieux donc et plus legierement,
> par us de bon antandemant,
> pourroit eschever franc voloir
> quan que le peut fere douloir.
> (ll.17681–84)

---

[67] Paré hazards that Nature's defence of free will is in part owing to Jean de Meun's rejection of the fatalism outlined in the condemnations issued by Étienne Tempier in 1270 and 1277 in *Les Idées*, p. 232.

(Free will then, by the exercise of good understanding, could better and more easily avoid whatever can make it suffer.)

A man with knowledge of his birth and his current situation will not need to concern himself with destiny, but can make his own fortune.

Yet immediately after this revelation, Nature makes a move that both sweeps aside the conflicts between free will and destiny and reveals their underlying significance. Following this discussion, Nature remarks:

> Des destinees plus parlasse,
> fortune et cas determinasse
> et bien vossisse tout espondre,
> plus opposer et plus respondre,
> et mainz examples an deïsse;
> mes trop longuement i meïsse
> ainz que j'eüsse tout finé.
> Bien est ailleurs determiné.
> Qui nou set a clerc le demande,
> qui leü l'ait et qui l'antande.
>
> (ll. 17697–706)

(I would speak more about destinies, I would settle the subject of Fortune and chance, and I would like very much to explain everything, to raise more objections, reply to them, and give many illustrations for them, but I would spend too much time before I finished everything. The good is decided elsewhere. He who does not know it may ask a clerk who had studied it and who may understand it.)

Nature's statement begs the question of whether 'bien' resides outside a discussion of free will, or whether Nature herself simply does not want to pursue a clerical question best discussed 'elsewhere', perhaps the university. Her refusal to bear out her discussion of fortune and chance may be an indication that her concerns with *voluntas* have been superseded by other, more pressing concerns. Her wager that human self-knowledge can trump destiny lays an emphasis on 'knowing thyself' rather than continence as the way to freedom, the good, and bringing the soul out of suffering. In philosophical and moral terms, God's foreknowledge and human cupidity cease to be the prime obstacles to freedom, replaced by the problem of being able to reflect upon oneself. It becomes clear that the poem, through Nature's lengthy discussion of free will and predestination, addresses the problem of the good while it explicitly claims to ward it off.

Although in the context of the poem's 'plot' the conversation between Nature and Genius seems to be removed from the concerns of the desiring Lover, love re-emerges as a core concern of Nature's confession. Free will and the capacity to resist evil is preserved for the person who knows himself entirely ('se connoit antierement'; l. 17762) and this knowledge allows him to love wisely ('aime sagement'; l. 17761). Love and knowledge are placed in a causal relationship: full knowledge enables love. In the *Summa theologiae* Aquinas asks 'whether knowledge is a cause of love', answering that

> some knowledge of a thing is necessary before it can be loved. That is why Aristotle says that sensory love is born of seeing a thing; and similarly, spiritual love is born of the spiritual contemplation of beauty or goodness. Knowledge is therefore said to be a cause of love for the same reason as is the good, which can be loved only when one has knowledge of it.[68]

Aquinas admits that perfect knowledge is not necessary for love, as one may love a thing better than it is known ('plus amatur quam cognoscatur'), for instance rhetoric or God.[69] But above Aquinas gives us to understand that spiritual love is caused by knowledge in the same way that knowledge of physical beauty sparks love. Our understanding of physical love allows us to understand spiritual love; one is the mirror of the other and knowledge is a necessary condition of love for humans and God alike. In contrast, Nature comments that dumb beasts are undoubtedly without self-knowledge ('se mesconnoissent par nature'; l. 17765). Yet she hazards that if they were given speech and reason, they would immediately challenge the mastery of men, refusing to submit to man's rule.[70] Most interestingly

---

[68] Aquinas, *Summa theologiae*, Ia IIae q. 27 a. 2: 'amor requirit aliquam apprehensionem boni quod amatur. Et propter hoc Philosophus dicit quod visio corporalis est principium amoris sensitivi. Et similiter contemplatio spiritualis pulchritudinis vel bonitatis, est principium spiritualis amoris. Sic igitur cognitio est causa amoris, ea ratione qua et bonum, quod non potest amari nisi cognitum.'

[69] Aquinas, *Summa theologiae*, Ia IIae q. 27 a. 2. Here Aquinas's theory of love and knowledge bears close comparison to Lacan's, as the theologian defines 'perfect love' as the apprehension of the appetite where a thing is 'loved as it is seen to be in itself' (in se apprehenditur ametur) — that is, in its being.

[70] In both Langlois's and Lecoy's editions of the *Rose*, the notes refer the reader to Boethius (Book II, pr. 5) on man becoming bestial if deprived of self-knowledge. Yet the source for animal rebellion if beasts were endowed with reason appears to be Aelred of Rievaulx's *De anima*, where he proves the supremacy of reason to the body: 'Et ut scias in comparatione rationis quam nihil possit corpus vel sensus, quis hominum unius muscae cavere posset insidias, si ipsa, ut homo, ratione vigeret? Quis ea invita quiescere, vel tute oculos posset aperire? [...] Nonne congregatis in unum feris ac volucribus, totum possent humanum genus delere, si aequales essent hominibus ratione?' (And in order that you know how the body or the senses are capable of nothing in comparison with reason, what human would be able to be safe from the plots of one fly, if this fly flourished with reason as a human does? Who could rest against the fly's will, or safely open his

in the context of her discussion of self-knowledge in beasts and men, she appears to equate the acquisition of knowledge, especially self-knowledge, with the task of writing, or at least implies that the obvious next step upon recognizing one's self is to realize the ability to write. For if beasts were given reason, the monkeys and marmots among them could work with their own hands ('ouvreroient de mains'; l. 17803) and rival humans in their craftsmanship; they could, Nature claims, be writers ('porroient estre escrivain'; l. 17805), thus perhaps unexpectedly completing the notion of 'working with one's hands' with the work of writing. The work that these newly rational animals would do is not only the work of making clothing and armour (so as to protect themselves against men), but the work of literary production. Writing is an imagined weapon in the arsenal of these newly rational, rebellious creatures. The result of self-knowledge for these animals is both a refusal of labour — the ox refuses the yoke — and a turning of that labour toward the necessary conditions of the exercise of free will: the destruction of humankind. The beasts undertake this action in whatever way they are able, from the buzzing fly to the writing marmot. Nature appears to subscribe to Aristotle's and others' dictum that reason, more than anything else, *is* man. But to reason she adds the important corollary of rational self-knowledge, the capacity for self-reflection, anticipating Genius by claiming writing as the activity that a rational creature should most fruitfully be engaged in.

However, this association of rationality, self-knowledge, and writing is complicated by Nature's excursus on mirrors further on in her 'confession'. This discussion of the fantastical characteristics of mirrors, showing both hidden truths and distorted realities, is the first of a series of episodes in which the poem appears to critique Aristotelian notions of contemplation as the greatest good. The stable connections that she has up to now created between rationality and self-reflection are troubled by her seeming 'digression' on optical phenomena. For in her discussion of optics, in which she defers to Aristotle's book, mirrors become agents of deception — confusing distances, size, and the location of actual objects.[71] Even when mirrors reveal truths, they appear to do so only in aid of

---

eyes? [...] If they were equal to humans in reason, is it not the case that with the birds and beasts all gathered as one, they could destroy all of humankind?' (*De anima*, in *Opera Omnia*, ed. by C. H. Talbot, bk II, 18–20, p. 713). Where both Aelred's and Jean's catalogues of rational, murderous beasts are somewhat terrifying, Jean's reads more sympathetically, acknowledging that the hypothetical animals are rebelling against forced servitude.

[71] Jane Chance Nitzsche notes that art is described pejoratively throughout Jean's *Rose* (especially falsity versus the truth of Nature). She contends that '[t]his discourse — on 'dreams', 'visions', and the artifice of mirrors — suggests obliquely that literature itself, peopled by

adulterous deception, as when Nature comments that if Mars and Venus had possessed the right kind of mirror, they could have magnified Vulcan's net and escaped his snare. Also particularly striking is Nature's discussion of the way that too much contemplation can create the appearance of false images outside the mind, in much the same way as mirrors can make images float in the air:

> voit l'an de ceus a grant planté
>
> .   .   .   .
>
> de trop panser sunt curieus,
> quant trop sunt melancolieus
> ou pooreus outre mesure,
> qui mainte diverse figure
> se font parair en eus meïsmes
> autrement que nous ne deïsmes
> quant des mirouers parlions,
> don si briefmant nous passions,
> et de tout ce leur samble lores
> qu'il sait ainsinc por voir defores.
> Ou qui, par grant devocion,
> en trop grant contemplacion,
> font apparair en leur pansees
> les choses qu'il ont porpansees,
> et les cuident tout proprement
> voair defors apertement.
>
>   (ll. 18314–32)

(One sees a great number of people who [are] [...] given to think too much in an unregulated way when they are very melancholy or irrationally fearful; they make many different images appear inside themselves, in ways other than those we told about just a short time ago when we were speaking about mirrors. And it seems to them then that all these images are in reality outside of them. Or there are those who, with great devotion, do too much contemplating and cause the appearance in their thought of things on which they have pondered, only they believe that they see them quite clearly and outside themselves.)

phantoms and images, is artificial, and even deceptive' (*The Genius Figure in Antiquity and the Middle Ages* (New York, 1975), p. 124). Alan Gunn, on the other hand, interprets Jean's depictions of such delusions as an attempt to ward them off, part of his aim in creating a 'true and fruitful image' reflected from the 'Mind of God' (*The Mirror of Love* (Lubbock, 1952) pp. 270–75). My reading falls somewhere in between; Jean is not here making a pronouncement about the ultimate falsity or truth of his art, or art in general, but rather exploring the possibilities and dangers of imagination, especially when confronted with love.

Here contemplation is a form of melancholia, a residing inside the self that results in the creation of false images. Thus rather than contemplation being defined as a rational thinking on the divine good, it becomes a sort of fantasmatic preoccupation with false images. The mistaken idea that an internal image is actually 'outside' (defores) oneself appears to be Narcissus's failure. Successful self-reflection demands a strict policing of the boundaries between inside and outside, self and other.[72] Love seems to function here as a limit case of the usefulness of mirrors. Although Nature opens up the possibility that self-knowledge may improve the life of man on earth, confer freedom, enable love and the ability to write, she also reveals the dangers inherent in such ideas. Artistic representations may be deceitful, excess of contemplation may lead to harmful phantasms, and a misguided sense of self will end in the acceptance of falsehoods rather than access to truth and good.[73]

Genius's response to Nature similarly contains foregrounded moments which appear to critique Aristotelian notions of the good and further presses the question of what is essential about humanity. The figure of Genius would seem to be particularly apt to provide a definition of the good life for man, given that as 'master of places, who sets all things at work according to their properties' (des leus iestes dex et mestres, | et selonc leur proprietez | tretouz en euvre les metez; ll. 16256–58) he also acts as a personification of human nature itself and as an embodiment of the 'genius' of humanness — in an Aristotelian sense, this characteristic is rational thought.[74] In the *Ethics* Aristotle claims in several places, in various formulations, that 'contemplation is the highest operation, since the intellect is the best element in us and the objects of the intellect are the best of the things that can be known'.[75] The *Rose*'s definition of genius as master of place and property seems a comfortable fit with Aristotle's teleological notion of human

---

[72] Sarah Kay argues that the demarcation of inside and outside is one of the key concerns of Guillaume's *Rose*, where the poet problematizes the limits of the self (*Subjectivity in Troubadour Poetry* (Cambridge, 1990), pp. 179–82).

[73] This distrust of contemplation may give support in a different context to Winthrop Wetherbee's claim that 'Jean's Nature seems scarcely to know herself', but rather views herself through human eyes ('The Literal and the Allegorical: Jean de Meun and the *De Planctu Naturae*' *Mediaeval Studies*, 33 (1971), 264–91 (p. 281)). Nature would be subject to the same faulty possibilities in vision and reflection as human beings.

[74] Nitzsche, *Genius Figure*, p. 97.

[75] Aristotle, *Ethica Nicomachea*, X. 8, ll. 18–19; 1177a19–21: 'Optima et enim hec operacio; et enim intellectus eorum que in nobis et cognoscibilium circa que intellectus.'

characteristics and the good. Yet Genius's speech points in multiple instances to the ways in which the notion of 'the good' can be misread, misappropriated, and misused — by tyrants, by their subjects, and ultimately by all humankind.

Genius takes the link between labour and writing foreshadowed by Nature and makes it concrete, if slightly overdetermined. He preaches of the duty men have to procreate and speaks, following Alain de Lille's *De planctu naturae*, in terms of the duty to write:

> quant il n'an veulent labourer
> por lui servir et honourer,
> ainz veulent Nature destruire
> quant ses anclumes veulent fuire,
> et ses tables e ses jaschieres,
>
> . . . .
>
> qu'el [tables] devandront toutes moussues
> s'el sunt en oiseuse tenues
>
> (ll. 19523–38)

(when they do not want to labor at serving and honoring Nature, but wish rather to destroy her by preferring to flee her anvils, her tablets and fallow fields [...] they [the tablets] will become all rusty if they are kept in oiseuse.)

Here we see a shift in the meaning of 'oiseuse' toward its more familiar definition of idleness, as here the idle tablets are not turned toward verbal frivolity, but rather not used at all. Writing, as metaphor for procreation, is the only way in which humankind might 'live forever' — everyone must write so that all might continue to live. The *oiseuse* that Guillaume imagined as the state of tension between the labours of loving and writing has been transformed into a much starker alternative to writing and (re)production. But then, Genius is a decidedly noncourtly figure, unsympathetic to the lyric conventions of unfulfilled and nonprocreative desire. For him, lyric stasis is not a satisfactory mode of desire — all should be for narrative and resolution. Lyric time is not for this world, but only for that *biaus parc* that one may hope to reach in the afterlife.

There has been much critical debate over whether Genius's sermon is to be taken ironically and how to reconcile his priestly function with his apparently cupidinous advice.[76] I err on the side of taking Genius seriously, if not as a

---

[76] Paré, *Les Idées et les lettres* (p. 321, and chaps 5–6, passim), takes Genius as not only a serious figure, preaching the gospel of Aristotelian 'naturalism', but as the key to the entire poem. For Paré, Genius reveals Jean de Meun's affinities with 'Averroists' such as Siger of Brabant and

mouthpiece for an authorial viewpoint. His 'naturalism' may be read as a screen
for exploring ideas of poetic labour and competing ideas of the good. Accordingly,
in Genius's sermon, the audience witnesses a collision of two versions of 'the
good', the courtly and the Christian. He exhorts:

> Pansez de mener bone vie,
> aut chascuns anbracier s'amie,
> et son ami chascune anbrace
>
> . . . .
>
> pansez de vos bien confessier,
> por bien fere et por mal lessier,
>
> . . . .
>
> Cil est saluz de cors et d'ame,
> c'est li biaus mirouers ma dame;
> ja ma dame riens ne seüst
> se ce biau mirouer n'eüst.
>
> (ll. 19855–72)

(Think of leading a good life; let each man embrace his sweetheart and each woman her
lover [...] think of confessing yourselves well, in order to do good and avoid evil, and call
upon the heavenly God whom Nature calls her master [...]. He is the salvation of body
and soul and the beautiful mirror of my lady, who would never know anything if she did
not have this beautiful mirror.)

Genius's definition of the 'bone vie' here is certainly not Christian and even
exceeds the courtly ethic with its emphasis on sexual procreation rather than
passion and play. Still, he presents it as the central message of the 'lovely Romance
of the Rose' which, according to Genius, preaches the gospel of sexual procreation
so that one may enter heaven. In urging his audience to confess he urges them to
take Nature as a model and states that Nature's own model is God himself,

Boethius of Dacia who supposedly subscribe to notions such as the virtues of sexual procreation
outside marriage and the possibility of achieving perfect happiness in this life. John Fleming takes
issue with Paré's thesis, arguing for the impossibility of Jean's embracing any morality at odds with
Christian ethics (*Romance of the Rose*, pp. 214–20). Fleming cites Rosemond Tuve for support,
as she argues that Genius and Nature are held up as examples of the domination of inadequate
ideas concerning love and the good; see *Allegorical Imagery: Some Medieval Books and Their
Posterity* (Princeton, 1966), p. 262. Robertson understands Genius as 'merely the inclination of
created things to act naturally' (*Preface*, p. 200). Sylvia Huot notes that medieval readings often
revolve around the question of whether Genius's sermon can be reconciled with Christian
doctrine, without recourse to satire or parody (*Medieval Readers*, p. 174).

inverting the usual image of Nature as God's mirror. God here is at the service of Nature, imparting knowledge much as the 'Miroër aus Amoreus' teaches its readers. Genius asks his audience (and by extension the reader) not only to take in his sermon, but to memorize it the better to spread his gospel, which 'vient de bone escole' (comes from a good school; l. 19890). Playing the role of both priest and scholar, Genius outlines a method of reading that literalizes the notion that one should achieve self-knowledge through a self-reflexive relationship to literature. Genius's audience should absorb and actually become the text he has offered them, much as Nature creates an image in imitation of God's mirror.

While Genius seems to preach unreservedly the good of procreation, it becomes clear that his 'naturalism' does not condone selfish hedonism in any way. Genius's later discussion of sensual pleasure as the sovereign good espoused by the tyrannical Jupiter seems to stage a critique of Aristotelian ethics based on a fundamental misunderstanding of Aristotle's terms. After Genius's description of the lyric space of the *biaus parc* that awaits those who pursue the good (as procreation), he remarks that not even the golden age knew a paradise so beautiful and pure. Yet the fall from the golden age, occasioned by the castration of Saturn by Jupiter, fits neatly with Genius's thesis that procreation is the greatest good and that any strike against fertility is the greatest outrage. For in committing this sin against Nature, Jupiter inaugurated an age of vice and sorrow. In Genius's telling, Jupiter signifies an alternate definition of the pursuit of good — the pursuit of individual pleasure:

> car deliz, si conme il disoit,
> c'est la meilleur chose qui soit
> et li souverains biens en vie
> don chascuns doit avoir anvie.
> (ll. 20075–78)

(As he [Jupiter] said, delight is the best thing that can exist and the sovereign good in life; everyone should desire it.)

Jupiter here espouses a vulgar understanding of 'pleasure' as the good: pleasure as delight in food and other bodily pleasures, not in rational contemplation of the divine. Further, he has the relationship between pleasure and desire backwards — Aquinas, commenting on Aristotle's statement that 'the good is what all desire', affirms the perhaps surprising conclusion that pleasure is good *because* all desire it; it is not desired because it is good. For Aquinas, the good is convertible with the movement of the appetite. He does not deny that some men desire evil, but explains that they only desire evil because they believe it to be good; the evilness

of the object is therefore only incidental.[77] The force of teleology must come first
in the causality of Aristotelian ethics: things naturally tend toward the good,
people tend toward pleasure, and therefore we see that pleasure is the highest
good.[78] Aquinas remarks that Aristotle 'calls people in power tyrants because
those who are occupied with amusements do not seem to strive for the common
interest but for their own gratification [...]. Thus then happiness is said to consist
in pleasures of this nature because persons in power — whom men consider happy
— spend their time in them.'[79] Thus the corruption of the state corrupts the very
definition of happiness, rendering it impossible for men to live good lives. The
identification of the good with sensual pleasure is a misunderstanding rooted in
perversions of civic society — when tyrants are in power, the good is necessarily
obscured.

Furthermore, Jupiter's pursuit of his own pleasure is what leads to the fall from
the golden age, to the necessity for labour, and thus to the creation of the arts.

> Ainsinc sunt arz avant venues,
> car toutes choses sunt vaincues
> par travaill, par povreté dure,
> par quoi les genz sunt en grant cure.
> (ll. 20145–48)

(Thus have the arts sprung up, for all things are conquered by labor and hard poverty;
through these things people exist in great care.)

In Genius's mythology, Jupiter defines pleasure as the highest good and a sensual
good, and thus creates the necessity for labour. In a fallen world, the only way we
have to overcome the excesses of tyrants and the obscuring of the good is through
labour and 'art'. It is not an accidental irony that the very 'plowing' that Genius
was advocating earlier (on a literal level) is here the result of tyrannical corruption.

---

[77] Aquinas, *Ethicorum Aristotelis Expositio*, L. I, l. i, 9.

[78] This teleology leaves open the question of how we can know which pleasure is the ethical
pleasure to be pursued. Jonathan Lear reads the opening of the *Ethics*, where Aristotle introduces
the idea of the single ultimate good, as an 'inaugural instantiation' whereby he 'injects the concept
of the good' into our lives (*Happiness, Death, and the Remainder of Life* (Cambridge, MA, 2000),
p. 8).

[79] Aquinas, *Ethicorum Aristotelis Expositio*, L. X, l. ix, 2072: 'Vocat autem huiusmodi potentes
tyrannos, quia non videntur communi utilitati intendere, sed propriae delectationi, qui in ludis
conversantur [...]. Sic ergo felicitas in talibus consistit, propter hoc quod huiusmodi vacant illi, qui
sunt in potestatibus constituti, quos homines reputant felices.'

Genius differentiates between Jupiter's unproductive pleasure on the one hand and the productive labour of the arts and reproduction. Such work unites productivity and pleasure, where pleasure both accompanies activity and serves as its reward. If Genius's followers procreate, they will deserve entry into a revised version of Guillaume's garden of delight, where the murky, madness-inducing fountain of Narcissus is replaced by a health-giving, clear 'fonteine de vie' (l. 20491). Genius's garden is both earthly paradise and Christian heaven, but for all his protestations, it is also not unlike Guillaume's courtly garden. Genius criticizes the 'queroles qui faillirent' (carols that will pass away; l. 20325) contained in the trifle-filled garden of love, but his heavenly park will contain people 'chantant en parduableté | motez, conduiz et chançonnetes' (forever singing motets, conducti, and chansonettes; ll. 20626–27). The reward for all of this labour is a return to the lyricism of the garden of Oiseuse, this time with guaranteed permanence. Genius's paradise illustrates how close fallen desire is to divine joy and also captures some of the tensions between a traditional notion of rest as labour's reward and an Aristotelian ideal of continuous activity.[80] Genius thus offers his audience an ideal of literary self-reflection, earthly labour, and the final reward of pleasurable activity disconnected from productivity or the pursuit of a desired object.

Nature's and Genius's explorations of art's relationship to pleasure, self-reflection, and the contemplation of the good are recapitulated and re-evaluated in the episode of Pygmalion.[81] Where the Narcissus episode and the discourse of Nature both emphasize the dangers of sight and reflection gone awry, Pygmalion perhaps embodies sight as it emerges in Aristotle's guiding metaphor for pleasure: a perfected activity that is whole, complete, and grammatically perfect. Aristotle's image of the complete, pleasurable act of seeing is an image of a 'Narcissus made good' — a figure that several critics have seen to reside at the centre of Jean de

---

[80] Nicole Oresme, fourteenth-century translator and commentator on Aristotle, captures this ideal in his insistence on heaven as a place of activity where the blessed continually understand and will in God: 'beneurés ont ilecques continuelment operacion de entendement et de volenté en Dieu' (*Le Livre de Ethiques d'Aristote*, ed. by Albert Menut (New York, 1940), p. 517).

[81] Minnis calls Jean's Pygmalion 'the antithesis of Narcissus, this being part and parcel of a systematic recapitulation and redirection of Guillaume's major terms of reference' (*Magister Amoris*, p. 106). On Pygmalion, see also Roger Dragonetti, 'Pygmalion ou les pièges de la fiction dans le Roman de la Rose', in *La musique et les lettres* (Geneva, 1986), pp. 345–67, and Daniel Poirion, 'Narcisse et Pygmalion dans le Roman de la Rose', in *Essays in Honor of Louis Francis Solano*, ed. by Raymond J. Cormier and Urban T. Holmes (Chapel Hill, 1970), pp. 153–65.

Meun's *Rose*.[82] One of the promises upon which Pygmalion delivers is the potential for art to lead to self-recognition and thus the potential for rational contemplation to lead to virtuous pleasure in this life. Initially, there is no evidence to support the idea that Pygmalion's love for his statue is a love that is being celebrated by the poem. Pygmalion himself cries that his love is horrible and unnatural ('mes ceste amour est si horrible | qu'el ne vient mie de Nature'; ll. 20832–33). We are further told that Love had stolen his 'sans et savoir' (l. 20894), leaving him completely bereft of comfort and clearly bereft of sense and rationality. However, Pygmalion recognizes himself in the Narcissus myth, asking whether Narcissus did not love more foolishly than he, falling in love with his own face ('ama [...] sa propre figure'; ll. 20846–48). Pygmalion thus displays the capacity to recognize himself in an exemplum — if somewhat self-servingly — and identify his desires with those of the subject of the tale, learning from this example.

The reward of such identification is not immediate — we witness the way in which he uses literary precedent to justify the continuation of his own clearly unnatural desires. He decides that he is better off than Ovid's lover, better off than the troubadours, and continues the work of creation — dressing the statue in fine clothing. It appears at first as though Pygmalion's myth might serve to expose the fictions underlying conventional courtly desire, illustrating that although courtly lovers may hold out hope for a kiss and love returned, their far-off loves may as well be cold ivory statues — in Narcissus's desire for his reflection, Pygmalion's love for his statue, and in the courtly poet's love for his lady, the sexual relation does not exist. The gods are not happy with the sculptor, not because he is insane or perverse, but rather because the love is not mutual. Yet Pygmalion's renunciation of Chastity (chastity defined as an aspect of idleness by Genius) convinces Venus to give life to the statue, transforming her into the damsel Galatea.[83] The narrator describes how Galatea gave Pygmalion every pleasure and that he was finally happy. This pleasure is importantly described as mutual, part of an ongoing exchange of happiness.[84] The closing of this tale offers

---

[82] Sylvia Huot, *From Song to Book*, p. 98; See Brownlee, 'Pygmalion', p. 211, for a discussion of the Pygmalion fable as representative of 'the signifying power of ART, told 'successfully' on Art's own terms as defined by Jean's *Rose*'.

[83] Kay, focusing on the role of Venus in the digression, reads that tale as a derision of 'the inadequacy of masculine art, and masculine fantasy, when they join forces to confine women in the role of object' (*Rose*, p. 47).

[84] The reciprocal erotic encounter between Pygmalion and Galatea is discussed by Brownlee, 'Pygmalion', pp. 197–98.

simultaneously an erotic corruption of Aristotelian notions of pleasure and felicity as well as a narrative that describes how artistic labour might allow one to achieve self-knowledge and happiness.

For unlike Ovid's Pygmalion, Jean de Meun's sculptor is not motivated to escape corrupted women by taking refuge in his own pure creation; rather he simply desires 'son grant angin esprouver' (to prove his skill; l. 20792). He thus works his greatest talent upon the most appropriate and valuable material, creating beauty for its own sake. From this activity and creation, love is born. Love or desire does not pre-exist, looking for a suitable object, but rather is engendered through one's own dedication to one's art. As Aristotle explains, since love resembles activity, it only makes sense that 'those who excel in activity love and have the concomitants of love'.[85] The love of an artist for his creation is explored in Book IX of the *Ethics*, as an explanation for the observed phenomenon that benefactors seem to love those they have benefited more than these beneficiaries love their benefactors in return. Aristotle explains that the same inequality happens with craftsmen, 'for each one loves his product more than he would be loved by it were the product alive. Likewise, it occurs especially with poets who love their own poems, doting on them as their children'.[86] To this, Aquinas adds that 'poems partake of reason — by which man is man — to a greater degree than other mechanical works'.[87] Pygmalion's love for his sculpture thus partakes in a natural and ethical state of affairs, and it is only Galatea's equal love once she is vivified that exceeds this relationship. Rational activity, here aligned with artistic production, naturally leads to love; it is the love returned by the object itself that must be supplied by the artistic imagination, an imagination happily supplied by the poet. Jean de Meun, in his love for Guillaume's *Rose*, might thus be fantasizing a moment where his poem might come to life and might love him equally in return.[88] Such a fantasy might

---

[85] Aristotle, *Ethica Nicomachea*, IX. 7, ll. 22–23; 1168a20–1: 'Superexcellentibus autem utique circa actum sequitur amare et amicabilia.'

[86] Aristotle, *Ethica Nicomachea*, IX. 7, ll. 4–7; 1167b33–1168a3: 'omnis enim proprium opus diligit magis quam diligatur utique ab opere animato facto; maxime autem forte hoc circa poetas accidit, superdiligunt enim isti propria poemata, diligentes quemadmodum filios.'

[87] Aquinas, *Ethicorum Aristotelis Expositio*, L. IX, l. vii, 1845: 'Poëmata enim magis ad rationem pertinent secundum quam homo est homo, quam alia mechanica opera.'

[88] Douglas Kelly notes that Pygmalion's desire for his art 'resembles Jean de Meun working with Guillaume's material for the *Rose*' in *Internal Differences and Meanings in the 'Roman de la Rose'* (Madison, 1985), p. 76.

be seen to give shape to feminine desire, to the subject of contemplation who is thus both loved by God and loving, and to poetry as the optimal vehicle for experiencing this love. This happy conclusion is shadowed by the possibility that this returned love will always be a fantasy, and Jean thus dutifully follows the lineage of Pygmalion and Galatea through to the incestuous romance of Myrrha and Cynaras and the birth of Adonis. Whether the violent ending to the Pygmalion digression, with Cynaras pursuing Myrrha in a murderous rage, should give us pause in thinking about the relationship Pygmalion pursues with his own artistic creation, we are not given time to consider, for we are returned quickly to the matter at hand. Yet it is clear that Pygmalion's love for his creation, considered from another perspective, might return us to the problem of melancholic narcissism, his love for Galatea another mistaking of 'inside' for 'outside', and thus aptly ending in murder and incest.

As he picks up his narrative directly after the Pygmalion narrative, however, Jean reinforces its positive emphasis on love and labour by emphasizing his own labour and the labour of his reader. He refers to his 'work' and compares his narration to plowing a field:

> Bien orroiz que ce senefie
> ainz que ceste euvre soit fenie.
> Ne vos vuell or plus ci tenir,
> a mon propos doi revenir,
> qu'autre champ me convient arer.
>   (ll. 21183–87)

(By the time you have finished this work you will know what it means. But I won't keep you any longer on this subject; I should return to my story, since I must plow another field.)

Jean here takes Genius's metaphor of writing and makes it his primary meaning — plowing here signifies writing rather than sex, although Jean's writing will include an involved (somewhat laborious) metaphorical description of a sex act between Amant and the rose. The reader must complete the work of reading the poem — 'ceste euvre' — as Jean himself must complete his 'plowing'. One might read Jean's address to the reader that he will understand what the myth of Pygmalion or his lineage 'senefie' when he is done with the work as a prescription for proper reading and self-recognition in a narrative exemplum. Just as Pygmalion's procreative, fruitful labour may be contrasted with Narcissus's folly, we might contrast the proper reading practices of both Pygmalion and the reader of the *Rose* with the first Lover's failed reading of the Narcissus myth.

Of course, the final procreative labour of the poem is the consummation of the affair between Amant and the Rose. The sex act is compared humourously with the labours of Hercules, and is in general represented as a strenuous bit of work.[89] And it concludes productively with the apparent impregnation of the rose and the awakening of the narrator. This fruitful union is both optimistic — an imagining of earthly fulfilment of desire — and fearful, filled with the uneasy humour that overlays the violence that such fulfilment might wreak. And although the open-endedness of Guillaume's poem is finally closed, both by the capture of the rose and the waking of the Dreamer, Jean does not offer a final resolution of the question of the desiring subject's ethical relationship to pleasure, the good, or the self. On a fairly overt metaphorical level, Jean's poem functions as a parody of Aristotelian theories of happiness, dissecting the all too easily imagined results of an ethics based on pleasurable activity as the achievable sovereign good. Yet if one reverses the metaphorical and literal levels, a reversal common in Jean's poem, this parody becomes a quite serious investigation of the ethical possibilities of the labour of reading and writing — both acts of creation in the poem. Whereas explicit acts of reading and writing in Guillaume's *Rose* typically express or perpetuate unattainable desire, creative labours bear fruit in Jean's continuation. We might read this contrast not only as a result of Jean's satire of the euphemisms of romance, but also as an aspect of and further contribution to the reception of the new Aristotle. The fruition reached through labour at the poem's end is both grammatically perfect and ethically flawed — an apt representation of the good in a period trying to come to grips with Aristotle's moral philosophy. The irony of these flaws, however, should not obscure the very real possibilities for ethical reading that Jean's poem holds out. This version of ethical reading does not seek a moral or even a practical example of living well, but rather a reflection upon oneself and one's desires, bringing with it the pleasure that comes with the labour of rational contemplation. The activity itself disposes one to love, and is perhaps an act of love, though it is — as both Nature and Lacan remind us — prone to give way to fantasm, misapprehension, and even hate. This duality will become a

---

[89] References to sex as 'labour' or 'work' are common euphemisms in medieval Romance languages. Such euphemism is used not only by Genius, but by La Vielle, who recommends that the couple, when they 'work' ('se seront mis an l'euvre'; l. 14263) should work carefully so that each should have his or her pleasure and strain toward the good ('et s'antredoivent entr'atendre | por ansamble a leur bonne tendre'; ll. 14269–70). The emphasis on reciprocity in both content and language (e.g., the repeated use of the prefix -*entre*) prefigures the reciprocal erotic encounter between Pygmalion and Galatea. See also Dragonetti, 'Pygmalion', p. 365.

distinctly late-medieval way of thinking about ethics, dependent upon a deliberate yoking together of love, intellectual activity, and pleasure.

Lacan's narrative of medieval Aristotelianism gives us an Aristotle who charges the body with jouissance and knowledge, and charges contemplative self-reflection with mystical ecstasy and narcissism. The questions raised in medieval Aristotelian commentaries and only partially resolved (how can contemplation be valued for its own sake? how can human happiness exist outside of love of God? what does it mean for pleasure to be the greatest good?) are taken to a variety of extremes in Jean de Meun's *Rose*. In the poem's various conversations and narratives, we witness self-sacrificing desire, teleological drive toward possession, love as action and love as rest, self-reflection as madness, and self-knowledge leading to love. Jean's *Rose* gets to the heart of late-medieval questions about how to understand the relationship between bodily and intellectual pleasure, self-love, love of others, and love of God — without resolution, but resolutely on the side of working through the Aristotelian valorization of labour, this-worldly desires and goods, and poetry that de-sublimes some of courtly love's most cherished metaphors. The new self-aware, active Narcissus limned by Jean's poem may experience desire as mutually delightful and productive or one-sided and destructive. Erotic desire shored up by the new philosophical language of human happiness may open avenues toward jouissance that need not be deferred, but these paths are fraught with potential for misapprehension. What remains clear, however, is that the *Rose* in its widespread and long-lasting influence bequeathed vernacular poetry a decidedly intellectual erotics, creating a tradition that would include Gower's confessing lover, framed by concerns for the common good; Chaucer's Troilus and Criseyde, wondering about freedom and 'felicite' while they romance; and Deguileville's *Pèlerinage de la vie humaine*, where we find an Aristotle intellectually unmanned by Sapience's broken mirror. Fourteenth-century poetry continued to speak in the shared vocabulary of lovers and clerks, and questions of how one should define and experience love, delight, pain, and desire continued to offer fodder for all of the medieval discourses oriented toward human happiness.

Washington University, St Louis

MEDIEVAL RHETORIC DELIVERS; OR,
WHERE CHAUCER LEARNED HOW TO ACT

Martin Camargo

Like many specialists in medieval literature, I first came to rhetoric in search of something equivalent to medieval literary theory. My particular interest was in medieval conceptions of genre: I was studying Middle English epistolary love lyrics at the time and needed help determining which poems in direct address might have been intended by their authors or recognized by their readers as letters.[1] I sought that help in the vast medieval corpus of rhetorical texts on letter writing known as the *ars dictaminis*. However, because so many of the rhetorical texts that interested me had never been published in printed editions, I soon found myself deeply immersed in the manuscript tradition and on my way to becoming as much a specialist in the history and theory of medieval Latin rhetoric as in Middle English literature. Moreover, when one studies rhetorical

This essay had its beginning in a brief contribution to a panel on medieval performance organized by Mary Carruthers in April 2005. I have delivered conference-paper versions at the annual conference of the American Society for the History of Rhetoric (Boston, November 2005) and the Fourth International Conference for the Study of *Piers Plowman* (Philadelphia, May 2007); longer versions as plenary lectures at the annual conference of the Medieval Association of the Pacific (Salt Lake City, February 2006), the international conference 'Classics in the Classroom' (Sydney, July 2006), and the conference 'Texts and Contexts' (Columbus, September 2006); and extracts from the lecture version at the interdisciplinary conference 'Rhetoric Beyond Words' (Oxford, March 2006) and the mini-conference '"Gladly Lerne, Gladly Teche": A Celebration of John Fleming, Scholar, Teacher, Friend' (Princeton, June 2006). I want to thank the organizers of these meetings for the opportunity to share my ideas and the participants for their enthusiastic responses. For their helpful suggestions, I am especially grateful to Rita Copeland and Marjorie Curry Woods.

[1] Martin Camargo, *The Middle English Verse Love Epistle* (Tübingen, 1991).

treatises in their codicological context, it is difficult to view them only as repositories of theoretical doctrine and illustrative examples. Signs of their intended and actual use are everywhere: in the marks of ownership, the glosses and marginalia, and even the other texts copied alongside them. Thanks to a prolonged exposure to the manuscripts, eventually my research on medieval rhetoric took what could be called a 'pedagogical turn', as I began to focus my attention more and more on who was teaching these texts, how they taught them, to whom, and toward what ends.

That line of questioning gave new prominence to features of the treatises I had previously neglected. One such feature is the medieval rhetoricians' frequent use of 'play' in their teaching. As I looked more closely at the way in which these teachers employed play-acting or impersonation, in particular, it became clear that more was at stake than merely illustrating a bit of stylistic lore or livening up a conventional lesson. What I will argue here is that, at least some of the time, the role-playing that features more or less prominently in one variety of medieval rhetorical textbook was part of a deliberate and systematic programme for training students in oral performance. Such training took place at a specific point in the study of the language arts and had practical applications at the next levels of study and in the work sphere of the professionally literate.

These views run counter to a persistent, if perhaps weakening consensus about medieval rhetoric. Performance or 'delivery' certainly was an important component of medieval rhetoric's classical antecedent. Called either *pronuntiatio* (which emphasized its first constituent: voice) or *actio* (which emphasized its other constituent: gesture), delivery was the fifth and final canon of Roman rhetoric. In other words, it was on a par with invention, arrangement, style, and memory as a fundamental category of rhetorical doctrine. Quintilian includes a lengthy discussion of delivery in his *Institutio oratoria* (XI. iii), though during the Middle Ages the briefer treatment in the anonymous *Rhetorica ad Herennium* (III. xi. 19–xv. 27) was better known. Cicero, who personified rhetoric for the Middle Ages, has this to say about delivery in *De oratore*, his most mature reflection on the rhetorical art: 'Delivery [...] is the dominant factor in oratory; without delivery the best speaker cannot be of any account at all, and a moderate speaker with a trained delivery can often outdo the best of them' (III. lvi. 213).[2] Training in delivery

---

[2] Cicero, *De oratore*: *'De oratore', Book III; 'De fato'; 'Paradoxa stoicorum'; 'De partitione oratoria'*, trans. by H. Rackham, 2 vols (Cambridge, MA, 1942), II, 169; 'Actio [...] in dicendo una dominatur; sine hac summus orator esse in numero nullo potest, mediocris hac instructus summos saepe superare' (p. 168).

was important enough in antiquity that a special category of teachers — the *phonasci* — existed to provide it (they are mentioned in *Rhetorica ad Herennium,* III. xi. 20).

The fall of Rome swept away or radically transformed the legal, political, and cultural institutions that sustained Roman rhetoric and with them the educational system that had trained Roman orators. The educational system that developed to replace it, according to the standard argument, had little room for training in rhetoric and even less for training in oral performance. Despite a steadily growing body of evidence to the contrary, the view persists that medieval rhetoric was chiefly concerned with producing written texts. If public speeches were the form taken by 'primary rhetoric', so the story goes, then medieval rhetoric was 'secondary rhetoric' that reduced the five canons of classical rhetoric to diminished versions of invention and arrangement, and placed most of its emphasis on style. Memory and delivery atrophied from disuse as medieval pedagogues subjected rhetoric to a process of aestheticization that George Kennedy famously dubbed 'letteraturizzazione'.[3]

Rarely does a long-standing scholarly consensus prove groundless, and this one rests in part on a perceptible blurring of the boundaries that separated rhetoric from the other two arts of the medieval trivium: grammar and logic. Already in antiquity rhetoric was prone to being partially absorbed by one or both of the neighbouring verbal arts, and this tendency was exacerbated during the Middle Ages. In medieval curricula and classroom practices, it is particularly difficult to spot the point where instruction shifts to rhetoric from grammar, a discipline that is fundamentally bound up with writing, as attested by its very name — from *gramma*, Greek for 'letter'.[4] Nonetheless, even at the most elementary levels of the grammar course, students were required to speak, and by attending to the different speaking skills required of students at each stage in their progression through the grammatical curriculum, we can clarify the seemingly vague boundary between grammar and rhetoric.

At the most elementary levels of instruction, grammar students were drilled in the most passive forms of memory and delivery. Their task was to memorize the

---

[3] George Kennedy, *Classical Rhetoric and Its Christian and Secular Tradition from Ancient to Modern Times* (Chapel Hill, 1980), pp. 108–19 (2nd edn, revised and enlarged (Chapel Hill, 1999), pp. 127–36). See also the influential version of this argument in Brian Vickers, *In Defence of Rhetoric* (Oxford, 1988), pp. 214–53.

[4] Martin Irvine (with David Thomson), '*Grammatica* and Literary Theory', in *The Cambridge History of Literary Criticism*, II: *The Middle Ages*, ed. by Alastair Minnis and Ian Johnson (Cambridge, 2005), pp. 30–33.

elements of Latin morphology, syntax, vocabulary, and prosody well enough to recite them back to the schoolmaster verbatim. Any deviation from the rule counted as an error and was discouraged with the threat of corporal punishment. At the most advanced stages of grammar instruction, by contrast, the emphasis shifted from analysis to synthesis, from breaking texts down into their constituent elements to recombining those elements to produce new texts, which students then presented orally to the master and the other students in the class. If the initial stage was grammar defined as the 'principles for writing and speaking correctly' (ratio recte scribendi et loquendi), this final stage was rhetoric, in fact if not always in name.[5]

In between these two extremes, students were trained in grammar as the 'science of interpreting' (scientia interpretandi), which encompassed not only a good deal of analysis and rote memorization of rules but also practice in oral recitation. During this intermediate stage of their elementary education, medieval students moved from mere recitation, which aspired to nothing more than correct content and pronunciation, to what could justly be called rhetorical delivery, which strove to communicate understanding of a text's tone and meaning through voice and gesture. The manuscript copies of the canonical texts that medieval students were assigned to read and interpret clearly indicate that medieval training in textual interpretation included practice in performance. In her 1996 book *Medieval Reading: Grammar, Rhetoric and the Classical Text*, Suzanne Reynolds studies the various notations that guided students through their oral recitations of complex classical poems such as Horace's *Satires*.[6] More recently, Jan Ziolkowski has discussed the practice of neuming such texts, in particular Virgil's *Aeneid* — a practice that he shows to have been fairly widespread from the tenth through the twelfth centuries. This musical notation was converted into oral performance in a variety of ways: it was 'employed to highlight accent or stress in pronunciation, syntactic function or word order in grammar, and emphasis in rhetoric',[7] and even at times to help schoolboys sing or chant the marked

---

[5] See Irvine (with Thomson), '*Grammatica* and Literary Theory', pp. 15–41, for an excellent brief overview of medieval grammar; and Rita Copeland, *Rhetoric, Hermeneutics and Translation in the Middle Ages* (Cambridge, 1996), on the fluid boundary between the disciplines of grammar and rhetoric.

[6] Suzanne Reynolds, *Medieval Reading: Grammar, Rhetoric, and the Classical Text* (Cambridge, 1996).

[7] Jan Ziolkowski, '*Nota Bene:* Why the Classics Were Neumed in the Middle Ages', *Journal of Medieval Latin*, 10 (2000), 74–114 (pp. 78–79).

passages.[8] In other words, the purpose behind this neuming and some of the practices described by Reynolds was the same: to facilitate interpretive, expressive delivery of the annotated text.

Before they ever turned their hands to text production, therefore, medieval students were (1) thoroughly habituated to regarding texts — particularly, but not exclusively, poetic texts — as scripts for performance and (2) well practised in the techniques of oral interpretation. It comes as no surprise, then, that the textbooks used to teach composition in the Middle Ages share those same assumptions and imply or, more rarely, describe those same classroom practices. Whether or not they expressly treat delivery, all medieval rhetoric textbooks teach the art of composing 'performable' texts. Moreover, what evidence we have strongly suggests that medieval rhetoric students actually performed the texts they were assigned to compose. Whatever form these texts took, whether sermons, letters, or poems in quantitative or rhythmical verse, they would have been delivered orally, probably from memory, and critiqued for their delivery as well as for their content, structure, and style.

Of the three main genres of medieval rhetorical textbooks, one might expect the arts of preaching (*artes praedicandi*) to concern themselves most explicitly with oral performance. As a rule, these treatises focus primarily on how to divide and elaborate on the biblical 'theme' of a sermon; but many of them do treat matters related to delivery, if only in passing. For example, the thirteenth-century *Ars concionandi* (Art of Public Speaking) of Pseudo-Bonaventure observes that a preacher does well to choose biblical passages in the second person.[9] Marianne Briscoe speculates that this is 'because the verbs in the theme can be spoken to the audience as exhortations or set in a quasi-dramatic frame with the preacher addressing or speaking in the person of some figure in Scripture'.[10] The Dominican Humbert de Romans (*c.* 1200–77) is more explicit in his *Liber de*

---

[8] Ziolkowski, '*Nota Bene*', pp. 93–98. See also Jan Ziolkowski, 'Women's Lament and the Neuming of the Classics', in *Music and Medieval Manuscripts: Paleography and Performance; Essays Dedicated to Andrew Hughes*, ed. by John Haines and Randall Rosenfeld (Aldershot, 2004), pp. 128–50; 'Between Text and Music: The Reception of Virgilian Speeches in Early Medieval Manuscripts', *Materiali e discussioni per l'analisi dei testi classici*, 52 (2004), 107–26; and '*Nota Bene*': *Reading Classics and Writing Melodies in the Early Middle Ages*, Publications of the Journal of Medieval Latin, 7 (Turnhout, 2007).

[9] [Bonaventure], *Ars concionandi*, in *S. Bonaventurae opera omnia*, 9 (Quaracchi, 1901), pp. 8–21 (p. 8).

[10] Marianne Briscoe, *Artes praedicandi*, Typologie des sources du moyen âge occidental, 61 (Turnhout, 1992), p. 33.

eruditione praedicatorum (Treatise on the Formation of Preachers), observing that
while preachers need to use discretion in deciding how loud to speak and which
gestures to employ on a given occasion, for any successful preaching they must
have a sonorous voice, fluency of speech, a measured pace, the ability to speak
simply and concisely, and a sensitivity to the audience's needs.[11] Delivery also
receives more extensive consideration in some of the fourteenth-century arts
of preaching written in England. For instance, Robert of Basevorn's *Forma
praedicandi* (Model of Preaching) includes brief remarks on modulation of voice,
appropriate gesture, and timely humour (chap. 50).[12] The Oxford theologian
Thomas Waleys devotes even more space to the subject in his *De modo componendi
sermones* (On the Method of Composing Sermons), which provides detailed and
practical advice on topics ranging from varying one's diction to practising the
delivery of one's sermon in advance (chap. 1).[13] One of the most influential arts of
preaching, Alain de Lille's *Summa de arte praedicatoria* (Compendium on the Art
of Preaching; late twelfth century), advises preachers to adapt the content of their
sermons to the needs and abilities of particular audiences but tells them nothing
about the most effective strategies for communicating that message through oral
delivery.[14] Presumably, such advice would have been provided orally by the
teachers who used these textbooks in their instruction.[15]

A concern with performability, if not advice on performance itself, is central
to a second major genre of medieval rhetoric textbook, the arts of letter writing
(*artes dictandi*). The reason for this emphasis can be traced to the very origins of
the *ars dictaminis*, as Ronald Witt reminds us: 'Since the major impetus behind
the growing demand for letter-writing came from the increasing organisation
of political and economic power, *ars dictaminis* from the outset was orientated
towards oral presentation of the message within a formal setting. Official
communications, particularly important letters, were usually read aloud by

---

[11] Humbert de Romans, *Liber de eruditione praedicatorum*, trans. by Simon Tugwell, in *Early
Dominicans: Selected Writings* (New York, 1982), pp. 179–370 (pp. 218–20).

[12] Thomas-M. Charland, *Artes praedicandi: Contribution à l'histoire de la rhétorique au moyen
âge* (Paris, 1936), p. 320.

[13] Charland, *Artes praedicandi*, pp. 331–41.

[14] Alain de Lille, *Summa de arte praedicatoria*, ed. by Jacques-Paul Migne, *Patrologiae cursus
completus [...] Series Latina*, 221 vols (Paris, 1844–64), CCX (1855), cols 110–98 (cols 184–98).

[15] The best concise surveys of the medieval arts of preaching are Marianne Briscoe, *Artes
praedicandi*, pp. 11–76; and James J. Murphy, *Rhetoric in the Middle Ages* (Berkeley and Los
Angeles, 1974), pp. 269–355.

recipients or in the recipient's presence, thus taking on the appearance of a speech at the moment of communication.'[16] The very structure of a medieval letter is based on the parts of an oration, as defined by the Roman rhetoricians, and distinctive features of epistolary style, most notably the patterned clause endings of the *cursus*, are valued for their effects on a listening audience. In fact, when a medieval art of speech making (*ars arengandi*), arose in thirteenth-century Italy, it took its origins from the *ars dictaminis* and prescribed speeches that look like nothing so much as letters minus the personal greeting (*salutatio*).[17]

A third genre of rhetorical textbook that consistently addresses oral delivery is the one most closely tied to the study of literature and hence most closely aligned with grammar: what Douglas Kelly calls the 'arts of poetry and prose' and James J. Murphy the 'preceptive grammars'.[18] Their concern with delivery is probably due to their position in the curriculum. Students would come to them fresh from their experiences with oral interpretation of canonical texts and ready to practise the same techniques on texts of their own composition. Looking ahead, the skills they would have refined by performing the exercises in general composition prescribed by the arts of poetry and prose would have prepared them to deliver letters or sermons and perhaps even to conduct effective disputations at the next stage of the arts curriculum: the study of dialectic.

What may be the latest of the eight surviving arts of poetry and prose,[19] the *Poetria* (Poetics) by the Swede Matthias of Linköping, is unique in theorizing the integral place of delivery within the arts of poetry and prose. Writing between 1318 and 1332, probably while a student in Paris, Matthias draws on the scholastic

---

[16] Ronald G. Witt, 'The Arts of Letter-Writing', in *Cambridge History of Literary Criticism* (see n. 4, above), pp. 68–83 (p. 70).

[17] For a more detailed introduction, see Martin Camargo, *Ars Dictaminis, Ars Dictandi*, Typologie des sources du moyen âge occidental, 60 (Turnhout, 1991).

[18] Douglas Kelly, *The Arts of Poetry and Prose*, Typologie des sources du moyen âge occidental, 59 (Turnhout, 1991); James J. Murphy, *Rhetoric in the Middle Ages* (Berkeley and Los Angeles, 1974), pp. 135–93.

[19] The extant medieval arts of poetry and prose, in approximate chronological order: (a) Matthew of Vendôme, *Ars versificatoria* (before 1175); (b) Geoffrey of Vinsauf, *Documentum de modo et arte dictandi et versificandi* (late twelfth century?); (c) Geoffrey of Vinsauf, *Poetria nova* (composed *c.* 1200, revised before 1213); (d) Gervase of Melkley, *De arte versificatoria et modo dictandi* (1213–16); (e) John of Garland, *Parisiana Poetria* (composed *c.* 1220, revised 1231–35); (f) Eberhard the German, *Laborintus* (after 1213, before 1280); (g) Matthias of Linköping, *Poetria* (1318–32); (h) Anonymous, *Tria sunt* (after 1256, before *c.* 1400).

commentary tradition[20] to distinguish between the 'essentials' (essencialia) and the 'accidentals' (accidentalia) of poetics, that is, between what is particular to poetry and what poetry shares with other types of writing. As accidentals common to all forms of writing, Matthias specifies the 'ways of reciting, arranging, amplifying and shortening'.[21] If his discussion of these accidentals is cursory, he goes on to say, that is because they have already been treated in detail in Geoffrey of Vinsauf's *Poetria nova* (New Poetics), the most popular of the medieval arts of poetry and prose, and in its classical model, Horace's *Ars poetica*.[22] Anyone who has reached the stage in the curriculum where he is ready to study the essentials of poetry, as Matthias's chief source Aristotle defines them, already will have learned the accidentals, including the 'ways of reciting', from one or both of these texts or from another text like them.

In fact, Geoffrey of Vinsauf's *Poetria nova*,[23] written in Latin hexameters and preserved in more than two hundred manuscripts, is the art of poetry and prose that treats delivery most directly and extensively; but all of them contain material that can help us understand (1) what made a text performable in the Middle Ages and (2) how medieval rhetoric teachers guided their students as they actually performed their compositions. The concern for performability is most evident in such prominent features of their teaching as (a) their emphasis on those stylistic ornaments that most appeal to the ear, (b) their proscription of those stylistic 'vices' that produce cacophony or impede listening comprehension, and (c) their advocacy of well-marked transitions that orient listeners to the sequence of discrete, sharply articulated parts of the performed text. Equally important, most of their textbooks contain multiple examples of highly performable texts, in particular those that illustrate the various techniques for amplifying one's subject matter.

When Geoffrey of Vinsauf classifies the ten tropes as 'ornamented difficulty' (ornata difficultas) and the other thirty-five figures of speech as 'ornamented facility' (ornata facilitas), he bases the distinction in part on the relative difficulty

---

[20] See Päivi Mehtonen, 'Essential Art: Matthew of Linköping's Fourteenth-Century Poetics', *Rhetorica*, 25 (2007), 125–39.

[21] Matthias of Linköping, *Poetria*, ed. and trans. by Birger Bergh, in *Magister Mathias Lincopensis, Testa Nucis and Poetria*, Samlingar utgivna av Svenska Fornskriftsällskapet, ser. 2, 9: 2 (Arlöv, 1996), p. 45; 'modos recitandi, ordinandi, prolongandi et abbreuiandi' (p. 44).

[22] Matthias of Linköping, *Poetria*, pp. 72–73.

[23] Geoffrey of Vinsauf, *Poetria nova*, ed. by Edmond Faral, in *Les arts poétiques du XIIᵉ et du XIIIᵉ siècle* (Paris, 1924), pp. 197–262; hereafter cited as PN.

and ease of aural comprehension.[24] Eberhard the German, drawing on Geoffrey's teaching in his own verse treatise, *Laborintus* (The Labyrinth), further explains that easy style may be achieved with or without ornament (ll. 431–32), but the ornamented easy style 'sounds sweet in the ear' (l. 440).[25] By contrast, the ornamented difficult style appeals more to the mind than the senses: it is characterized by figures whose effects are derived from transferred meaning rather than pleasing sounds. The nineteen figures of thought also fall under 'ornamented facility', but it is overwhelmingly the figures of speech, the stylistic ornaments that rely on patterned sounds, that dominate in the model texts that medieval rhetoric teachers provided in their textbooks. These figures include various kinds of repetition, including rhyme; various kinds of transplacement, including paronomasia or punning; and various mimetic techniques, including those that imitate spoken dialogue. Numerous treatises devoted solely to the figures of speech confirm the importance of such figures in the medieval pedagogy of performability. Marbod of Rennes's *De ornamentis verborum* (On the Figures of Speech; late eleventh century) is an early and especially influential

---

[24] The rhetorical figures, from *Rhetorica ad Herennium*, IV. xiii. 19–lv. 69: (a) Tropes: onomatopoeia (*nominatio*), antonomasia (*pronominatio*), metonymy (*denominatio*), periphrasis (*circumitio*), hyperbaton (*transgressio*), hyperbole (*superlatio*), synecdoche (*intellectio*), catachresis (*abusio*), metaphor (*translatio*), allegory (*permutatio*) [Geoffrey of Vinsauf's 'ornamented difficulty'; PN 765–1093]; (b) Other figures of speech: epanaphora (*repetitio*), antistrophe (*conversio*), interlacement (*complexio*), transplacement (*traductio*), antithesis (*contentio*), apostrophe (*exclamatio*), interrogation (*interrogatio*), reasoning by question and answer (*ratiocinatio*), maxim (*sententia*), reasoning by contraries (*contrarium*), colon or clause (*membrum*), comma or phrase (*articulus*), period (*continuatio*), isocolon (*compar*), homoeoptoton (*similiter cadens*), homoeoteleuton (*similiter desinens*), paronomasia (*adnominatio*), hypophora (*subiectio*), climax (*gradatio*), definition (*definitio*), transition (*transitio*), epanorthosis (*correctio*), paralipsis (*occultatio* or *occupatio*), disjunction (*disiunctum* or *disiunctio*), conjunction (*coniunctio*), adjunction (*adiunctio*), reduplication (*conduplicatio*), synonymy or interpretation (*interpretatio*), reciprocal change (*commutatio*), surrender (*permissio*), indecision (*dubitatio*), elimination (*expeditio*), asyndeton (*dissolutum* or *dissolutio*), aposiopesis (*praecisio*), conclusion (*conclusio*); (c) Figures of thought: distribution (*distributio*), frankness of speech (*licentia*), understatement (*deminutio*), vivid description (*descriptio*), division (*divisio*), accumulation (*frequentatio*), refining (*expolitio*), dwelling on the point (*commoratio*), antithesis (*contentio*), comparison (*similitudo*), exemplification (*exemplum*), simile (*imago*), portrayal (*effictio*), character delineation (*notatio*), dialog (*sermocinatio*), personification (*conformatio*), emphasis (*significatio*), conciseness (*brevitas*), ocular demonstration (*demonstratio*) [b. and c. = Geoffrey of Vinsauf's 'ornamented facility'; PN 1094–1587].

[25] 'Talis planities dulcis in aure sonat': Eberhard the German, *Laborintus*, ed. by Faral, in *Arts poétiques* (see n. 23, above), pp. 337–77 (p. 351); my translation.

example.[26] Geoffrey of Vinsauf's *Summa de coloribus rhetoricis* (Compendium on the Rhetorical Colours; late twelfth century)[27] is only one of the many short treatises on the same topic that followed in Marbod's footsteps.

Most arts of poetry and prose not only defined and illustrated the stylistic ornaments one ought to cultivate but also devoted some space to the stylistic faults one ought to avoid (e.g., PN 1920–42). Nearly all such treatises include among those 'vices' a group of five or six that either offend the ear or impede aural comprehension. I will try to illustrate each of them with an *exemplum domesticum*, or 'homemade example', in English. The first of the cacophonous vices, hiatus or collision of vowels, can be illustrated with this snippet of dialogue from my as-yet-unwritten play *The Cockney Narcissus:* 'O, 'ello, Echo.' 'O, 'ello, Echo.' The second offence against the ear is the excessive repetition of the same consonant sound, especially if the consonant is an *l, m,* or *r.* I will illustrate this vice and a third offence against euphony, excessive repetition of the same ending, with another homemade example, this one from an 'Apostrophe to a Gossip Columnist': 'O radar reader! rumor reaper! ruder writer!' Geoffrey of Vinsauf points out that the fourth cacophonous vice — excessive repetition of the same word — like the previous three, is a case of ornament gone wild: 'The moderate repetition of words is an adornment; whatever is excessive is a thing remote from adornment' (PN 1934–35).[28] A fifth vice in the standard group could be called an excessive version of the figure hyperbaton or incongruous word order, as in 'Hyperbaton this is, excessive, surely'. It is difficult to say whether this vice offends more against euphony or ease of comprehension. In order to illustrate the sixth and final vice, the use of excessively long periodic sentences, which interfere with a listener's ease of comprehension, any one of the sentences characterized by subordinate clauses, parenthetical asides, and passive constructions that my wife (formerly a professional editor in the New York publishing industry) revised out of the original draft of this paper to improve its performability would have sufficed.

---

[26] Marbod of Rennes, *De ornamentis verborum*, ed. and trans. (Italian) by Rosario Leotta, in *Marbodo di Rennes, 'De ornamentis verborum'; 'Liber decem capitulorum': Retorica, mitologia e moralità di un vescovo poeta (secc. XI–XII)* (Florence, 1998), pp. 1–25.

[27] Geoffrey of Vinsauf, *Summa de coloribus rhetoricis*, ed. (in part) by Faral, in *Arts poétiques* (see n. 23, above), pp. 321–27.

[28] *'Poetria nova' of Geoffrey of Vinsauf*, trans. by Margaret F. Nims (Toronto, 1967), p. 86; 'Moderata resumptio vocum | Est color: omne quod est nimium res absque colore': PN, ed. by Faral, p. 256:

Avoiding sentences like the preceding is one way of keeping listeners from getting lost. A more positive strategy is to provide them with easily recognized signposts. Medieval composition teachers frequently address this feature of performable texts by providing lists of words and phrases suitable for marking transitions between sections of texts. Such lists are a regular feature in the arts of letter writing, because letters usually had five or more parts, each of them fulfilling a distinct rhetorical function. When the arts of poetry and prose explicitly address the same need, they tend to focus on the transition between the general proverb or exemplum that might open the text and its application to the specific subject matter to be developed in the body of the text. Geoffrey of Vinsauf's prose textbook has the fullest treatment of this technique,[29] which it calls 'connecting' or 'continuing' (continuatio); but sharply delineated transitions characterize all but the shortest model compositions found in such treatises and clearly represent a basic feature of what could be called the pedagogy of performability.

From sources that include John of Salisbury's reminiscences about his teacher Bernard de Chartres as well as the statutes of medieval English schools, we know that such compositions actually were performed in medieval classrooms.[30] Though detailed descriptions of such performances are rare, some idea of what they might have been like can be derived from the texts themselves. The most performable types of text were those that provided the greatest scope for both stylistic abundance and emotional excess, as Marjorie Curry Woods demonstrates in her studies of medieval schoolboys impersonating tragic heroines.[31] Similarly, Jan Ziolkowski found that passages of great emotional intensity, notably the laments of tragic heroines such as Dido's in Book IV of the *Aeneid*, were those most likely to be neumed in medieval manuscripts, as a guide to future performances.

The same dramatic intensity characterizes another popular type of school exercise, the invective against ill-qualified teachers. In his *Poetria nova*, Geoffrey

---

[29] Geoffrey of Vinsauf, *Documentum de modo et arte dictandi et versificandi*, ed. by Faral, in *Arts poétiques* (see n. 23, above), pp. 265–320 (pp. 268–71).

[30] John of Salisbury, *Metalogicon* (1159), I. 24; Strickland Gibson, *Statuta antiqua universitatis oxoniensis* (Oxford, 1931), p. 171.

[31] Marjorie Curry Woods, 'Rape and the Pedagogical Rhetoric of Sexual Violence', in *Criticism and Dissent in the Middle Ages*, ed. by Rita Copeland (Cambridge, 1996), pp. 56–86; 'Boys Will Be Women: Musings on Classroom Nostalgia and the Chaucerian Audience(s)', in *Speaking Images: Essays in Honor of V. A. Kolve*, ed. by Robert F. Yeager and Charlotte C. Morse (Asheville, NC, 2001), pp. 143–66; and 'Weeping for Dido: Epilogue on a Premodern Rhetorical Exercise in the Postmodern Classroom', in *Latin Grammar and Rhetoric: From Classical Theory to Medieval Practice*, ed. by Carol Dana Lanham (London, 2002), pp. 284–94.

of Vinsauf provides an example that includes a rare glimpse of how a teacher might have coached his students through an actual performance. The passage occurs in Geoffrey's discussion of apostrophe, a technique of amplification that is highly suited to dramatic presentation. In characteristically playful fashion, Geoffrey embeds his apostrophe on a pretentiously precocious master within a larger apostrophe to his students — on the subject of performing apostrophes — that includes guidance on appropriate tone of voice and gestures. Further complicating matters — and adding to the fun — Geoffrey interrupts the model apostrophe on the topic 'Boys are raised up and made masters' with asides or miniature apostrophes to his students. To understand what Geoffrey is doing and even to keep track of the frequent shifts from one level of apostrophe to another and finally to pure gesture, it is best to perform the text as Geoffrey might have delivered it orally to his students. As an alternative, I have underscored the parts of the passage that refer directly to the manner in which the classroom exercise should be delivered:

> If you wish to rise up in full strength against the ridiculous, assail them in this form of speech: offer praise, <u>but in a facetious manner</u>; reprove, but with wit and grace; <u>have recourse to gestures, but let these be consistently fitting</u>. Give your speech teeth; attack with biting force--<u>but let your manner rather than your lips devour the absurd</u>. Lo, what was hidden in darkness will be revealed in full light. A lively theme is under discussion: *'Boys are raised up and made masters.'* <u>Let their 'masterly status' evoke laughter</u>:
>
> *Now he sits, loftily graced with the title of master, who up to now was fit for the rod. For laymen, the cap on his head guarantees him authentic; as do the cut of his robes, the gold on his fingers, his seat at the head, and the crowd in his study.*
>
> <u>You can laugh at the absurd situation</u>; it is indeed a ridiculous thing:
>
> *By his own and by popular verdict this is a learned man. But you perceive the same thing that I do: he is a very ape among scholars.*
>
> <u>I said that in a whisper, let no one hear it aloud</u>.
>
> *He boasts of himself, indeed, and rattling on, promises marvels. Hurry up, one and all; now the mountain's in labour, but its offspring will be only a mouse.*
>
> <u>Going before him, bid the master good day; but smile, too, at times, with a sidelong glance. Mock him with a kind of 'beak' of your hands;</u>[32] <u>or pull a wry mouth, or draw in your nostrils: for such expressions of ridicule it is fitting to use not the mouth but the nose</u>.

---

[32] I have replaced Nims's version ('Mock him with the ciconia's sign of derision') with a more literal translation of Geoffrey's Latin: 'quodam rostro manuum quasi pinse' (PN 452, adopting Nims's correction of Faral's *punge* to *pinse*).

Revelling in its stylistic excess, apostrophe cries out for dramatic performance, and Geoffrey concludes his apostrophe on apostrophe by enumerating four popular modes of performance that it facilitated in medieval classrooms, each with its distinctive associated emotion:

> Apostrophe varies its countenance thus: with the mien of a magistrate it rebukes vicious error; or it languishes in tearful complaint against all that is harsh; or is roused to wrath over some great crime; or appears with derisive force in attacking buffoons. When evoked by causes such as these, apostrophe contributes both adornment and amplification. (PN 431–60)[33]

Dozens of school texts contain analogues of Geoffrey's annotated example, in which scholarly pretensions are mocked with theatrical derision. The stage directions in Geoffrey's version may even indicate role playing, with one schoolboy doing the mocking and another playing the object of mockery. Throughout the *Poetria nova* Geoffrey provides examples of the other three modes of apostrophe: magisterial rebuke of error (276–323), expression of outrage at crimes committed (e.g., 382–85, 472–87, 517–22), and tearful complaint about harsh misfortune (368–430). The last of these he illustrates in a lament for the death of King Richard Lionheart that became famous enough to have been parodied by Chaucer nearly two hundred years later. In such exercises, apostrophe was used together with other figures to heighten the drama and the level of emotion. The same strategy can be seen in an exercise in which Geoffrey uses the thirty-five figures of

---

[33] '*Poetria nova*', trans. by Nims, pp. 31–32, with my changes in formatting; 'Contra ridiculos si vis insurgere plene, | Surge sub hac specie: lauda, sed ridiculose; | Argue, sed lepide gere te, sed in omnibus apte; | Sermo tuus dentes habeat, mordaciter illos | Tange, sed irrisos gestus plus mordeat ore. | Ecce, quod in tenebris latuit, sub luce patebit. | Strenua res agitur: *pueri tolluntur in altum | Et fiunt domini.* Moveat dominatio risum: | *Han sedet egregie donatus honore magistri | Aptus adhuc ferulae. Laicis authenticat illum | Pileus in capite, species in vestibus, aurum | In digitis, sedes in summo, plebs numerosa | In studio.* Ridere potes de ridiculoso: | Quoddam ridiculum est: *Tam se quam judice vulgo | Doctus homo est.* Sed idem sentis quod sentio: quaedam | Simia doctorum est. Clam dixi, ne quis aperte | Audiat. Ipse tamen se jactitat osque revolvens | Mira quidem spondet. Omnes accurrite: jam mons | Parturiet, sed erit tandem mus filius ejus. | Praeveniens illum salvere jubeto magistrum. | Nec minus interdum transverso lumine ride; | Vel quodam rostro manuum quasi pinse [Faral: punge]; vel oris | Rictum distorque; vel nares contrahe: tales | Ad formas non ore decet, sed naribus uti. | Sic igitur variat vultum: vel more magistri | Corripit errorem pravum; vel ad omnia dura | In lacrimis planctuque jacet; vel surgit in iram | Propter grande scelus; vel fertur ridiculose | Contra ridiculos. Ex talibus edita causis | Et decus et numerum lucratur apostropha verbis': PN, ed. by Faral, pp. 210–11.

speech in sequence to construct a coherent text (PN 1098–1217). The resulting
poem is divided into three parts, each of them punctuated by an apostrophe —
first to the fatal apple and Adam who tasted it (1098–1116), then to the Devil
(1139–44, 1169–71), and finally to Christ (1175–82). While the entire poem is
a showpiece of verbal 'sound effects', the hyperdramatic apostrophes stand out
like strategically placed crescendos. When read silently, especially by a modern
reader, these massed figures seem tedious and overblown; but the effect would
have been different in a live performance. To pursue the musical analogy, one
could call such compositions 'operatic'. Anyone who comes to an opera expecting
verisimilar dialogue will find the arias similarly overblown and repetitious, but
that would be to miss the point.

Other techniques besides apostrophe were used in isolation or in combination
to enhance the performability of school exercises. To mention only one example,
the persistent use of dialogue in the illustrative examples may point to even more
elaborate classroom role-playing, perhaps involving student and master or more
than one student speaking by turns. Geoffrey of Vinsauf provides several mini-
dramas in the *Poetria nova*. One of them, a dialogue between a lazy man and his
master, actually derives from Terence (1366–80). Another, apparently an exchange
between a debtor and his impatient creditor, is usually glossed in the manuscripts
as representing a writer who pleads for more time to complete his composition
(1745–48).[34] Still another brief example, which I will quote for illustration, leaves
no doubt about the student identity of the interlocutors. It first appears in
Geoffrey of Vinsauf's prose textbook *Documentum de modo et arte dictandi et
versificandi* (Instruction in the Method and Art of Composing in Prose and in
Verse; II. 3. 168)[35] and is repeated in both Gervase of Melkley's *De arte versificatoria
et modo dictandi* (On the Art of Versifying and the Method of Composing in
Prose)[36] and the anonymous *Tria sunt* (Worcester Cathedral, Chapter Library, MS
Q.79, fol. 129ᵛ):[37] 'Are you crying?' 'I'm crying.' 'Will you be quiet?' 'No!' 'I'm
going to call the teacher.' 'Go ahead!' 'Do you want me to call the teacher?' 'What

---

[34] Personal e-mail from Marjorie Curry Woods.

[35] Geoffrey of Vinsauf, *Documentum de modo*, ed. by Faral, p. 317: "'Fles — Fleo'"; "'Nonne taces — Non'"; "'Vado vocare magistrum. — Vade'"; "'Magistrum visne vocem? — Quae mihi cura? Voca'".

[36] Gervase of Melkley, *De arte versificatoria et modo dictandi*, ed. by Hans-Jürgen Gräbener, in *Gervais von Melkley: 'Ars poetica'* (Münster, 1965), p. 28, ll. 5–17.

[37] I am preparing a critical edition and translation of this work, which takes its title from the incipit 'There are three'.

do I care? Call him!' The paired model letters in the arts of letter writing also would have lent themselves to this kind of interactive performance. Indeed, it is quite possible that teachers would have assigned different students to compose each half of the exchange, allowing them to impersonate a wide range of persons, from popes and emperors, to soldiers and swineherds, and — no great stretch here — students and their parsimonious relatives.

As noted earlier, oral performance of such texts would have highlighted their emotional dimension. Cues for expressing emotional intensity are especially evident in another of the extended exercises from Geoffrey of Vinsauf's *Poetria nova* (1280–1527). Built around the nineteen figures of thought, again deployed in their standard textbook sequence, the poem is a veritable anthology of set pieces suitable for performance. The speaker begins with an apostrophe to the pope (1280–1304), then speaks in the pope's persona (1305–24), then addresses a tightly structured harangue to the pope (1325–44), and later acts out a dialogue between the lazy man and his accuser (1366–80), impersonates the mockers of Christ's Passion (1389–1402), laments the Crucifixion in the voice of personified Nature (1411–15), and chastises recalcitrant humanity in yet another impassioned apostrophe (1424–28). In his own teaching, Geoffrey seems especially to have favoured performances that expressed outrage and rebuke. Hence, when he comes to discuss delivery per se, near the end of the *Poetria nova*, he devotes considerable space to the expression of anger. However, Geoffrey makes it clear that he is not encouraging his students to become angry themselves but rather to adopt a persona, to play a role: 'If you act the part of this man [that is, an angry person], what, as reciter, will you do? Imitate genuine fury, but do not be furious. Be affected in part as he is, but not deeply so. Let your manner be the same in every respect, but not so extreme; yet suggest, as is fitting, the emotion itself' (PN 2047–51).[38]

Although the other preceptive grammarians are less explicit about delivery than Geoffrey of Vinsauf, their stylistic doctrines and the illustrative models in their textbooks strongly suggest that they taught delivery in their classrooms. They did so because their students needed them to. Formal training in oral performance at the point where students completed their general mastery of Latin had practical value, whether in preparing them to conduct oral disputations when

---

[38] '*Poetria nova*', trans. by Nims, p. 90; 'Personam si geris ejus, | Quid recitator ages? Veros imitare furores. | Non tamen esto furens: partim movearis ut ille, | Non penitus; motusque tuus sit in omnibus idem, | Non tantus; sed rem, sicut decet, innue': PN, ed. by Faral, p. 260

they moved on to the study of logic, to declaim letters that were structured like classical orations and intended to be read aloud in public, or to preach sermons.

Recent scholarship has confirmed that the practical application of rhetorical training in oral delivery was by no means limited to preaching and theological disputation. In her 1992 book *Rhetoric and the Origins of Medieval Drama*, for example, Jody Enders traces the persistent importance of delivery in the forensic rhetoric of the Middle Ages.[39] Like their classical antecedents, medieval lawyers relied on structured conflict, impersonation, gesture, manipulation of the audience's emotions, even costume and other elements of spectacle to persuade; and they, too, were often criticized for their 'histrionic' practices. Thomas Haye has argued that oral delivery was a necessary skill in political as well as legal contexts. His 1999 book *Oratio* brings together fourteen Latin texts or groups of texts, dating from the tenth through the fourteenth centuries, that show signs of having been delivered orally as speeches, whether in courtrooms, conclaves, palaces, town squares, or schoolrooms.[40] In my own work I have used literary texts in the vernacular, such as the *Chanson de Roland* and Chaucer's *Troilus and Criseyde*, to illustrate the common yet potentially complex relation between the written text and the oral delivery of medieval letters.[41]

I will conclude by considering briefly some other literary examples that simultaneously highlight the qualities of performable texts that were taught in medieval composition classes, draw attention to the fact that expertise in oral delivery was a product of the schoolroom, and/or comment on the persons who were most likely to employ the techniques imparted by the arts of poetry and prose. As Joyce Coleman demonstrates in her 1996 book *Public Reading and the Reading Public in Late Medieval England and France*, Geoffrey Chaucer, like most authors writing in the fourteenth century, 'expected both his contemporary and future audiences to hear his books'.[42] Though typical in this 'aurality', Chaucer stands out among medieval vernacular poets in his explicit self-consciousness about the rhetorical dimension of poetry.[43] In no other work of his does that self-

---

[39] Jody Enders, *Rhetoric and the Origins of Medieval Drama* (Ithaca, 1992).

[40] Thomas Haye, *'Oratio': Mittelalterliche Redekunst in lateinischer Sprache* (Leiden, 1999).

[41] Martin Camargo, 'Where's the Brief?', *Disputatio*, 1 (1996), 1–17.

[42] Joyce Coleman, *Public Reading and the Reading Public in Late Medieval England and France* (Cambridge, 1996), p. 148.

[43] Among the many studies of Chaucer and rhetoric, Beryl Rowland's article is unusual in focusing on delivery. Although she cites some of the same evidence that I do, the thrust of her

consciousness engage more frequently with issues of oral performance than in the *Canterbury Tales*. This stands to reason, since the premise of the work is that each tale in the collection is performed orally. As master of ceremonies and 'horseback editor',[44] the Host is particularly attuned to what makes a good or a bad oral performance. Usually his standards are simple and commonsensical — lively stories are entertaining, monotonous delivery is boring — but occasionally he exhibits knowledge, however limited, of formal training in rhetorical delivery. For example, when he invites the Clerk of Oxford to tell a tale, he knows enough about his likely training in the *ars dictaminis* to warn him not to use it in present company:

> Youre termes, youre colours, and youre figures,
> Keepe hem in stoor til so be ye endite
> Heigh style, as whan that men to kynges write.
> Speketh so pleyn at this tyme, we yow preye,
> That we may understonde what ye seye.
>   (CT IV. 16–20)[45]

Though Harry Bailey envisages the Clerk appropriately using 'high style' when 'writing' to more socially elevated persons such as 'kings', his concern that the Clerk might employ that same style on the road to Canterbury is a reminder that even letters in the high style were composed for oral delivery. Whatever their effect on a more sophisticated listening audience, the dense wordplay and complicated syntax of that style will only bewilder him and, he implies, the other pilgrims in the company.

Despite the Host's anxiety, the Clerk's tale of patient Griselda does not exhibit features of the medieval performative style of rhetorical display to an unusual degree. If we look for pilgrims who do speak like schoolboys who absorbed and retained Geoffrey of Vinsauf's lessons on oral performance, we find them instead in the Pardoner and the Nun's Priest. Like the schoolboy reciting his composition

---

argument is that Chaucer's texts were significantly less ambiguous for the medieval audiences for whom he performed them in person than they are for later readers who must interpret them for themselves. See Rowland, '*Pronuntiatio* and Its Effect on Chaucer's Audience', *Studies in the Age of Chaucer*, 4 (1982), 33–51.

[44] Alan T. Gaylord, '*Sentence and Solaas* in Fragment VII of the *Canterbury Tales*: Harry Bailley as Horseback Editor', *PMLA*, 82 (1967), 226–35.

[45] Chaucer's *Canterbury Tales* are quoted from *The Riverside Chaucer*, ed. by Larry Benson and others, 3rd edn (Boston, 1987); hereafter cited as CT.

before the master,[46] the Pardoner knows his speech by heart and therefore is able to deliver it clearly and forcefully:

> 'Lordynges,' quod he, 'in chirches whan I preche,
> I peyne me to han an hauteyn speche,
> And rynge it out as round as gooth a belle,
> For I kan al by rote that I telle.'
>
> (CT VI. 329–32)

Standing 'lyk a clerk in [his] pulpet' before the 'lewed peple' (CT VI. 391–92), he not only speaks in a loud (hauteyn) voice but also employs a rhythmical cadence that is echoed in the perfectly regular iambic feet of the line in which he describes it.

The Pardoner also has taken pains to develop a repertoire of stagey gestures that reinforce the effects of his stern words, just as Geoffrey of Vinsauf's mocking gestures complemented his debunking of a pretentious young schoolmaster:

> Thanne peyne I me to strecche forth the nekke,
> And est and west upon the peple I bekke,
> As dooth a dowve sittynge on a berne.
> Myne handes and my tonge goon so yerne
> That it is joye to se my bisynesse.
>
> (CT VI. 395–99)

He encourages his fellow pilgrims to share the delight he takes in making a spectacle of himself, as he ostentatiously stretches out his neck, sweeps his gaze back and forth across the audience — nodding all the while, and gesticulates energetically with his hands to emphasize his ready words. His enthusiasm is so great that we probably should imagine him enacting the very gestures he describes, even as he describes them.

---

[46] Cf. Thomas Waleys, *De modo componendi sermons*, ed. by Charland, *Artes praedicandi*, p. 334: 'Non enim decet praedicatorem, nec etiam est auditoribus utile, ut sic loquatur sicut puer qui suum *Donatum* recitat, non sciens nec intelligens ea quae loquitur aut quae dicit' (It is not proper for a preacher, nor is it profitable for his audience, that he speak like a boy who is reciting his Donatus, not knowing nor understanding what he is saying or what it means). On this and other points of contact between the two works, see Martin Camargo, 'How (Not) to Preach: Thomas Waleys and Chaucer's Pardoner', in *Sacred and Profane: Essays on Chaucer and Middle English Literature*, ed. by Robert Epstein and William Robins (Aldershot, 2008). Claire M. Waters, *Angels and Earthly Creatures: Preaching, Performance, and Gender in the Later Middle Ages* (Philadelphia, 2004), also notes that Thomas Waleys pays special attention to delivery (see especially pp. 92–95).

The memorized speech that the Pardoner dramatically delivers as his 'tale' also exhibits some of the most distinctive qualities of performable texts, as medieval rhetoricians conceived them. Especially prominent is his frequent use of apostrophe to express righteous indignation.[47] A self-styled bad man | good rhetorician, the Pardoner boasts that he's not sincerely outraged by the sins he attacks, most of which he practises himself (CT VI. 423–34). As Geoffrey of Vinsauf counselled, the Pardoner is not an angry man; he's only impersonating one, as part of a virtuoso performance. When he becomes angry in earnest, after the Host ignores his rhetorical persona and insults his physical person, the result is not eloquence but speechlessness (CT VI. 956–57).

If Geoffrey of Vinsauf's advice on performing anger is evoked by the Pardoner, his model for expressing grief through apostrophe is explicitly invoked by the Nun's Priest. In a tale whose very genre — the beast fable — smacks of the schoolroom,[48] self-conscious rhetoric is everywhere on display. The 'Nun's Priest's Tale' could rightly be called Chaucer's *ars poetica,* a poem that explores and explodes conventional notions of the poet's craft. As in the Pardoner's prologue and tale, artificially enhanced oral performance is a prominent target for satire. The crafty fox teaches the vain rooster Chauntecleer how to deliver his song with maximum effect, directing him to stand on tiptoes, stretch forth his neck, and, most important, close his eyes, only to conclude the rhetoric lesson by snatching his pupil in his jaws. At this moment, the tale's emotional climax, the speaker pauses for a series of apostrophes to Destiny, Venus, Geoffrey of Vinsauf, and

---

[47] Apostrophes from 'The Pardoner's Tale': 'O glotonye, ful of cursednesse! | O cause first of oure confusioun! | O original of oure dampnacioun | Til Crist hadde boght us with his blood agayn!' (CT VI. 498–501); 'O glotonye, on thee wel oghte us pleyne! | O, wiste a man how manye maladyes | Folwen of excesse and of glotonyes, | He wolde been the moore mesurable | Of his diete, sittynge at his table' (CT VI. 512–16); 'O wombe! O bely! O stynkyng cod, | Fulfilled of dong and of corrupcioun! | At either ende of thee foul is the soun. | How greet labour and cost is thee to fynde!' (CT VI. 534–37); 'O dronke man, disfigured is thy face, | Sour is thy breeth, foul artow to embrace, | And thurgh thy dronke nose semeth the soun | As though thou seydest ay "Sampsoun, Sampsoun!"' (CT VI. 551–54); 'O cursed synne of alle cursednesse! | O traytours homycide, O wikkednesse! | O glotonye, luxurie, and hasardrye! | Thou blasphemour of Crist with vileynye | And othes grete, of usage and of pride! | Allas, mankynde, how may it bitide | That to thy creatour, which that the wroghte | And with his precious herte-blood thee boghte, | Thou art so fals and so unkynde, allas?' (CT VI. 895–903).

[48] See Peter W. Travis, '*The Nun's Priest's Tale* as Grammar-School Primer', *Studies in the Age of Chaucer: Proceedings*, 1 (1984), 81–91, and Edward Wheatley, *Mastering Aesop: Medieval Education, Chaucer, and His Followers* (Gainesville, 2000), especially pp. 52–123.

finally the hens who are Chauntecleer's 'wives', before returning to the story
proper with one of those clear transitional signposts that are a hallmark of
medieval performativity:

> O destinee, that mayst nat been eschewed!
> Allas, that Chauntecleer fleigh fro the bemes!
> Allas, his wyf ne roghte nat of dremes!
> And on a Friday fil al this meschaunce.
>   O Venus, that art goddesse of plesaunce,
> Syn that thy servant was this Chauntecleer,
> And in thy servyce dide al his poweer,
> Moore for delit than world to multiplye,
> Why woldestow suffre hym on thy day to dye?
>   O Gaufred, deere maister soverayn,
> That whan thy worthy kyng Richard was slayn
> With shot, compleynedest his deeth so soore,
> Why ne hadde I now thy sentence and thy loore,
> The Friday for to chide, as diden ye?
> For on a Friday, soothly, slayn was he.
> Thanne wolde I shewe yow how that I koude pleyne
> For Chauntecleres drede and for his peyne.
>   Certes, swich cry ne lamentacion
> Was nevere of ladyes maad whan Ylion
> Was wonne, and Pirrus with his streite swerd,
> Whan he hadde hent kyng Priam by the berd,
> And slayn hym, as seith us *Eneydos*,
> As maden alle the hennes in the clos,
> Whan they had seyn of Chauntecleer the sighte.
> But sovereynly dame Pertelote shrighte
> Ful louder than dide Hasdrubales wyf,
> Whan that hir housbonde hadde lost his lyf
> And that the Romayns hadde brend Cartage.
> She was so ful of torment and of rage
> That wilfully into the fyr she sterte
> And brende hirselven with a stedefast herte.
>   O woful hennes, right so criden ye
> As whan that Nero brende the citee
> Of Rome cryden senatoures wyves
> For that hir husbondes losten alle hir lyves —

> Withouten gilt this Nero hath hem slayn.
> Now wole I turne to my tale agayn.
>
> (CT VII. 3338–74)

Like the apostrophes in Geoffrey of Vinsauf's *Poetria nova*, including the one on which it is modelled (PN 368–430), the passage cries out for oral performance. Indeed, the speaker leaves little doubt that his purpose here is less to lament convincingly than to demonstrate how well he has learned to perform lamentation and to credit, with a rhetorical compliment (CT VII. 3347–54), the source of his excellent instruction. Despite his disclaimer, he shows himself to be an apt pupil, at least until his excessive schoolboy zeal induces him to carry the exercise a step too far. As *exclamatio* is piled on *exclamatio* in oral performance, it is difficult to resist speaking more and more quickly and in a progressively louder voice. This relentlessly building emotional intensity is further amplified by the figures anaphora and rhetorical question (*interrogatio*) and by the refrainlike invocations of Friday, which portentously (and irreverently) link Chauntecleer's with Christ's Passion. From a schoolboy's perspective, the next move, signalled by the limp expletive 'Certes', is understandable and perhaps inevitable. Having cast himself in the role of perennial *discipulus* to the *magister* Geoffrey of Vinsauf, the speaker shifts to the obligatory form of schoolroom histrionics, the bereaved woman's lament. However, he shows himself too much the schoolboy by insisting on showing off his learned repertoire of suitably tragic antique heroines, such as the Trojan women and Hasdrubal's wife, before trying to sustain or build on the rhetorical excitement he had so skilfully generated. When he finally apostrophizes the 'woful hennes', comparing them to the wives of Roman senators slain by Nero, the energy has dissipated beyond recovery, and what began as mock-tragic hyperbole ends in abrupt, comic anticlimax.

We should not assume too readily that such humour is meant to dismiss the performable style or the techniques for performing it that Chaucer would have learned as a schoolboy. Medieval tastes are not modern tastes, and Chaucer as often caters to them in earnest as in game. The very features that are chided in the Host's words to the Clerk and parodied in the tales of the Pardoner and the Nun's Priest dominate *Troilus and Criseyde*, the poem that was considered Chaucer's masterpiece in his lifetime and for centuries thereafter. Moreover, it was precisely the most 'performable' parts of *Troilus and Criseyde* — the apostrophes, extended complaints, letters, and other rhetorically heightened and emotionally charged set pieces — that medieval and early-modern readers and listeners often valued most. What my twenty-first-century undergraduate students find most tedious and overwrought in the poem, their fifteenth- and sixteenth-century counterparts marked for special attention, excerpted in their commonplace books, and imitated in their own compositions.[49] It is impossible to know exactly how Geoffrey Chaucer himself would have performed such texts for a live audience. However, if we could somehow set in motion the famous 'Troilus Frontispiece' (Cambridge, Corpus Christi College MS 61, fol. 1; early fifteenth century) and recapture the gestures and sounds of the performance it depicts, I suspect that what we would see and hear would not differ all that much from what Geoffrey of Vinsauf had in mind as he put his thirteenth-century schoolboys through their paces.

University of Illinois

[49] See, for example, C. David Benson and Barry A. Windeatt, 'The Manuscript Glosses to Chaucer's *Troilus and Criseyde*', *Chaucer Review*, 25 (1990), 33–53; Camargo, *Middle English Verse Love Epistle*, especially pp. 87–125; and Barry Windeatt, *Oxford Guides to Chaucer: Troilus and Criseyde* (Oxford, 1992), pp. 360–82. Alice S. Miskimin, *The Renaissance Chaucer* (New Haven, 1975), is not as informative on this topic as her title would imply, but see pp. 230–38.

RHETORIC'S WORK:
THOMAS OF MONMOUTH AND
THE HISTORY OF FORGETTING

Hannah R. Johnson

One who tells the truth does not strain in telling it:
What is hard is first fabricating falsehood, then speaking.

—Peter Abelard, *Carmen ad Astralabium*

Near the end of his account of the life and miracles of William of Norwich, Thomas of Monmouth records a case of blasphemy punished. Thomas tells us that a certain man named Walter, his fellow monk in the Norwich priory, made a habit of disparaging the 'sanctitati atque miraculis' (holiness and miracles; VII. 272) of little William.[1] Though repeatedly warned to stop mocking

I would like to thank the individuals who took the time to read and comment on this article before its appearance in print: D. Vance Smith, Kathleen Davis, Michael Wood, Eric Johnson, Jeffrey J. Cohen, Kellie Robertson, Dan Morgan, Johnny Twyning, Amy Murray Twyning, Kim Stern, Amanda Irwin Wilkins, and of course David Lawton and the anonymous reader at *New Medieval Literatures*. Its faults remain my own, but I have benefited from the feedback of so many patient and thoughtful readers.

[1] I cite the nineteenth-century edition and translation by Augustus Jessopp and Montague James throughout, still the only modern edition available of MS Cambridge Add. 3037. I quote both their Latin edition and their English translation, and signal any emendations in the footnotes. On occasion I have silently changed some transcriptions for ease and convenience (e.g., *obliuio* to *oblivio*). My citations include the book number (identified by its Roman numeral), followed by the page number on which both English and Latin appear. Thomas of Monmouth, *The Life and Miracles of St William of Norwich*, trans. by Augustus Jessop and Montague James (Cambridge, 1896).

the saint, Walter never listened. Finally, after being visited in a dream by William and soundly beaten by the saint for his sin, he awoke in terror and 'membris omnibus vehementissimam doloris sensit gravedinem' (felt the smart of severe pains all over him; VII. 273), the blows just as real as if he had borne them while awake. The import of this account as 'quasi generale universis commonitorium' (a sort of general warning to all; VII .273) is clear to Thomas, William's *secretarius*: 'Temerarium enim valde est in sanctos dei verbis maledicis tam audacter invehi, quos ab ipso domino tot ac tantis miraculis tam patenter constat glorificari' (It is the height of rashness to attack the saints of God thus boldly with abusive words, since we so plainly see them glorified by many and great miracles by the Lord Himself; VII. 273). These remarks, which appear near the end of William's hagiography, carry an important subtext. In the mid-1150s, as Thomas was most likely composing William's *Vita*, Norwich Cathedral was still a new foundation, just over sixty years old, and had no patron saint.[2] This was a problem that would have been remedied if William's cult had been more widely accepted, but by Thomas's own testimony, it appears that the boy was nearly forgotten in Norwich before Thomas's arrival, probably sometime in or just after 1149.[3] What is more, 'Blessed William' is the subject of controversy within the priory, and Thomas's claims for his holiness — that he is 'plainly' glorified by God — are not universally accepted by those around him.

The blasphemer Walter appears in the seventh and final book recording William's life and miracles, but he is only one of a number of sceptics who are featured in the course of Thomas's narrative, and their motivating resistance

---

[2] Joe Hillaby discusses the need for a patron saint as a possible motive for the Norwich Cathedral monks to take up the story of William. See Joe Hillaby, 'The Ritual-Child-Murder Accusation: Its Dissemination and Harold of Gloucester', *Jewish Historical Studies*, 35 (1997), 69–109 (pp. 72 and 82). Previous accounts vary considerably in their views of the specific circumstances of composition, but they all date the text to the years around 1150–55. Gavin Langmuir dates the composition of the first Book to 1150, and that of Books II–VI to 1154–55. See Gavin Langmuir, 'Thomas of Monmouth: Detector of Ritual Murder', *Speculum*, 59 (1984), 820–46, later reprinted in Gavin Langmuir, *Toward a Definition of Antisemitism* (Berkeley and Los Angeles, 1990), pp. 209–36. John McCulloh argues for dating the composition of the whole work to 1154–55, arguing that the text was composed following King Stephen's death in 1154 and was available no earlier than 1155; Emily Rose follows this dating. John M. McCulloh, 'Jewish Ritual Murder: William of Norwich, and the Early Dissemination of the Myth', *Speculum*, 72 (1997), 698–740; and Emily Rose, 'The Cult of St. William of Norwich and the Accusation of Ritual Murder in Anglo-Norman England' (unpublished doctoral dissertation, Princeton University, 2001; abstract in *Dissertation Abstracts*, 62 (2001), 283-A).

[3] Langmuir, 'Thomas of Monmouth', p. 827

directly influences the grounds of his claims about the dead boy and shapes the
course of his work. Thomas of Monmouth's account of William's death and
afterlife is best remembered as a story of insistent and uncontested slander — it
is the most extensive written account of a ritual murder accusation in medieval
Europe.[4] Yet I would argue that the problem of doubt is so fundamental to the
Vita that Thomas's narrative can be read as a contest between the intellectual
scepticism of Christian monks and what Thomas describes as 'simplicity', and
that this contest is at least as important, from Thomas's point of view, as the
more obvious competition in the text between Jewish unbelief and Christian
faith.[5] In Thomas's account, scepticism stands for crippling epistemological and

---

[4] The question of the precise origins of the ritual murder accusation continues to exercise
scholars who work on the topic, with sometimes surprising results. John McColloh, building on
arguments advanced by Israel Yuval, suggests that Thomas may have composed his account only
after rumours about William's demise had reached the Continent and circulated there, and builds
a case for parallel but separate strands of transmission of the story ('Jewish Ritual Murder', p. 728).
Yuval himself even suggests that Thomas's account is necessarily as long and detailed as it is
because he needs to convince an English audience less familiar with accusations of this sort than
their contemporaries on the Continent (Israel Yuval, *Two Nations in Your Womb: Perceptions
of Jews and Christians in Late Antiquity and the Middle Ages* (Los Angeles, 2006), p. 170). Yuval
is perhaps best known for advancing the controversial argument that the ritual murder accusation
was inspired by Christian understanding of contemporary Jewish messianism and the memory
of several communal acts of Jewish self-sacrifice in the face of violent assaults by Christians around
the time of the First Crusade. These ideas were initially outlined in an article and have now been
included in his recent book, especially pp. 135–204. For the original article, see Israel Yuval,
'Vengeance and Damnation, Blood and Defamation: From Jewish Martyrdom to Blood Libel
Accusation', *Zion*, 58 (1993), 33–96; English summary, pp. vi–viii. Responses appeared in a
follow-up issue: *Zion*, 59.2–3 (1994), pp. 129–350; English summaries, pp. x–xvii. Yuval's
rejoinders, in turn, appear at pp. 351–414; English summaries, pp. xvii–xx. For a review of some
earlier theories about the origins of the accusation, see Gavin Langmuir, 'Historiographic
Crucifixion', *Les Juifs au regard de l'histoire: Mélanges en l'honneur de Bernhard Blumenkranz*, ed.
by Gilbert Dahan (Paris, 1985), pp. 109–27, later reprinted in Gavin Langmuir, *Toward a
Definition of Antisemitism* (Berkeley and Los Angeles, 1990), pp. 282–98. Friedrich Lotter is more
interested in the influence of Thomas's text. He provides a useful overview of the work and its
impact in Friedrich Lotter, '*Innocens Virgo et Martyr:* Thomas von Monmouth und die
Verbreitung der Ritualmordlegende im Hochmittelalter', *Die Legende vom Ritualmord*, ed. by
Rainer Erb (Berlin, 1993), pp. 25–72.

[5] I use the words *doubt* or *disbelief* to refer to Christian sceptics, and the word *unbelief* to refer
to Thomas's portrayal of Jewish scepticism, which is for him ultimately linked to Jews' refusal of
Christ's incarnation as the son of God, and the common Christian belief that the Jewish people
were responsible for the Crucifixion. Since the Jews are members of a separate religion, it makes
logical sense to refer to their 'unbelief' rather than doubt, since doubt or disbelief implies a

spiritual uncertainty, while faithful ways of knowing ensure certain understanding and bestow confidence. In Book I, the forces of scepticism are represented by the Jews of Norwich who, Thomas alleges, kill William in mockery of the faith of Christians. But from Book II onward, the rhetoric of scepticism within the *Vita* is produced by Christian reason, and is represented as the questioning of Christian monks. What Thomas offers us is a kind of disputation by stealth that reinforces his claims about the sanctity of a dead local boy but also serves to critique contemporary intellectual developments associated with the so-called twelfth-century Renaissance.[6] Thomas's debate with critics is one-sided, conducted with amplified rhetorical language and sly imputation, but it effectively communicates the stakes of this contest between reason guided by the dictates of faith and reason that appeals to human logic. During a period when the presentation of evidence is becoming increasingly important in evaluating claims of sanctity, Thomas values pious 'simplicity' over intellectual enquiry. At a time of prolific literary production emphasizing the piety and martyrological zeal of Christian saints, he narrates the *inventio* of a 'martyr' who does not choose, but only passively reflects his 'cause'. And in a climate that underscores the importance of credible witnesses, he reveals that his critics openly question his own honesty.

Thomas's efforts to persuade and convince — his rhetoric — are efforts of highly evolved stylization, developed in response to sophisticated objections among his contemporaries that can be partially reconstructed — if only partially — from

questioning of something one has formerly accepted or feels obligated to accept. I do, however, understand 'scepticism' as a characteristic of both doubt and unbelief in this context. For a discussion of religious doubt elaborated in the course of an argument about how Christians' reservations concerning their own belief system encouraged them to attribute malevolent qualities to Jewish unbelievers, see Gavin Langmuir, *History, Religion, and Antisemitism* (Berkeley and Los Angeles, 1990). Jeremy Cohen describes how Jewish unbelief gradually came to be reclassified between the twelfth and thirteenth centuries as a form of 'heresy', first in a general sense of departing from Christian belief, and later as an accusation that Jews had been led astray from the 'true' practice of an authentic Judaism itself with Christian attacks on the Talmud (Jeremy Cohen, *Living Letters of the Law: Ideas of the Jew in Medieval Christianity* (Berkeley and Los Angeles, 1999), especially pp. 147–66 and pp. 317–63).

[6] The term has been in use and perennially debated since the publication of Charles Homer Haskins's 1933 book *The Renaissance of the Twelfth Century* (Cambridge, MA; repr. 1955). For a general summary of the basic conceptual problems, see R. N. Swanson, *The Twelfth-Century Renaissance* (Manchester, 1999), pp. 1–11. For a summary of the major claims for the period, and an interesting revision of their terms, see Stephen C. Jaeger, 'Pessimism in the Twelfth-Century "Renaissance"', *Speculum*, 78 (2003), 1151–83.

his arguments against them. There is very little we can say we know about the circumstances Thomas describes in twelfth-century Norwich based on his account alone, but we can reconstruct what a reasoned twelfth-century critique of the ritual murder accusation might have looked like in contemporary terms. Paradoxically, in the absence of a secure ground of reference for the events depicted in Thomas's work, his partisan rhetoric may constitute the text's only stable location of meaning. I am less interested in the fact of rhetorical manipulation (something previous analyses have taken for granted anyway) than in the methods used to anchor such manipulations, methods that reveal as much as they erase about the arguments exchanged between Thomas and his contemporary critics. What Thomas most wants to forget is the work of rhetoric itself, the multitude of ways in which, as author, he shapes his narrative to his desire even as he writes it. Thomas recasts opposition as blasphemy, links doubting Christians with unbelieving Jews, and encourages us to forget any distance between the paired terms. His other rhetorical feats, his sleights of hand and acts of selective forgetting, continue an agenda of social critique and suggest the incompatibility of sceptical enquiry with true Christian faith.

Previous analyses of William's *Vita* have largely ignored Thomas's tactical rhetorical effects in their search for the origins of the ritual murder accusation in Europe.[7] In their drive to answer this question, scholars do not often pause to consider that Thomas's fictional 'embellishments' may extend beyond accusing the Norwich Jews of William's murder to his representations of certain figures within the priory or accounts of his own activities.[8] Gavin Langmuir criticizes the

---

[7] See, for instance, my references in n. 3, above. Langmuir's account is still the pre-eminent effort at reconstructing Thomas's investigation.

[8] This is not to suggest that other scholars have not noticed the presence of such sceptics — in point of fact, Thomas's opponents are routinely mentioned by other writers in passing, yet no one has attempted the kind of reconstruction I present here. For a few such references, see McCulloh, 'Jewish Ritual Murder', p. 732; Langmuir, 'Thomas of Monmouth', pp. 843–44; and Hillaby, 'The Ritual-Child-Murder Accusation', pp. 74–75. Benedicta Ward mentions these critics and points out that Thomas assembles around himself an alliance of monks devoted to William's cause (Benedicta Ward, *Miracles and the Medieval Mind: Theory, Record, and Event, 1000–1215* (Philadelphia, 1982), p. 70). Jeffrey J. Cohen characterizes those who fail to support William's sanctity as 'acting Jewish' (in Thomas's terms) through their refusal to participate in the fledgling cult, a remark that supports my own conclusions in tracing the rhetorical links Thomas establishes between sceptical Christians and Jews. While Cohen does explore some of the text's rhetorical effects in imagining a united Christian community, he does not develop this particular idea further (Jeffrey J. Cohen, 'The Flow of Blood in Medieval Norwich', *Speculum*, 79 (2004), 26–65 (pp. 58–59 and 63); this article was later incorporated into Cohen's book, *Hybridity,*

naiveté of analyses that once sought to use Thomas's account to determine 'what really happened' in Norwich *c.* 1144. Yet in many respects, he and other scholars make use of the narrative in much the same way, extrapolating from it what Thomas 'really did' in his work of investigation and reporting.[9] While the narrative probably does reflect critical aspects of the investigation from Thomas's point of view, and Langmuir does an admirable job of analysing the occulted rhetoric of Thomas's work, it remains true that scholars have been insufficiently attentive to the rhetorical character of the work itself. Thomas's account of Walter's conversion also enacts one of a handful of *historiae oblivionis* — histories of forgetfulness — that haunt the strange narrative of 'Saint' William of Norwich, and reveal a surprising connection between Thomas and his modern critics.[10] In our rush to examine his anti-Jewish means, modern readers have often forgotten to attend to Thomas's limited, and even mundane, ends. And we have followed Thomas in consistently undervaluing the argumentative force of his critics in our pursuit of Thomas himself — his motives, his influences, his successes or failures. It is tempting to identify a kind of critical amnesia at work in such a consistent devaluation — an amnesia that suggests our focus on the origins of anti-Semitism may have encouraged us to overlook potential contexts of resistance.[11] By calling

Identity, and Monstrosity in Medieval Britain: On Difficult Middles (New York, 2006), pp. 109–73). Monika Otter's discussion mentions the presence of sceptics in the text and highlights particular aspects of its stylization — she describes Thomas's use of the conventions of *inventio*, including a set of formalized narrative tropes, to structure his text (Monika Otter, *Inventiones: Fiction and Referentiality in Twelfth-Century Historical Writing* (Chapel Hill, 1996), pp. 21–57).

[9] In his discussion of such matters as Thomas's battles with Prior Elias, the treatment of sceptics, and the state of the body, Langmuir reveals something of a literalist bias in his reading of the text ('Thomas', pp. 230–34). Jeffrey J. Cohen, by contrast, is careful to stress the narrative's ideological, imaginative purpose over any problematic claims to its being 'a truthful record' of events ('Flow of Blood', p. 45).

[10] I borrow this phrase from D. Vance Smith, 'Irregular Histories: Forgetting Ourselves', *New Literary History*, 28 (1997), 161–84 (p. 168). I sometimes render this rather loosely as 'histories of forgetting'.

[11] I am currently working on a separate project that examines a critical shift visible in the study of medieval Jewish-Christian relations. Scholars like Israel Yuval and Elliott Horowitz are making a deliberate move away from an emphasis on Jewish suffering and the implicit rebuttal of inflammatory accusations against Jews, and emphasizing instead Jewish agency, self-determination, even aggression. Although I am not writing about Jewish experience here, the present article follows this general trajectory away from apologetics and toward the re-examination of historical and narrative evidence. The genealogy of this development within Jewish studies may be traced back to Salo Baron's famous description of the 'lachrymose model' of Jewish history, but also to

attention to what Thomas has covered over, I pick up the threads of a counter-narrative just visible in the rhetorical warp and weft of his text. The resulting reconstruction traces the outlines of a short history of forgetfulness.

Thomas of Monmouth's most enduring claim is that at Easter time in 1144, the Jewish community of Norwich kidnapped a young boy named William, kept him hidden for a short time in one of their houses, and then crucified him in imitation of Christ. William's body was discovered in the woods outside the town, and he was eventually recovered and buried in the monks' cemetery next to the cathedral, but only after a sequence of hurried burials and reburials in the unconsecrated ground of Thorpe Wood, his original resting place. The monk Thomas arrived at the priory a few years after the boy's death, conducted his own investigation into these events, and managed to have William moved into the monks' chapter house, and later the cathedral itself, calling him a martyr for Christ. As author of William's *Vita*, Thomas presents his case for William's sanctity as the logical outcome of careful enquiry, but it is built upon a foundation of circumstantial evidence that was not lost on his contemporaries. In his account of the sceptic Walter's conversion described above, Thomas helpfully highlights the nature of the other monk's transgressions against the saint: he mocked William's holiness and miracles. William's *sanctitas* and *miraculi* are the very topics Thomas says are disputed by his antagonists within the priory, the same qualities that are supposed to confirm the child's status as a martyr. In addition to expressing such doubts, Thomas points out a third problem with his opponents — 'depravandi consuedtudine' (their habit of corrupting others; VII. 272). Even some years into

David Nirenberg's more recent critique of the tendency to read events 'less within their local contexts than according to a teleology leading, more or less explicitly, to the Holocaust'; David Nirenberg, *Communities of Violence: Persecution of Minorities in the Middle Ages* (Princeton, 1996), pp. 4–5. In addition to Yuval's work cited above, see Elliott Horowitz, *Reckless Rites: Purim and the Legacy of Jewish Violence* (Princeton, 2006). If there were any doubt about the real potential for political (or at least politicized) repercussions from academic work in this area, the recent Ariel Toaff controversy should have allayed it. Toaff unleashed a storm of criticism with his thesis that the ritual murder accusation might have had some limited basis in reality among some Ashkenazic Jews in Italy. The debate over the book involved important questions of academic method, but was also clearly influenced by the afterlife of the legend and bound up in fears about the links between medieval and modern anti-Jewish hatreds. Toaff's book, released only in Italian, sold out and has not been re-printed. See David Abulafia's review of Ariel Toaff's *Pasque di Sangue*, 'Libels of Blood', *The Times Literary Supplement* (London), 2 March 2007, p. 11.

his campaign to establish William as 'unicus ac peculiaris [...] patronus' (sole and special patron; III .156) of Norwich, Thomas is troubled by detractors.

In the face of such scepticism, Thomas establishes the importance of faithful 'simplicity' as a value to be cherished. He challenges his opponents to 'audiant [...] rerumque vertitatem simplicitatis intuentes oculo glorie sanctorum detrahere amodo [*sic*] conquiescant' (hear [...] the truth of the facts, and look at them with the eyes of simplicity — and henceforth let them cease to detract from the glory of the saints; II. 61). The 'truth of things' is apparent when 'simplicity' is one's guide. His enemies, 'qui caninum dentem simplicitati nostre imprimunt' (who leave the impress of their currish teeth upon our simplicity; II. 60), refuse to hear the truth of what has been established, according to Thomas, by 'manifest proofs' (*manifestis indiciis*).[12] Indeed, if one examines *rerum veritatem* with 'the careful eye of simplicity', then 'quid aliud videns videt' (what else will it see by seeing; II. 64) but the truth of William's martyrdom? An appropriate attitude toward the evidence, the ability to see what is 'manifest' in the world and discern through this the hidden nature of everyday events, also shows a proper faithful simplicity. Thomas believes and hopes that the diligent *lector*, having followed his work of enquiry, will be drawn on to agree with his conclusions. Like the Prior of St Pancras in Lewes, who offered to purchase William's relics for his own institution after inquiring 'plenius ac diligentius' (very fully and carefully; I. 49) into the case, this ideal reader should be led to remark, 'quid aliud inter hec nimirum perpenderet, nisi quia sanctissimus ille puer in obprobrium Christi a iudeis revera occisus fuisset?' (What else could he infer with all this before him, but that the most holy boy had in very truth been killed by the Jews as an insult to Christ? I. 49). We are encouraged to forget that such a conclusion might involve as much self-interest on Thomas's part as it does for the Prior of St Pancras, who says that at his priory, they would protect William (and profit from him) as a 'treasure' (thesaurum; I. 50).

The monks who wash William's body prior to its reburial in the priory cemetery rightly interpret the ambiguous signs before them, according to Thomas: 'certa et manifesta in eo martyrii deprehensa sint indicia' (they perceived certain and manifest indications of martyrdom in him; I. 52). *Certa et manifesta* is a conceptual pairing that appears over and over again in Thomas's narrative — he emphasizes the certainty of his knowledge repeatedly, and in diverse ways. He

---

[12] Thomas is quick to associate this 'simplicity' with himself, as when he indicts those 'qui simplicitatis ac pure conscientie gesta depravare non cessant' (who cease not from making light of the efforts of simplicity and a pure conscience; II. 61).

speaks of 'signa certissima [...] et manifesta' (most certain and manifest signs; I. 21), which often follow in the wake of his work of 'diligentius inquirentes' (enquiring very diligently; I. 21) into events.[13] Each of his witnesses, he claims, reports what he or she knows to be true — 'pro certo cognoverat' (I. 30) — so that Thomas can claim he reports such accounts only after 'eisdem referentibus audiens et revera verum esse cognoscens' (hearing it from their lips and knowing it to be certainly true; I. 30) himself. Like Thomas, his witnesses investigate, ask questions, and draw conclusions in the hope of obtaining certain knowledge, of knowing about past events *pro certo*. And a few of these witnesses, Thomas insists, know of events through the evidence of their own eyes. Thomas's text enacts a few dramas of seeing and then being cut off from sight at the very threshold of certainty. This motif takes on a striking theatricality when Thomas recounts what a Christian servant inside the Jew's house is alleged to have seen:

> Hostio [*sic*] interaperto puerum posti affixum, quia duobus non potuit, oculo uno videre contigit. Quo viso exhorruit factum; clausit oculum et illi hostium [*sic*].

> (Through the chink of the door [she] managed to see the boy fastened to a post. She could not see it with both eyes, but she did manage to see it with one. And when she had seen it, with horror at the sight she shut that one eye and they [the Jews] shut the door; I. 90.)[14]

Such dramatic moments of eyewitnessing stop just short of the actual sight of William's *passio*, but Thomas musters all of his rhetorical skill to bring his narrative as close to certainty as possible using circumstantial evidence.

Thomas's emphasis on what is certain and manifest presents a deliberate contrast with the uncertainty and confusion of his opponents in the text, both Jewish and Christian. He reports several conversations among the Norwich Jews — none of which he claims to have witnessed, but probably still accounted

---

[13] The full sentence reads: 'Et nos rem diligentius inquirentes et domum invenimus et rei geste signa certissima in ipsa deprehendimus et manifesta' (I.21). My rendering of the phrase 'signa certissima [...] et manifesta' differs somewhat from that of Jessopp and James, who refer to 'most certain marks'.

[14] Before this, William's cousin is supposed to have 'iterque illius oculis explorans, et ad iudeos intrare et post intrantum statim hostium claudi certissime conspexit' (watched him on his way with her eyes, saw him go into the Jews and after his entrance actually saw the door shut close behind him; II. 89). Here he repeats a claim he made earlier (I. 19) about what the cousin was supposed to have seen, but goes on to multiply the witnesses: 'then on the day before his death he went among the Jews *in the sight of many people* [*multis cernentibus*], and after that no one saw him outside the door (II. 89); emphasis mine.

as 'true' parts of his narrative, in keeping with the common medieval practice of assigning imagined speeches to historical figures on the basis of what seemed 'suitable' to their character type.[15] It is a form of licit (though generally limited) stylization that reveals a great deal regarding Thomas's beliefs about Jews. Following William's death, Thomas asserts, the Norwich Jews met to decide what to do with his body and 'dubitantibus illis et quid faciant nichil [*sic*] adhuc pro certo habentibus' (were in doubt and quite uncertain what they should do; I. 23). Their momentary confusion as they are left in doubt (*dubitantibus*) echoes Thomas's remarks about those Christians who are doubtful of his story, while the language he invokes here — *nihil [...] pro certo* — explicitly reverses his own formula for his certain knowledge of events and witnesses. Thomas claims that the Jews present at the meeting discuss various options for the body's disposal, but since nothing can be decided, further discussion is put off until the next day. At that time, still 'quid agerent prorsus adhuc ignorantibus' (quite undecided what they should do; I. 24), the Jews appeal to one of their *auctoritates*, who gives a speech highlighting their anxiety, general timidity, and the uncertainty of their living situation. This drama of fear, uncertainty, and the appeal to an earthly authority is acted out several times, as when the Jews of Norwich are called before the ecclesiastical synod at which they have been accused of William's murder (I. 48), and again when a certain man comes to Norwich asking about the location of the boy's remains (II. 70–71).[16]

---

[15] See, for instance, the discussion in Ruth Morse, *Truth and Convention in the Middle Ages* (Cambridge, 1991), pp. 99–124; 172–78. Thomas does say at one point that 'sicut ab aliquo eorum postmodum didicimus' (we learnt [about this] afterwards from one of them; I. 24), but I think this is pure rhetoric and may even signal that he feels he is pushing the authorial license for inventing speeches a bit far. He never ties his evidence for these conversations to a named witness, as he does with so many of his claims. The likeliest candidate for this mystery informant would be the Jewish convert Theobald, who is supposed to have told Thomas about the ancient pedigree of alleged nefarious Jewish practices (II. 93–94). But Theobald (assuming he existed) was supposed to be from Cambridge, and Thomas never says he came to Norwich, though some recent commentators have assumed he became a monk there. Langmuir makes some of these connections as well, though he argues that if Theobald were a Norwich monk, Thomas would surely alert us to this fact ('Thomas of Monmouth', pp. 835–37).

[16] Thomas claims that two Jews were discovered by a Christian while on their way to dispose of the body and became 'non modico terrore perculsis et ad omnes occursus novum parturientibus horrorem' (extremely terrified and conceived new fears at every meeting with anyone they saw; I. 28). Once again, the Jews meet together, being 'quid faciant prorsus ignorant' (quite at a loss what course to take; I. 28), and appeal to an earthly authority for help — this time John, the Norwich sheriff. The transition from fear and uncertainty to an appeal to earthly authority is also

Everyone associated with the Jews in Thomas's narrative is ruled by uncertainty. The identity of the messenger sent to entice William away from his home is ambiguous: Thomas tells us 'christianum nescio sive iudeum' (I am not sure whether he was a Christian or a Jew; I. 16). The Christian servant who tells Thomas that she worked in the house where William was killed is morally unmoored by the events she claims to have witnessed, 'Dumque sic an revelet an taceat dubia decernit, tandem terror interveniens revelandi ausum compescuit' (hesitating whether she should make the disclosure or keep silence, [until] at last her fear of revealing the matter prevailed; II. 90). Her fear prevailed, that is, until Thomas persuaded her to talk to him. Thomas also portrays his opponents within the priory as being uncertain and in doubt, and their confusion parallels that of the Jewish unbelievers in his story. The fruits of reliance on human reason instead of 'the eye of simplicity' are disorientation, uncertain knowledge, and a multiplicity of conflicting voices. Thomas even dramatizes the conversion of his alleged informant, the Jew from Cambridge called Theobald, in these terms. Thomas says that Theobald perceived with his intellect or recognized (*cernere*) the significance of William's miracles (II. 94).[17] Becoming afraid, just as his Jewish confreres do in other parts of the narrative, Thomas reports Theobald saying that simply by 'conscientum meam consulens' (consulting my conscience; II. 94), he is led to certain knowledge of Christianity and converts.[18] Thomas's claim here is a powerful rhetorical blow against his Christian sceptics, since he suggests that a Jew can perceive the truth of William's merits simply by consulting his conscience, whereas Thomas's co-religionists are unable to do the same.

In his characterizations of both Jews and sceptical Christians, Thomas frequently returns to the idea of *malevolentia* — spite, ill will.[19] His Christian

---

implied when a Jewish creditor is murdered and the matter is brought before the king (II. 96–110), though Jewish anxiety and timidity are not explicitly referenced this time.

[17] The text reads: 'gloriosa miraculorum cernerem magnalia que beati martiris Willelmi meritis virtus operatur divina' (I became acquainted with the glorious display of miracles which the divine power carried out through the merits of the blessed martyr William; II. 94). The Jessopp and James translation of *cernere* as 'became acquainted with' does not seem to capture the force of the verb's association with the work of recognition and seeing with the mind's eye. For Thomas it is important that this witness recognizes the truth of his argument in an immediate, forceful way.

[18] Jessopp and James render this phrase as 'following the dictates of my conscience' (II. 94).

[19] There is significant overlap in the specific language Thomas brings to bear in his discussion of the alleged activities of the Norwich Jews and those of his Christian rivals, which emphasizes their ill will (*malevolentia*) and envy. Thomas says that his opponents, 'qui perverso ducti spiritu'

adversaries are not motivated by a desire for the truth or certain knowledge, he suggests, but are guilty of a willful ingratitude that clouds their perception: 'ingrati beneficiis divina etiam in quantum prevalent vel ausi sunt magnalia sub palliate voto religionis adnullare vel imminuere sive saltem depravare non nunquam conantur' (thankless for heaven's gifts, they try, so far as they can or dare, under the garb of religion to make little or nothing of divine mysteries, or, at least, to turn them to ridicule; II. 58). Though his fellow monks are dedicated to God, Thomas implies that under the sharp knives of their intellects, always 'Ad vituperandum prompti ac precipites' (ready and eager to find fault; II.57–58), the holy is annulled (*adnullare*), diminished (*imminuere*), or perverted (*depravare*). Instead of creating faithful knowledge, they undermine what others believe they already know. When Thomas portrays his own arguments as 'rationum allegationis [...] spirituales' (spiritual claims of reasoning; II. 58), he is implicitly criticizing his Christian critics' reliance on human reason, which was closely identified with the emerging scholastic practices of the contemporary schools.[20] His opponents are unable to 'see' the truths of the faith properly because they are incapable of using 'the reason of faith'. This is William of St Thierry's polemical

(led away by a spirit of perversity; I. 5) proceed with '*malivole* [*sic*] *intentionis*' (II. 60) and persecute him with all the 'invidiorum versuta malivolentia [*sic*]' (the crafty malice of the envious; II. 61). Thomas claims that the Jews are motivated by a '<tali ma>lignitatis spiritu' (a malignant spirit; I. 21), harbour a 'malignitatis sue propositum' (malignant purpose; I. 16), and are subject to an 'innatam sibi christiani nominis invidiam' (inborn hatred [or envy] of the Christian name; I.22). This is the only time Thomas refers to any 'innate' feelings of enmity among the Jews he slanders, though otherwise similar formulas appear throughout Thomas's account. Jeffrey J. Cohen links *innatus* with 'a hunger for Christian blood' ('Flow of Blood', p. 48). Thomas also suggests that the Norwich Jews are cunning, much like his critics within the priory. See I. 16 ('versute machinationis sue conflantes astutiam') and I. 45, where the 'messenger' who originally took William away is described as 'versutissimi'. *Malignitatis, invidia, malitia, versutus* — this shared vocabulary of description is not overwhelming within the *Vita*, but it does create an important rhetorical link between the Christian sceptics whose doubts Thomas rebuts and the Jews, whom he views as *christiani nominis hostes* — enemies of the Christian name (I. 28).

[20] Jessopp and James translate 'rationum allegationes [...] spirituales' as 'spiritual weapons of reasoning' (II. 58). This reading makes logical sense in the context of the passage, in which Thomas compares himself to a new David setting out to confound his opponents, 'the abusive Philistines'. However, I want to emphasize the association between *allegatio* and argumentation, the idea of advancing allegations or claims, alleging by way of proof, extending even to *allegatio*'s sense of sending out or despatching something — in this case sending forth an interpretation of events.

formulation for a properly Christianized use of human reason.[21] While his opponents are 'duri corde et ad credendum tardi' (hard of heart and slow to believe; II. 85) and insult William's miracles, Thomas views his own claims from a lofty position of certainty: 'Nos equidem ut sanctum veneramur quem nos revera sanctum cognovimus' (As for us, in very truth, we reverence as a saint him whom in deed we *know* to be a saint; II. 61, translators' emphasis).[22] It is from this secure height that Thomas claims he is ministering to 'dubitantium incredulitas' (the unbelief of doubters; II. 93) those poor souls who fluctuate in uncertainty.[23]

Not only are his opponents uncertain of the truth and changeable in their opinions; they cannot even agree on an alternative version of events, according to Thomas. He moves from the arguments of the first (*primis*) group of doubters, on to others (*alios*), who make their own arguments, to a third class (*terciis*; II. 87–88). Rhetorically, he distinguishes between what may be parts of the same argument in this way, responding to the remarks of those who think a pauper boy unlikely to be a saint, answering those who object that there is no evidence William exhibited special virtue during his life, and finally making a long and complex series of counter-arguments in response to those 'a quibus et quare interemptus sit incerti sunt' (who are uncertain by whom and why he [William] was made an end of; II. 88).[24] All of these objections are complementary, and speak to William's disputed status as a martyr for Christ. But by presenting them in this way, moving from the arguments of some, to others, and then on to still 'others', Thomas multiplies his opponents and implies that they are divided, a set of cacophonous voices 'barking' at him from the margins of the text, and 'qui gloriosissimi martyris Willelmi ledentes famam imminutione quadam sanctitatis indebitam laudem laudisque promotionem pro posse suo supprimunt et minuendo

---

[21] Alarmed by the rise of scholastic methods — particularly dialectic — and the citation of classical texts in key areas like theology and philosophy, he writes, 'The reason of faith [...] is to put all human reason after faith or to reduce reason to captivity in obedience to faith, and not to ignore the limits of that faith our Fathers established, nor to disregard them in any way' (cited in Stephen Ferruolo, *The Origins of the University: The Schools of Paris and Their Critics, 1100–1215* (Stanford, 1985), p. 74).

[22] Jessopp and James render 'duri corde et ad credendum tardi' somewhat differently, as 'hard and slow of heart to believe'.

[23] See also the references at II. 95 to 'dissolving' doubts and strengthening faith: 'incredulorum dissoluitur dubietas' and 'quo fides corroboretur dubitantium'.

[24] This sentence is worth reproducing in full: 'Terciis denique respondemus, eis scilicet qui crudeliter quidem occisum sciunt, sed quoniam a quibus et quare interemptus sit incerti sunt, iccirco [*sic*] nec sanctum nec martirem dicere presumunt' (II. 88).

persequuntur' (doing all they can to stop the spread of his [William's] renown and persecute him by making light of him; II. 60–61). He attempts to shift the burden of proof from himself, as advocate of the would-be saint, to those who doubt William's sanctity, a neat trick in a period when the determination of sanctity is becoming increasingly vested in the upper echelons of the church hierarchy.

In characterizing his opponents this way, Thomas surreptitiously enters into contemporary intellectual debates about the balance between reason and faith in a proper understanding of the world. He suggests that his detractors, like the contemporary products of the Paris schools, have reversed the proper order of things by subordinating faith to reason and demanding rational proofs for matters that are the proper province of faith. One of the ironies of Thomas's text is that even as he appears to ally himself with contemporary critics of scholasticism, he highlights a few of the very dangers of innovation that such men feared. Thomas invokes the simplicity of faithful belief in the service of a novelty — his narrative of ritual murder — unsupported by any Christian tradition. Thomas acknowledges the unprecedented character of his narrative, asserting that 'novo scilicet operi veniam concedendam' (some indulgence ought to be allowed for this novel attempt; I. 2) and even suggests that this novelty may have entertainment value for his readers, since he hopes 'lectionem novam desiderantes invitem' (that I may tempt those who wish for something new to read; I. 2–3). Thomas knows very well that the claim of novelty is a potentially damning characterization in ordinary medieval discourse, though he seems to feel that his theological purpose overrides such considerations.[25] He adduces the importance of faith in constituting Christian ways of knowing, but his account is not sanctioned by any Christian authority and has no historical standing. Of course, it must be said that Thomas never accuses his opponents of being imprisoned by scholastic reason. He addresses one critic as a detractor (obtrectator; I. 5), says that his foes are envious and full of malice, and represents their criticisms as unworthy. And yet the objections he attributes to his opponents can be read, I suggest, as the sceptical arguments of medieval intellectuals. They are perhaps even products of the prestigious French schools subsequently transplanted to a new English cathedral foundation as part of the general Norman movement toward ecclesiastical reform.[26]

---

[25] In his Prologue, Thomas refers to the duty of every Christian to publish the deeds of the saints (I. 4), and later remarks on his desire to instruct those who are properly disposed to hear his message.

[26] For the divisions among the Norwich clergy along ethnic lines and the association between the cathedral and its 'Continental monks', see Jeffrey J. Cohen, 'Flow of Blood', pp. 50–52.

Nevertheless, it is important to avoid casting this conflict in black and white, as a case of progressive intellectuals pitted against a religious reactionary. Thomas's opponents are sceptical of his account, but not because they doubt the actual occurrence of miracles or the suspect status of unbelievers.[27] Instead, they appear to doubt William's status as a martyr on specific grounds and openly question Thomas's reliability as a reporter of events. While we cannot assume that Thomas represents his critics fairly, it is likely that he brings forward most of their major objections in his efforts to answer them. In Book II, he provides a roll call of arguments against William's sanctity and accusations against himself, accusations he proceeds to refute. The first of these critiques is that 'Presumptuosum nimis est quod universalis ecclesia non recipit tam audacter suscipere et non sanctum pro sancto habere' (It is very presumptuous to maintain so confidently that which the church universal does not accept and to account that holy which is not holy; II. 59), a clear objection to William's status as a saint or martyr. Thomas also defends his claims against accusations of novelty when he says, 'Neque quispiam que dico his tanquam [*sic*] rebus suo tempore insuetis cordis aures et fidei diligentiam avertat' (now let no one withhold his attention from these things that I assert, because they are matters not usual in his own time; II. 64).

Thomas speaks repeatedly of those who 'cum promulgarentur miraculis insultabant, eaque ficticia esse dicebant' (mocked at the miracles when they were made public, and said that they were fictitious; II. 85), and appears to reveal more than he intends when he says, 'nemo veris me non vera cudere sive interkalare [*sic*] existimet, nemo nugarum vel mendatiorum compilatorem appellet' (let no man think I am interpolating or passing off for true that which is untrue; let no man call me an inventor of trifles or falsehoods; II. 74). Thomas says that some of his critics even 'nos deliros autumant' (pretend that we [William's supporters] are mad; II. 61), while another objection is that 'a quibus et quare et qualiter occisus sit prorsus in incerto fluctuamus [...] si a iudeis vel aliis penaliter constet occisum' (we [the sceptics] are entirely uncertain and doubtful by whom and why, and how he [William] was killed [... and whether] he was killed in punishment by Jews or

---

[27] Brian Stock's discussion of the complex interaction of different cultural practices of reasoning on religious matters is very revealing here, particularly where he analyses Guibert de Nogent's early-twelfth-century work *De pignoribus sanctorum*. Medieval thinkers, while they were quite capable of rational discussion and problem-solving, lived in a world that sometimes exhibited different standards for what constituted the rational than our own. See Brian Stock, *The Implications of Literacy* (Princeton, 1983), pp. 244–52.

anyone else; II. 86). This diversity of complaints covers the whole spectrum of Thomas's claims, from the manner of William's death to the character of Thomas himself. While it is impossible to say precisely how this rhetoric of doubt was justified since Thomas does not represent these claims in any great detail, we can reconstruct from these remarks some basis for a set of coherent objections to the ritual murder accusation in twelfth-century terms.

This reconstruction must begin by bringing to notice what Thomas encourages us to forget. He engages in a systematic redefinition of key terms like 'martyr' and 'cause' over the course of his debates with critics, even as he elides or erases the significance of these changes. When Thomas's opponents accuse him of 'accounting that holy which is not holy' (II. 59), their criticism appears to consist of two parts: William is not venerated by the church, and (as both a consequence and a complement of this claim) his sanctity is not certain but is in dispute. On both counts, Thomas subtly reworks the terms of the debate. On the first count, the accusation that, because William's cult is not more generally known, Thomas is 'presumptuous' to call him a saint, he is quick to stage the conflict as a matter of the local versus the global:

> Et ut verum fatear, preter gloriosam virginem dei matrem et baptistam Iohannem atque apostolos, paucis sanctorum attribuitur quo ubique terrarum quibus christiani nominis floret religio ipsorum notitia propaletur.

> (And to say the truth, saving only the glorious Virgin mother of God and John the Baptist and the Apostles, of few of the saints can it be said that the knowledge of them is spread over all the earth whereon the religion of the Christian name prevails; II. 59–60.)

He goes on to invoke the names of other prominent English saints to reinforce his claim, asking, 'Nunquid illud celebre beatissimi regis et martyris Eadmundi gloriosique confessoris Cuthberti nomen in partibus Anglie universis innotuit Grecie populis sive Palestine?' (Is it the fact that the famous name of the most blessed King and Martyr Eadmund or of the glorious Confessor Cuthbert, renowned in every part of England, is equally well known among the people of Greece or Palestine?; II. 60). Thomas suggests that the criticism is a slight against a local English saint whose renown, like that of most northern saints, has simply not travelled throughout the Christian world.[28]

---

[28] Some might see the residue of an anxiety about the status of insular cults in the wake of the Norman Conquest in this reference to English saints. Norman scepticism regarding certain English saints was a long-standing scholarly commonplace, though S. J. Ridyard suggested some time ago that earlier claims on this subject have often been inflated or mistaken. See Susan J. Ridyard, '*Condigna Veneratio:* Post-Conquest Attitudes to the Saints of the Anglo-Saxons', in

We should question the adequacy of this rebuttal. The majority of regional saints achieve notoriety because they have a popular following that emerges (or, perhaps less kindly, *appears* to emerge) spontaneously.[29] At the very least, clerical encouragement of a cult usually develops alongside some degree of popular devotion. When Thomas's contemporaries complain that he is wrong 'to account that holy which is not holy', they may have been drawing attention to the fact that he is quite openly reverse-engineering a cult for William, first by having his remains translated to a more public place, then by seeking out miraculous accounts from those around him. Thomas himself acknowledges the general lack of popular interest in William's case when he says, 'Hoc quippe miraculo beati martyris Willelmi revivixit memoria, que paulatim decrescens, in cordibus universorum fere funditus iam fuerat emortua' (assuredly by this miracle the memory of the blessed martyr William revived, for it had gradually been waning, yea in the hearts of almost all it had almost entirely died out; II. 84).[30] And his contemporaries cannot have failed to notice that William's first miracles are reported among the priory's extended *familia* — monks and their relations, priory servants, and benefactors — in other words, the people who would be most easily influenced by Thomas's stories.

Proceedings of the Battle Conference 1986, ed. by R. Allen Brown, Anglo-Norman Studies, 9 (London, 1987), pp. 179–206. In the context of this passage, where Thomas also refers to the limited notoriety of Roman and Gaulish saints, it is unlikely that insular insecurity is the primary issue. Thomas's status concerns may have much more to do with his desire to establish William as a patron saint for Norwich Cathedral. See Joe Hillaby's argument to this effect ('The Ritual-Child-Murder Accusation', pp. 72–73). The use of saints' lives to improve or reinforce institutional standing and corporate identity has been discussed at length where twelfth-century historical writing is concerned. See, for instance, Antonia Gransden, *Historical Writing in England,* 2 vols (London, 1974), I, 105–35 (Gransden also refers to Norman scepticism with references to Lanfranc at pp. 105–06); Otter, *Inventiones*, pp. 21–35; Jocelyn Wogan-Browne, *Saints' Lives and Women's Literary Culture* (Oxford, 2001), pp. 57–79.

[29] It is perhaps easiest to see the importance of a popular following in cases in which the institutional church discourages a particular cult in the face of persistent public support. For an overview of a number of such cases, see André Vauchez, *Sainthood in the Later Middle Ages*, trans. by Jean Birrell (Cambridge, 1997), pp. 147–56.

[30] There are some other indications of this basic lack of recognition within the text as well. See, for instance, the story of a man who goes searching for William's shrine after his son receives a vision, only to discover that no one appears to recognize the story, or know anything about a shrine. It is only in the wake of a public accusation against the Jews in an ecclesiastical synod that the family is able to locate the saint (II. 67–74).

The second and more fundamental objection regarding William's status is the matter of his 'martyrdom', which Thomas tries to establish by arguing that William is one of those who have suffered on behalf of the Christian faith. As both Thomas and his critics know, the question of William's sanctity rises and falls on his status as a martyr for Christ, and Thomas's opponents remind him more than once, 'pena martirem non facit, sed causa' (it is not the pain but the cause that makes the martyr; II. 86).[31] William, they maintain, displayed no special sanctity during his life, when he was only 'pauperculum atque neglectum' (a poor neglected little fellow; II. 85).[32] Furthermore, 'quis indubitanter credat viventem illum pro Christo mortem appetisse, vel pro Christo illatam pacienter sustinuisse?' (who could confidently believe that this lad courted death for Christ's sake, or bore it patiently for Christ's sake when it was inflicted upon him? II. 86). In advancing this objection, they point to an obvious weakness of Thomas's account, in which William appears to suffer all manner of indignities without any sign of resistance or presentiment. A logical literary model for Thomas's account would be the narratives of early Christian martyrs so popular in Anglo-Saxon England, many of which were being rewritten in the twelfth century, around the same time Thomas produced his text. In these narratives, the unbelieving persecutor and his Christian victim often engage in a religious debate over the martyr's body, while the martyr resists in both body and spirit.[33] In William's *Vita,* there are no debates in which the saint taunts, ridicules, or

---

[31] The same qualification is repeated at II. 96: 'Quod autem opponitur, *martirem pena non facit sed causa*' (editors' emphasis).

[32] Patricia Healy Wasyliw points out that most medieval child saints are reported to have been precocious in their religious devotion and observance. See Patricia Healy Wasyliw, 'The Pious Infant: Developments in Popular Piety during the High Middle Ages', *Lay Sanctity, Medieval and Modern: A Search for Models*, ed. by Ann W. Astell (Notre Dame, 2000), pp. 105–15, especially pp. 108–14. Aside from several remarks about William's 'innocence', Thomas makes only a few modest claims for his piety — on this count, I disagree with Healy Wasyliw's suggestion that 'Thomas took care to construct a pious *pueritia* for William' (p. 114). If one contrasts William's relatively bland characterization in Thomas's *Vita* with the other saints Healy Wasyliw discusses, or indeed compares it with the demonstration of piety through simple song by Chaucer's 'littel clergeon', it appears that any case for William's special religious devotion is weak. See also Patricia Healy Wasyliw, 'Martyrdom, Marder and Magic: Child Saints and Their Cults in Medieval Europe' (unpublished doctoral dissertation, State University of New York at Binghamton, 1993; abstract in *Dissertation Abstracts*, 54 (1993), 640-A).

[33] See Wogan-Browne, *Saints' Lives*, pp.106–22. She also briefly considers ritual murder accusations as martyrological narratives similar to those she analyses throughout her work, and labels them 'a less reputable subgenre of *passio*' (p. 120).

converts his tormentors.[34] Thomas sidesteps this convention entirely — in fact his
victim is even incapable of speaking because Thomas claims that a 'teseillun'
(teazle; I. 20) is used to gag him during his sufferings.[35] Thomas's opponents may
have been dissatisfied with this missing element of the martyrological story — or
rather the absence of any sign of William's knowing acceptance of his own sacrifice.[36]
Certainly their remarks, as reported by Thomas, point to the importance they placed
on the victim's intentionality in determining the martyr's status — that he 'courted
death' and 'bore it patiently for Christ's sake'. Thomas's sceptical opponents
understand the cause (*causa*) of martyrdom as the martyr's religious cause, his
spiritual vocation: the martyr must die *for* something in order for his death to
exhibit his virtues.

In Thomas's account, William appears to suffer without deliberate intentionality
at all, and Thomas's constant references to his 'simplicity' and 'innocence' in fact
encourage the view that he may be incapable of achieving the martyr's knowing
acceptance. Thomas responds to this obvious difficulty by redefining the term
martyr — he formulates a different definition of the term both literally and
figuratively, by redefining the requirements for martyrdom, and also by making
an argument by analogy for the 'truth' of William's death as an *imitatio Christi*.
In addition, he consciously situates William's story within a particular genre,
aligning it with the traditions of saintly *inventio*.[37] But in the course of defending

---

[34] There is, however, an interesting substitute in the conversion of the Jew Theobald, which
Thomas discusses in Book II.

[35] William's uncle, Godwin Sturt, apparently later capitalized on this instrument as a relic,
using it to extort money from the locals. Thomas describes how he is chastised for its misuse in
Book V (pp. 192–93).

[36] Joe Hillaby has suggested that Thomas's putative Welsh origins influenced the structure
of his narrative and that the Welsh saints' penchant for taking vengeance for personal slights by
supernatural means may have seemed out of place or strange in the life of an English saint. He says
that 'William's miracles, as described by Thomas, were those of a Welsh saint' ('The Ritual-Child-
Murder Accusation', p. 71). (The case of Walter's vision of revenge, discussed above, is one of a
few such moments in Thomas's *Vita* of William.) This is an intriguing possibility, though the
claim requires further analysis, particularly since other saints, including some of the Anglo-Saxon
variety, were quite capable of taking revenge against tomb-violators or other offenders. The case
of Etheldreda is frequently discussed. For the methods of revenge commonly employed by Welsh
saints, see Elissa R. Henken, *The Welsh Saints: A Study in Patterned Lives* (Cambridge, 1991).

[37] Monika Otter remarks that in his confrontation with sceptics, 'One thing Thomas can do
to strengthen his case is to pattern the narrative on standard hagiographic models' (*Inventiones*,
p. 39). She also describes Thomas's *Vita* as 'the most thorough and skillful exploitation of the
inventio model' among his contemporaries (p. 38). One of the conventional expectations of this

himself against the doubters of his narrative, Thomas inadvertently signals what most disturbs him about the case, and it has less to do with William's status as a martyr than the apparent injustice of an untimely death. Relinquishing for a single key moment his claim that Jews killed the boy in an act of theologically motivated spite, Thomas tells us that 'qui certis vulnerum indiciis, quisquis ea fecerit, quibusdam quasi argumentis revera occisus comprobatur' (by the certain marks of his wounds, *whoever may have inflicted them,* he is proved as it were by sure arguments to have indeed been slain; II. 64, emphasis mine). He also remarks, 'quomodocunque res gesta fuerit, id tamen pro certo tenemus, quoniam durissimis attrectatus modis tandem occisus sit' (let the matter *have happened as it may,* we hold it for certain that after being handled in the cruellest manner he was slain at last; II. 65, emphasis mine). In spite of being in the midst of a retreat from his most explosive claim, Thomas still manages to deploy the vocabulary of certain knowing here; 'by the certain marks of his wounds', it is 'proved by sure arguments', and we must 'hold it for certain' that his death was a violent one.

Thomas needs the Jews to play the role of the bad pagans in this martyrological narrative, but even without them, he suggests, the cruelty and injustice of this death render it a kind of special martyrdom. These slips of rhetoric, in which Thomas implies that William's death is singular regardless of *how* it happened, suggest that the death itself carries a transcendental value for him. André Vauchez reviews a number of medieval cults inspired by the death of a person under tragic circumstances, including a woman killed by her husband, travellers murdered far from home, and even a dog who faithfully served his master.[38] He includes

---

model is that the community will show it has 'earned' its saint by the difficulties encountered in finding him — in Thomas's narrative, his account of his efforts to overcome the initial opposition to the cult, especially his conflicts with the prior, are supposed to serve this function of showing that the community (via Thomas, of course) has earned its claim to William. For Thomas's account of his battle of wills with his first prior, Elias, see esp. III. 127–28 and IV. 172–74. The boy's remains were moved to the monks' chapter house with the Bishop's approval, but Elias never seems to have become a supporter.

[38] Vauchez, *Sainthood,* pp. 148–54. Vauchez states: 'However diverse the circumstances, two fundamental elements are found in every story: the shedding of blood and the glaring injustice of their death' (p. 151). Healy Wasyliw remarks: 'By the eleventh century, martyrdom as a route to sanctity was practically unattainable in western Europe, and the veneration of murder victims was increasingly considered inappropriate' ('Pious Infant', p. 106). Jeffrey J. Cohen refers to the special emotional appeal of such circumstances when he calls the body of a dead child 'the most troubling of cadavers' ('Flow of Blood', p. 41). Langmuir remarks on the difficulty of this unanswered

William as one of these individuals, a case like the others in which 'pity provokes piety'. Vauchez goes on to remark, 'The large number of popular "martyrs" we encounter in the Middle Ages suggests that the word encompassed very different realities', and proposes that the clergy may occasionally have borrowed religious language to dress up a narrative whose specific Christian content 'seemed to them to be dubious'.[39] Of course, in William's case, there is no popular following whose accounts must be revised — it is Thomas himself who structures the narrative and engenders wider interest in the cult at a time when it had been all but forgotten.

But in order for his narrative to withstand the scrutiny of his peers, Thomas understands that he must introduce suitable Christian content to his story, and not rely on the pity it inspires alone. By using the word *causa* in a subtly different way than his opponents, Thomas recasts his own argument as an answer to theirs. He tells us, 'Nempe penarum indicia in sancti Willelmi corpore percepimus, quarum causam fuisse patet Christum, in cuius contumeliam penaliter sit occisus' (Assuredly we have seen the marks of the sufferings on the holy William's body, but it is plain that the cause of those sufferings was Christ, in scorn of whom he [William] was condemned and slain; II. 96). The 'cause' of William's death was Christ because his death was a re-enactment of the original model, according to Thomas. The 'cause' here is a literal one that leads to a symbolically overdetermined effect — it has almost nothing to do with William's active adoption of the 'cause' of Christ, the criterion put forward for martyrdom by Thomas's opponents.[40] From Thomas's point of view, this argument trumps his

question as well ('Thomas', pp. 820–21). For an example of a successful cult formed on the pity/piety model, see André Vauchez, 'Anti-Semitism and Popular Canonization: The Cult of St. Werner', *The Laity in the Middle Ages: Religious Beliefs and Devotional Practices*, trans. by Margery J. Schneider, ed. by Daniel Bornstein (Notre Dame, 1993), pp. 141–52. For other remarks on the formation of cults considered inappropriate by contemporaries, see Hillaby, 'The Ritual-Child-Murder Accusation', p. 76; Ward, *Miracles and the Medieval Mind*, pp. 129–31; Nancy Partner, *Serious Entertainments: The Writing of History in Twelfth-Century England* (Chicago, 1977), pp. 191–92. For a study of the holy dog Guinefort, see Jean Claude Schmitt, *The Holy Greyhound*, trans. by Martin Thom (Cambridge, 1983).

[39] Vauchez, *Sainthood*, pp. 151, 152

[40] Thomas stages what is fundamentally an argument by analogy in his defence of William's martyrdom. This argument is largely implicit: if Christ died having received certain wounds, and one of his believers received these wounds also, then that believer must be holy, not precisely as Christ was, but in a similar manner. Comparable arguments by analogy populate the literary disputations between Christians and unbelievers like Jews and pagans that were in vogue during this period. Within disputation texts, this kind of argument takes a specific form: if Jews could

opponents' discourse of doubt because of its symbolic aptness and power. William's suffering, its powerful clustering of signs as an imitation crucifixion, signals to Thomas not only the reality of an authentic martyrdom, but the highest or ultimate 'cause' of his religious worldview.[41] The sense of Thomas's deliberate deployment of this meaning of *causa* is reinforced by his use of the word elsewhere in the narrative, where *causa* appears in its primary sense of

believe in various natural phenomena easily observed around them, Christians reasoned, then they should be able to believe in miracles like the virgin birth and the Incarnation. Over time, the presumed reasonableness of belief in these doctrines gave rise to the idea of the unreasonableness of unbelief where they were concerned. Ironically, however, Thomas's disputation by stealth unhinges the typical presentation of such questions by featuring Christian intellectuals as adversaries of true Christian knowledge rather than its champions. Anna Sapir Abulafia makes a convincing case that such literary debates were designed largely as intellectual exercises in which Christians explored a new-found interest in confirming the tenets of their faith with intellectual arguments, and refuted the doubts of their co-religionists as well as those outside the faith. Thomas makes self-interested use of such tools for very specific ends, importing a few overtones of this genre into his own literary production in much the same way many medieval hagiographies borrow tropes from romance. He occupies a complex position within the larger movement toward the 'Christianization of reason' she describes (Anna Sapir Abulafia, *Christians and Jews in the Twelfth-Century Renaissance* (London, 1995), pp. 34–47 and 77–93). For a summary of the literature discussing the extent to which the twelfth century witnessed a major deterioration in Christian-Jewish relations, see Jeffrey J. Cohen, 'Flow of Blood', p. 42, n. 63. Christopher Ocker describes this work of analogy indirectly, when he links medieval injunctions to identify with and imitate Christ to the appeal of the ritual murder accusation for Christian audiences. The alleged victims of such crimes appear to be 'ennobled by imposing the syntax of Christ's passion' on their deaths (Christopher Ocker, 'Ritual Murder and the Subjectivity of Christ: A Choice in Medieval Christianity', *Harvard Theological Review*, 91 (1998), 153–92 (p. 170)).

[41] In fact, when Thomas remarks that 'the heavenly crown' of martyrdom 'is bestowed in return for special merits of some special persons' in addition to those who 'strive lawfully', he may have the wounds in mind — and specifically the shedding of blood — as William's 'special merits'. If so, this would qualify as another example of his subtle redefinition of key terms in his argument. The Latin reads: 'procul dubio constat solis legitime certantibus celestis bravii coronam repromitti, et tamen pro meritis singulorum singulis retribui' (II. 62–63). Thomas does mention the example of the Holy Innocents, but curiously does not capitalize on an explicit comparison between William's 'martyrdom' and theirs. Vauchez mentions the 'mere shedding of innocent blood' as an apparent criterion for sanctity in popular estimation (*Sainthood*, p. 155), and *The Golden Legend*, produced over a century after Thomas's text, may encode some sense of this when de Voragine tells us that the Holy Innocents 'suffered innocently and unjustly', and links this to a reference from the Psalms about 'pour[ing] out' blood (Jacobus de Voragine, *The Golden Legend: Readings on the Saints*, trans. by William Granger Ryan, 2 vols (Princeton, 1993), I, 56). Also see n. 37, above.

advocacy.[42] Instead of the intentionality of the martyr himself, Thomas emphasizes the intentionality of his persecutors, who allegedly re-enact a crucial event from Christian history. Indeed, Thomas suggests that this work of re-enactment is their 'cause', taken up out of a desire for revenge: he claims that they must scorn Christ in this way 'ut sic suas in illum ulciscantur iniurias cuius mortis causa ipsi et a sua exclusi sunt patria' (so they might avenge their sufferings on him; inasmuch as it was because of Christ's death that they had been shut out of their own country; II. 93).[43]

It is clear to Thomas (if not to everyone else) that the only group capable of redeploying the signs of crucifixion in this way are Jews, irrevocably separated from the Christian community and yet implicated in its foundation. Thomas imagines one of the accused speaking to other Jews following William's death: 'Non enim verismile videtur quod aut christiani de christiano, aut iudei talia fieri aliquatenus voluissent de iudeo' (It will not seem probable that Christians would have wished to do this kind of thing to a Christian, or Jews to do it to a Jew; I. 24–25). With remarks like these, Thomas points to the divided character of the two communities, who may share physical spaces, but are understood to act and think on behalf of entirely different causes. The suggestion that these two communities are at ideological war with one another points to what Thomas sees as the allegorical aptness of his theory: the Jews of Norwich are supposed to persecute William as a kind of literal re-enactment, making him a *memento* of another crucifixion that they also regard as the death of one who was simply a man. By refiguring William's death as a martyrdom, Thomas hopes to show a new triumph of Christian understanding over alleged Jewish literalism that parallels the way the two communities interpret the significance of the Crucifixion: the Jews of Norwich supposedly kill a boy, but Thomas resurrects a saint, someone more than human, from his remains, just as the Jews believe Christ died a man, while Christians proclaim that he is the son of God.

Thomas's struggle with his critics depends upon his own credibility as a reporter of events. Saintly *inventiones* and catalogues of miracles are supposed to be true relations about the past, and Thomas signals his commitment to the truth-telling

[42] Thomas tends to deploy the term in its legal sense, referring, for instance, to the priest Godwin's support of the 'cause' of the martyr before the ecclesiastical synod where he first accuses the Jews of murder (I. 43).

[43] See Israel Yuval's argument on this key topic, *Two Nations in Your Womb*, especially pp. 161–74.

function of his narrative at every turn. He has followed all of the evidentiary procedures of the period quite self-consciously, and his text resounds with the signs of his investigations, moving beyond the commonly accepted phrases about 'credibilium [...] virorum' (men who were to be believed; II. 57), to the insistent refrain: 'Quod ego Thomas monachus Norwicensis, eisdem referentibus audiens et revera verum esse cognoscens, scripto tradere curavi' (All which I, Thomas, a monk of Norwich, after hearing it from their lips and knowing it to be certainly true, have been careful to hand down in writing; I. 30). At one point he remarks of his method that he did not record some of the many miracles performed at William's tomb because 'plenam veri certitudinem non prevaluimus indagare. Porro ea presenti placuit interserere libello que nos visu sive auditu pro certo cognouimus' (we were not able to arrive at any certainty about the facts. Those, however, we resolved to insert in the present book [...] we were fully assured of, either by what we saw or what we heard; III.162).[44] This rhetorical ploy is not unique to Thomas and signals both the fullness of the saint's miracles and his own discrimination and discernment in reporting them.[45] Most importantly, Thomas highlights his reliance on eyewitness testimony to substantiate his claims, always his own or someone else's who communicates directly to him. He is seldom more than one degree removed from the miraculous events he reports. From Thomas's perspective, the evidence is transparent and doubt is unreasonable. The signs of holiness were shown by miracles, these miracles were witnessed by many (*testificata*), they were made public (*promulgarentur*), and they were written down (*scripta sunt*).

In both history and hagiography, the reliability of witnesses and the extent to which their testimonies could be trusted, in either the mundane or the sacred realms, was an important topic of contemporary concern.[46] Differentiating the miraculous from the wondrous, *miraculi* from *mirabilia*, was an important

---

[44] Here is another variation on the same theme: 'sive diligenti indagatione a viris credibilibus pro certo scire potui, omnino nichil presentibus scriptis commendare curavi' (I have been careful to set down in this present writing nothing but what I myself saw or else know for certain from diligent enquiry of men to be trusted; II. 64).

[45] For a brief discussion of the procedures of witnessing and accreditation undertaken by compilers of miracles, see Ronald Finucane, *Miracles and Pilgrims: Popular Beliefs in Medieval England* (London, 1977), p. 70–71, 100–02.

[46] Jeanette Beer discusses this issue at some length. See Jeanette Beer, *Narrative Conventions of Truth in the Middle Ages* (Genève: Librairie Droz, 1981), especially pp. 23–34. See also Partner, *Serious Entertainments*, pp. 116–18.

epistemological issue with spiritual ramifications, and often this work came down to the issue of reliable testimony. Caroline Walker Bynum has suggested that between the eleventh and the thirteenth centuries, there was increasing scope for naturalistic explanations for unusual phenomena, but acknowledges, following Vauchez, that

> There was not in fact a sharp enough sense of what the regularities of nature were to allow for testing individual miracles as *contra* or *supra* the ordinary course of things. Hence the authenticating of saints tended to fall back on testing the character — the veracity and dependability — of witnesses.[47]

Medieval historians were concerned with evaluating the truth of miraculous reports, and both Nancy Partner and Monika Otter draw attention to the efforts of certain twelfth-century English historians (notably William of Newburgh), to analyse such accounts on the basis of available testimony.[48] Partner summarizes this state of affairs when she writes that 'in the twelfth century the evaluation of testimony rather than laws of probability was central to the problem of authenticating prodigies'.[49]

Medieval people also understood that it would be possible for a witness to report something sincerely without always being correct. This is one reason why a witness's credibility was so often emphasized. But this consideration only makes Thomas's reports of his critics' remarks all the more damning: he is not just accused of 'getting it wrong' but of deliberately 'interpolating or passing off for true that which is untrue', of being 'an inventor of trifles or falsehoods' (II. 74). Thomas's elaborate efforts to substantiate his claims with tropes of eyewitnessing and careful procedure are also fairly common methods of authentication, though Monika Otter is one of a long line of critics to suggest that Thomas 'is virtually

---

[47] Caroline Walker Bynum, 'Miracles and Marvels: The Limits of Alterity', in *Vita Religiosa im Mittelalter*, ed. by Franz Felten and Nikolas Jaspert (Berlin, 1999), pp. 799–817 (p. 809). Bynum describes even a 'flattening' or 'naturalizing' of unusual occurrences ('The Limits of Alterity', pp. 807–11). Also see Bynum, 'Wonder', *American Historical Review*, 102 (1997), 1–26 (pp. 10–12). Vauchez highlights the cautious and sometimes sceptical cast of mind adopted by ecclesiastical officials regarding miraculous stories, once these began to be evaluated by papal commission (pp. 481–98). While Vauchez's examples are drawn from a slightly later period, this attitude of cautious reservation is reminiscent of what Thomas describes among his contemporaries.

[48] Partner, *Serious Entertainments*, pp. 114–40; Otter, *Inventiones*, pp. 102–07.

[49] Partner, *Serious Entertainments*, pp. 116–17.

obsessed with clues and corroborating detail'[50] — in other words, he has the look of someone who is protesting too much. Of course, I have already mentioned the novelty of this case and suggested that Thomas's account of William's 'martyrdom' was out of keeping with the kind of narrative expected for a martyr during this period. It is also possible that Thomas's account, because it is modern, is being held to a higher standard of evidentiary investigation and testimony by his peers. This idea goes hand in hand with the novelty of the narrative: there is no sense of tradition here to reinforce the status of Thomas's claims.

In addition to his elaborate evidentiary apparatus, Thomas attempts to fall back on one of the few other 'authorities' available to him, the authority of common report. Thomas suggests at several points in his narrative that 'everybody knows' about the ritual murder accusation already or, if they are unaware of the specifics, they already 'know' that Jews are capable of doing something very much like it.[51] By suggesting that such activities are an open secret, Thomas tries to play down the novelty of his own narrative.[52] Of course, 'testimony' of this kind is not considered as reliable as eyewitness testimony from credible individuals, something Thomas acknowledges with his innuendoes about the behaviour of William's mother when she learns of his death:

> Porro quicquid [*sic*] animo suspicabor iam pro certo habens, quodque ymaginabatur quasi visu compertum asserens, facto per vicos et plateas discursu et materno compulsa dolore universos horrendis sollicitabat clamoribus.

> (And so, assuming everything to be certain which she suspected and asserting it to be a fact, as though it had actually been seen — she went through the streets and open places and, carried along by her motherly distress, she kept calling upon everybody with dreadful screams; I. 42.)

---

[50] Otter, *Inventiones*, p. 41.

[51] For instance, see: Godwin Sturt's claims in synod (I. 42–43), and Thomas's report about those who come out to see 'the boy lately killed by Jews' (II. 70), even before the formal accusation was made.

[52] This is an issue with important interpretive implications for scholars like John McCulloh and Israel Yuval. Yuval has argued that rumours and stories circulated among Christians about Jewish acts of ritual self-sacrifice in 1096, that these contributed to the formation of the legend, and that Thomas is transmitting such Contintental rumours to an English audience (Yuval, *Two Nations in Your Womb*, pp. 161–72). McCulloh emphasizes the existence of separate strands of rumour circulating about the Norwich case before Thomas composed his text (McCulloh, 'Jewish Ritual Murder'). With the benefit of hindsight, it might have appeared to Thomas as if everyone knew about the legend from the beginning.

Thomas appears to be insensible to the similarities between this behaviour and his own, but it may also be true that he is trying to distinguish his 'diligent' investigations from the simple credence of individuals like William's mother or the other citizens of Norwich who repeat common knowledge to one another. Thomas argues that 'everybody knows' about ritual murder already, yet it is difficult to evaluate the truth value of a claim whose rhetorical function within his narrative is so pronounced. The fact that William's cult never became very popular seems to militate against the idea that everyone knew about the accusation — and believed it — before Thomas arrived. What is insidious about Thomas's novel account, of course, is the effect to which his work of textualization contributes. Thomas is accused of manufacturing fictions, but he contributes to a process of canonization, in which novel claims gain authority with repetition — tellings and retellings eventually create new cults, and periodic outbreaks of violence.

Thomas's ambitions within the monastery are also clearly linked to the success of this cult. He says he is accused of presumption by the other monks for advancing his claims for William's sanctity, but we may well wonder if the charge springs as much from his manner as his cause. After all, he is insistent and demanding in opposing his prior, and he gathers about himself a coterie of monks who operate as his allies, though their identities are far from certain.[53] Thomas works aggressively on William's behalf, seeking out those who knew him, paying him honours, and offending priory officials in the process. He forces Prior Elias's hand by repeating an account of his vision in which the boy William demands that the prior speak to the bishop about a translation into the chapter house — essentially going over the prior's head. Thomas may have been angling for some higher office within the priory, but it is not clear that he ever received one. Of course there may have been something less concrete than a priory office at stake. Not only does Thomas remind us again and again that it is *ego Thomas* who preserves these

---

[53] Ward counts at least six members of Thomas's 'circle', drawing on his own account to name fellow monks who are said to have participated in some way in the verification of William's sanctity, sometimes directly (e.g., by having visions), and sometimes indirectly, for instance by reporting the deathbed confessions of witnesses (Ward, *Miracles and the Medieval Mind*, p. 70). This is not an unreasonable conclusion, but it is possible that at least a few of these individuals had such dreams or other experiences without having been 'partisans' per se, or even that a few of their reports were reinterpreted or appropriated by Thomas in some way after the fact. The exception may be the monk Wicheman, who acts as a consistent link between Thomas and some of the witnesses in the narrative (Langmuir, 'Thomas of Monmouth', pp. 833–34).

accounts, he also names his greatest enemy quite clearly — it is *oblivio* (II.65). Whether or not Thomas covets an office of leadership, he understands that his position in the community is tied to William's — oblivion for one means oblivion for the other. As much as the narrative works to rescue William, to save him for posterity, it also resurrects another figure for us — William's earthly double, *ego Thomas*.

Thomas stresses his own importance to William's cult, not just in the process of gathering evidence and interviewing witnesses, but in being favoured with messages from the martyr himself. The Latin reveals a common catchphrase, whose repetition builds a powerful rhetorical effect: 'quorum numero *ego Thomas* interesse merui' (III. 121); '*ego Thomas*, qui beati martiris tunc secretarius eram' (III. 142).[54] Thomas's insistence on his own presence at several moments in the text appears in addition to constant reminders of his activities as recorder of miracles. He is repeatedly singled out by the saint and has his special status confirmed in visions reported by other people — William describes him as 'Thomam meum' (III. 143) and 'secretarium meum Thomam' (IV. 175).[55] Many of Thomas's explicit references to himself as narrator occur near the saint's special identification of him within the text, so that at certain points the *Vita* seems to resound with variations on the melody of *ego Thomas* and *Thomam meum*. It is not difficult to see the extent of Thomas's intense personal investment in William's cult, and, given that level of investment, to understand why he sees any perceived slight to the saint as the most intimate kind of insult to himself.

Medieval critics' doubts about Thomas's credibility as a reporter of events reinforce modern commentators' basic agreement that he is an unreliable narrator. Benedicta Ward calls Thomas 'a sly and secret manipulator of events',[56] while Langmuir remarks that 'The *Life* tells us what he wanted to believe happened, but not necessarily what really did happen'.[57] Many a historian would dismiss these remarks as modern psychologizing, but they are assessments drawn from the rhetoric of Thomas's text, a rhetoric that reveals more than it means to and implicates its author in a web of contemporary controversy that hardly paints him in a positive light. It seems likely that Thomas also pushed his rhetoric too far by contemporary standards. His peers would have had a subtle sense of how to

---

[54] The examples are easily multiplied. See III.127; IV. 169; and IV. 174.

[55] Also see IV. 168 and IV. 171.

[56] Ward, *Miracles and the Medieval Mind*, p. 69.

[57] Langmuir, 'Thomas of Monmouth', p. 829

evaluate 'proper' embellishments from improper, appropriate innovation on a textual model from inappropriate *fabula*. This finely tuned sense of discrimination is not something easily recovered now. We understand true and untrue in definitive terms, and we understand the canons of relativism, but the complex negotiations, reciprocal confirmations, and overlap of genres involved in advancing medieval truth claims are another animal altogether. One of the things Thomas reveals is that his critics among the Norwich monks broadly agreed with modern assessments of his unreliability, although their reasons for doing so were somewhat different from ours.

It is easy to forget that only Books I and II of the *Vita* focus on Thomas's extended argument for William's sanctity, while Books III–VII are premised on a kind of forgetting of the originary crime, allowing it to recede into the background as toothaches and fluxes, paralyzed limbs, and painful swellings come to the fore. This is the work of establishment and consolidation Thomas sought to do with his narrative — Books I and II are the toll, the tax he had to pay to his critics in order to move on to these miraculous accounts. In the end, Thomas merely requires the Jews, as former martyrologists needed bad pagans, in order to do his work. The real meaning of William's death for Thomas lies in his mundane accounts of the miraculous, and how these reassert the coherence of his community and his place in that community.[58] In their drive to locate some glimmer of insight into historical events beneath Thomas's rhetoric, scholars have forgotten his critics and his modest aims as William's advocate. An unpleasant truth obscured by this act of forgetting is that beneath the rhetoric may lie only more rhetoric, with no secure ground of historical reference to offer outside the bounds of Thomas's debates. He reminds us of his own role in the text by his constant, obtrusive presence, and instead of composing a narrative that allows us to forget his work of persuasion, he announces his partisanship through his defensive tone. But if we attend to that rhetoric carefully, we can just hear, at the very margin of our historical perception, the contrary voices of Thomas's twelfth-century critics. It is at this margin between memory and erasure that we must interrogate rhetoric's work.

University of Pittsburgh

---

[58] Jeffrey J. Cohen presents an argument to this effect, suggesting that the narrative is supposed to heal ethnic and racial divisions within Norwich by offering a vision of Christian unity: 'The *Vita* records Thomas's attempt to envision, foster, and promulgate a harmonized community, but it also reveals that this unity of which he at times seems so confident was neither as monolithic nor as enduring as he desired' ('Flow of Blood', p. 64).

PROPHETIC LANGUAGE AND ETYMOLOGICAL DISCOVERY IN THE WORK OF RICHARD VERSTEGAN

Hannah Crawforth

O n the wilds of the heath, Lear's Fool recites a prophecy anticipating a chaotic time to come in which 'priests are more in word than matter', when there are 'No heretics burn'd but wenches suitors', and 'bawds and whores do churches build'.[1] It is by these signs of religious dissolution that the imminence of an apocalyptic moment will be made known: 'Then shall the realm of Albion | Come to great confusion'.[2] An apocalypse, in the etymological sense

I am extremely grateful to Anthony Grafton for reading an earlier draft of this article. His clarifications on points of difference between antiquarians and ecclesiastical historians were extremely helpful, as were his suggestions for further reading within the history of chronology, a tradition to which Verstegan is indebted. I am conscious that had space allowed I could have explored these issues further. A version of this essay was delivered at the 'Medieval/ Renaissance: Rethinking Periodization' Conference held at the University of Pennsylvania on 11 November 2006. I am very grateful to the organizers of this event, Jennifer Summit and David Wallace, and to Rita Copeland, Margreta De Grazia, and David Lawton, for their insightful questions and comments. I would like to thank Kathleen Davis, Jeff Dolven, Nigel Smith, and an anonymous reviewer at *NML* for their detailed and thought-provoking readings of drafts of this paper. Graham Parry kindly offered his time and many helpful suggestions. Susan Wolfson provided support at a crucial juncture. Lisa Jardine gave invaluable advice and I owe her and all at the Centre for Editing Lives and Letters, Queen Mary, London, my thanks for providing me with an intellectual home whilst writing this essay.

[1] William Shakespeare, *King Lear* (1605), in *The Riverside Shakespeare*, ed. by G. Blakemore Evans with J. J. M. Tobin, 2nd edn (Boston, 1997), III. ii. 81, 84, 92.

[2] Shakespeare, *Lear*, III. ii. 85–86.

of the word, is 'an uncovering or a disclosure', a literal revelation of something that has been there all along.[3] The fact that we recognize the signs of its coming reflects this familiarity. The Fool's speech draws upon the tradition of Galfridian prophecy stemming from the *Vita Merlini* of Geoffrey of Monmouth (*c*. 1090–1155).[4] He also alludes to the widespread interest in political prophecy focused upon dynastic succession that culminated in a frenzy of speculation around the death of Elizabeth I.[5] In the model of historical time the Fool evokes here, the events of the future are simply the prophecies of the past, uncovered.[6]

Shakespeare treats this temporal model, the modus operandi behind centuries of exegetical work, and central to the self-mythologizing rhetoric of the Tudor monarchs, with scepticism however. 'This prophecy shall Merlin make for I live before his time', the Fool declares, in a characteristically shrewd but apparently nonsensical remark.[7] His predictions are foreshadowed by a poem known as

---

[3] Alison Shell, *Catholicism, Controversy and the English Literary Imagination, 1558–1660* (Cambridge, 1999), p. 24. The Greek root of the word is related to that for *veil*.

[4] The figure of Merlin usefully combines elements of several types of prophet, pre-Christian, Old Testament and political. Jan Ziolkowski, 'The Nature of Prophecy in Geoffrey of Monmouth's *Vita Merlini*', in *Poetry and Prophecy: The Beginnings of a Literary Tradition*, ed. by James L. Kugel (Ithaca, 1990), pp. 150–62 (p. 157). See also A. O. H. Jarman, 'The Merlin Legend and the Welsh Tradition of Prophecy', in *The Arthur of the Welsh: The Arthurian Legend in Medieval Welsh Literature* (Cardiff, 1991), pp. 117–46.

[5] The most notorious example of this is perhaps the 'HEMPE' prophecy, recalled by Francis Bacon: 'The trivial prophecy, which I heard when I was a child, and Queen Elizabeth was in the flower of her years, was, When hempe is spun England's done: whereby it was generally conceived, that after the princes had reigned, which had the principal letters of that word hempe (which were Henry [VIII], Edward [VI], Mary, Philip, and Elizabeth [I]), England should come to utter confusion; which, thanks be to God, is verified only in the change of the name; for that the King's style, is now no more of England but of Britain' (Francis Bacon, *The essayes or counsels, ciuill and morall* (London, 1625), pp. 214–15). Two variant versions are recorded in a collection published north of the border: 'When *HEMPE* is come, and also gone, | *SCOTLAND* and *ENGLAND* shalbe all one'. 'Praised be God alone, for *HEMPE* is come & gone, | And left vs olde *ALBION*, by peace joyned in one' (Merlin Ambrosius, *The Whole Prophecies of Scotland, England, France, Ireland and Denmarke* (Edinburgh, 1617), A2ʳ).

[6] As Bart Van Es has put it, 'By imagining some ancient source and attributing to it a vision of action that had, in reality, already come and gone, past events could [...] be envisaged as a certain future.' Van Es gives an extremely helpful overview of the relationship between prophetic texts and historical interpretation in Elizabethan England in his chapter '"By Cyphers, or by Magicke Might": Prophecy and History', in Bart Van Es, *Spenser's Forms of History* (Oxford, 2002), pp. 164–96 (p. 164).

[7] Shakespeare, *Lear*, III. ii. 95.

'Chaucer's Prophecy', with which Shakespeare's first audiences may well have been familiar:

> Whan feyth failleth in prestes sawes
> And lordes hestes ar holden for lawes
> And robbery is holden purchas
> And lechery is holden solas
> Than shal the lond of albyon
> Be brought to grete confusioun.[8]

In the light of 'Chaucer's Prophecy', the parodic nature of the Fool's speech becomes all the more apparent. The fact that his prophecy is itself anticipated by the lines attributed to Chaucer adds a further layer of irony. Even a prophecy must be prophesied. Shakespeare not only appears to parody those prophetic doomsayers who delight in predicting that England's current religious and political actions will bring about disaster, but his Fool also mocks the ancient and persistent practices of exegesis itself. When *King Lear* was first performed in 1605, key passages of scriptural prophecy had become vigorously contested sites of polemical debate. Ecclesiastical historians of varying religious persuasions sought to verify their differing faiths by matching events in the history of the church to the prophecies of Daniel and the Book of Revelations.[9] Thus for Renaissance theologians the study of history and the exegesis of prophecy mutually reinforced one another.

---

[8] *The Complete Works of Geoffrey Chaucer*, ed. by Walter Skeat, 7 vols (Oxford, 1894), I, 46. As Skeat notes, Chaucer's authorship of these lines is highly unlikely. Instead, they were most probably added by one of his early editors in order to fill a space on a printed page. It is possible that the attribution to Chaucer occurred in a manuscript copy, where, Seth Lerer explains, 'the ascription of a poem to Chaucer and the compilation of a text itself were often due to circumstances more commercial or political than literary. Some poems carry Chaucer's authorship simply to make a manuscript more attractive to a potential buyer. Some poems also carry his name because he was one of the few named authors in the vernacular' (Seth Lerer, *Chaucer and His Readers: Imagining the Author in Late-Medieval England* (Princeton, 1993), p. 119).

[9] Particularly popular among reformers, including Martin Luther, was the idea that the four monarchies mentioned by Daniel corresponded to four major empires, each less noble than the last. Protestant theologians interpreted this passage to mean that the world had been in decline ever since its earliest 'Golden Age', before the church became corrupted. The seventh chapter of Jean Bodin's *Methodus* offers a 'Refutation of those who postulate four monarchies and the golden age' (*Method for the Easy Comprehension of History*, ed. and trans. by Beatrice Reynolds (New York, 1945), pp. 291–302).

The first part of this essay examines the workings of prophetic language in the work of the Catholic writer Richard Verstegan (1548–1640) and his Protestant polemical adversaries.[10] Verstegan published his best-known work, *A Restitution of Decayed Intelligence* (1605), in the year of *Lear*'s first performance. Born Richard Rowlands in London, he lived in England under Mary Tudor and the Elizabethan settlements before having to flee England in 1583 after the arrest of his collaborators in the publication of Thomas Alfield's account of Edmund Campion's martyrdom.[11] He spent the remaining fifty years of his life in exile, returning to his Dutch roots and taking his grandfather's name.[12] From 1587 until his death he lived in Antwerp, where he found a role as an intelligencer providing his contacts across Europe with information about Catholic interests in England via his regular newsletters.[13] Scholarly attention has thus far focused largely on Verstegan's contribution to early-modern debate about the status of the English vernacular.[14] This essay builds upon Donna B. Hamilton's important insight that much of *A Restitution* responds to Protestant texts, considering the linguistic operations of prophecy as a means of understanding Verstegan's methodological approach to historiography itself.[15] The second half of this paper explores a very

---

[10] Verstegan lived for over ninety years, an exceptional span by any standards but particularly by those of the seventeenth century. Indeed, Verstegan's life is so lengthy that some have been inclined to attribute his later Dutch works to a son, a postulated Richard Verstegan the younger. I follow Paul Arblaster's *Oxford Dictionary of National Biography* entry here in rejecting this hypothesis. Paul Arblaster, 'Verstegan [Rowlands], Richard (1548x50–1640)', in *Oxford Dictionary of National Biography*, ed. by H. C. G. Matthew and Brian Harrison (Oxford, 2004).

[11] Thomas Alfield, *A True Report of the Death and Martyrdom of M. Campion, Jesuite and Prieste, & M. Sherwin & M. Bryan, Preists* [sic], *at Tilborne the first of December, 1581* (London, 1582).

[12] Verstegan's father had adopted the name Rowlands when fleeing as a refugee himself from Gelderland. See again Arblaster, *ODNB*, 'Verstegan'.

[13] See *The Letters and Despatches of Richard Verstegan*, ed. by Anthony G. Petti (London, 1959), p. xviii.

[14] Verstegan's is cited by Richard F. Jones in his seminal study *The Triumph of the English Language: A Survey of Opinions Concerning the Vernacular from the Introduction of Printing to the Restoration* (London, 1953), especially pp. 220–22. Paul Arblaster has recently published the first full-length monograph to address the whole range of Verstegan's writing: Paul Arblaster, *Antwerp and the World: Richard Verstegan and the International Culture of Catholic Reformation* (Leuven, 2004).

[15] Donna B. Hamilton, 'Richard Verstegan's *A Restitution of Decayed Intelligence* (1605): A Catholic Antiquarian Replies to John Foxe, Thomas Cooper and Jean Bodin', *Prose Studies: History, Theory, Criticism*, 22 (1999), 1–38.

different polemical use of language, that of etymological discovery, a method that both draws upon and modifies the model of prophetic language I outline below. I ask why Verstegan was increasingly drawn to this linguistic device in the course of his long literary career.

The case of Lear's Fool is illustrative of the way the past erupts into, or interrupts, the present moment in the language of prophecy. To borrow Allen J. Frantzen's phrase, the prophecies of the past are paradoxically both 'ancient and continuous with the present'.[16] Prophetic language situates the past in anticipatory relation to the present whilst simultaneously insisting upon a disjunction between these two temporalities, our separateness from the 'ancient'. It reveals what has been there all along, operating according to a synchronic model of time in which past and present momentarily coexist. Etymological discovery is, contrastingly, about exploring the space in between past and present, charting ongoing development and the evolution of language across time. It is concerned with the traceable past, and a diachronic reconstruction of linguistic traces through history. Despite these contrasting operational models, prophetic language and etymological discovery are not mutually exclusive, and nor is it fair to say that the two modes align themselves neatly with the opposing rhetorical strategies of Protestant and Catholic writers. My intention is rather to show how these two approaches to language each offer particular resources to the polemicist of either doctrinal affiliation. I suggest that the work of Richard Verstegan provides just one example of the way in which those engaged in early-modern religious debate were able to exploit the workings of the English language across time, from the instantaneous moment of revelation to the longer evolution of linguistic development, in the service of their ideological ambitions.

Babylonian Prophecy: A Polemical Battle

When Shakespeare wrote his parody of 'Chaucer's Prophecy', he could rely on his audience's awareness of a long-standing polemical dispute with which the poem had become associated. A doctrinal tradition dating back to the writings of Jerome and Augustine held that the description of Babylon in Revelations foretells the decadence of Rome at the height of its Empire.[17] Elizabethan Protestant reformers

---

[16] Allen J. Frantzen, *Desire for Origins: New Language, Old English, and Teaching the Tradition* (New Brunswick, 1990), p. 22.

[17] A more detailed account of this is given in Richard Bauckham, *Tudor Apocalypse* (Oxford, 1978), pp. 18, 56–59. Bauckham lists some of the early-modern texts that use Revelations,

extended this interpretation to apply it analogously to the contemporary Roman Church. Thus the prominent Reformist writer John Bale, for example, in a prefatory epistle to his *Actes of Englysh Votaryes* (1560), notes 'the shame of Babilon (which now is the Romish churche)'.[18] He goes on to recount 'An olde prophecy of Merlyne dysclosed': 'That after the manyfolde irrupcions of straungers, the kynges of thys realme should be ones againe crowned with the Dyademe of Brute, & beare hus auncyent name, the new name of straungers so vanishing away.'[19] In this vision the Reformation will restore England to the purity of faith held by the ancient Britons, before the invasion of the Saxon 'straungers':

> Fre was that power from the great whores dominion (which is the Rome churche) tyll the violente conquest of the Englysh Saxons, whiche they hadde of the Britaynes for their iniquities sake. And noew (prayse be unto that Lorde) it is in good way to that freedom agayne, and would fullie attaine therunto, were here heithnysh yokes in religion ones throwne a syde, as I doubt it not but they wyl be within shorte space[...]. And as concerning the returne of the name, marke in thys age the wrytynges of learned men, and ye shall well percyue the chaunge, for nowe commonly do they wryte us for Englyshemen Brytaynes.[20]

A reversion to the name of 'Brytaynes' is the sign that Merlin's prophecy of a restored pre-Catholic English faith is coming to fruition. Again, the recognition of this sign reminds us that an apocalypse implies the uncovering of something that has always existed.

Richard Verstegan enters into this debate in one of his frequent communications to the Jesuit priest Robert Persons, written in April 1593. In an apparently deliberate allusion to 'Chaucer's Prophecy', Verstegan says that he is planning to write a work entitled '"The second confusion of Babilon"', or alternatively, 'I might call it "The

Chapter 17, to identify Babylon with Rome, including William Fulke's *A Sermon Preached at Hampton Court: Wherein is playnly proved Babilon to be Rome* (London, 1572), which was reprinted five more times in the ensuing decade. Other works in this tradition are Laurence Deios, *That the Pope Is Antichrist* (London, 1590); John Dove, *A Sermon Preached at Paules Crosse* (London, 1594); and Georg Sohn, *A briefe and learned treatise conteining a true description of the Antichrist* (Cambridge, 1592). See Bauckham, *Tudor Apocalypse*, p. 103.

[18] John Bale, *The Actes of English Votaryes* (London, 1560), bk II, 'To the Reader', n.p.

[19] Bale, *The Actes of English Votaryes*, bk I, fols 50ᵛ–51ʳ. The frequent attribution of such prophecies to Merlin has already been evidenced by Shakespeare's play upon the idea.

[20] Bale, *The Actes of English Votaryes*, bk I, fols 50ᵛ–51ʳ.

Confusion of Albion"'.[21] Verstegan's idea, as he goes on to explain, is to reverse the commonplace Reformist identification of the Roman Church with Babylon. Instead he will argue that it is more appropriate to compare modern-day England to this symbol of corruption, particularly given the contemporary poetic identification of England as Albion.[22] The fact that the two words are near perfect anagrams adds further weight to this argument. 'Albion might, by transposing the letters, seme to be Babilon', Verstegan observes, 'the one name conteyneth the very same letters of the other, one letter only doubled for there is no letter in the one that is not in the other.'[23] Whilst Verstegan downplays somewhat the anagrammatic association between these words as 'a toy in my head', in fact it is crucial to his rhetorical strategy, providing ultimate validation of his argument. The linguistic correspondence between these words is the sign by which one recognizes the prophecy of Babylon coming to fruition in current-day England. It is worth noting the prophetic power with which language is imbued here. 'Albion' and 'Babilon' are inherent within one another, and their anagrammatic congruence makes this fact explicit with the force of a revelation. We should again keep in mind the etymological root of 'apocalypse' in the Greek for 'uncovering' here. In the same way that 'Albion' is already present in 'Babilon', Verstegan suggests, so the corruption of this ancient city can already be witnessed in Elizabethan England.[24]

---

[21] The projected text was never produced. *Letters and Despatches*, p. 142. Verstegan's familiarity with 'Chaucer's Prophecy' is further evidenced by a reference to the poem in an epistle 'To the Indifferent Reader' prefaced to his tract, *A Declaration of the True Causes*. He writes that '*thus leaving the reader out of the matter ensuing (with some addition of something here omitted) to make a commentarie upon* Chaucers *prophesie, I wish him well to fare from Colen the 26 Marche 1592*' (Richard Verstegan, *A Declaration of the True Causes of the Great Troubles, Presupposed to be Intended against the realme of England* (Antwerp, 1592; facsimile repr. Ikley, 1977), p. 5).

[22] A typical example of this can be seen in Gabriel Harvey's commendatory poem to Spenser's *Faerie Queene*, where he writes of 'Elyzas blessed field, that Albion hight'. See Gabriel Harvey [Hobynoll], 'To the Learned Shepeheard', appended to Edmund Spenser, *The faerie queene Disposed into twelve books, fashioning XII. morall vertues* (London, 1590), p. 597.

[23] *Letters and Despatches*, p. 142.

[24] The anagrammatic revelation of Babylon in Albion recalls the workings of the 'HEMPE' prediction, and 'Chaucer's prophecy', which both depend upon this principle of uncovering through the processes of deciphering an acronym, to reveal the series of Tudor monarchs encoded therein, or completing a rhyme, to establish a parallel between 'albyon' and 'confusioun'.

Verstegan's belief in the revelatory rhetorical powers of such linguistic 'toys' is clear elsewhere, for instance when he denounces Burghley's grandson for openly scoffing at the Bible and encouraging 'folkes to spell the name of God backward'.[25] Robert Southwell, with whom Verstegan corresponded up until the Jesuit priest's martyrdom in 1595, attaches similar importance to anagrammatic devices, asking in the 'Epistle to His Father', 'Shall we gorge the devil with our fairest fruits and turn God to feed on the filthy scraps of his leavings? What is this but to spell God backward and of a God to make Him a dog, a blasphemy that would cause any Christian ear to glow?'[26] Similarly, in his poem 'The Virgin's Salutation', Southwell argues that the emphasis upon the divine grace of Mary in the Catholic faith is endorsed by the fact that 'Spell *Eva* backe and *Ave* shall you finde, | The first began, the last reverst our harmes'.[27] But faith in the prophetic force of such verbal play is not restricted to Catholic writers. In his *Actes of Englysh Votaryes*, for example, John Bale offers the observation that 'Roma' is 'amor' spelt backwards in support of his claims that sexual corruption is rife within the Catholic Church.[28] By deriving his proposed rhetorical strategy from the anagrammatic resemblance of 'Albion' to 'Babilon', Verstegan subverts a construct frequently employed by Protestant polemicists.

By turning the Reformers' arguments upon themselves, Verstegan harnesses the polemical power that derives from positioning the present as the fulfilment of earlier prophecy. In Verstegan's case, his reversal of the Protestant argument exposes a political rhetoric that conflates linguistic congruity with historical continuity. Verstegan's proposed work will take its intellectual impetus from both existing Protestant publications and recent Catholic arguments, taken 'oute of

[25] *Letters and Despatches*, p. 40.

[26] Robert Southwell, *The Triumphs over Death [...] Together with the Epistle to His Father, the Letter to His Brother, the Letter to His Cousin 'W.R.', and a Soliloquy*, ed. by John William Trotman, The Catholic Library, 8 (London, 1914), p. 55.

[27] The stanza continues: 'An Angels witching wordes did *Eva* blinde, | An Angels *Ave* disenchants the charmes, | Death first by womans weakenes entred in, | In womans vertue life doth now begin' ('The Virgin's Salutation', ll. 1–6, in *The Poems of Robert Southwell, S. J.*, ed. by James H. McDonald and Nancy Pollard Brown (Oxford, 1967), p. 5).

[28] Bale, *Actes*, bk II, 'To the Reader', n.p. The Catholic writer Thomas Stapleton branded him 'baudy Bale' owing to his allegations of sexual abuse of monks and altar-boys by the clergy. See *The history of the Church of Englande: Compiled by Venerable Bede, Englishman*, trans. by Thomas Stapleton (Antwerp, 1565), fol. 4ʳ.

sundry our late Englishe hereticall bookes'.[29] In deliberately rewriting the long interpretative tradition associating Rome with Babylon, Verstegan makes clear to his polemical adversaries that exegesis is itself susceptible to revision, dependent not so much upon the prophetic utterances of the past as the interpretative strategies of the present. Verstegan's project suggests that he understands historiography as an act of rewriting in a highly politicized sense, the language of the debate serving as an ideological battleground. He seeks here to recast the terms of this debate, which are reinscribed even as they are employed, a common tactic amongst polemicists.

Verstegan's letter demonstrates the productive intersection of his antiquarian and linguistic interests with his role as a Catholic propagandist. His ingenious reinterpretation of each piece of evidence linking Babylon to the Roman Church exploits this wide-ranging knowledge. 'The 7 hilles', described as a feature of Babylon in Revelations, he writes, 'are seaven kinges, *ergo* not seaven hills; and unto seaven kinges' govermentes hathe Albion bene devyded, and Roome never.'[30] In *A Restitution of Decayed Intelligence*, Verstegan will list the 'Seaven Kingdomes of the Saxons in Britaine', and his familiarity with Anglo-Saxon history here furnishes Verstegan with a parallel between England's heptarchic past and the allegorical seven kings of Scripture.[31] His proposal continues with a description of the Whore of Babylon, symbolically identified with the pope in Protestant exegesis: 'Also that the woman sat uppon a rose coloured beast, and the rose is the armes or banner of England'.[32] Again, Verstegan's multiple talents are summoned to advance his theory, in this case his skills as a linguist (he knew at least nine languages). Verstegan rejects the standard translation of the Vulgate *coccineam* as 'scarlet', rendering the word instead as 'rose'. The decision enables him to invoke the emblem of the Tudors and, of course, to align the 'woman' in this reading with Queen Elizabeth I. Verstegan inserts an additional slur upon Elizabeth's virginity when he renders the scriptural proclamation 'that the woman was drunken with the blood of saintes, and said, "*sedeo regina, et vidua non sum, et luctum non videbo*"' by declaring 'so dothe she sit as a queene, and is neither widow, wyf nor

---

[29] *Letters and Despatches*, p. 142.

[30] *Letters and Despatches*, p. 142.

[31] These are '*Kent, South-Saxons, East-English, West-Saxons, East-Saxons, Northumbers*, and *Mercians*'. See Richard Verstegan, *A Restitution of Decayed Intelligence: In antiquities; Concerning the most noble and renowmed English nation* (Antwerp, 1605), pp. 132–33. All subsequent references are to this edition and are cited parenthetically in the text.

[32] *Letters and Despatches*, p. 142.

maid'. Literally the Latin text reads more like 'and I am not a widow and I will not suffer loss'.[33] Whilst this possibly implies that the Queen will never marry, it certainly does not insinuate, as Verstegan does, that she is not a 'maid'. Literature is yet another field Verstegan works in and across.[34] Like many of his contemporaries, he treats poetry as a source of historical fact and notes at one point that the Anglo-Saxons often chose to write important historical documents in verse, 'commonly in meeter, belike to be kept the better in memorie' (p. 146). By approaching scriptural prophecy from such a wide-ranging viewpoint, Verstegan is able to uncover an alternative interpretation that has lain within the text all along.

Etymological Discovery in the Restitution

'Because Verstegan was an English Catholic living in exile', Richard W. Clement has written, he 'was on the margin in his own day and has remained there, deserving little more than a footnote in modern historical scholarship.'[35] This marginal status might be said to typify not merely Verstegan's life but post-Reformation English Catholicism as a whole. Ethan Shagan has recently suggested 'an unfortunate and unproductive barrier within early modern historiography' exemplified by the early-modern period's 'inflammatory' subtitles: 'the age of Reformation', the 'age of religious wars', or the 'confessional era'. The result is what Shagan calls the ghettoization of Catholicism as an 'historical subfield'.[36] Shagan calls instead for 'a post-confessional, post-revisionist approach' that includes Catholic historiography, a methodology also advocated by Alison Shell, who believes that an 'historical wrong has been done to Catholics', and that the corrective to this lies in the 'unmasking of prejudice, and the dissection of its

---

[33] My translation. See *Letters and Despatches*, p. 142.

[34] Verstegan's allusion to 'Chaucer's Prophecy' is one of many references to Chaucer in his work attesting to an interest in Middle English poetry. See for example Verstegan, *A Restitution*, pp. 200, 203–04, 211, and 247. Lydgate and Gower are also mentioned.

[35] Richard W. Clement, 'Richard Verstegan's Reinvention of Anglo-Saxon England: A Contribution from the Continent', in *Reinventing the Middle Ages & the Renaissance: Constructions of the Medieval and Early Modern Periods*, ed. by William F. Gentrup (Turnhout, 1998), pp. 19–36 (p. 19).

[36] Ethan Shagan, Introduction to *Catholics and the Protestant Nation: Religious Politics and Identity in Early Modern England*, ed. by Ethan Shagan (Manchester, 2005), pp. 18 and 1.

imaginative complexities'.[37] Peter Lake adopts a similar strategy, asking that we embrace what he calls the 'Catholic effect'.[38] 'By reintegrating a variety of different Catholic perspectives, texts and voices into our account', Lake argues, 'the whole period can be made to look different: relatively familiar texts and events can be made to appear unfamiliar; established chronologies can be disrupted; the seemingly stable can be rendered unstable, the peripheral central and the central peripheral.'[39]

It is not merely Verstegan's religious convictions that have rendered him marginal to historical accounts of the English Renaissance. At a time when classicism was revered, Verstegan chooses to put aside arguments that Britain's origins can be traced back to Troy, rejecting this Graeco-Roman inheritance in order to celebrate England's Anglo-Saxon history.[40] In the *Restitution*, Verstegan follows Polydore Vergil in dismissing the popular argument that Brutus (from whom Britain was mistakenly said to take its name) was a nephew of Aeneas, 'descended from the *Trojans*, as heretofore believed to have been' (p. 94).[41] Instead, 'it standeth with far more likelihood of truth, seeing out of *Gallia* he came into *Albion*, that we hold him for some Prince of the same Country and Nation' (p. 94). Verstegan continues, 'And far more honourable it is for the *Britains* to derive their descent from so great, so ancient, and so honourable a people as the *Gauls* then were, than with so much obscurity & unlikelihood of

---

[37] Shagan, Introduction, p. 1. Shell, *Catholicism, Controversy and the English Literary Imagination,* p. 17.

[38] Peter Lake, 'From *Leicester His Commonwealth* to *Sejanus His Fall*: Ben Jonson and the Politics of Roman (Catholic) Virtue', in *Catholics and the Protestant Nation* (see n. 36, above), pp. 128–161 (p. 157).

[39] Lake, 'From *Leicester*', pp. 156–57.

[40] Verstegan takes his lead here from Tacitus's interest in so-called 'barbarian' peoples in the *Germania* (*c.* 100 AD). His description of the nobility of the Saxons owes much to Tacitus's account of the bravery of the 'Germani' in battle. See Tacitus, *Germania,* ed. and trans. by J. B. Rives (Oxford, 1999), p. 80. Writing in the fourth century AD, Eusebius depicts the Greeks themselves as 'barbarian', Aaron P. Johnson argues, in order to distinguish 'Christians as a restoration of the ancient Hebrews', legitimizing Christianity 'as rooted in antiquity and superior to other ethnic identities' (Aaron P. Johnson, *Ethnicity and Argument in Eusebius' 'Praeparatio Evangelica'* (Oxford, 2006), p. viii).

[41] Polydore's *Anglica Historia* (Basel, 1534) caused outrage by suggesting that the Trojan descent from Brutus was merely a myth. T. D. Kendrick, *British Antiquity* (London, 1950), chap. 6, and especially pp. 79–84. See also May McKisack, *Medieval History in the Tudor Age* (Oxford, 1971), pp. 99–102.

truth to seek so far-off to fetch their descent, and that from no better Ancestors than the poor miserable fugitives of a destroyed City' (pp. 94–95). In the sixteenth and seventeenth centuries, 'fetch' commonly meant 'to derive as from a cause or origin', a definition that recognizes that these histories may not be all they seem, offering only the deceptive appearance of a connection to an origin.[42] It is in this sense that Verstegan uses the word here, and his denunciation of these genealogies as fetched from 'far-off' further emphasizes the human work that has gone into the creation of such a narrative. Troy's history does not anticipate English history, Verstegan points out, and nor does the particular tragic nobility of the Trojans persist to the present day. Instead, Verstegan suggests, we should be aware that this account of the English past is artificially, even fictitiously, constructed. The English should rather take pride in a very different past, in Verstegan's view no less honourable: that of the Anglo-Saxon heritage he reconstructs here.

For the Protestant reformers, English history is characterized by interruptions. The years of Catholic primacy represent for them a break with the true Church, to which the country is only now returning. As already noted, Protestant polemicists attempt to claim that the 'pure' English Church existed long before the Pope Gregory sent his Roman missionary Augustine to the country. 'What had essentially been a revolutionary change in the structure of power was thus retrospectively justified in the late Tudor period as a return to an earlier position from which the Roman Church, not the English Church, had deviated', Angelika Lutz explains.[43] For Protestant ecclesiastical historians England's past holds a prophetic force, in which isolated moments of true faith anticipate Reformed values, from which they are clearly separated by intervening time. They argue that the Reformation uncovers (with all of the apocalyptic associations this evokes) a 'true' Church, long predating the Roman conversion of the Saxon kings, which has lain dormant in England since the mission of Joseph of Arimathea. This historiographical approach is in keeping with the prophetic understanding of language already encountered in their work, for example in John Bale's anagrammatic arguments, whereby latent meaning is instantaneously uncovered with the force of revelation.

[42] *The Oxford English Dictionary*, ed. by J. A. Simpson and E. S. C. Weiner, 2nd edn (Oxford, 1989), s.v. 'fetch', v., 6b.

[43] Angelika Lutz, 'The Study of the Anglo-Saxon Chronicle in the Seventeenth Century and the Establishment of Old English Studies in the Universities', in *The Recovery of Old English: Anglo-Saxon Studies in the Sixteenth and Seventeenth Centuries*, ed. by Timothy Graham (Kalamazoo, 2000), pp. 1–82 (p. 1).

But in the same way that Verstegan subversively appropriates this model in his letter, *A Restitution* modifies this sense of language, and of history. As we will see, the work moves beyond the model of prophetic language already described and favours instead a lexicographical approach based upon the etymological reconstruction of linguistic history. Just as Verstegan traces the 'true' English faith from the Augustinian conversion of the Anglo-Saxon king Ethelbert to the contemporary Catholic Church, so he traces spoken English of the present-day to its Anglo-Saxon roots. Whereas prophetic language insists on a distinct division between the moment of utterance, in which the future is foreseen, and the moment in which this prediction comes to pass, etymological reconstruction focuses on the gaps in between. These two modes of polemically motivated history display then quite different periodizing principles, reflected in the linguistic devices they use. Protestant historiography interprets certain key originary episodes in the past as anticipating the present, thus emphasizing the synchronicity of the two moments. Verstegan's response to this rhetorical strategy is to draw our attention to the diachronic disjunction between our historical beginnings and the present. While Protestant historiography focuses upon a return to the origins of the Church, before the corrupting influence of Catholicism took hold, and tells a story of degeneration, Verstegan's version of ecclesiastical history portrays a gradual and progressive development over time, guided by the hand of divine providence.[44] His etymological approach requires that the present and past be understood in relation to one another, indeed as creating one another. The intervening spaces are made visible as sites either for the exposition of semantic development, or for admitted speculation where the knowledge needed to trace this evolution is lacking.

As Graham Parry has written, the Anglo-Saxon language functions in *A Restitution* as 'an instrument of discovery [...]. By its means, place names and personal names yield up their meaning.'[45] But the notion of discovery is itself unstable at the time Verstegan writes. In its earliest senses the word *discover* was simply the negative of the verb *to cover,* and thus meant 'to reveal'. But during the sixteenth century the word begins to take on a different meaning, that most familiar to us today, first attested by the *OED* in 1555: 'To obtain sight or knowledge of (something previously unknown) for the first time; to come to the

[44] I am grateful to Anthony Grafton and Lisa Jardine for drawing my attention to this important distinction.

[45] Graham Parry, *The Trophies of Time: English Antiquarians of the Seventeenth Century* (Oxford, 1995), p. 64.

knowledge of; to find out'.[46] Parry's description of Anglo-Saxon lexicography as 'an instrument of discovery' in *A Restitution* is particularly apt, because in this work Verstegan modifies the model of prophetic language that implies an uncovering of something present all along (which he played upon in his letter of 1593). Instead he adopts an approach that seeks to 'discover' the Anglo-Saxon beginnings of the English language in this later sense of the word, which implies the finding out of something 'for the first time', the reconstruction of origins. Etymological discovery in this sense encompasses both an element of the prophetic force of language already explored in this essay, but adds to this model an aspect of re-creation that bridges the gap between linguistic roots and current usage. It is worth noting that when Polydore Vergil writes *De inventoribus rerum* in 1499, he does not seem to distinguish the concept of discovery from that of invention.[47] As a recent translator of *On Discovery* observes, 'The root sense of the Latin *invenire*, to come upon, is on the side of discovery, but the same verb also means to devise or invent.'[48] Of course, this idea of the novelty of discovery is in one sense an illusion, because the past is always with us and, as Verstegan makes clear, the Anglo-Saxon roots of English are evident in many words in current usage. But in another sense, what we encounter through lexicographical study is not a direct connection to any idealized notion of linguistic 'origins', as Edward Said describes them, 'divine, mythical and privileged', but rather the tracing of what Said terms 'beginnings', 'secular, humanly produced, and ceaselessly re-examined'.[49] These 'beginnings' genuinely are discovered 'for the first time' in Verstegan's

[46] The earliest attribution is to Richard Eden's translation of *The decades of the newe worlde or west India* (1555), *OED*, s.v. 'discover', v., 8. The last attestation for its early meaning 'To remove the covering (clothing, roof, lid, etc.) from (anything)' (*OED*, s.v. 'discover', v., 1) is 1628. It continues to mean 'To disclose or expose to view (anything covered up, hidden, or previously unseen), to reveal, show' (*OED*, 'discover', v., 3, 4) into the nineteenth century, but this usage is now virtually obsolete.

[47] When the work was first rendered into English by Thomas Langley in 1546, his title for the work similarly conflated invention and discovery. Thomas Langley, *An abridgement of the notable worke of Polidore Vergile conteygnyng the deuisers and first finders out aswell of artes, ministeries, feactes [and] ciuill ordinaunces, as of rites, [and] ceremonies, commonly vsed in the churche: and the originall beginnyng of the same* (London, 1546).

[48] Polydore Vergil, *On Discovery*, ed. and trans. by Brian P. Copenhaver (Cambridge, MA, 2002), p. xi. As Copenhaver points out, Langley used the word 'inventours' to mean 'those who found [...] without inventing anything'. In other words, those who discovered things.

[49] Edward Said, *Beginnings: Intention and Method* (New York, 1975), pp. xii–xiii, 5–6; qtd in Frantzen, *Desire for Origins*, p. 23.

lexicography, because it is his very act of etymological reconstruction that creates them.

Because it is the Saxon king Ethelbert who will be converted to Christianity by the Roman mission, representing the beginnings of the true English Church in his account, Verstegan awards supreme importance to the Saxon invasion of England. His description of their arrival is accompanied by an engraving and declaration that 'because these noble Gentlemen were the very first bringers and conductors of the ancestors of Englishmen into Britaine, from whence unto their Posterity the possession of the Countrey hath ensued, I thought fit here in pourtrature to set down their first Arrivall' (p. 116). However, Verstegan skims over both the subsequent Danish and Norman invasions, pronouncing their impact insignificant on the grounds that 'the Danes and Normanes were once one same people with the Germans, as were also the Saxons' (p. 187). Moreover, 'albeit it pleased God for the chasticement of the English people to permit the Normanes to have the victories in the battaile in *Sussex*, yet were they but a handful in regard of the whole English people which by the continuance of divers ages and descents were become the universall inhabitants over all the land' (p. 186).

This is reflected in the version of the history of the English language Verstegan constructs. He rapidly dismisses the linguistic impact of the Norman invasion, unlike that of the Saxons, observing that 'the French toung in *England* became not any where to bee the people Languages, only it left in our English tongue a mixture of divers French words' (pp. 180–81).[50] In his list of English surnames, Verstegan is careful to point out, 'I have not therefore found that ever [William the Conqueror] forced the Englishmen to leave their sirnames when hee made them lose their landes' (p. 280). While some instances of French naming conventions, such as the interpolation of *le* or *de* into a title, as in 'le Reve' or 'de Newton', are in evidence in the years immediately after the Conquest, 'it is not therefore to be thought that these were Normans with English sirnames, but that it only was (as yet it is) the French maner of writing sirnames both of their owne and of strangers, with *le* and *de*' (p. 281). Even this was a short-lived practice, Verstegan stresses, ending as soon as 'Englishmen and English maners began to prevayle unto the recovery of decayed credit' (p. 281). Finally, when obliged to

---

[50] Verstegan famously denounces Geoffrey Chaucer as 'a great mingler' of French and English. Chaucer, Verstegan writes, 'is of some called the first illuminator of the English tongue: of their opinion I am not', for 'Since the time of *Chaucer*, more Latin and French hath beene mingled with our tongue then left out of it', with the result that some say 'that it is of it selfe no language at all, but the scum of many languages' (pp. 203–04).

acknowledge that in fact quite a number of surnames in current English usage are French in origin, Verstegan presents the list in truncated form. He does not gloss the meaning of these names, whilst providing extensive annotations detailing the noble associations of Saxon names. Even this account is prefaced by an insistence that although 'some sirnames of good families remayning in *England* at this day' are French in origin, they are 'not found to bee in any list of such as came in with the Conquerour: and therefore may well bee thought to bee remayned of such gentlemen and others, as came into *England* out of *Henalt*, with Queene *Isabel* wife unto King *Edward the Second*', in the early fourteenth century (pp. 304–05). Verstegan endeavours to write the Norman element out of English history, and the English language, at every turn. Instead *A Restitution* discovers England's Saxon past. And by this claim I wish to invoke the sense of 'discovery' current when Verstegan was writing, which hints at invention, in addition to the idea of coming across a history that has been there all along.

Discovering Saxon English

Just as the work Verstegan proposes in his 1593 letter depends upon the Protestant polemical rhetoric it subverts, so *A Restitution* is in dialogue with texts that mobilize the history of Anglo-Saxon England to very different ends. Verstegan positions his narrative in contradistinction to that of Protestant historiography, a process he begins by undermining the authority of its most famous contemporary proponent, John Foxe. In the prefatory 'Epistle to Our Nation', Foxe is ridiculed for accepting the mythical Trojan origins of Britain as fact, 'for what is it other then an absurditie for an English Author to beginne his Epistle (to a huge volume) with *Constantine the great and mightie Emperor the sonne of Helen an English woman*, &c' (iv[v]).[51] Verstegan corrects this misapprehension, remarking that 'in truth, S. *Helen*, the mother of *Constantine* was no English woman, but a British woman, and in all likelihood never knew what English ment, for that she died more then an hundreth yeares before the English-Saxons came into Brittaine' (iv[v]). Verstegan is keen to establish early in *A Restitution* that the synthesis of 'English' and 'British' in Reformist historiography jeopardizes their whole enterprise because the English are descended not from the Britons but rather from

---

[51] A printed marginal note identifies Foxe as the author in question. His 'huge volume' of Protestant martyrology, *Acts and Monuments*, was very widely read, although it is now considered unlikely that a copy could be found in every church in England, as previously thought.

the Saxons, receivers of the Christian faith from Rome.[52] As Donna B. Hamilton has recently made clear, by correcting Foxe and his historiographical predecessors Verstegan 'called attention to the constructed nature of Protestant mythology'.[53] Elsewhere, Verstegan criticizes Luther himself on the grounds that 'he makes his owne fancy his Author, for another Author of more Antiquity than himselfe he can find none' (p. 156).

The most important misconception Verstegan wishes to address is that held by many 'English men (and those no idiots neither)' as to the origins of the English people (iv[v]). In speaking of the Saxons, these historians 'rather seeme to understand them for a kind of forraine people, then as their own true and meere Ancestors' (iv[v]–v[r]). Verstegan devotes considerable effort to correcting this misconception, employing his customary device of etymological reconstruction to discover the history inherent in the name 'Saxon', a history that reveals the bravery of the Saxons themselves. I have suggested that Verstegan traces the space between this Anglo-Saxon history and the present, rather than sympathetically identifying with selected isolated moments in the past, as Protestant historiographers tended to do. This is reflected in *A Restitution*'s lexicographical approach, which is one of charting the space in between a word's earliest instances and its current usage. Verstegan has a sophisticated understanding of linguistic change as it occurs over time, observing that 'it hath diverse times also happened, that the appellation of some of these people have come to be varied and changed', as well as of the multiplicity of possible interpretations of individual words (p. 17).[54] He dismisses three different proposed derivations of the term *Saxon,* counting himself among those 'smelling these denominations to be fabulous' (p. 17). He prefers instead the explanation '(though some hold it unlikely) of their use and wearing of a certaine kinde of sword or weapon invented and made bowing crooked, much after the

---

[52] Anne Dillon also notes the way in which reformist rhetoric appears to have 'regarded the terms British and English as interchangeable'. As she observes, 'Religious belief, inextricably tied to membership of a Church, was now a function of tribal ancestry' (Anne Dillon, *The Construction of Martyrdom in the English Catholic Community 1535–1603* (Aldershot, 2002), p. 333). Dillon's book provides the most searching analysis to date of Verstegan's own martyrological work, the *Theatrum Crudelitatum Haereticorum nostri temporis* (Antwerp, 1587), written in response to Foxe.

[53] Hamilton, 'A Catholic Antiquarian Replies', p. 5.

[54] 'But as all thinges under heaven do in length of time encline unto alteration and varietie, so do [*sic*] the language also', Verstegan observes (p. 194). He anticipates a key precept of the famous Grimm's Law, not fully articulated until the eighteenth century, in noting that over time Teutonic languages come to substitute 'the D for the T' (p. 9).

fashion of a sithe' (p. 21). There are two important reasons why Verstegan prefers this etymology. First, its 'proceeding of the bearing of armes' means that the name 'can no way seem dishonourable, but indeed very honourable' (p. 24). The name of the 'Saxon' people thus reflects a nobility of character crucial to Verstegan's argument that the 'true' English Church begins with their conversion. Second, this explanation can be traced right to the present day. Verstegan records a conversation with pre-eminent Catholic historian Justus Lipsius in which he confirms 'that a sithe is yet at this present in the Netherlands called a saisen' (p. 21). This continuity of usage allows Verstegan to construct narrative connections in the gap between ancient times and his own day. In an extension of *A Restitution*'s central argument, this enables him to claim that just as the word *saisen* has persisted into contemporary European vocabulary, so the nobility of the Saxons, enhanced and defined by their acceptance of Christian faith from Rome, is preserved by those English men and women who continue to profess this true Catholic faith.

The word lists that form the last three of *A Restitution*'s ten chapters are the first etymological glossaries of the Anglo-Saxon language ever to be printed. Today's scholars consider the lists remarkably accurate.[55] This is striking 'when we consider he produced his glossary in isolation', as Clement observes, 'unable to draw upon the manuscript glossaries produced by the Protestant scholars in the 1560s and 1570s, and unable to consult either contemporary English scholars or the vast majority of Anglo-Saxon manuscripts, all unavailable to him in England'.[56] In his glossary Verstegan traces the etymological root of the name *Antwerp* to that shared by the Anglo-Saxon verbal adjective 'Awarpen, or

---

[55] According to Philip H. Goepp, 615 out of the 685 words glossed in the word lists are correctly identified as Anglo-Saxon. See Philip H. Goepp, 'Verstegan's "Most Ancient Saxon Words"', in *Philologica: The Malone Anniversary Studies*, ed. by Thomas A. Kirby and Henry Bosley Woolf (Baltimore, 1949), pp. 249–55 (p. 249).

[56] Clement, 'Richard Verstegan's Reinvention of Anglo-Saxon England', p. 33. Whilst Clement is undoubtedly right that Verstegan did not have access to the manuscript collections and early drafts of an Anglo-Saxon dictionary compiled by the scholars of Archbishop Matthew Parker's household in the 1560s and 1570s, it is likely that he was able to draw upon the library of his friend in Antwerp, cartographer and antiquarian Abraham Ortelius. Amongst the Anglo-Saxon manuscripts thought to have passed through Ortelius's hands is an Aldhelm's *De laudibus virginitatis* with Old English glosses upon the Latin text that could feasibly have provided Verstegan with the means to reconstruct some of the vocabulary found in his word lists. See *The Old English Glosses of MS. Brussels, Royal Library, 1650 (Aldhelm's 'De Laudibus Virginitatis')*, ed. by Louis Goossens (Brussels, 1974), p. 8.

Awurpen', meaning '*Thrown or cast* (p. 209). The semantic origins of the name *Antwerp* are connected to this word, '*And-warp*, anciently *Hand-warpe*, took that name, as is said, of hands being there cut off, and cast into the River of Skeld' (p. 209). Verstegan's definition of 'Awarpen' encompasses local usage of the word in 'some parts of England' and admits multiple semantic meanings. Another dimension is added by his description of hands being cut off during the city's ancient history, which may have reminded Verstegan's first readers of the recent violent religious uprisings in Antwerp during the sixteenth century. Verstegan offers a comparable etymology of 'Antwerp' in his first published work, *The Post for Divers Partes of the World*.[57] Antwerp, he there tells us, 'which as some say, was kept of a Giant enhabiting therein [...] toke the name by a hande, which smitten of, was cast into the river Schelt'.[58] By the time Verstegan composed *A Restitution*, he had lived in Antwerp for nearly twenty years and, having arrived in the aftermath of the siege of the city, may have felt this account of the city's name less pertinent than its recent bloody history.

Verstegan's definition of 'Awarpen, or Awurpen' prompts him to recollect that '[w]e call in some parts of *England* a moul a *Mould-warp*, which is as much to say as a *cast-earth*, and when planks or boards are awry, we say they cast, or they *warp*' (p. 209). This passing reference to the '*Mould-warp*' invokes a Galfridian prophecy, commonly attributed to Merlin, which was extremely popular in the sixteenth century.[59] Also known as the 'Prophecy of the Six Kings', the mouldwarp prophecy describes a series of animals, the last of which would be the evil mole — or

[57] The work is effectively a travel guide that includes notes of antiquarian interest pertaining to each destination.

[58] Richard [Rowlands] Verstegan, *The Post for Divers Partes of the World* (London, 1576), p. 33. There is a more detailed discussion of this mythical history of the city of Antwerp and origins of its name in the first book of Joannes Goropius Becanus, *Origines Antwerpianæ* (Antwerp, 1569).

[59] The mouldwarp prophecy was supposedly used by the Percy-Glendower rebels to justify their actions against Henry IV. Shakespeare expects his audiences to pick up on this allusion when Hotspur denounces the superstitious Glendower in *1 Henry IV*: 'Sometimes he angers me | With telling of the moldwarp and the ant, | Of the dreamer Merlin and his prophecies, | And of a dragon and a finless fish, | A clip-wing'd griffin and a moulten raven, | A couching lion and a ramping cat, | And such a deal of skimble-skamble stuff | As puts me from my faith' (William Shakespeare, *1 Henry IV* (1596–97), in *The Riverside Shakespeare*, III. i. 146–53). Shakespeare is drawing here upon his source, Holinshed, who holds that the rebels conspired against King Henry IV on the basis of 'a foolish credit given to a vaine prophesie [...] the deviation (saith *Hall*) and not the divination of those blind and fantasticall dreames of the Welsh prophesiers'. See Geoffrey Bullough, *Narrative and Dramatic Sources of Shakespeare*, 8 vols (London, 1957–75), IV, 185.

mouldwarp — whose fate it is to be driven from the land by a dragon, a wolf, and a lion, who would then divide England into three parts, to be shared amongst themselves.[60] This was usually interpreted as referring to the succession of English monarchs following King John. Henry III was said to be figured by a lamb, for instance, and Edward I by the dragon. Subsequent monarchs are characterized as a lion, goat, and ass, according to popular understanding of the prophecy, until '[f]inally a Mouldwarp, or Mole (Henry IV), shall become ruler of the land', A. G. Dickens explains.[61] This conventional interpretation of the mouldwarp prophecy was however challenged by those who opposed the reforms of Henry VIII, who dubbed him the mouldwarp.[62] Keith Thomas goes so far as to brand this alternative reading an 'article of faith' amongst Catholics.[63]

What I wish to draw attention to here is that whilst this interpretation of the mouldwarp prophecy would obviously have held certain attractions for Richard Verstegan, his interest here is not so much in the mythology attached to the word *'Mould-warp'* as in the history of the word itself. Whilst there is an additional polemical charge added to the word by its association with the language of prophecy, Verstegan chooses not to devote his time to this but rather to explicating the relationship between the word *'Mould-warp'* and other etymologically related terms, tracing the Anglo-Saxon root words through to present-day usage. Verstegan's methodology might thus be described as a move away from a purely revelatory conception of semantic meaning (although words do continue to hold something of this power for him), and toward a view of language as a means of discovery, of re-creating the links that bind the past to the present. His emphasis falls on the fact that to this day, 'We call in some parts of *England* a moul a

---

[60] Keith Thomas, *Religion and the Decline of Magic: Studies in Popular Beliefs in Sixteenth and Seventeenth Century England* (London, 1971), p. 399. A. G. Dickens notes the Galfridian qualities of the prophecy: 'it represents historical figures by animals, and the political story by wars and adventures between them' (A. G. Dickens, *Lollards and Protestants in the Diocese of York 1509–1558* (London, 1959), p. 127).

[61] A. G. Dickens, *Lollards and Protestants*, p. 127.

[62] This despite arguments to the contrary that if, as was generally accepted, Henry III, was the first of the six kings, the prophecy could not possibly extend to the Tudor monarch. Wilfrid Holme, in his long poem *The Fall and Evill Success of Rebellion [...] Written in old English Verse* (London, 1536), defends Henry VIII on precisely these grounds. See A. G. Dickens, *Lollards and Protestants*, p. 128.

[63] 'In fact', Thomas writes, 'prophecies of one kind or another were employed in virtually every rebellion or popular rising which disturbed the Tudor state' (Thomas, *Religion and the Decline of Magic*, pp. 399–400, 398).

Mould-warp' (p. 209), an assertion supported by the fact that in the first manuscript dictionary of the Anglo-Saxon language, produced by Laurence Nowell, his gloss of *aWeorpan & toWeorpan*, is 'To cast awaye'.[64] Writing some forty years before Verstegan, Nowell's definition of the Saxon *Wandwyrp* as 'A molle, a molde-warpe' further backs up his suggestion that the word is in current use.[65] Laurence Nowell's manuscript glosses have a notoriously strong Lancastrian bias, reflecting the fact that the word was most widely employed at this time in the north and the Midlands, limited, as Verstegan says, to 'some parts of England'.

The regional and historical variation Verstegan goes out of his way to include in his etymology of *awarpen* is indicative of his wider pluralist methodology. At the same time, he writes distinctly out of his own marginal position as a Catholic exiled from early Jacobean society. Indeed, one of the most revealing aspects of Verstegan's lexicographical analysis of Anglo-Saxon vocabulary in *A Restitution* is the way in which he suggests a prehistory to the language of contemporary Catholicism, which serves to endorse the continuing practices of the outlawed faith. As Hamilton suggests, when read in this light the glossary 'is as deeply inflected with Verstegan's religious-political priorities as the first half of *A Restitution*'.[66] Among the Old English words that Verstegan glosses, we find *Afgod,* meaning 'An Idoll', along with *Afgodnes,* 'Idolatry', for example (p. 207). Verstegan's word lists also hint at the Catholic ritual of praying upon beads in its etymological explication of the word *Bead,* or *Gibead,* originally meaning simply 'Prayer' (p. 209). 'Hereof commeth the name of Beades (they beeing made to pray on)', Verstegan notes, whilst also drawing attention to the semantically related ancient origins of 'Going on Pilgrimmage', or 'Bead-faring' (p. 209). The archetypal prayer of Catholicism, the Hail Mary, is also shown to trace its roots back to the Anglo-Saxon 'Hael or Haile' (p. 224). 'Our Ancestors', we are told, 'vsed it in steede of *Aue,* as a word of most well wishing, as when they

---

[64] Here, as elsewhere, Nowell gives an example supporting this usage: '*From ælcum ʒodes dæle aworpene.* Deprived of suche part as belongeth to God'. Nowell's dictionary remained unpublished until the twentieth century. Laurence Nowell, *Vocabularium Saxonicum*, ed. by Albert H. Marckwardt (Ann Arbor, 1952), p. 179.

[65] Nowell, *Vocabularium Saxonicum*, p. 179.

[66] Hamilton makes the important point that the acknowledged oddities in Verstegan's selection and organization of words in his lists of glosses become more explicable 'once one begins to surmise that Catholic interests guided Verstegan's procedures' (Hamilton, 'A Catholic Antiquarian Replies', p. 15).

sayd *Haile Mary*, &c' (p. 224).[67] These are just some examples of Verstegan's carefully constructed attempt to demonstrate precedents for these practices by carefully situating Catholicism's vocabulary within the history of the English language. As these words have remained in steadily evolving usage from Anglo-Saxon times to the present day, Verstegan suggests, so the church they belong to should continue uninterrupted.

As I have shown, the differing temporal models implied by prophetic language and etymological discovery have particular resonances for Verstegan and his polemical adversaries, resonances which differ in accordance with their disparate beliefs about the history of the true Church. Prophetic language, in which the past is revealed in the present as something that has been there lying dormant all along, has particular significance for Protestant writers, who emphasize the interruption to right religion in England by years of Catholic predominance. Etymological discovery, spanning the space in between present usage and past precedent in the native roots of the English language, offers Richard Verstegan a means of establishing the uninterrupted progress of the Catholic Church from the Saxon conversion up to the present day, as he seeks to justify a continuation of Catholic practices. I do not mean to suggest universally that prophetic language, with its verbal 'toys', the anagram and the acronym foremost amongst them, was the preferred rhetorical device of Protestants, or that etymological discovery was favoured by Catholics. As we have seen, Verstegan and his Counter-Reformation allies repeatedly adopt the rhetorical devices of their opponents in an attempt to win the polemical battle of the day. His subversion of the reformists' commonplace identification of Rome with Babylon through the anagrammatic relationship of Albion and Babylon is just one instance of this. And whilst Verstegan brought to a broad readership a new interest in the Anglo-Saxon origins of the English language, his work was predated by that of lexicographers (such as Laurence Nowell working for Archbishop Parker) who sought to use language as 'an instrument of discovery', to borrow Parry's words once more, to very different ends. What I wish to emphasize is the way in which, for writers of both religious convictions, the function of language across time, be that the providential time of prophecy and revelation or the continuous chronological time of ongoing etymological development, provides an analogy for thinking through their relation to history. This relation changes depending upon the polemical aims of any given text, with broad trends giving way to moments of subversion and even

---

[67] See also Hamilton, 'A Catholic Antiquarian Replies', p. 16.

playfulness. Verstegan's dismissal of these linguistic devices as 'toys' captures something of this. But as we have seen, prophetic language and etymological discovery are dangerously sharp weapons in the armoury of early-modern polemicists.

Princeton University

FROM *CHANSON DE GESTE* TO MAGNA CARTA: GENRE AND THE BARONS IN MATTHEW PARIS'S *CHRONICA MAJORA*

Heather Blurton

T he thirteenth-century chronicler Matthew Paris never minded noting when things were going from bad to worse, and the mid-thirteenth century offered plenty of grist for his mill. It saw the Mongol invasions in the 1240s, the failure of the awaited apocalypse of 1250, several disastrous crusades, the violent struggles between the papacy and the Holy Roman Emperors, and, perhaps most importantly for England, the decades-long power struggle between the king and his barons, which had as its highlights King John's concession of Magna Carta in 1215 and the 1258 baronial rebellion led by Simon de Montfort. Matthew Paris's *Chronica majora* is one of the most important historical sources for the conflicts between barons and kings in thirteenth-century England, and this article proposes to take the entry for the year 1253 as a case study in order to suggest that it offers a sophisticated reading of the ideology of the political and legal relationship between the English barons and the English king in the events leading up to the baronial rebellion of 1258.

The year 1253 is an important moment in the *Chronica* because it contains the only extant text of the 1253 confirmation of Magna Carta by Henry III, alongside the witnessing of an oath of excommunication against anyone who defied its terms.[1] Even more interestingly, in this entry, Matthew follows the account of the confirmation of Magna Carta with a manifestly fictive episode that describes the rupture of homage between a knight and the king who has refused him both

---

[1] The text is included in Matthew Paris's 'appendix' to the *Chronica majora*, the *Liber additamentorum*.

honourable treatment and legal justice. Briefly, in this episode, the king's malicious counsellors convince him to confiscate a loyal knight's goods. When the outraged son of the knight murders one of the counsellors in the heat of passion, the king has him hung without trial while the knight is absent seeking securities.[2] In other words, Matthew juxtaposes Magna Carta 1253 with an episode that is modelled as a stock scene from the Old French epic of revolt, from *chanson de geste*.

This, at least, is how this article will read the brief episode of a loyal knight and an unjust king. It will argue that the *Chronica majora*'s *chanson de geste* follows the description of the confirmation of Magna Carta in 1253 in order to perform an intervention into that precise political moment. In this entry, the *Chronica* contrasts the competing genre of *chanson de geste* in order to highlight the themes of rebellious barons and unjust kings. This narrative's appropriation of the tropes of *chanson de geste* functions as political analysis of the mid-thirteenth-century power dynamic between the king and the baronage of England.[3] In his presentation of the events of 1253, we may read Matthew as engaging with a contemporary discourse of rebellion that was taking place across generic boundaries — in *chanson de geste*, but also in charter and chronicle. In the tropes that the *Chronica majora* appropriates from Old French epic, we can read, I propose, Matthew's equivocal response to the politics of baronial revolt between 1215 and 1258. While Matthew's deployment of the tropes of *chanson de geste* is a forceful assertion of the right of the barons to rebel against the king, it may simultaneously contain a subtle acknowledgement of the fact of royal power. Finally this article will suggest that considering the deployment of different genres in the *Chronica majora* may offer one way of better understanding Matthew Paris's modes of historical analysis.

---

[2] For the full story, see below, pp. 121–23.

[3] Although this article will use the word *baron* to refer to the rebel barons both of 1215 and of 1258, doing so does create an artificial opposition between baron and king. As Claire Valente summarizes: 'As far as the various ranks of society are concerned, resistance to John, even among the baronage was not universal, which is why one should speak of "opposition" barons, not barons generally. Thirteen of the thirty-seven most important barons rebelled at some point during 1215–17; about forty barons (out of about 200 in all) can be confidently assigned to the opposition, the same number to the king. Thus it seems that the baronage was fairly evenly divided. Also important were knights, who made up the main fighting forces, but probably less than a quarter of knights joined the revolt' (Claire Valente, *The Theory and Practice of Revolt in Medieval England* (Aldershot, 2003), p. 62).

The juxtaposition of Magna Carta 1253 with an episode drawing on the tropes of *chanson de geste* suggests that Matthew understands *chanson de geste*, particularly the so-called 'rebellious barons cycle', to be a genre that takes up the question of the right of feudal barons to employ rebellion as a political tool in order to modify royal behaviour and/or royal policy. In England, the right of barons to rebel against the king had been recently enshrined in Chapter 61 of Magna Carta 1215, which provided a legal mechanism for baronial distraint of the king, stating:

> Et si nos excessum non emendaverimus, vel, si fuerimus extra regnum, justiciarius noster non emendamverit infra tempus quadraginta dierum computandum a tempore quo monstratum fuerit nobis vel justiciario nostro, si extra regnum fuerimus, predicti quatuor barones referant causam illam ad residuos de illis viginti quinque baronibus, et illi viginti quinque barones cum communa tocius terre distringent et gravabunt nos modis omnibus quibus poterunt, scilicet per capcionem castrorum, terrarum, possessionum et aliis modis quibus poterunt, donec fuerit emendatum secundum arbitrium eorum, salva persona nostra et regine nostre et liberorum nostrorum; et cum fuerit emendatum intendent nobis sicut prius fecerunt.

> (And if we, or our justiciar, should we be out of the kingdom, do not redress the offence within forty days from the time when it was brought to the notice of us or our justiciar, should we be out of the kingdom, the aforesaid four barons shall refer the case to the rest of the twenty-five barons and those and twenty-five barons with the commune of all the land shall distrain and distress us in every way they can, namely by seizing our castles, lands, and possessions, and in such other ways as they can, saving our person, and those of our queen and of our children, until, in their judgement, amends have been made; and when it had been redressed they are to obey us as they did before.)[4]

This clause, however, was subsequently dropped from the reissues of 1216, 1217, and 1225.[5] In the *Chronica majora*'s account of the events surrounding the 1253 confirmation, Henry III expresses discontent with even the remaining version, when, in a dramatic scene, he rejects Magna Carta as impinging on his sovereignty. No sooner are the sentences of excommunication threatened to those who would violate the terms of Magna Carta, but Henry threatens to do just that:

---

[4] James Clarke Holt, *Magna Carta*, 2nd edn (Cambridge, 1992), pp. 470, 471 (text and translation by Holt).

[5] Holt notes, however, that the abandonment of clauses may not have been received as of any particular import, because '[t]he re-issues of the charter seem to have convinced many that its principles were more important than its variants; hence they gave it a continuous history going back to Runnymede' (James Clarke Holt, 'The St Albans Chroniclers and Magna Carta', in *Magna Carta and Medieval Government* (London, 1985), p. 277).

Soluto autem sic concilio, rex confestim pessimo usus consilio, omnia praedicta cogitabat infirmare. Dictum namque est illi, quod non foret rex, vel saltem dominus in Anglia, si supradicta tenerentur, et expertus est rex J[ohannes] pater eius, qui mori praeelegit quam sic pessundari calcibus subditorum.

(Thus, the council was dissolved, and the king at once, taking the worst of advice, sought to invalidate all the proceedings. For he had been told that, if the above conditions were kept, he would not be a king, or even a lord in England, and that his father John had found that out, and he preferred death to being thus trodden under foot.)[6]

Henry's threat to break faith with his barons is then followed in the 1253 entry by the story of a dispossessed knight who withdraws homage from his king. Matthew's inclusion of this story in the context of the 1253 confirmation of Magna Carta that he alone records invites a consideration of the themes of Magna Carta through the perspective of *chanson de geste*. Reading Magna Carta alongside *chanson de geste* is a fascinating study because it reveals the extent to which the thematic preoccupations of each are shared. Magna Carta 1215 itself reads somewhat like a *chanson de geste*, with its insistent demands for royal justice, its expulsion of traitors from the royal court, and its exhortations to rebellion.[7] The scenario of this *chanson de geste* episode in the *Chronica majora* is precisely that imagined in Magna Carta, most specifically in Chapter 39, the element that came to be seen as constitutive of the core of baronial demands. Chapter 39 encapsulates the crisis at the centre of the *Chronica majora*'s narrative, stating:

Nullus liber homo capiatur, vel imprisonetur, aut disseisiatur, aut utlagetur, aut exuletur, aut aliquo modo destruatur, nec super eum ibimus, nec super eum mittemus, nisi per legale judicium parium suorum vel per legem terre.

(No free man shall be taken or imprisoned or disseised or outlawed or exiled or in any way ruined, nor will we go upon him or send against him, except by the lawful judgement of his peers or by the law of the land.)[8]

---

[6] Matthew Paris, *Chronica Majora*, ed. by H. R. Luard, Rolls Series, 7 vols (London, 1872–83), V, 378 (hereafter cited as Luard); *Matthew Paris's English History*, trans. by J. A. Giles, 3 vols (London, 1852–54), III, 27 (hereafter cited as Giles). It should be noted, however, that Giles's translation is not based on Luard's edition.

[7] There is evidence that Magna Carta was promulgated in the vernacular. This raises the question of whether it might be possible to trace points of contact at the lexical level between the language of vassalage and rebellion employed in *chanson de geste* and that of the vernacular redactions Magna Carta. Unfortunately, there are only two extant Anglo-Norman versions and none in English. See James Clarke Holt, 'A Vernacular-French Text of Magna Carta 1215', *English Historical Review*, 89.351 (1974), 346–64, and his *Magna Carta*.

[8] Holt, *Magna Carta*, p. 460; 461. Chapter 39 becomes Chapter 29 in the 1225 reissue, which was used in 1253. Matthew Paris's version of the text in the *Liber addimentorum* of the

This narrative that Matthew offers for 1253, and which I have been referring to as a *chanson de geste*, is worth quoting at length in order to highlight its integrity as a self-contained narrative unit. The story is set on crusade. During a truce, a loyal and dutiful French knight asks his king's permission to launch an attack against the Saracens. Upon his successful return to court, he is accused by jealous knights at court of having made too much money off the adventure and, worse, of keeping it for himself. The king, on the advice of his counsellors, subsequently appropriates the knight's spoils. Following the seizure of his goods, the knight addresses the king:

'Domine, omnia mea tua sunt, immo et ego tuus. Videtur tamen mihi justius, ut ipse bonis gaudeat adquisitis, qui pro ipsis caput et vitam exposuit adquirendis. Haec enim, ut perpendo, verba excitarunt quidam desides et formidolosi cubicularii vestry ac consiliarii, vobis blandientes, et ut vobis placeant blandientes.' Prosiliens igitur unus ipsorum in medium quos sic reprehenderat, et ebulliens in ira megn, convitia multa in ipsum exaggeravit, dicens, 'Talia dicens mentiris per medium gulae tuae foetentis, qui domini regis collaterales ignaviae redarguis et proditionis'; addens quod malus miles esset, fugitivus et victus, quod est in Gallicana lingua *recreant*, et hoc verbum maximae offensionis inter eos. Cum autem haec audisset quidam miles junior, audax et strenuous, filius videlicet militis accusati, ira accensus nimia prosiliit in medium, et non se capiens prae ira, ore reboante ait, 'O pro cerebro Dei, et tu degener et imbellis talis ausus es verba patri meo me praesente et audiente proferre!' Et subito extrahens sicam quam bajulavit, scilicet hanelacium, ipsum concito eviseravit, et in ipso furore exiliens, se in ecclesiam causa defensionis recepit. Hoc autem videns pater, doluit quasi usque ad mortem, et procidens ad pedes regis ait; 'Nunc, domine mi reverentissime, experienda est regalis clementia vestra, si parcere dignemini huic facto impetuoso. Ego enim stare paratus sum curiae vestrae judicio, ac humiliter juri pariturus'. Cui rex; 'Reperi super hoc idoneos fidejussores'; et dum iret pater, filius ejus subito a Regis satellitibus extractus est subito, et sine judicio curiae subito suspendus. Et cum redisset pater cum fidejussoribus, juri parere per omnia paratus, vidit filium suum jam suspensum et mortuum, quod etiam procurarunt ejus inimici, ut pater videns filium extinctum magis angeretur. Contrmuit igitur prae angustia, et vix ora resolvens; 'Quid hoc est, domine mi rex?' ait. 'Suspendisti, vel suspendi conniventibus oculis filium meum absque judicio permisisti? Non possum patrem dissimulare. Ubi nam ecclesiae reverentia? Ubi curiae Francorum justicia? Quaecunque me avito jure in Francia contingent, necnon et homagium, et quae nuper ense meo adquisivi, tibi resignans derelinquo'. Et ante expectatum, equum velocissimum ascendens, lateribus equinis non parcendo, se ad quondam Soldanum contulit, haecque omnia ipsi seriatim intimavit. Qui respondit; 'Confugisti ad me? Nunquam tibi deero. Pando tibi sinum refugii et protectionis'. Extunc igitur additus est paganorum exercitui, factus apostata formidabilis, et secundum illud quod scribitur, 'Ira est libido ulciscendi',

Chronica majora contains one very interesting textual variant: it amends the troublesome *vel* of 'nisi per legale judicium parium suorum vel per legem terre' to *aut* (Holt, 'The St Albans Chroniclers and Magna Carta', p. 280).

extunc intendit ultioni vigilanter, et factus de amico familiari inimicus, regem et exercitum suum inaestimabiliter dampnificavit, non cessans donec qui filiam suum suspenderunt interemisset. Sic, sic igitur ex invidia ira generator, et ex ira homicidium propagator.

('My lord, all my possessions, and even myself, are yours; but it appears to me that it would be more just for him to enjoy the wealth he has gained who has exposed his body and life in gaining it. These proceedings, it is my belief, have been provoked by some lazy and cowardly chamber gentlemen and advisors of yours, who flatter and fawn on you to give you pleasure'. One of these whom he thus reproached, at hearing this speech, leapt forth into the midst of those assembled, and boiling with rage poured forth invectives against the knight, saying, 'In uttering such words you lie in your foul throat, when you accuse the body servants of our lord the king of idleness and treachery'; and added, 'that he the accuser was a bad knight, a recreant and defeated one', in the French language, a *méchant*, which was a most offensive epithet amongst them. At this speech, the son of the accused knight a young, bold, and brave cavalier, sprang up in the midst of them, and unable to restrain himself with rage, cried with a voice of thunder, 'By God's brains, you degenerate and impotent wretch, do you dare to utter such words to my father in my presence and hearing?' and suddenly drawing a small sword, or dagger which he wore, at once stabbed him in the belly, and rushing forth still mad with rage, fled to a church for protection. His father, on seeing what was done, was deeply grieved, and falling at the king's feet, said, 'Now, my most revered master, will your royal clemency be proved, if you will deign to pardon this infuriated deed; as for me, I am ready to abide by the judgment of your court, and to submit to its jurisdiction'. Then replied the king, 'Find proper securities in the matter'. Whilst he was gone for the purpose, his son was dragged from the Church by the king's agents, and hung at once without any trial or judgment, and when the father returned with his sureties, prepared to obey the law in every respect, he saw his son hanging and already dead, which his enemies had managed in order the more to grieve the father by the sight of his dead son. His limbs trembling with agony, and speaking with difficulty, he at length exclaimed, 'what is this? my lord king? Have you hung, or connived at, or permitted the hanging of my son without trial or judgment? I cannot dissemble my feelings as a father. Where is the reverence due to the Church? Where is the justice of the French courts? Whatever belongs to me in France by ancestral right, as also my homage to you, and what I have lately acquired with my sword I resign to you and leave you myself. So saying, he suddenly mounted a swift horse, and not sparing the spur he fled to a certain soldan, and related all these proceedings in detail. Then said the soldan, 'You have fled to me, and I will never fail you; I open the bosom of refuge and protection'. He at once then joined the army of the Pagans and became a formidable apostate, proving the truth of the proverb, 'Anger is the desire for vengeance'. From that time he entirely devoted himself to revenge, and his friendship being changed to especial hatred, he did immeasurable injury to the king and his army, nor did he desist from his purpose until he had slain those who had hung his son. Thus, then, does envy beget anger, and anger propagate murder.)[9]

---

[9] Luard, V, 386–87; Giles, III, 33–34.

Although related as history, this narrative — with its story of a loyal knight treated unjustly by his king at the instigation of sycophants at court, who subsequently renounces his allegiance to the king and then fights against him — is a stock episode of *chanson de geste*. In addition to its emplotment, the narrative encodes several clues as to its generic affiliation: stylistically, it is narrated almost entirely in the direct discourse characteristic of *chanson de geste*, the story originates at the French court, includes an encounter with Saracens, and perhaps most tellingly, indexes the vocabulary of *chanson de geste* with its quotation of the French term for the insult to the knight, who is called a *recreant* 'in Gallicana lingua' (in the French language). *Recreant* is a deeply evocative term in this context. It is, for example, the term Guerri uses as the insult that stirs Raoul de Cambrai to action in his eponyomous *chanson de geste*: 'Raoul clama malvais et recreant' (He called Raoul a coward and a break-faith).[10] This incident takes place at the court of King Louis, who has unjustly deprived Raoul of his patrimony, and Raoul is only barely prevented from renouncing homage.

The invocation of the term *recreant* here suggests further that the plot of this story is not only that of a *chanson de geste*, but more specifically, of a *chanson de geste* of the 'rebellious barons' cycle. This characterization itself belongs to the thirteenth century. Bertrand de Bar-sur-Aube, the thirteenth-century author of *Girart de Vienne*, which is itself a *chanson* of the 'rebellious barons' group, identifies three thematic groupings of *chanson de geste*: the Charlemagne cycle, the Guillaume d'Orange cycle, and the cycle of the rebellious barons. Bertrand writes:

> N'ot que trois gestes en France la garnie
>
> . . . .
>
> Des rois de France est la plus seignorie,
> et l'autre après, bien est droiz que je die,
> fu de Doon a la barbe florie,
> cil de qui molt ot baronnie.
> El sien lingnaje ot gent fiere et hardie;
> De tote France eüsent seignorie
>
> . . . .
>
> La tierce geste qui molt fist a prisier
> fu de Garin de Monglenne au vis fier.

---

[10] *Raoul de Cambrai*, ed. and trans. by Sarah Kay (Oxford, 1992), l. 517. Of course it is impossible to draw a straight line between *chanson de geste* and romance: in Chrétien de Troyes' *Yvain*, Yvain declares that he would rather have been called 'recreant' than to have fought against Gawain in judicial combat.

De son lignaje puis je bien tesmoignier
Que il n'ot coart ne lannier
Ne traitor ne vilein losangier.

(There are only three *gestes* in abundant France

. . . .

The most lordly is of the Kings of France,
And the other after that, it is right that I tell,
Is of Doon of the full beard,
He of Maience, which has many barons.
The people of his lineage are proud and strong,
They have lordship over all France

. . . .

The third *geste*, which many hold in esteem,
Was of Garin de Monglane, him with the proud face.
Of his lineage I am well able to testify,
Which has neither coward nor craven,
Nor traitor nor coarse flatterer.)[11]

The first *geste* that Bertrand itemizes here, 'des rois de France', or the
Charlemagne cycle, has as its defining characteristic the strong presence of
Emperor Charlemagne and a celebration of the feats of his armies against the
Saracens. This cycle is epitomized by its most famous *geste,* the *Chanson de
Roland*: here Charlemagne faces threats from without (in the form of the Saracens
of Spain) and from within (in the form of the traitor Ganelon) but emerges with
his kingdom and his rule intact. The third cycle that Bertrand lists here, as that of
Garin de Monglane, is more commonly referred to as the Guillaume d'Orange
cycle. It coalesces around the figure of Guillaume d'Orange (who is the putative
great-grandson of Garin de Monglane), a loyal but much-abused vassal of Louis
the Pious. In the face of a range of insults, from lack of appreciation to
dispossession, Guillaume perseveres in exhorting the weak and easily flattered
Louis the Pious to live up to the example of strong and fair rule set by his father,
Charlemagne. Dominique Boutet notes about the *Chanson de Guillaume* that
while Guillaume often finds himself opposing the king, he is never opposing royal

---

[11] Bertrand de Bar-sur-Aube, *Girart de Vienne*, ed. by Wolfgang van Emden (Paris, 1977), ll.
11; 13–18; 46–50; my translation. See also William C. Calin, *The Old French Epic of Revolt:
Raoul de Cambrai, Renaud de Montaban, Gormond and Isemberd* (Geneva, 1962), p. 9.

power: on the contrary, Guillaume reproaches Louis with not exercising royal power strongly enough.[12]

Finally the *Geste de Doon de Maience* offers a name of familial affiliation for a loosely knit group of *chansons de geste* that have as their common and defining feature a rupture in homage between an unjust king and a disposed knight.[13] 'If, as a whole', Alan Hindley and Brian Levy note in their introduction to the genre, 'this cycle lacks the same kind of coherence as that of Guillaume d'Orange, it nevertheless contains some of the most violent and sombre of the epics, dealing as it does with the tragic consequences of disloyalty and *désmesure*'.[14] Wolfgang van Emden anatomizes the structural elements common to what he terms 'the Old French epic of revolt' as follows: in the first instance, 'the hero is received with favour by the king or wins that favour by his services' but subsequently 'a quarrel, which may involve a close relation of the king and/or the vassal and which causes the former to treat the latter unjustly, changes the king's favour into hatred.'[15] This series of events, which provides the problematic for the plotting of the epic of revolt is exactly that which is represented in Matthew Paris's *précis*, as the anonymous knight first wins the king's favour then breaks with him over the execution of his son. The episode in the *Chronica majora* is further embellished with another presence familiar from Old French epic — those bad counsellors who gain the ear of a weak king through flattery, the traitors at court — 'vilein losangiers'. And just to drive the point home, they speak in the vernacular of the literature from which they came when they insult the knight by calling him a *recreant*.

Thus, this episode finds its analogue in such *chansons de geste* as *Raoul de Cambrai,* where the action is set in motion by the disinheritance of the baby Raoul. This initial act of royal injustice sets off a train of events, where the

---

[12] Dominique Boutet, 'Les chansons de geste et l'affermissement du pouvoir royal (1100–1250)', *Annales*, 37 (1982), 3–14 (p. 7).

[13] Ailes notes that while originally these stories were not related, the impulse over time was to form them into a family group and to give them a shared genealogy — normally in relation to Ganelon — hence the appellation of this cycle after a fictive ancestor (Marianne Ailes, 'Traitors and Rebels: The Geste de Maience' in *Reading Around the Epic: A Festschrift in Honour of Professor Wolfgang van Emden*, ed. by Marianne Ailes, Philip E. Bennett, and Karen Pratt (London, 1998), pp. 41–68).

[14] Alan Hindley and Brian Levy, *The Old French Epic: An Introduction* (Leuven, 1983), p. xiv.

[15] Wolfgang van Emden, 'Kingship in the Old French Epic of Revolt', in *Kings and Kingship in Medieval Europe*, ed. by Anne J. Duggan (London, 1993), p. 309.

murder of Bernier's mother causes him to break the tie of vassalage with Raoul and, ultimately, to kill him. In revenge, Raoul's heir, Gautier, hunts down Bernier and his family, the Vermandois. In *La Chevalerie Ogier de Danemarche*, when a squabble over a game of chess results in the murder of Ogier's son by Charlemagne's son, Ogier is refused justice and thus revolts against the king. Likewise Renaut de Montauban is refused justice by Charlemagne in his eponymous *chanson*. In *Girart de Roussillon*, perhaps the earliest of the texts of the rebellious barons cycle, Girart, like Raoul, is unjustly deprived of land that he does not hold in fief from the emperor.[16] While in no two *chanson de geste* is the precise catalyst of the action the same, they all share these structural elements: the scenario of a dramatic scene at court where an accidental disaster or an act of royal injustice results in loyalty being withdrawn is exactly one of these elements. These *chansons* have in common the representation of a refusal of homage on the part of a baron who seeks not glory or material gain, but to right a royal injustice.[17]

In his recapitulation of these tropes of the Old French epic of revolt in the *Chronica majora*, Matthew implicitly admits the possibility of rebellion as a response to royal injustice. He supports, perhaps, through the invocation of the rebellious barons of the literary tradition, rebellion on the home front. What the genre of *chanson de geste* offers him is the ability to consider in a fictional space the issues raised on the eve of the baronial rebellion of 1258. This specific episode allows Matthew to consider the question of the barons' right to rebel that had been raised in Magna Carta 1215. It further enables a consideration of the line between rebellion and treason as well as a broader engagement with the theoretical question of the relationship of the ruler of the realm to the law of the land. In his consideration of these issues, we see Matthew formulate an equivocal response to the legality of baronial rebellion: this response follows *chanson de geste* in its sympathy for baronial transgression but simultaneous acknowledgement of the fact of royal power.

These *chansons* of the rebellious barons cycle extend the tension inherent in the relationship between Louis the Pious and the long-suffering Guillaume d'Orange to one logical extreme: how far may a king push his vassal before the

[16] *Girart de Rousillon* and *Raoul de Cambrai* are from the second half of the twelfth century; *Renaut de Montaban* and *La Chevalerie Ogier* are from the first half of the thirteenth.

[17] In my understanding of the ideological work of *chanson de geste*, I am indebted to William Calin, *The Old French Epic of Revolt*, Sarah Kay, 'Chanson de Geste' in the Age of Romance (Oxford, 1995), and Robert M. Stein, *Reality Fictions: Romance, History and Governmental Authority, 1025–1180* (Notre Dame, 2006).

vassal gains the right to push back? The passage quoted above by Bertrand de Bar-sur-Aube responds implicitly to this question when it emphasizes that in the genealogy of Guillaume d'Orange there is 'ne traitor ne vilein losangier'. The rebellious barons cycle also responds to this question and in the same terms — if with a different answer. The rebellious barons may be rebels, but this cycle emphatically asserts that they are not traitors. Adalbert Dessau's seminal article on treason in the *chanson de geste* frames the theme thusly:

> Numerous *chansons de geste* describe an instance of feudal betrayal in which the *loiaus om*, the faithful vassal, fights against the traitor; in such epics, this judicial battle, whether duel or not, constitutes the main subject and frame of the poem's action. It is interesting to note that in most conflicts thus described, the guilty party is not the vassal.[18]

One very interesting aspect of these *chansons de geste*, when read in the context of 1253, is exactly this insistence on distinguishing between rebels and traitors. As William Calin notes in his study of the genre:

> [T]he authors distinguish carefully between the *rebels*, nobles of upright heart misbehaving only to protect their just rights, and the *traitors*, who act purely out of maliciousness against right and the moral law.[19]

In this genre, the rebel baron is, by definition, not a traitor. The traitors tend to be associated with the king's court, and they fight on the side of the king. What they are betraying is therefore not their king or their feudal vows, but a more abstract ideal of right, of justice. The rebel barons paradoxically uphold and remain single-mindedly true to this ideal even as they may break their vows to their feudal lord and engage in activities that alienate them from the very society whose ideals they alone are represented as defending. Thus in *Girart de Roussillon*, Girart, in revolt against Charlemagne because of the murder of his father by one of Charlemagne's closest counsellors, and ambivalent about making peace with him, asks the anxious question: 'Eu comment amerai rei tant felon?' (How am I to love such a felon king?). The quelling response he receives is 'Ja ne seras retaz de mespreson, | Vers ton lige segnor de traiciun' (Do not let yourself be accused

---

[18] Adalbert Dessau, 'L'idée de la traihson au moyen âge et son rôle dans la motivation de quelques chansons de geste', *Cahiers de civilisation médiévale*, 3 (1960), 23–26 (p. 24); trans. by Fredric L. Cheyette as 'The Idea of Treason in the Middle Ages', in *Lordship and Community in Medieval Europe: Selected Readings* (New York, 1968), pp. 192–209 (p. 194).

[19] Calin, *The Old French Epic of Revolt*, pp. 116–17. See too the discussion by Marianne Ailes, in 'Traitors and Rebels', where she notes, 'In the epics of revolt the family of rebels stands in opposition to the traitors. In these texts we find a general sense of antagonism between the traitors and the rebels' (p. 46).

of treason against your liege lord).[20] This careful distinction between rebel and traitor functions to suggest that while treason is always wrong, there may be situations where it is legitimate for a vassal to rebel against his *seigneur*.

The representation of traitors at court in *chanson de geste* is apposite to read into the *Chronica majora* because it seems to reflect very much the situation at the court of Henry III in the years leading up to the rebellion of 1258. Thus the separation between the knight who fights for his own glory and the knights who remain with the king and who retain his confidence in the story Matthew tells in the *Chronica majora*, as in the rebellious barons cycle of the *chanson de geste*, may have been imagined as analogous to the contemporary situation. There the barons of the realm felt excluded from positions of intimacy with the king, and, just as importantly, from positions of power within the kingdom, while the inner chambers of the king were imagined to be peopled with 'alien knights' and, in reality, a new class of royal administrator. Henry was criticized, by Matthew in particular, for promoting the interests of 'foreigners' against those who Matthew refers to as his 'natural' subjects.[21] In the entry for 1251 Matthew describes how

> Dominus rex diatim, et non jam paulatim, dilectionem suorum hominum amisit naturalium. Patrissans enim manifeste, omnes quos potuit attraxit alienigenas et ditavit, et spretis ac spoliatus Anglicus alienos introduxit.
>
> (At this time, the king day by day lost the affection of his natural subjects; and that not now by degrees: for, openly following the example of his father, he enticed all the foreigners he could to his side, enriched them, and, despising and despoiling his English subjects, intruded aliens into their place.)[22]

---

[20] *La Chanson de Girart de Roussillon*, ed. and trans. by Micheline de Combarieu and Gérard Gouiran (Paris, 1993), ll. 2997, 3006–07, my translation. Stein describes this incident in much greater detail (*Reality Fictions*, pp. 185–203).

[21] The question of desirability of counsellors of court to advise the king was a long-standing issue during the reign of Henry III, especially since his minority rule was, of course, handled by counsellors. As late as 1244, ten years into Henry's personal rule, the project known as the Paper Constitution was mooted — and included in the *Chronica majora*. This plan called for an elected council of four members to advise the King (Michael Prestwich, *English Politics in the Thirteenth Century* (London, 1990), p. 23, and C. R. Cheney, 'The 'Paper Constitution' Preserved by Matthew Paris', in *Medieval Texts and Studies*, ed. by C. R. Cheney (Oxford, 1973), pp. 231–41).

[22] Luard, V, 229; Giles, II, 437. While Matthew harps on nationality as the determining factor in baronial discord, this may not necessarily have been the only aspect. Powicke, for example, argued that these interloping barons were distinguished less by nationality than by the fact that they were essentially courtiers, 'household men taking over the offices of state'. Prestwich agrees with Matthew, however, that the contemporary perception was that the important distinction

The jealous advisors who hold the ear of Matthew's fictive king may well recall these 'alien' knights.

But the evocation of the rebellious barons of *chanson de geste* in this episode addresses a larger issue than that of the 'alien' knights at the court of Henry III. It addresses the dynamic at the heart of Magna Carta. Magna Carta had attempted to remind the king of the legal rights enjoyed by the barons. The constant confirmations of Magna Carta throughout the thirteenth century kept the language of baronial rights current, and 1253 was just such a year of confirmation. In this episode's framing of the conflict between king and vassal, and its placement in 1253, it demands to be read more largely in the context of the politics of Henry III's 'personal rule' of 1234–58: that is, the years between the end of Henry's minority and the baronial rebellion of 1258. In the *Chronica majora* Matthew is generally understood to take the side of the barons against the king. Vaughan, for example, writes:

> In sympathy with his own position, Matthew always supports aristocratic corporations similar to his own against those exercising power over them: he takes the side of the canons of Lincoln against their bishop, the monks of Canterbury against their archbishop, and even the barons against their king.[23]

While the entry for 1253 is very obviously a personal critique of Henry and more generally a critique of the abuse of royal prerogative, we can read in its appropriation of the tropes of *chanson de geste* not simply a defence of the

---

was that of nationality. He attributes Powicke's opinion to his desire 'to see the thirteenth century as an era of internationalism to match the post war idealism of the period when he wrote' (see the discussion in Prestwich, *English Politics in the Thirteenth Century*, pp. 79–80). It seems to me possible that both of these historians are correct and that what was essentially anxiety about 'new men' taking over administrative roles at court was articulated through discourse of xenophobia. See also Huw W. Ridgeway, 'King Henry III and the 'Aliens,' 1236–72', in *Thirteenth-Century England II*, ed. by P. R. Coss and S. D. Lloyd (Woodbridge, 1986), pp. 81–92, and Michael Clanchy, *England and Its Rulers* (Oxford, 1998), pp. 188–91. Carpenter argues that Henry did not favour alien knights in 'King, Magnates, and Society: The Personal Rule of Henry III, 1234–1258', *Speculum*, 60 (1985), 39–70, especially p. 57.

[23] Richard Vaughan, *Matthew Paris* (Cambridge, 1958), p. 137. See also Antonia Gransden, who writes: 'From beginning to end Matthew has a consistent attitude to centralized authority in church and state. He opposes it. He criticizes the pope and any ecclesiastic who interfered with established privileges. Not since the days of William Rufus had a chronicler had such an implacable attitude towards royal power' (Antonia Gransden, *Historical Writing in England, c. 550–c. 1307* (London, 1974), p. 367), and Galbraith, who characterizes St Albans historiography as '*apologia pro baronis*' (Vivian Hunter Galbraith, *Roger Wendover and Matthew Paris* (Glasgow, 1970), p. 20).

baronial right to rebellion, but a sophisticated treatment of the relationship between this right and the fact of royal power.

Joel T. Rosenthal has written from an historian's point of view about the role that accusations against royal counsellors, and their characterization as traitors, played in medieval baronial rebellions. He sees accusations directed against the king's 'wicked advisers' as rhetoric that served to justify baronial intervention, while at the same time deflecting criticism from the royal person to royal policy. He argues:

> Medieval government was impregnated with many political myths, and the constant allegations against the king's wicked advisors can be seen as one of these. By using a theme which did not attack the king or the basic social structure of the state, the barons effectively ritualized their rebellion and thereby minimized the scope of their attack upon order and authority.[24]

Accusations against traitors at court, in other words, must be understood to be about policy change, rather than regime change.

Although Rosenthal is writing about historical, rather than literary, baronial revolts, accusations against traitors at court play a similar role in *chanson de geste*. Even while these texts propose the possibility, indeed the necessity, of baronial correction of royal inadequacies, another characteristic of the genre is that, in the cycle of the rebellious barons, royal power always triumphs, even when — or perhaps especially when — it is in the wrong. Calin notes this feature of the genre, summarizing the way in which rebellion in these narratives is never ultimately successful:

> [I]n the majority of cases the feudal family does not gain a provisory victory or any victory at all, and if Raoul and Isembard are killed and Renaud, Girard and Ogier turn to the Church, it is the direct result of their crushing defeat in secular battle.[25]

Raoul de Cambrai, for example, may win back his ancestral lands, but his efforts to do so result in his murder. Even the most prototypically loyal of the vassals, Guillaume d'Orange, ends his days in monastic withdrawal from political life, as does the rebellious Girart of Roussillon, the erstwhile founder of the cathedral at Vézelay. The position of the king, by contrast, hardly changes.

If the presence of traitors at court plays a mitigating role in the attack on royal power that these rebel knights launch, it may, in this context, therefore be

[24] Joel T. Rosenthal, 'The King's "Wicked Advisers" and Medieval Baronial Rebellions', *Political Science Quarterly*, 82 (1967), 595–618 (p. 600).

[25] Calin, *Old French Epic of Revolt*, p. 140.

significant that the *Chronica majora's* version of *chanson de geste* backs away from offering a dramatic moment of the reassertion of royal power. The episode in the *Chronica majora* ends, as it were, *in media res*: rather than providing the reconciliation (or death, or *moniage*) demanded by the genre, the episode instead, in a sense, restarts, with the story of a stolen horse at the siege of Damietta:

> Huic consimillimia pestis jam quadraginta annis elapsis contigit, de quodam Templario, pro uno equo desiderabili sibi violenter ablato, transfugium ad Sarracenos faciente, cui nomen Ferrandus, in armis strenuo et consilio circumspecto, per quem primo Damiatam amiserunt, sed et omnem honorem infeliciter Christiani; sed tandem cum submersioni patuissent, commotis visceribus, ne culpa unius in tot milia redundaret, subvenit perituris.

> (A very similar disaster occurred forty years previously, when a certain Templar, named Ferrand, a man brave in fight and prudent in council, in consequence of a valuable horse having been forcibly taken from him, deserted to the Saracens, and through him the Christians unhappily lost Damietta in the first place, and finally all the honour they had gained; but at length, when they were in danger of drowning, his bowels of compassion were touched, and he assisted those who were on the point of perishing, that the fault of one might not be avenged on so many thousands.)[26]

This story, reading itself like the epitome of a lost *chanson de geste*, may refer back to the capture and loss of Damietta during the Fifth Crusade of 1217–21, but it simultaneously brings the narrative up to date with the defeat of Louis IX's Seventh Crusade and the decisive loss of Damietta in 1250. It provides the resolution that the story of the first knight lacks, but it significantly refuses to name the initial antagonist in a plot where so much surely depends on who took the horse. It consequently erases the central narrative of conflict between a king and his vassal and focuses instead on the consequences of rebellion. The originary incident of the narrative fades beside its successful resolution in the 'compassion' of the wronged Templar. In doing so it turns away also from the formal aspects of *chanson de geste*, which depend for their emotive impact precisely on having the fault of the king 'avenged on so many thousands'.

How, then, do we read the absence of the scene of reconciliation so essential to the *chanson de geste*? Should this absence be read as a rejection of this reconciliation and of the generic assertion of the irresistibility of royal power? With his choice of *chanson de geste*, Matthew may bow to the inevitable on the irresistibility of royal power, but with his choice of an ending he selects baronial

---

[26] Luard, V, 387; Giles, III, 33. Luard notes that this story is not included in Wendover's version of the siege of Damietta, but that Wendover instead follows a story found in Oliver of Paderborn's chronicle.

compassion over royal clemency as the solution to political violence. Royal power is similarly questioned by means of the competing model of kingship offered by the pagan king to whom our first knight flees. The contrast between the noble Saracen whose ethics are more Christian than the Christians who fight him and the ignoble traitors at the centre of the king's court is, of course, a staple of thirteenth-century imaginative literature. Here, the soldan to whom the knight flees is a foil to the king he abandons. This noble Saracen demands neither feudal vows nor knightly service, but simply promises, 'I will never fail you.'[27]

This promise clearly frames a wish-fulfilment fantasy for a thirteenth-century rebellious baron; however, in its narrative context it opens the door to a cycle of violence as the knight fights against those who have wronged him, one by one. And while this fantasy resolution has obvious appeal, the text nevertheless seems to prefer a legal model for resolving tensions between a king and his vassal. Specifically, it centres the ideal of Chapter 39 of Magna Carta that a baron must be tried by a jury of his peers.

In Matthew's *chanson de geste*, as in the rebellious barons cycle more generally, the insult delivered by the king to his vassal centres around a question of law and punishment. Matthew's story further moves this theme to the spotlight: the king never speaks, there are no names, no families, and, importantly, no territories. Although the setting is putatively the court of the French king on crusade, in their anonymity the actors become exemplary figures and 'a certain knight' becomes all knights. So in some ways the episode vacillates between the tropes of *chanson de geste* and the tropes of Magna Carta, and it ends up being less about the conflicting demands of individual loyalties, or about conflicts between individual and communal desires, and more about the law and the proper administration of law and justice. In abrogating the right to dispense justice to himself, this fictional king is adhering to the kind of feudal code rejected by Magna Carta, which is above all concerned with the right to administer justice in the realm. As Claire Valente indicates in *The Theory and Practice of Revolt in Medieval England*,

> The crisis of Magna Carta was to a great extent a conflict over the king and his relationship to the law, the king insisting on his rights, the opposition insisting on his subordination to the law.[28]

---

[27] Both Sarah Kay and Michael Heintze note that the theme of the traitors at court 'takes over from that of Christian-Saracen combat from about the middle of the 12th century' (Kay, '*Chanson de Geste*' in the Age of Romance, pp. 179–80; Michael Heintze, *König, Held und Sippe* (Heidelberg, 1991), p. 207).

[28] Valente, *Theory and Practice*, p. 65.

In other words, Matthew frames here in a fictional mode the contemporary debate about whether the king is above the law or subject to it. In the *Chronica majora*'s representation of Henry III's dismissal of Magna Carta in 1253, Henry implicitly imagines himself as above the law: under the provisions of Magna Carta, he feels, 'he would not be a king'.[29] In the *chanson de geste* episode, the king acts on just this belief, hanging the knight's son 'without trial or judgement'.[30] The implicit view of this rendition of the appropriate dispensation of royal justice is that for the king to set himself above the law is simultaneously to transgress the law and is an act that requires baronial counteraction.[31] Thus even though the knight's son is clearly guilty of murder, the sympathy of the episode lies with the knight, who asks, 'Where is the justice of the French courts?'[32]

The question of the quality of royal power is not new to the mid-thirteenth century, of course. The view that the will of the king is not the law finds a classic and early formulation in John of Salisbury's *Policraticus,* but it coexisted with the development of ideas of sacral kingship.[33] It is into exactly this aporia that *chanson de geste* makes its entry in the twelfth century. Recently, several scholars have offered sophisticated analyses of the ideological work of *chanson de geste*. The work of Dominique Boutet, Sarah Kay, and Robert M. Stein, in particular, combines to give a picture of a genre that rather than being an oral remnant of a distant Carolingian past is, on the contrary, heavily invested in the present. Thus

[29] Giles, III, 27.

[30] Giles, III, 33.

[31] And it is perhaps worth recalling here that the ultimate catalyst of the baronial rebellion of 1258 was Henry's refusal of justice to one of his barons, John fitz Geoffrey (Carpenter 'King, Magnates, and Society', p. 46).

[32] Giles, III, 33.

[33] The seminal discussion of this issue is, of course, Ernst Kantorowicz, *The King's Two Bodies: A Study in Medieval Political Theology* (Princeton, 1957). See James Clarke Holt, 'The Barons and the Great Charter', *English Historical Review*, 70.274 (1955), 1–24, for the ways in which these ideas, percolating throughout the twelfth century, make their appearance in Magna Carta. This debate would come to be a hot-button issue later in Henry's reign. In the aftermath of 1258, the suspicion was mooted that Henry had been advised to rule as if he were above the law. It was claimed that the Lusignan faction had suggested to the King that he was above the law (Luard, VI, 406–09), but the historical record contains no comment from Henry himself. Like their medieval counterparts, modern scholars likewise debate the issue. Michael Clanchy has interpreted Henry's actions during his personal rule as evidencing absolutist tendencies (Michael Clancy, 'Did Henry III Have A Policy?', *History*, 53 (1968), 207–19). In rebuttal to this view, Carpenter argues just the opposite ('King, Magnates, and Society', p. 40).

chanson de geste (like romance and history) in the twelfth century anticipates the ideological role that Gabrielle Spiegel has identified as belonging to thirteenth-century vernacular prose historiography:

> The 'romancing of the past' in vernacular historiography also addresses sentiments of loss and decline that plagued the French aristocracy in the opening decades of the thirteenth century, as the rise of a newly powerful monarchy threatened its traditional autonomy and sought to limit its exercise of traditional political and military roles. From this perspective, the rise of vernacular prose historiography entailed the quest for a lost world of aristocratic potency.[34]

If *chanson de geste* as a genre is one aspect of an aristocratic response to the development of a government based less on aristocratic consensus and military support and more on the bureaucratisation of power, then, Dominique Boutet argues, it is a fundamentally conservative response. Throughout twelfth-century *chanson de geste*, he notes, the theme of the rebellious vassal grows in importance. At the same time, these rebellious vassals are increasingly contrasted with unjust kings who abuse royal power.[35] Around 1200, Boutet further argues, the theme of the royal abuse of power deepens, and the role of the traitors is enlarged.[36] Boutet nevertheless suggests that, despite a changing focus, *chanson de geste* demonstrates a deep ideological homogeneity ('profonde homogénéité idéologique').[37] Rather than reading the representation of the king in *chanson de geste* as reflecting the rise and fall of the strength of the French monarchy, Boutet sees *chanson de geste* as desiring a king who is both good and strong. Thus, when the monarch is weak, the genre exhorts him to be strong. When the monarch is strong, the genre exhorts him also to be good.[38]

It is perhaps this assessment of royal power in which the *Chronica majora* seeks to implicate itself by means of its appropriation of the tropes of *chanson de geste*. While Matthew seems to agree that the king should be 'good', however, he equivocates on 'strong'. Indeed, as Robert M. Stein has recently suggested, in some ways, the relative strength of the monarchy may be beside the point. Stein argues:

---

[34] Gabrielle Spiegel, *Romancing the Past: The Rise of Vernacular Prose Historiography in Thirteenth-Century France* (Berkeley and Los Angeles, 1995), p. 3.

[35] Boutet, 'Pouvoir Royal', p. 10.

[36] Boutet, 'Pouvoir Royal', p. 12

[37] Boutet, 'Pouvoir Royal', p. 13; my translation.

[38] By means of contrast, Boutet further notes a generic difference to romance, especially Arthurian romance, where the ideal of kingship has little to do with strength in governing, but rather emphasizes personal worth ('Pouvoir Royal', p. 13).

The contradiction that inhabits these representations of royalty does not lie simply in an indecision on the part of the traditional nobility about whether it would be better to have a weak or strong king. It lies rather in a fundamental contradiction within the conceptualization of sovereignty itself: on the one hand the king is *sui generis*, a sacral figure, and on the other hand he is a lord like other lords, *primus*, to be sure, but *inter pares*. Briefly, is the king part of the realm, a power, however superior in strength, in essence like any other power in the realm, or is he a singularity, a power comparable to no other and therefore transcendent to the realm he holds?[39]

This, clearly, is the debate into which Matthew implicitly enters, and in which he sees Magna Carta as playing an important role. While it cannot be said that Matthew forcefully argues the point, his imagination of a *chanson de geste* scenario implies a quite trenchant critique of royal power, suggesting simultaneously that the wronged baron may rightfully renounce homage to his king and that the king must give due consideration to the law.

Thinking about the intervention of *chanson de geste* into an historical moment characterized by what Kay has termed 'baronial resistance to the successful imposition of royal power'[40] may suggest that one reason for the continued strength of *chanson de geste* as a generic form into the thirteenth century and beyond is that the political crisis into which it attempts to intervene is itself continuing in recognizable forms. Although often treated in scholarly accounts as a primitive genre driven out of fashion by the more sophisticated courtly romance, the manuscript evidence shows that, even when not composed during the thirteenth century, the *chansons de geste* retained their popularity throughout its course. The thirteenth century, not the twelfth, marks the height of vernacular book production of *chanson de geste*, and this was especially true in England. *La Chanson de Guillaume*, for example, regarded as one of the earliest and most important *chansons de geste*, is extant only in a thirteenth-century English manuscript.[41]

Indeed, part of the cultural understanding of the events of the mid-thirteenth century was to cast them as *chanson de geste* — or to recast them into imaginative literature: 'the men of this period', writes J. C. Holt, 'were prolific in providing

[39] Stein, *Reality Fictions*, p. 183.

[40] *Raoul de Cambrai*, ed. by Kay, p. lxvi; also the discussion in Stein, *Reality Fictions*, chap. 4, 'From Romance to Epic'.

[41] Hindley and Levy, *The Old French Epic*, p. xi; Joseph Duggan, 'The Manuscript Corpus of the Medieval Romance Epic', in *The Medieval Alexander Legend and Romance Epic*, ed. by Peter Noble and others (Millwood, NY, 1982), pp. 29–42, and Ian Short, 'An Early French Epic Manuscript: Oxford, Bodleian Library, French e. 32', in ibid., pp. 173–91.

subjects for *gestes*.'[42] William the Marshal, Fulk fitz Warin, John de Courcy, Ranulf of Chester, and even Eustace the Monk all found an afterlife in literature as well as in history.[43] These texts dwell on literary representations of the dramatic moment of defiance: for example, in his eponymous *chanson de geste*, Fulk fitz Warin renounces his fealty to King John:

> Donqe dit sire Fouke al roy: 'Sire roy, vous estes mon lige seignour e a vous su je lïé par fealté tant come je su en vostre service, e tan come je tienke terres de vous; e vous me dussez meyntenir en resound, e vous me faylez de resound e commun[e] ley, e unqe ne fust bon rey qe deneya a ces franke tenauntz ley en sa court; pur quoi je vous renke vos homages.'[44]

> (Then Sir Foulke said to the king: 'Lord King, you are my liege lord, and I am bound by fealty to you whilst I am in your service and as long as I hold lands from you. You ought to maintain my rights, and yet you fail me both in rights and in common law. He was never a good king who denied justice to his free-born tenants in his court. For this reason I relinquish my homage.')[45]

Matthew himself revisits precisely these tropes in the aftermath of the baronial rebellion of 1258. In the *Chronica majora* entry for 1258, Matthew narrates a story about Simon de Montfort that echoes the emplotment of his 1253 narrative of the wronged knight. An incident breaks out between the Simon de Montfort and William of Valence in which:

> Et adhuc convicia in comitem Legrecestriae magis multiplicans, ipsum fuisse veterem proditorem et mentitum fuisse, ausus est palam coram rege et multis magnatibus contumeliose protestari. At comes ira accensus et stomachatus respondit, 'Non, non, Willelme, non sum filius proditoris sive proditor; dissimiles fuere nostri genitores'.

> (William continued to utter reproaches against the earl of Leicester, and with more earnestness, and dared openly, and in the presence of the king and the nobles, to assert that the earl was an old traitor, and had lied. To this the earl, inflamed with anger and

---

[42] Holt, 'The Barons and the Great Charter', p. 24. Valente notes too that 'resort to violence against unjust kings was also [...] positively celebrated in medieval English romance' (*Theory and Practice of Revolt*, p. 12).

[43] Holt, 'The Barons and the Great Charter', p. 24, n. 4.

[44] *Fouke le Fitz Waryn*, ed. by E. J. Hathaway and others, Anglo-Norman Text Society (Oxford, 1975), p. 24.

[45] *Two Medieval Outlaws: Eustace the Monk and Fouke Fitz Warin*, trans. by Glyn Burgess (Woodbridge, 1997), p. 112. *Fouke le Fitz Waryn* survives as a fourteenth-century prose redaction of a thirteenth-century verse *chanson de geste* (*Fouke le Fitz Waryn*, p. 91).

vexation, replied, 'No, no, William, I am not the son of a traitor, nor a traitor myself; our fathers were not alike'.)[46]

Simon then attempts to attack William, but, in this instance, is prevented by the king's intervention. This parallel emplotment aligns Simon de Montfort, the leader of the baronial rebellion of 1258, with the wronged knight of 1253 and with the rebel baron of *chanson de geste*.

The sympathy of this episode for the wronged knight, despite the fact that he has broken the rules to engage in private warfare and despite the fact that he has purposefully offended the king's counsellors, is explained by Matthew's impulse to narrate the episode through the tropes of *chanson de geste*. Moreover, *chanson de geste* does not simply dovetail in its vague outlines with the concerns of the contemporary history of baronial rebellion between 1215 and 1258: the tropes and language of *chanson de geste* powerfully recall those of Magna Carta. Matthew's gesture is deliberate. In the words of Hayden White: 'By the very constitution of a set of events in such a way as to make a comprehensible story out of them, the historian charges those events with the symbolic significance of a comprehensible plot structure.'[47] While any act of narrative necessarily takes place within a set of pre-existing tropes that render it intelligible, in the chronicle entry for 1253 Matthew exaggerates this effect, explicitly offering *chanson de geste* to his readers by way of an interpretive stance.

Matthew has long been recognized as interested in experimenting with modifications to the chronicle form — through the appendices of the *Liber additamentorum*, through epitomizing, visual indexing, and illustration, for example. I would add genre to this list. Matthew, like all medieval historians, narrates events that are fictional, or semifictional, alongside events that are more or less historical. It makes sense in this context to think about the historian's turn to literature as a specifically historical mode of representing events and making them intelligible — in this instance by invoking the affinities of historical events with more literary models and forms. *History* and *literature* are useful terms only if we think of them not as truth and falsehood, but as two modes of narrative representation that make very different truth claims. Matthew is quite aware of these truth claims, and he is interested throughout the *Chronica majora* in experimenting with genre as a way of articulating meaning within the chronicle

---

[46] Luard, V, 677; Giles, III, 268–69. William de Valence is one of King Henry's Lusignan half-brothers, thus at the centre of complaints of Henry's favouritism at court.

[47] Hayden White, *The Tropics of Discourse: Essays in Cultural Criticism* (Baltimore, 1978), p. 92.

structure.[48] Matthew's consideration of the power struggles between royal and baronial power in the mid-thirteenth century through the lens of *chanson de geste* may thus be read as constituting a complex mode of political analysis. Reading for the genre throughout the *Chronica majora*, therefore, may suggest similar ways of reconceptualizing Matthew Paris's historical methodology.

The University of York

---

[48] Helen Cooper, for example, has noted Matthew's appropriation of the tropes of romance in his use of the Havelok story as a model through which to narrate as assassination attempt on the life of Henry III (Helen Cooper, *The English Romance in Time: Transforming Motifs from Geoffrey of Monmouth to the Death of Shakespeare* (Oxford, 2004), p. 325). And I have argued elsewhere that Matthew uses a similar technique with his accounts of the Mongol invasions of Central Europe in the 1240s. By borrowing the representational strategies of the Marvels of the East tradition, Matthew transforms the Mongols into cannibalistic Tartars; see Heather Blurton, *Cannibalism in High Medieval English Literature* (New York, 2007).

USK AND THE GOLDSMITHS

Marion Turner

T homas Usk, scribe, lawyer, author, factionalist, sergeant-at-arms to the king, victim of the Merciless Parliament, and early reader of Chaucer was also, we now know, salaried clerk to the Goldsmiths' Company in London.[1] Usk was working for the Goldsmiths — copying their accounts and wearing their livery — in the years when he was also actively supporting John Northampton, controversial mayor of London, and shortly before he wrote his *Appeal* (1384) and the *Testament of Love* (1385–87).[2] In what ways might this new information about Usk — discovered in 2004 by Caroline Barron — matter to us as scholars of medieval culture? What light might this fact throw on the medieval cultural world, on Usk's writings, and on Chaucerian reception? Using this newly unearthed information as a lens on the interplay between commerce and culture in late-fourteenth-century London, in this essay I explore the livery

I did most of the work for this essay while I held a Research Fellowship from the Leverhulme Trust in 2006, and I would like to thank the Trustees of the Leverhulme for their generosity. I also want to thank Paul Strohm and Elliot Kendall for commenting on drafts of this essay, and Caroline Barron for many conversations about Usk and London.

[1] For information about Usk, see Paul Strohm, 'Politics and Poetics: Usk and Chaucer in the 1380s', in *Literary Practice and Social Change in Britain, 1380–1550*, ed. by Lee Patterson (Berkeley and Los Angeles, 1990), pp. 83–112. For Usk's Goldsmith connections, see Caroline M. Barron, 'Review of Lisa Jefferson (ed.), *Wardens' Accounts and Court Minute Books of the Goldsmiths' Mistery of London 1334–1446*. Woodbridge: Boydell Press, 2003', *Urban History*, 32 (2005), 173–75.

[2] See Ruth Bird, *The Turbulent London of Richard II* (London, 1949) for discussion of mayoral politics at this time. Usk seems to have worked for the Goldsmiths from 1380–83. Northampton was mayor during these years; Brembre took over after the 1383 election (mayoral years ran from October).

companies as sites for literary reception and production, and think about the implications of bringing these companies more prominently into the cultural mix. At the same time, I am concerned with texts' relationship with other kinds of cultural production integral to livery companies, such as pageantry, processions, and gifting. The resonances that a word or image had in its own historical moment can never be wholly recovered, but can be understood more fully by exploring the cultural and material environment from which the text emerged. Historicism and close reading are therefore, in my view, inseparable.

The contours of the world in which Chaucer's texts were born look different now. We now know that Chaucer's earliest known scribe (Adam Pynkhurst), the first known owner of a *Canterbury Tales* manuscript (John Brynchele), and the earliest known reader of *Troilus and Criseyde* (Thomas Usk) were all employed as scribes for major London livery companies. Pynkhurst, copier of Ellesmere and Hengwyrt and possibly the addressee of Chaucer's poem to 'Adam Scriveyn', worked regularly as scribe for the Mercers in the 1380s and 1390s, and maybe until 1427.[3] Brynchele, who bequeathed his copy of the *Canterbury Tales* to a fellow tailor in 1420 but may have owned this text for decades before his death, was clerk for the Tailors from sometime before 1398 until 1420.[4] Thomas Usk, who was reading *Troilus* either when it was in progress or very soon after, was sworn scribe to the Goldsmiths in the early 1380s.[5] The repeated appearance of

[3] See Linne Mooney, 'Chaucer's Scribe', *Speculum*, 81 (2006), 97–138. Pynkhurst wrote the Mercers' Petition in 1387/8, and 'what appears to be his hand kept the accounts for the Mercers' Company from 1391 to 1393 and may be the hand that continued recording their annual accounts until 1415 and sporadically thereafter until 1427' (p. 98). Ellesmere and Hengwyrt have generally been dated to after Chaucer's death; for bibliography for the idea that they were made before 1400, see Mooney, ibid., p. 97, n. 2. For discussions of 'Adam scriveyn' see especially Carolyn Dinshaw, *Chaucer's Sexual Poetics* (Madison, 1989), pp. 3–27, and Alexandra Gillespie, 'Books', in *Oxford Twenty-First Century Approaches: Middle English*, ed. by Paul Strohm (Oxford, 2007), pp. 86–103.

[4] Brynchele's will is mentioned by Furnivall in *The Fifty Earliest English Wills*, ed. by F. J. Furnivall, Early English Text Society, o.s. 78 (London, 1882), p. 136. Matthew Davies discusses Brynchele's role as the first-known clerk of the Merchant Tailors Company, emphasizing the fact that he was originally a tailor, not a professional clerk, and discussing his skills and salary, in Matthew Davies and Ann Saunders, *The History of the Merchant Tailors' Company* (Leeds, 2004), pp. 43, 275.

[5] I compare Pynkhurst and Usk in Marion Turner, 'Conflict', in *Oxford Twenty-First Century Approaches* (see n. 3, above), pp. 258–73, especially pp. 261–66. For discussion of Usk as early reader of Chaucer see p. 270 and n. 40. For Usk's use of *Troilus* see Marion Turner, *Chaucerian Conflict: Languages of Antagonism in Late Fourteenth-Century London* (Oxford, 2006), chap. 4.

guild scribes amongst Chaucer's earliest readers, copiers, and consumers adds a new dimension to our understanding of Chaucer's circles. There are very few people who we can say were definitely reading Chaucer in his lifetime. Those whom we can identify mainly comprise chamber knights and London officials.[6] We are also now accustomed to the idea that 'bureaucratic service in the English fourteenth and fifteenth centuries was a first home of the vernacular literary culture of Langland's and Chaucer's generation, and that the activities of those bureaucrats participating in it were substantially, not just accidentally, literary'.[7] Katherine Kerby-Fulton and Steven Justice have explored the world of scriveners and legal clerks who worked in civil service jobs and actively engaged with texts by men such as Chaucer and Langland. We need to consider the London livery companies as another home for these clerks and to think of such scribes as go-betweens, connecting seemingly disparate cultural worlds. Through examining the world inhabited by Usk, Pynkhurst, and Brynchele, the world in which they read, copied, and perhaps shared and discussed Chaucer's writings with other guild members, we can understand more about the conditions in which Chaucer's books were produced. Men such as Pynkhurst and quite possibly Usk were copiers as well as readers, and the collaborative nature of medieval authorship increases the significance of the cultural assumptions and interests of these men.[8] Scribes had the power to shape texts and to guide literary taste.[9] The guild experiences — political,

---

[6] See Strohm, *Social Chaucer* (Cambridge, MA, 1989), pp. 24–83, and Derek Pearsall, *The Life of Geoffrey Chaucer* (Oxford, 1992), pp. 181–85.

[7] Katherine Kerby-Fulton and Steven Justice, 'Langlandian Reading Circles and the Civil Service in London and Dublin 1380–1427', *New Medieval Literatures*, 1 (1997), 59–83 (p. 59).

[8] In other words, scribes had active roles in textual production. This is discussed by several scholars; for instance, Seth Lerer comments on 'the blurring of distinctions between author, scribe, compiler, and commentator', in *Chaucer and His Readers* (Princeton, 1993), p. 13. See also D. F. McKenzie, *Bibliography and the Sociology of Texts*, 2nd edn (Cambridge, 1999). In 'Conflict', I discuss the creativity of these particular scribes. For the idea that Usk may have had access to *Troilus* as a work-in-progress, see Ramona Bressie, 'The Date of Thomas Usk's *Testament of Love*', *Modern Philology*, 26 (1928), 17–29 (p. 29), and J. A. W. Bennett, *Middle English Literature*, ed. and completed by Douglas Gray (Oxford, 1998), p. 347.

[9] Kathryn Kerby-Fulton and Steven Justice write that the reception of Ricardian literature 'was shaped by, and around the interests of, some scribes to whom we owe a good many of our important texts', suggesting specifically that Scribe D may have been 'helping to create or at least direct and shape, the desires of those who would be the *cognoscenti* of Ricardian writing' ('Scribe D and the Marketing of Ricardian Literature', in *The Medieval Professional Reader at Work: Evidence from Manuscripts of Chaucer, Langland, Kempe, and Gower*, ed. by Kathryn Kerby-Fulton and Maidie Hilmo (Victoria, 2001), pp. 217–37 (pp. 226, 223)). Similarly, Derek Pearsall

social, and cultural — of scribes such as Pynkhurst must have conditioned their tastes, interests, and assumptions, and they in turn then had the power to influence cultural trends through their work in the book trade. Indeed, just as we cannot divide artisan scribes from creative authors, so there is often no clear separation between other 'artisans' and designers/artists. The fact that the artist of the Wilton Diptych shared techniques with goldsmiths reminds us that goldsmiths themselves were creative and artistic in their work; Marian Campbell comments on the 'reciprocity' between painters and metalworkers at this time.[10] The work of scribes and of goldsmiths (and of other guildsmen such as tailors) was often creative.

The scribes who read and worked on guild writings and vernacular poetry simultaneously — and who themselves were often guild members — are crucial lynchpins for the interplay between the livery companies and Ricardian poets.[11] They also connect Chaucer's personal mercantile environment — the world of his father and of the customs house — with his texts: Usk, Pynkhurst, and Brynchele read Chaucer and worked for merchants. The diversity of the networks in which these scribes were involved illustrates the fact that mercantile and court circles constantly overlapped: Mooney suggests that Pynkhurst and Chaucer could possibly have met through John Organ, mercer and collector of the wool custom, *or* through the court, where Pynkhurst's father and Chaucer held positions.[12] Pynkhurst also exemplifies the overlap between the government writing offices and the mercantile world as he worked with Hoccleve *and* with the Mercers.[13]

A variety of Ricardian writings were flying about in the dynamic world of the company scribes, and the clerks with whom I am concerned had mutual literary interests that stretched further than the *Canterbury Tales* and *Troilus*. Brynchele, Usk, and Pynkhurst all knew Boethius in English translation, Pynkhurst copied

writes that in the fifteenth century tastes were 'predicted and shaped and nurtured' by the producer, and that this built on fourteenth century practices ('Introduction', in *Book Production and Publishing in Britain 1375–1475*, ed. by Jeremy Griffiths and Derek Pearsall (Cambridge, 1989), pp. 1–10 (p. 3)).

[10] Marian Campbell, 'White Harts and Coronets: The Jewellery and Plate of Richard II', in *The Regal Image of Richard II and the Wilton Diptych*, ed. by Dillian Gordon and others (London, 1997), pp. 95–114, notes at pp. 297–310, p. 307, n. 138.

[11] Usk wore the livery of the Goldsmiths; Brynchele was a member of the Tailors' company before he became their clerk; Pynkhurst was a member of the Scriveners' company.

[12] Mooney, 'Chaucer's Scribe', pp. 111–13, 119.

[13] He and Hoccleve (who was, of course, a clerk of the Privy Seal) were two of the scribes who worked on Cambridge, Trinity College Library, R.3.2 (a copy of Gower's *Confessio amantis*).

Gower and Langland manuscripts, and Usk knew Gower's writings and possibly Langland's too.[14] We might also note that the only contemporary person named in *Piers Plowman* is John Chichester, who was Mayor of London and a goldsmith, and whose wife's bequests of money, hangings, tapestries, and cushions to the Goldsmiths' company were written up by Usk. A little later, one of Langland's early known readers was a mercer, Thomas Roos.[15]

Usk's own writings are illuminated in diverse ways by Barron's discovery. The relevance of connecting biography to literary interpretation is often dubious, and reliance on biography can encourage simplistic understanding of causes and effects.[16] But the reductiveness of some biographical approaches does not mean that life is never relevant to art or that the material conditions of the production of a book can be dissociated from its meaning. Rather than using biographical information in order to prove and to validate a recoverable authorial intent, one can understand this material as contributing to a 'habitus', a 'scheme of dispositions' that encompasses the tastes, skills, and assumptions of a group.[17] Biography can help to

[14] Brynchele bequeathed two copies of Boethius, one Latin and one English, and Usk draws extensively on Boethius in the *Testament*. For manuscripts copied by Pynkhurst see <http://www.medievalscribes.com/scribes.html>. For Usk's knowledge of Gower see Joanna Summers, *Late-Medieval Prison Writing and the Politics of Autobiography* (Oxford, 2005), pp. 32–36. There is debate about whether or not Usk knew Langland's work; this is discussed by the editor in Thomas Usk, *The Testament of Love*, ed. by R. Allen Shoaf (Kalamazoo, 1998), pp. 14–17. Subsequent references to the *Testament* (cited by book, chapter, and line number) and to the *Appeal* (cited by line number) are to this edition.

[15] Caroline Barron, 'William Langland: A London Poet', in *Chaucer's England: Literature in Historical Context*, ed. by Barbara Hanawalt (Minneapolis, 1992), pp. 91–109 (p. 96), T. F. Reddaway and Lorna E. M. Walker, *The Early History of the Goldsmiths' Company 1327–1509* (London, 1975), pp. 289–91, *Wardens' Accounts and Court Minute-Books of the Goldsmiths' Mistery of London*, ed. by Lisa Jefferson (Woodbridge, 2003), pp. 202–03. Barron speculates that '[p]erhaps [Langland] knew Chichester, or had received some hospitality at his house?' ('William Langland', p. 96). The reference to Chichester is in *Piers Plowman*, B. 13. 270. Thomas Roos left a copy of *Piers Plowman* to his son in 1433; see Barron, 'William Langland', pp. 97–100, and Carol M. Meale, '*The Libelle of Englysche Polyce* and Mercantile Literary Culture in Late-Medieval London', in *London and Europe in the Later Middle Ages*, ed. by Julia Boffey and Pamela King (London, 1995), pp. 181–227 (p. 187).

[16] As Ruth Evans writes: 'Nothing is more irritating than the crude reduction of the intricate surface of Chaucer's poetry to the effects of his personal circumstances, real or imagined' ('Chaucer's Life', in *Chaucer: An Oxford Guide*, ed. by Steve Ellis (Oxford, 2005), pp. 9–25 (p. 10)).

[17] The idea of the 'habitus' is especially used by Pierre Bourdieu and is a key concept in *Outline of a Theory of Practice*, trans. by Richard Nice (Cambridge, 1977). Kellie Robertson

illuminate the cultural environment of texts; it can enhance our understanding of the depth of the textual world inhabited by an author and his or her writings. Usk, furthermore, goes out of his way to foreground the interplay between his life and his texts. The *Testament of Love* is poised between the literary and the documentary, between the fictitious and the factual. Usk moves between conventional tropes of courtly love and Boethian complaint, and highly specific autobiographical detail about, for instance, his employers' failure to pay his travelling expenses. Perhaps financially specific comments such as 'Who yave thee ever ought for any rydynge thou madest?' (I. 6. 730) or 'whiche of hem [...] ever thee refreshed by the valewe of the leste coyned plate that walketh in money' (I. 6. 720–21) even reveal an account-keeping habit of mind, a transference from his work for the Goldsmiths. The *Testament* exemplifies the difficulties in defining a text by genre or by modern disciplinary categories. Usk stages the *Testament* as an ornamental and philosophical tract, but he also presents it as a petition, a way of achieving direct political rewards for himself by revealing his side of the story; he has turned his life into a narrative and that narrative may well have had real political results in his life.[18] A fuller understanding of Usk's life illuminates the text in surprising ways: one of the most interesting aspects of the *Testament* is the fusion of the material and the abstract, especially in Usk's use of imagery.

Usk's (and Chaucer's) cultural milieu encompassed things such as jewels, plate, robes, books, and props, and performances including plays, pageants, feasts, ridings, and mummings. All of these things and events were bound up with political and economic necessity, with propaganda, self-fashioning, patronage, and faction. While much scholarship tends to separate (and to hierarchise) strands of culture, much can be gained from considering late-medieval writings as embedded within the full range of the cultural, political, and social life of London and

---

discusses the difference between using biography 'in the name of a author-subject who exhibits full agency in his writings' and using it to understand a 'habitus'. She suggests that 'Chaucer' is 'also made up of the statutes that he enforced, the writs that he wrote and received and the habits of thought that such work encouraged'; see her 'Authorial Work', in *Oxford Twenty-First Century Approaches* (see n. 3, above), pp. 441–58 (p. 453–54).

[18] Strohm discusses the interplay between Usk's texts and life in *Hochon's Arrow: The Social Imagination of Fourteenth-Century Texts* (Princeton, 1992). Writing about the *Appeal*, he comments, 'Although a textually created identity can (and in this case did) propel its subject to prominence on a real stage, it remains vulnerable to the vicissitudes of textuality itself — to revision, resistant reading, capricious treatment by those upon whose encouragement it depends, or loss of place to an alternative textual tradition or generic rival' (p. 146).

Westminster. Things, events, and texts interpenetrate, overlap, and act on each other in extraordinary ways. This essay seeks to tease out some of the interplay between Ricardian literary culture and the livery companies, with a particular focus on Usk and his Goldsmith environment. In the next section, I explore the changing cultural world of the livery companies in the late fourteenth century to establish some of the reasons why scribes and texts found 'homes' there at this time. I then analyse the *Testament of Love* in the light of our new knowledge about Usk, thinking particularly about the materiality of Usk's language. Finally, this essay will look at the *Appeal*, and will consider how our understanding of Usk's political position is changed by Barron's discovery.

The Livery Companies and Cultural Production

Thinking about companies such as the Goldsmiths and the Mercers as early 'homes' for Ricardian literature, crucibles in which books were consumed and produced, encourages us to consider both the physical environment and the cultural world of the companies. Things changed for the livery companies in the late fourteenth century and the changes enabled the companies to engage more fully with textual culture by employing scribes and keeping documents in more regular ways, and to advertise their own products and wealth through new forms of hospitality and cultural display. The acquisition of halls was especially decisive in the companies' cultural development. Although they were not legally permitted to own land as companies, in the second half of the fourteenth century some of the great guilds began to acquire significant land and property portfolios held by trustees and feoffees. Guild members were increasingly able to come together as a group in an established and exclusive place. After the second Statute of Mortmain in 1391, many of the companies sought and gained royal charters which gave them the right to hold land in mortmain and to become incorporated. This allowed them to expand their property holdings, and to challenge the church as suitable administrators of benefactions.[19] The guilds became important London landlords, and members often left generous legacies of property to their company. From the second half of the fourteenth century, then, the livery companies were not just imitating, but were actually becoming great households, landowners for whom display and patronage were important ways of self-fashioning. The halls were places where guild members could hold their annual great feast, could write and

[19] Caroline Barron, *London in the Later Middle Ages* (Oxford, 2004), p. 209.

keep their records, could store funds and treasure, could conduct administration, and could generally 'enjoy the style of communal living that members of the retinue of a great lord might experience in his household'.[20] The hall provided a place where scribes could work and this production of texts could share a space with other aspects of guild life and culture. Both the Goldsmiths and the Tailors were among the first companies to build halls, doing so in the middle of the fourteenth century.[21] Usk mentions the Goldsmiths' Hall in the *Appeal* and we now know that it was a regular place of work for him, a site of writing. From at least 1391, the Mercers met regularly in the hall of the Hospital of St Thomas of Acon, and in the early fifteenth century they purchased a little room from the hospital, which became known as Mercers' Hall.[22] Putting together Pynkhurst's connection with the Mercers and his involvement in a property transaction at the hospital in 1385, Mooney has suggested that St Thomas of Acon may also have been Pynkhurst's regular working space.[23] The Mercers' official account book was started in 1391–92 — a 1347 document was copied into it, presumably from loose leaves[24] — which further enforces the idea that meeting regularly in a fixed place went alongside attention to writing and record-keeping.

The newly constructed halls were places for administrative business and textual production and they also hosted spectacular displays of wealth and culture in the guise of feasts. Owning a hall enabled companies such as the Goldsmiths to mobilize culture and social capital for commercial and political ends. The hall provided a setting for cultural and social interaction between court and city, a chance for a livery company to demonstrate its own investment in beautiful and

[20] Barron, *London*, p. 217.

[21] The Goldsmiths constructed their hall in 1366; see Reddaway and Walker, *Early History*, p. 30. The Tailors may even have been meeting on their site from 1332, otherwise from 1347 when it was settled on the fraternity's trustees. In 1392 the company gained its licence of mortmain. Excavations suggest that the hall itself was built in the second half of the fourteenth century. See Davies, *History of the Merchant Tailors*, pp. 14–16.

[22] See John Watney, *The Mercers' Company* (London, 1914), p. 5, John Watney, *Some Account of the Hospital of St Thomas of Acon in the Cheap, London, and of the Plate of the Mercers' Company* (London, 1892), p. 36, Jean Imray, *The Mercers' Hall*, with an Introduction by Derek Keane, ed. by Ann Saunders, London Topographical Society, 143 (London, 1991), pp. 6, 13, and Anne F. Sutton, *The Mercery of London: Trade, Goods and People, 1130–1578* (Aldershot, 2005), pp. 73–74.

[23] Mooney, 'Chaucer's Scribe', p. 111.

[24] Mooney, 'Chaucer's Scribe', p. 110, n. 54.

lavish things and to advertise its own products. In 1379–80, for instance, the Goldsmiths held a feast for Lady Isabelle, Edward III's daughter, her young daughter Philippa, who was married to Robert de Vere (Richard II's favourite, who became one of the casualties of the Merciless Parliament), Lord Latimer, erstwhile chamberlain of the royal household who had been impeached in 1376, Robert Hales, High Master of St John of Clerkenwell (who was to be killed in the Peasants' Revolt), and the Mayor of London, John Philipot.[25] Only the presence of the king himself or a prince of the blood could have made this gathering more illustrious; it is no surprise that 'les ditz gardayns furount a grauntz costagez' (the wardens had great expenses).[26] Presumably the feast included various kinds of entertainment; unfortunately the items of expenditure are not specified, but there may well have been performances and music as there would be at a similar feast held at a royal or noble household.[27] An agreement was made within the guild that each year the wardens should either hold a feast or pay a penalty; the following year the penalty was four pounds, which might give us some idea of what this feast cost.[28]

Not only were the Goldsmiths' guests exceptionally important, they were also interestingly varied — men and women, people of court and city, people who had had opposite allegiances only a couple of years earlier (when Philipot opposed Gaunt and Latimer was strongly of Gaunt's party).[29] Further, while many

---

[25] *Wardens' Accounts*, pp. 184–85.

[26] *Wardens' Accounts*, pp. 184–85.

[27] Anne Lancashire notes, 'When London in turn — the civic government itself or its most influential livery companies — held civic banquets at which it feasted royalty, nobility, visiting dignitaries from abroad, and important Crown administrators, it must have provided similar entertainments [to those put on at court]' (Anne Lancashire, *London Civic Theatre: City, Drama, and Pageantry From Roman Times to 1558* (Cambridge, 2002), p. 63). Janet Coleman mentions this particular feast, in *English Literature in History 1350–1400: Medieval Readers and Writers* (London, 1981), p. 55.

[28] *Wardens' Accounts*, pp. 190–91.

[29] Latimer was one of those accused in the Good Parliament of (illegitimate) profiteering; he was impeached and imprisoned, but pardoned later in 1376 when Gaunt re-established his authority. Philipot, Brembre and Walworth, were organized against the group with which Latimer was associated, a group that included the notorious Richard Lyons. (For Lyons's connections with Chaucer's father and with Chaucer himself see Pearsall, *Life of Geoffrey Chaucer*, pp. 14, 16.) At this point (the mid-1370s) Northampton also gave support to Brembre and others in the court of aldermen. See Simon Walker, *The Lancastrian Affinity 1361–1399* (Oxford, 1990), p. 63, and Gerald Harriss, *Shaping the Nation: England 1360–1461* (Oxford, 2005), pp. 439–43. Discussing

goldsmiths were to be strongly associated with Northampton and with protesting against Brembre, here their guests include Philipot, connected with Brembre through work and family, and Philippa, the wife of one of the principal targets of the Merciless Parliament.[30] In other words, these are not the kind of people that one might expect the Goldsmiths to host if one considered their principal factional affiliations in London over the subsequent few years. The diversity of the people gathered for this feast might caution us to remember that things could change very quickly, that different members of the same company could have different affiliations, and that allegiances were always flexible and somewhat treacherous; the 'parties' in London were so unstable as to be almost nonexistent as entities.[31] Members of the great livery companies always retained close connections with diverse members of the royal family and the highest aristocracy; they and these most important customers needed each other.[32]

But it is also true that the three guilds whose scribes had certain connections with Chaucer's books were amongst the most politically volatile companies in Ricardian London: large numbers of the Goldsmiths, Mercers, and Tailors ranged themselves alongside Northampton and supported the civic unrest after Brembre's election. An inquisition from Northampton's trial specifies that his supporters conspired together at locations including St Thomas of Acon (i.e. the Mercers' de

Thomas Haxey, A. K. McHardy comments that 'links can often be traced between individuals who were apparently at loggerheads on political matters', a comment that has general relevance for contemporary society and politics ('Haxey's Case, 1397: The Petition and its Presenter Reconsidered', in *The Age of Richard II*, ed. by James L. Gillespie (Stroud, 1997), pp. 93–114 (p. 108)).

[30] Robert de Vere was later (in 1387) to repudiate his wife, to the fury of her royal relatives. So, in a case in point of the mixed and varying allegiances in contemporary politics, we might associate Philippa more with her uncles (such as Gloucester) than her husband. See Nigel Saul, *Richard II* (New Haven, 1997), p. 122.

[31] T. F. Tout comments on the 'danger of overemphasising the permanence of medieval parties' (T. F. Tout, *Chapters in the Administrative History of Medieval England* (Manchester, 1928), III, 462). See also Pamela Nightingale, *A Medieval Mercantile Community: The Grocers' Company and the Politics and Trade of London 1000–1485* (New Haven, 1995), pp. 2–4, and Pamela Nightingale, 'Capitalists, Crafts, and Constitutional Change in Late Fourteenth-Century London', *Past and Present*, 124 (1989), 3–35 (pp. 29–31).

[32] Ralph Hanna writes that in the fourteenth century 'symbiotic mercantile-magnatial-royal relationships, in excess of those previously in place from the luxury trade, were created' (*London Literature: 1300–1380* (Cambridge, 2005), p. 128).

facto hall), the Tailors' Hall, and the Goldsmiths' Hall.[33] It is evident that these halls were sites of politicking and that the three companies that were especially connected with Chaucer's texts were also the three companies most implicated in the civic upheavals of the 1380s. Chaucer's early readers — as well as copies of his books and perhaps the sites of their production — were located at the heart of London's political maelstrom.

The Tailors in particular spread their social tentacles widely and this may have brought together diverse readers of Chaucer in the years immediately after his death. In the late fourteenth century and especially in the fifteenth century, the Fraternity of St John the Baptist of Tailors and Linen-Armourers, to give it its full title, recruited large numbers of influential members from outside the craft itself (including Henry V and his brothers).[34] Bearing in mind the fact that at some point between the late fourteenth century and 1420 the clerk to the company acquired a *Canterbury Tales* manuscript, the admission of Thomas Chaucer to the fraternity in 1411–12 is of great interest.[35] Several scholars have suggested that Thomas had some control over his father's papers and that he may have played a part in bringing out early copies of the *Canterbury Tales*.[36] The Tailors' Hall may have been a place where commissions and textual production were discussed, and if Thomas had a connection with Ellesmere — Manly and Rickert write that he 'is logically the person to have had [Ellesmere] made' — Pynkhurst's Mercers might enter this network.[37] Thomas also had close relations with Lydgate who was to pen mummings for both the Mercers and the Goldsmiths.[38] We do not

---

[33] Bird, *Turbulent London*, pp. 135–36.

[34] Davies, *History of the Merchant Tailors*, pp. 19–20.

[35] Matthew Davies, personal communication.

[36] Pearsall writes that it is 'reasonable' to think that Thomas 'had a part in bringing out an early edition of *The Canterbury Tales*' (*Life of Geoffrey Chaucer*, p. 280). John H. Fisher comments that Thomas 'could have had both opportunity and motive for commissioning a group of scribes to sift through his father's [papers]' in order to create presentation copies. 'Animadversions on the Text of Chaucer, 1988', *Speculum*, 63 (1988), 779–93 (p. 789). See also J. M. Bowers, 'The House of Chaucer and Son: The Business of Lancastrian Canon-Formation', in *Medieval Perspectives: The Proceedings of the Southeastern Medieval Association, 6*, ed. by Edith Whitehurst Williams (Richmond, KY, 1991), pp. 135–43.

[37] *The Text of the 'Canterbury Tales'*, ed. by John M. Manly and Edith Rickert (Chicago, 1940), I, 159. Sutton mentions a connection between Thomas Chaucer and a mercer in *Mercery of London*, p. 168.

[38] For a discussion of Lydgate's mummings see Maura Nolan, *John Lydgate and the Making of Public Culture* (Cambridge, 2005), pp. 71–119. Lydgate wrote a poem to Thomas Chaucer,

know how strong Thomas Chaucer's link with the Tailors was, but Thomas and Brynchele's simultaneous connection both with the company and with Chaucer's writings does support the idea that the livery company halls were sites for literary discussion, production, and exchange.[39] The information that we can glean about the livery companies' cultural interests and involvement from the late fourteenth century onward suggests that the commissioning and production of Lydgate's mummings around 1430 was part of a long continuum of active cultural engagement on the part of the great guilds.[40]

The development of the halls in the second half of the fourteenth century allowed the Goldsmiths and their fellows to demonstrate their wealth and their cultural tastes in the form of the decor of the hall, the tapestries, and the plate, as well as through providing entertainments. Indeed, the actual things that companies such as the Mercers, Tailors, and Goldsmiths produced — luxury cloths, robes, plate and jewels — were themselves part of the culture of display and spectacle, and the companies could showcase their work at social and cultural occasions.[41] The companies also employed the same men as the court did to help to create images of their own taste and importance: Gilbert Prince, for instance, was a painter who worked extensively for John of Gaunt and then for Richard II (to the extent that he is usually referred to as the king's painter), and he also

'Ballade at the Departyng of Thomas Chaucyer on Ambassade in-to France'. See Derek Pearsall, *John Lydgate (1371–1449): A Bio-bibliography* (Victoria, 1997), p. 20.

[39] Another member of the fraternity with literary interests was Adam Usk, who joined in 1399–1400. I am indebted to Matthew Davies for this information.

[40] Scholars have discussed the participation of city merchants in literary culture in the mid- and late fifteenth century in some detail; see for instance Sheila Lindenbaum, 'London Texts and Literate Practice', in *The Cambridge History of Medieval English Literature*, ed. by David Wallace (Cambridge, 1999), pp. 284–309 (pp. 301–04), and Lerer, *Chaucer and His Readers*, pp. 88–89. Less attention has been paid to companies' and merchants' literary and other cultural pursuits a little earlier.

[41] Writing about the early and mid-fourteenth century, Hanna comments: 'at this period, it is difficult to conceive of mercantile-industrial City and royal Westminster as anything other than interconnected, not oppositional. City artisans are involved in royal projects — not just books, but other handcrafts like masonry and tapestry. And the Court persistently interpenetrates the City, not simply through such ceremonial as Edwardian tournament, but spatially. Courtly people were not necessarily residents of palatial Westminster, but within the City, where they would have met daily, perhaps even attended church with, Londoners' (*London Literature*, p. 124).

worked for the Goldsmiths and appears in their accounts.[42] He had cultural interests himself, and was a book owner.[43]

Moving on from the importance of the hall, another change for the livery companies was that pageantry, mumming, and drama were heavily encouraged in Richard II's reign.[44] The companies were now involved much more intensively in public cultural display than heretofore.[45] The year 1377 was almost certainly the first occasion on which guild-sponsored pageants were staged for a royal entry,[46] and this innovation was part of a general increased concern with cultural display. The great companies were involved in cultural practices such as staging spectacles and pageants, funding and performing mummings before the king, elaborate gift-giving, and feasting.[47] The livery companies' cultural role was expanding at the

---

[42] Prince pays the Goldsmiths forty shillings in 1384–85 (*Wardens' Accounts*, p. 212); my guess is that this was for some overpayment for work that he did for them (which could have been very similar to his court work, painting minstrels' trumpets, banners, designs for cloths, etc.). For Prince's court work, see Dillian Gordon, *Making and Meaning: The Wilton Diptych* (London, 1993), p. 72. His work is also mentioned in several articles in *Regal Image* (see n. 10, above). For connections between Prince and Simon Burley, see Maude Violet Clarke, 'Forfeitures and Treason in 1388', *Transactions of the Royal Historical Society*, ser. 4, 14 (1931), 65–94 (p. 72).

[43] For Prince's book-owning, see V. J. Scattergood, 'Literary Culture at the Court of Richard II', in *English Court Culture in the Later Middle Ages*, ed. by V. J. Scattergood and J. W. Sherborne (London, 1983), pp. 29–43 (p. 43).

[44] For a discussion of drama, spectacle, processions, and pageantry in late-medieval London and of the connections between guilds and cultural production, see Lancashire, *London Civic Theatre*; for Richard's involvement, see especially pp. 55–56. Public plays were regularly performed in the late fourteenth century but by the early fifteenth century had been replaced by private, indoor drama. See also Meale, '*Libelle*'.

[45] However, for London oligarchs' possible engagement with other forms of cultural performance more than a century earlier, see Rosamund Allen's suggestion that King Horn was first recited at a celebration for the appointment of a sheriff or alderman in London in the 1270s. See Rosamund Allen, 'The Date and Provenance of *King Horn*: Some Interim Reassessments', in *Medieval English Studies Presented to George Kane*, ed. by Edward Donald Kennedy, Ronald Waldron, and Joseph S. Wittig (Cambridge, 1988), pp. 99–125 (p. 125).

[46] See Gordon Kipling, *Enter the King: Theater, Liturgy, and Ritual in the Medieval Civic Triumph* (Oxford, 1998), pp. 6, 28. Sheila Lindenbaum also discusses the 'steady growth of urban ceremony from the late fourteenth century when power began to be concentrated in an oligarchy in London and other places' (Sheila Lindenbaum, 'Ceremony and Oligarchy: The London Midsummer Watch', in *City and Spectacle in Medieval Europe*, ed. by Barbara A. Hanawalt and Kathryn L. Reyerson (Minneapolis, 1994), pp. 171–88 (p. 178)).

[47] For instance, the Goldsmiths incurred heavy expenditure on minstrels and owned a collection of musical instruments — notes in the accounts refer to 'l'amendement des trompes'

same time as they began to employ regular scribes who recorded their cultural practices and who were also engaged in vernacular literary production and consumption (which also, of course, went through a period of unprecedented growth at this time). Indeed, the culture of visual display overlapped with literary culture in diverse ways: books often functioned as luxury *objets d'art* and took their place in the gift-giving conventions that also went alongside mummings and entries; poetry, like drama and pageants, was often performed and performative; visual spectacle was bolstered by the written word in diverse ways.[48]

Occasions such as royal entries gave companies opportunities to advertise their own status and also to display some of their own wares, such as the gold bejewelled clasps that the Goldsmiths all wore at Queen Anne's entry, quoted below.[49] This might be compared with the way guilds used mystery plays in other cities: the plays often enabled guilds to display and advertise their goods. In York, Beverley, Newcastle, and Norwich, the Goldsmiths' Company staged the 'Adoration of the Magi', which allowed them to offer their own gold goods to the Christ child.[50] The mystery plays, like royal entries, provided a public space in which guilds could

(repair of the trumpets) in 1381–82 (*Wardens' Accounts*, pp. 194–95). See also Reddaway and Walker, *Early History*, p. 78. Reddaway writes that by 1403, the Goldsmiths 'had spent heavily on its minstrelsy, the most obvious piece of ostentation open to a craft. It had bought [...] instruments valuable enough to have a special chest brought for their safe-keeping, and it paid its minstrels well'. For the Mercers' expenditure on mummings see, Lancashire, *London Civic Theatre*, pp. 42, 46.

[48] Scribes profited from the growing need to record civic spectacles in writing — through captions, programmes, and accounts in prose and poetry. Barron discusses the fact that entries and pageants were lucrative for scriveners, increasingly so in the fifteenth century (*London*, p. 22).

[49] Goldsmiths did most of their trade in the English market not abroad (see Reddaway and Walker, *Early History*, p. 49), and members of the court were, of course, important customers.

[50] See Kathleen Ashley, 'Sponsorship, Reflexivity and Resistance: Cultural Readings of the York Cycle Plays', in *The Performance of Middle English Culture: Essays on Chaucer and the Drama*, ed. by James J. Paxson, Lawrence M. Clopper, and Sylvia Tomasch (Cambridge, 1998), pp. 9–24 (p. 16). She adds, 'Such a relationship between the craft and its play has been seen at the very least as an advertisement for the guild's goods or services (a kind of "trade propaganda") or — more positively — as a symbolic association which might have ritual efficacy by effecting a real "transfer of grace" to performers and producers'. See also Alan D. Justice, 'Trade Symbolism in the York Cycle', *Theatre Journal*, 31 (1979), 47–58 (p. 50). Considering the specific model of gift-giving as an emblem of service (represented by the Magi), it is worth noting that the cult of Epiphany and the Magi was particularly important to Richard II, partly because Epiphany was also his birthday. See Olga Pujmanová, 'Portraits of Kings Depicted as Magi in Bohemian Painting', in *Regal Image* (see n. 10, above), pp. 247–66 (p. 262–63).

advertise to a large audience while also associating themselves with culture, and with civic or religious duty.[51] The concept of using aesthetic form to self-promote, and ultimately to gain business and jobs, can be compared to writers' inclusion of petitionary elements in their texts, or to their gifting of elaborate presentation copies to potential or actual patrons.

The cultural interests and expenditure of the Goldsmiths during Usk's tenure are showcased in the account of the arrival of Queen Anne in 1382; in the Goldsmiths' records Usk recorded this procession immediately before recording the regularizing of his own position with the company.[52] Examining this record gives us a sense of the cultural world that infused Usk's imaginary and that, I argue below, impacted on his imagery. He writes:

Feat a remembrer qe le vendirdy aprés le feste del Epiphanie cest an les meire et aldermans et comunes furent arrayés pur chevacher encontre la Reyne, soer al Emperour, et par cause qe touz les miesters de la cité avoyent en charge q'ils ne duissent avoyr autre vesture qe rouge et blank, les orfevers furent arrayez de mesme les colours, et pur ceo qe touz autres miesters avoy[e]nt divers conisances, les ditz orfevers furent en le rouge partie barrés de selverwir et poudrés de treys foylles d'argent [de] perles, et chescun homme de mesme le miester al nombre de vii avoy[e]nt sur le senestre partie grauntz nouches d'or et de perreye et sur lour testes chapelles coverés de rouge et poudrés des ditz treys foylles. Queux chevacheront ovec la royne parmy la cité et les ditz gardeyns payeront devers custages pur mesme le chevaché c'est assavoir:En primes, a les vi mynstralles — lx s.

> Item, pur vesture de mesme les mynstralles — xxiiii s. v d.
> Item, pur foylles a diaprer a geter sur le royne — v s.
> Item, pur selverskynnes — iii s. iiii d.
> Item, al porter de Seint Bartholomeu et soun servant — xiiii d.
> Item, a un peyntour pur les garnementz des mynstralles — ii s. ii d.
> Summa: iiii li. xvi s. i d.

---

[51] Barron writes, 'Royal entries, victory processions, and marriages were occasions when the London craftsmen could display their wares to the king, the court, the aristocracy, country gentry, and foreign visitors' (*London*, p. 22).

[52] 'Feat a remembrer qe par comune assent de tut le companye Thomas Usk feut resseu d'estre clerk de mesme le companye et juré feut a mesme le companye et ordiné feut q'il duist avoyr par an soun vesture et i marc pur loyalment servyr mesme le companye en lours affaires etc' (Memorandum that by common consent of the whole company Thomas Usk was admitted as clerk of the same company and was sworn to the said company, and it was ordained that he should receive each year clothing and 1 mark for his loyal service to the same company in their affairs etc.): *Wardens' Accounts*, pp. 198–99. Note that 'Usk' is transcribed as 'Vok' in this edition. Usk's hand can be found in the Goldsmiths' accounts between 1380 and 1383 (Caroline Barron, personal communication). His association with the company was formalized in 1381–82, when he was sworn in.

Et feat a remembrer qe desuis Chepe feut un somercastelle bien arrayés, pendant en quel furent treys virgyns pur geter foylles, quel castel costa:

> En primes, pur vi verges de rouge pris le verge xviii d.
> i verge et i quarter rouge, pris le verge — xxx d.
> iii verges blank, pris le verge xxviii d.
> Johan Garoun pur carpentrie — xliii d.
> Item, pur i corde — vi s. viii d.
> Item, pur selverskynnes — viii s. x. d. ob.
> Summa, xxxv s. ix d. ob.
> dount ressu pur le drap et le corde — x s.

Feat a remembrer qe les ditz gardeyns ount resseu de la companye pur les ditz costages encontre la venue de la dite royne — vii li.

(Memorandum that on the Friday after the Feast of the Epiphany this year [11 January, 1382 n.s.] the Mayor, aldermen and the commons were arrayed to ride in procession with the Queen, the Emperor's sister, and whereas all the city misteries were instructed that their clothing must be of red and white, the goldsmiths were dressed in these same colours, and since all the other misteries had various cognizances, the goldsmiths had the red part of their clothing barred with silver wire and powdered with silver pearl trefoils, and each of the seven score men of the said mistery wore on their left side a large gold clasp with gemstones, and on their heads they wore chaplets covered in red material powdered with the said trefoils, and they rode with the queen throughout the city, and the said wardens paid various expenses for the said riding as follows:

> Firstly, to the 6 minstrels — 60s.
> Item, for the clothing of the same minstrels — 24s. 5d.
> Item, for leaves to be diapered to throw over the queen — 5s.
> Item, for 'silverskins' — 3s. 4d.
> Item, to the porter of St Bartholomew's and his servant — 14d.
> Item, to a painter for the minstrels' ornaments — 2s. 2d.
> Total: £4 16s. 1d.

Memorandum also that a summer-castle was set up in Cheap and well decorated, and three virgins leaned out of it to throw leaves, and this castle cost:

> Firstly, for 6 yards of red cloth at 18d. the yard —
> 1 ¼ yards of red cloth at 30d. the yard —
> 3 yards of white cloth at 28d. the yard —
> John Garoun, for carpentry work — 43d.
> Item, for a rope — 6s. 8d.
> Item, for 'silverskins' — 8s. 10 ½ d.
> Total: 35s 9 ½ d.
> of which has been received for the cloth and the rope — 10s.

Memorandum that the said wardens have received from the company for the said
expenses at the arrival of the said queen — £7.)[53]

These account entries give us an idea of the kind of entertainment put on by
London and its great livery companies. This public display for the entry of Anne
of Bohemia involved music and minstrels who performed with decorated
ornaments; it also included pageantry with elaborate props — a movable tower
erected on Cheap sounds impressive — and performers (the virgins strewing
confetti over the Queen). Clothing was also important — the guildsmen of the
city wore the livery of the city, and also marked their own guild identity with
intricate display. The Goldsmiths took their clothes very seriously, processing
garbed in silver wire, silver pearl trefoils, gold clasps, and jewels over the red and
white livery of the city of London. Clearly, this lavish spectacle staged the city as
a site of splendour, entertainment, and generosity; it constructed London as a
place of culture and hospitality, while also emphasising its wealth and importance.
The record reveals how enthusiastically the Goldsmiths used cultural performance
to advertise their own products (metals and jewels). Usk was to attempt to use
culture in similar strategic ways when he wrote his *Testament*.

Writing down what happened — as Usk was paid to do — memorializes it for
future wardens and generations of Goldsmiths, and sets a standard of guild
cultural performance. Discussing urban spectacle, Barbara Hanawalt and Kathryn
L. Reyerson comment on 'the significance of writing down ceremonies', adding
that '[w]ith a written record, the ceremonial process can become more fixed, less
spontaneous'.[54] Committing a record of guild cultural display to parchment
emphasises the fact that the guild should continue to reproduce these standards
of display in the city in order to maintain its cultural position. Indeed, the
Goldsmiths' accounts record that in 1377, at Richard's coronation, the
Goldsmiths' pageant included a castle, minstrels, maidens, and some kind of foil
probably used as gold leaves.[55] This sounds very similar to the spectacle produced
for Anne of Bohemia five years later, which also involved minstrels, maidens, a
movable castle, and scattering leaves. Writing down such details let future
generations know what was expected of them to maintain the honour and
standing of the guild. Similarly, the wardens suggested after the feast in 1379 that

[53] *Wardens' Accounts*, pp. 196–99.

[54] Barbara A. Hanawalt and Kathryn L. Reyerson, 'Introduction', in *City and Spectacle* (see
n. 46, above), pp. ix–xx (p. xviii).

[55] *Wardens' Accounts*, pp. 178–79.

the wardens should each year hold a lavish feast or else pay a fine (as mentioned above); the company was trying to enforce regular expenditure on cultural display. This anxiety about making sure that expense was equally incurred reveals the businesslike mentality behind the distribution of largesse.

Work, gifts, culture, and commerce were consistently linked for livery companies. These companies presented possible customers with beautiful examples of their skills, often alongside performances of various kinds, in the expectation of encouraging future purchases. We see this model in diverse forms: spectacle accompanied by gifts dominated Richard's public relationship with the city. In his reconciliation with London in 1392, for instance, pageantry and costume was the order of the day and all accounts of the festivities emphasize the importance of gift-giving.[56] In return, the following year Richard embarked upon a spending spree, repaying Londoners' generosity by scattering his own largesse in the city.[57] This reciprocity was central to the relationship between livery companies and their royal or aristocratic customers: all parties in the exchange were aware that the gifts had strings attached. They were examples of work and that work had to be paid for. But the conventions of masking the economics of the relationship between company and customer were upheld, partly by surrounding gifts with cultural elaboration. Production and *cultural* production were intertwined in this world:[58] gifts, laboured over by skilled craftsmen, were presented as part of a procession accompanied by musicians,[59] or as part of mumming.[60] Gifts and the

[56] Caroline M. Barron, 'The Quarrel of Richard II with London 1392–7', in *The Reign of Richard II: Essays in Honour of May McKisack*, ed. by F. R. H. Du Boulay and Caroline M. Barron (London, 1971), pp. 173–201. Kipling writes that the ceremony 'consisted entirely of dramatized gift-giving', discussing the 'seemingly endless series of opulent, symbolic gifts' (*Enter the King*, p. 118).

[57] Barron, 'Quarrel', p. 197.

[58] Louise Fradenburg makes the point that the sovereign 'is created in and through the inventive activity of his subjects, he depends upon their willingness to "produce" him as unique, both through works of imagination and works of labor' (Louise Fradenburg, *City, Marriage, Tournament: Arts of Rule in Late-Medieval Scotland* (Madison, 1991), p. xii).

[59] In 1371, for instance, three goldsmiths supplied the city with plate which they presented to the Black Prince after a ceremonial riding accompanied by music (Reddaway and Walker, *Early History*, p. 38).

[60] Important characteristics of mumming included disguising, gift-giving, and game-playing. It burgeoned under Richard and fell under suspicion in the reign of Henry IV. Prohibitions against mumming issued in the late fourteenth century aimed not at preventing mumming but at maintaining its exclusivity for more important Londoners. See Nolan, *John Lydgate*, pp. 78–80, p. 113, and Lancashire, *London Civic Theatre*, p. 41.

city were thus consistently associated both with work and labour and with cultural performance and spectacle.[61]

The embedding of cultural practices within economic exchange (for instance, in 1392 the Londoners put on pageants and gave gifts in the *expectation* of recompense soon afterward) lay at the heart of the cultural world of the livery companies.[62] Their cultural life also tended to be 'visual and public': their cultural practices (pageants, clothing, gifts) were for display, they glittered and shone and drew the eye.[63] This clear understanding of culture as material, commercial, beautiful, and ostentatious underpins Usk's *Testament of Love*.

'The Testament of Love'

The *Testament* refracts Usk's working life. This book is a thing, an aesthetic object that can help Usk to get ahead; both as a display object and as a demonstration of his probity and intelligence it can assist Usk in his construction of an image of himself. Indeed, Anne Middleton has argued that the content of Usk's book was firmly wedded to its material form, that at times Usk's ideas were subject to the necessities of formal layout. Middleton adds that 'Usk's care with these features

[61] For the way that cultural production was increasingly seen as entwined with work and everyday life, see Steven Justice, *Writing and Rebellion: England in 1381* (Berkeley and Los Angeles, 1994), p. 117, Richard Firth Green, *Poets and Princepleasers: Literature and the English Court in the Late Middle Ages* (Toronto, 1980), especially pp. 111, 203–06, and M. B. Parkes, 'The Literacy of the Laity', in *Literature and Western Civilization: The Mediaeval World*, ed. by David Daiches and Anthony Thorlby (London, 1973), pp. 555–77 (p. 572).

[62] The competitive reward-based structure of the Puy earlier in the century (which was dominated by the Mercers and formed a model for the conceit of the *Canterbury Tales*) also exemplifies a commercial attitude to cultural production. The Puy may well have taken place in 'The Tumbling Bear', a tavern that seems to have functioned as an informal hall for the Mercers at this date. See Anne F. Sutton, 'The Tumbling Bear and its Patrons: A Venue for the London Puy and Mercery', in *London and Europe* (see n. 15, above), pp. 85–110. Sutton discusses the fact that John de Cheshunt, third prince of the Puy, also owned this tavern. By 1407, the Bear was called the Maydeneshead, in tribute to the Mercers' emblem; it was located in the heart of the Mercery. The dominance of mercers in the Puy is discussed by Hanna in *London Literature*, p. 36. Note also that Thomas Becket's family had owned the land on which the Hospital of St Thomas of Acon and Mercers' Hall were built. See Sutton, *Mercery of London*, p. 6.

[63] Charles Phythian-Adams writes, 'The essence of culture in the late medieval city was that it was visual and public' (Charles Phythian-Adams, *Desolation of a City: Coventry and the Urban Crisis of the Late Middle Ages* (Cambridge, 1979), p. 112).

of layout and ornament imply that he considered them aspects of the work's expressive and communicative form' — for Usk, she suggests, the way the book looked was integral to how it could and should be read and interpreted.[64] Similarly, abstract philosophical concepts are fully embedded within the literal and the material within the *Testament*. If we turn to Usk's favourite images, the intertwining of things and thought, jobs and ideas, is striking. Two images that resonate throughout the *Testament* are the knot in the heart and the Margarite pearl.[65] The love knot — 'the knotte of al goodnesse' — contains a wealth of conceptual meaning, but it is also reminiscent of a scribal signature, as J. A. W. Bennett has noted.[66] The idea of the scribal knot was that it made a signature unique. Usk's guarantee of philosophical, even divine, integrity thus comes in the guise of a proof of *professional* integrity.

In the same way, the Margarite pearl, Usk's central motif and object of desire, has manifold biblical and literary associations but is also a material, high-status luxury object. He repeatedly describes the pearl in detail:

> [A] Margarit peerle that is so precious a gemme, whit, clere and lytel, of whiche stones or jewel the tonges of us Englissh people tourneth the right names and clepeth hem 'Margery perles.' [...] [T]he Margarite is a lytel whyte perle, throughout holowe and rounde and vertuous, and, on the see sydes in the more Britayne, in muskle shelles, of the hevenly dewe the best ben engendred; in whiche by experience ben founde thre fayre vertues. One is, it yeveth comforte to the felyng spyrites in bodily persones of reason. Another is good: it is profytable helth ayenst passyons of sorie mens hertes. And the thirde, it is nedeful and noble in staunchyng of bloode, there else to moche wolde out ren. To whiche perle and vertues me lyst to liken at this tyme Philosophie with her thre speces, that is, natural and moral and resonable, of whiche thynges hereth what sayne these great clerkes. (III. 1. 25–39)

This excerpt from a much longer passage about the physical and moral properties of the pearl illustrates its polysemous significance for Usk; he is explicit in describing it as a real jewel with mystical properties and as a philosophical symbol.[67] Usk's position as employee and intimate of the Goldsmiths reminds us

[64] Anne Middleton, 'Thomas Usk's "Perdurable Letters": The *Testament of Love* From Script to Print', *Studies in Bibliography*, 51 (1998), 63–116 (p. 91).

[65] Shoaf comments, 'After the Margarite, the most important as it is also the most unusual image in *TL* is that of the knot [...]. The Margarite and the knot are the most extensive and fully-developed of Usk's images' (*Testament*, ed. by Shoaf, pp. 10, 12).

[66] Bennett, *Middle English Literature*, p. 350. See also *Testament*, ed. by Shoaf, pp. 10–11.

[67] Summers writes that for Usk, the Margarite pearl 'forms the object of the narrator's religious and secular devotion, a priceless jewel with associations of courtly veneration, perfection,

that pearls would be familiar to him as material objects of display and exchange as much as they were familiar to him as religio-literary tropes.[68] Felicity Riddy and Helen Barr have both considered the material aspects of the jewel and jeweller in *Pearl*, suggesting that we should think about the social and economic aspects of the poem's emphasis on luxury jewels.[69] Much can be gained by extending this kind of analysis to the *Testament of Love*. Riddy explores the emphasis on opulence in *Pearl* and writes that the poem 'is positioned at the meeting-point between aristocratic and urban values'. She adds that 'the high culture sustained by the luxury system is the product of exchange between craftsmen, merchants, and aristocrats, between the court and the city. The narrating voice of *Pearl*, shifting between jeweller and courtly love is an acknowledgement of this.'[70] Similar negotiations are apparent in Usk's life and text. Usk himself was a Londoner with guild associations who sought the favour of the king, and the guild with which he was associated was one that engaged in particularly extensive trade and gifting with aristocrats and the court. Indeed, he had long had connections with the court as well as with London: in his *Appeal*, he tells us about hurrying from the city to see John of Gaunt (ll. 125–26, 179), and we have seen that livery companies such as the Goldsmiths had social and cultural as well as professional ties with the court. Usk's choice of a pearl as his unifying image beautifully links the different aspects of his career and aspirations — it is a product of the city, which can be used to demonstrate kingly power, to adorn the court. Jewels, like plate, were mobile objects, bought and sold but also offered as homage and dispersed as patronage.[71] Just as *Pearl* can be compared to a jewel in its beauty and complexity,[72] so the *Testament of Love* is like the jewels and plate presented by the city to the king as objects of homage and signs of dedication.

---

and the spiritual worth inherent in the biblical pearl-of-great-price tradition' (*Late-Medieval Prison Writing*, p. 28).

[68] Goldsmiths often had special expertise in jewellery; for instance, Adam Bamme was one of three experts in jewels who appraised those offered as security for a loan by Richard II in 1383. See Reddaway and Walker, *Early History*, p. 277.

[69] Felicity Riddy, 'Jewels in Pearl', in *A Companion to the 'Gawain'-Poet*, ed. by Derek Brewer and Jonathan Gibson (Cambridge, 1997), pp. 143–55; Helen Barr, '*Pearl* — or "The Jeweller's Tale"', *Medium Aevum*, 69 (2001), 59–79.

[70] Riddy, 'Jewels', pp. 150, 149.

[71] Riddy, 'Jewels', p. 150.

[72] Riddy, 'Jewels', p. 147.

Usk roots his image of the pearl in material reality; for instance he reminds us of sumptuary laws and of the literal value of pearls when he tells us: 'no wight is worthy suche perles to weare but kynges or princes or els their peres' (I. 3. 333–34). The specific reference to wearing pearls is especially relevant to Usk's life if we remember that the Goldsmiths, Richard, and Richard's followers all decked themselves in pearls in the late fourteenth century.[73] In the account of the Goldsmiths' extravagant livery worn for Anne's entry in 1382, Usk wrote out a description of the silver pearl trefoils that decorated the guildsmen's outfits.[74] Richard wore pearls on his robes in 1385 (at exactly the time at which the *Testament* was probably being penned). At this date, Richard ordered robes with white harts embroidered on them in pearls for the Feast of the Purification of the Virgin.[75] Richard's use of pearls for such a purpose demonstrates the fluid symbolism that could attach to such luxury items both as signs of wealth and authority and as symbols of religious and spiritual purity. Indeed, Richard had a particularly strong belief in the importance of the luxury system as something integral to his sacral view of kingship.[76] Scholars such as Lee Patterson have discussed Richard's view of patronage as a tool for demonstrating his own magnificence, rather than supporting the nobility as vital political agents and landowners in their own right.[77] His artistic patronage too, which produced

[73] Discussing the *Testament*, Summers comments on Richard's special affinity with pearls, (*Late-Medieval Prison Writing*, pp. 52–53).

[74] The fact that the Goldsmiths wore pearls as distinctive livery for this civic procession and display might remind us of the description of a civic procession in which the participants wore pearls as livery in *Pearl*. This poem depicts a 'prosessyoun' (l. 1096) in the 'noble cité' (l. 1097) in which everyone is crowned 'of the same fasoun' (l. 1101) and is decorated with 'perles' (l. 1102) with a 'blysful perle' (l. 1104) on each participant's breast. Their clothing is described as 'livrés' (l. 1108) and the participants themselves are 'aldermen' (l. 1119).

[75] This is mentioned in John M. Bowers, 'Pearl in its Royal Setting: Ricardian Poetry Revisited', *Studies in the Age of Chaucer*, 17 (1995), 111–55 (p. 138). The long, red velvet gown was embroidered with harts in pearls and crowns in gold thread, and represents the earliest known public use of harts by Richard as king. See Kay Staniland, 'Extravagance or Regal Necessity?: The Clothing of Richard II', in *Regal Image* (see n. 10, above), pp. 85–93 (p. 91).

[76] This relates to what Saul has termed 'the fusion of secular and religious ideas that is so vital to an understanding of Richard II's kingship'. See Nigel Saul, 'Richard II's Ideas of Kingship', in *Regal Image* (see n. 10, above), pp. 27–32 (p. 27).

[77] Lee Patterson discusses Richard's concept of the nobility as 'an embodiment of the king's magnificence', rather than as an independent body controlling land; hence his refusal to give Gloucester land and his creation of a baron without a barony ('Court Politics and the Invention

objects such as the Wilton Diptych, the coronation portrait, his and Anne's tomb, his glorious robes, and the remodelled Westminster Hall, focused on the production of objects that reflected, enhanced, and promoted his own majesty.[78] The language that he used to create new honours in the parliament of 1385 reveals a view of patronage that connects luxury objects, particularly jewels, with political patronage, and with Richard's own elevated view of kingship. When bestowing an earldom on Michael de la Pole, he states (in the Rolls of Parliament):

> Credimus namque nostram coronam regiam tanto pluribus micare gemmis, et preciosis coruscare lapidibus, quanto viris virtuosis et strenuis, presertim consilio prepollentibus, in partem solicitudinis regie ad fasses honorum evocatis.

> (For we believe our royal crown to glitter with many gems and shimmer with precious stones in so far as virtuous and active men, especially those excelling in counsel, on the king's behalf are summoned to high office to strengthen the management of public affairs.)[79]

He continues to emphasize that the name of this earl should 'honori nostri diadematis' (honour our diadem) and to state that de la Pole has been promoted 'corone nostre regie decorem' (for the adornment of our royal crown). Richard here constructs his subjects as jewels, who become part of the royal regalia. Such a comparison suggests that the display of kingship is integral to kingship itself. Commissioning the production of luxury objects is perhaps not essentially different from bestowing titles and positions on subjects. Usk's production of a book and his construction of his putative patron as a jewel while hoping for a royal appointment can be seen as very much part of a continuum of Richard's worldview, one that was supported and sustained by the producers of luxury

---

of Literature: The Case of Sir John Clanvowe', in *Culture and History 1350–1600: Essays on English Communities, Identities and Writing*, ed. by David Aers (New York, 1992), pp. 7–41 (p. 17)). See also Anthony Tuck, *Richard II and the English Nobility* (London, 1973), especially pp. 84–85.

[78] On the Wilton Diptych, see *Regal Image* and Gordon, *Making and Meaning*; on the coronation portrait, see Jonathan Alexander, 'The Portrait of Richard II in Westminster Abbey', in *Regal Image* (see n. 10, above), pp. 197–206; on the tomb see Phillip Lindley, 'Absolutism and Regal Image in Ricardian Sculpture', in *Regal Image*, pp. 61–83; on Richard's robes, see Staniland, 'Extravagance or Regal Necessity?'; on Westminster Hall, see Christopher Wilson, 'Rulers, Artificers and Shoppers: Richard II's Remodelling of Westminster Hall', in *Regal Image*, pp. 33–59.

[79] 'Richard II: Parliament of October, 1385: Text and Translation', in *The Parliament Rolls of Medieval England*, ed. by C. Given-Wilson and others, 16 vols, CD-ROM (Leicester, 2005), III, 207.

goods, such as the Goldsmiths. Usk metaphorically desires to be a jewel on the royal diadem, and to serve the Margarite pearl, but quite literally he desires a jewelled badge, such as those pearled badges in the possession of Henry of Derby; Roger Mortimer, Earl of March; Margaret, Duchess of Burgundy; and Sir John Golafre, modelled by Richard in the Wilton Diptych.[80] He may even have received one.[81] In the *Testament*, as in *Pearl*, the jewels mean many things, but on one level they are indeed jewels.

Clothing was also part of the luxury culture, and Usk repeatedly uses imagery relating to clothes, especially livery, in the *Testament*.[82] The unworthy are 'not clothed of my lyvery but unleful lustye habyte' (II. 14. 1364–65), Jupiter has 'in his warderobe bothe garmentes of joye and of sorowe' and can 'clothe thee in blysse' (II. 9. 910–12), and through long service 'is the consynance of my lyvery to al my retynue delyvered' (I. 5. 493–94).[83] As with the pearl, Usk uses metaphors that represent real, tangible rewards and favour in his own life. The repeated mentions of livery are especially important, as Usk himself wore the Goldsmiths' livery and sought to wear the king's; clothing, like a pearl badge, was a material mark of favour.[84]

The concreteness of Usk's imagination is also evident in his use of imagery recalling visual arts; he imagines and discusses such lavish artwork in Book II, Chapter 13 of the *Testament* when he writes:

> Our noble God, in glyterande wyse, by armony this worlde ordeyned as in purtreytures storied with colours medled in whiche blacke and other derke coloures commenden the golden and the asured paynture. (ll. 1303–05)

---

[80] For the pearled white harts owned by Henry, Mortimer, Golafre, and Margaret, see Campbell, 'White Harts', p. 102. On the Wilton Diptych, the antlers on the hart worn by Richard are tipped with pearls.

[81] As far as we know, white hart badges were not distributed by Richard during Usk's lifetime; but other badges certainly were, especially indeed at the time when Usk was in favour. See Saul, *Richard II*, pp. 265–66.

[82] *Pearl* also includes mention of livery as discussed above, n. 74.

[83] Presciently, writing several years before Barron's discovery of Usk's Goldsmith connections, Summers writes of the reference to livery in Book II that: 'It also conjures up the economically and politically powerful guilds who also wore liveries at this time' (*Late-Medieval Prison Writing*, p. 45).

[84] In the crisis of 1387, which led to Usk's death, Richard sought to whip up support through the distribution of badges. See *The Westminster Chronicle 1381–1394*, ed. by L. C. Hector and Barbara F. Harvey (Oxford, 1982), p. 186.

In other words, God has ordained a balance in the world, just as paintings use contrast to show colours to their best advantage. The kind of painting or illumination that Usk is imagining is lavishly adorned with gold and azure (as was the Wilton Diptych).[85] Here, Usk invites the reader to visualize what he is describing as a painting, or even a pageant, a cultural production adorned with expensive colours. He expresses a sense of the divine by describing a luxury cultural object, again demonstrating his own belief in the 'holiness of the luxury system'.[86] Similarly, in *Pearl*, the description of the heavenly Jerusalem seems to be influenced by contemporary illuminations in Apocalypse manuscripts.[87] This is particularly manifest when the dreamer mentions the wall of jasper that 'glent as glayre' (l. 1026), referring to the egg-white used to glaze manuscript illuminations.

The descriptions of paintings, illuminations, or pageants in words might also remind us of the fact that ceremonies and rituals may have been written about in the form of descriptive programmes. Maurice Keen argues that this was the case for entries such as Henry V's after Agincourt, and this is part of Keen's more general argument that the rise of literacy in the late Middle Ages enabled the elaboration of visual culture, as the written word was 'empowering visual display'.[88] The development of guild pageantry and civic drama is thus part of the same cultural flowering that produced the outpouring of written vernacular texts in these

[85] Pigments used in the Wilton Diptych included azurite and gold leaf; see Ashok Roy, 'The Technique of the Wilton Diptych', in *Regal Image* (see n. 10, above), pp. 25–135 (pp. 133–34). (Of course, the Wilton Diptych itself was almost certainly produced in the late 1390s, about ten years after Usk's death, but it gives us an example of the highest-quality art available at this time.) Indeed, the Diptych specifically reveals the art of the goldsmiths; Marian Campbell comments that 'the art of the goldsmith permeates both the style and the content of the [Wilton] Diptych to a notable extent: in its exceptional rendering of *ronde bosse* enamel, in its use of *pointillé* and in its precisely observed depiction of jewellery' ('White Harts', p. 110). *Ronde bosse* was the most fashionable type of enamelling at this time, and can be seen in the way that the paint is raised above the surrounding area on the body of the hart on Richard's brooch in the Diptych. *Pointillé*, also known as pouncing or stippling, was standard in high quality Parisian goldsmiths' work at this time and also known in England; it can be seen in the hart's antlers, the mantle of the Christ Child, and the gold backgrounds to the figures (p. 109).

[86] Riddy, 'Jewels', p. 152.

[87] See R. Field, 'The Heavenly Jerusalem in *Pearl*', *Modern Language Review*, 81 (1986), 7–17, Muriel A. Whitaker, '*Pearl* and Some Illustrated Apocalypse Manuscripts', *Viator*, 12 (1981), 183–96, and Sarah Stanbury, 'Visions of Space: Acts of Perception in *Pearl* and in Some Late Medieval Illustrated Apocalypses', *Mediaevalia*, 10 (1988), 133–58.

[88] Maurice Keen, 'Introduction', in *Heraldry, Pageantry, and Social Display in Medieval England*, ed. by Peter Coss and Maurice Keen (Woodbridge, 2002), pp. 1–16 (pp. 5, 8).

decades.[89] The *Testament* was produced by someone who had seen, or even participated in, civic processions and tableaux,[90] and who was paid to write down descriptions of such events. Usk's imagination was conditioned by the luxury culture of display that knitted together court and city, part of the 'broadly performative culture' of late-medieval England, and he was accustomed to transforming these visual spectacles into writing.[91]

Vernacular books themselves were visual objects, most strikingly in the case of presentation copies with elaborate miniatures. Middleton has suggested that the *Testament* was a carefully made book, and that Usk was a 'connoisseur and designer, if not a direct practitioner of every level of the textmaker's art'.[92] Certainly, his inscription of his name into the fabric of the text (in his acrostic) suggests that he conceived of his text as a visual object, and Middleton believes that the book was 'relatively refined and ornate as a made object', suggesting that Ellesmere and the more elaborate Gower manuscripts might be suitable comparisons.[93] Texts could also, of course, be performed, when the poet's body became part of the spectacle of the cultural event, and they could also be combined with wall paintings.[94] Like jewels, texts could take their place as valuable items in the gift-exchange culture. Discussing the connections between beauty, commodities, and poetry in the 'Miller's Tale', Maura Nolan writes that books

[89] Keen discusses 'the interplay of written word and visual presentation at work in this newly literate age, to their mutual enrichment' ('Introduction', p. 7).

[90] Usk certainly participated in ridings; see below.

[91] Claire Sponsler's comment about medieval drama could be applied to other aspects of medieval culture as well. She writes: 'Should we reconsider the tendency of theatre historians to view "medieval drama" as a distinct and identifiable cultural category rather than an activity that merges — both in practice and in the documents that record that practice — with other creative activities produced within a broadly performative culture?' ('Drama in the Archives: Recognizing Medieval Plays', in *From Script to State in Early Modern England*, ed. by Peter Holland and Stephen Orgel (Basingstoke, 2004), pp. 111–30 (p. 114)).

[92] Middleton, '"Perdurable Letters"', p. 95.

[93] Middleton, '"Perdurable Letters"', p. 95.

[94] See, for instance, John Trevisa's comment about those places 'where þe Apocalips ys ywryte in þe walles and roof of a chapel boþe in Latyn and yn Freynsch', presumably referring to depictions of Revelation that included both wall-paintings and parts of the text (John Trevisa, 'Dialogus inter dominum et clericum', in Ronald Waldron, 'Trevisa's Original Prefaces on Translation: A Critical Edition', in *Medieval English Studies Presented to George Kane* (see n. 45, above), pp. 285–99 (pp. 289–94, 292)). Lydgate wrote several poems to be inscribed on walls; see Lindenbaum, 'London Texts', p. 297.

functioned as tangible symbols of their owners' wealth and prestige, communicating visually a message that the text inside the covers could not be relied on to produce, depending on its purpose and frame. Like 'perling' and 'latoun', books are not things-in-themselves so much as they are representations of things — and people, places, actions, objects, events. They are, as Francesca famously reminds us, go-betweens.[95]

The book as a gift represents Usk's stature and potential; like the figure of the scribe or messenger himself, it moves between different groups, bonding them together, and conferring obligations.

Like his erstwhile Goldsmith masters, who went all-out in the 1382 royal entry with their movable tower, employment of multiple artisans, lavish costumes, and vast expenditure, Usk fully understood the power of constructing oneself through aesthetic form, of gaining position through demonstrating one's cultural sensibilities. Usk enthusiastically took on the idea of using cultural production to get ahead economically. One of his strategies for gaining the attention of the royal party and a royal appointment was producing this book, a strategy that would seem especially sensible to someone who had witnessed the way that the livery companies and London as a whole used gifts in their relationship with the court. Usk articulates his views on the presentation of gifts in the book itself: with open cynicism, Lady Love advises petitioners to use gifts as a way of getting ahead. She tells how she counsels her servants to write letters, make songs, learn manners, and 'to yeve gret yeftes and large' (I. 2.199) to gain the favour of their loved ones/sovereigns.[96] Usk is here explicit about the economic value of gifts: they are presented in the expectation of a return.

The *Testament of Love* is a demonstration of Usk's imaginative abilities but it is also presented as a product of immense work; Usk sees culture and labour as inseparable. He is keen to emphasize that his book truly is a labour of love, involving so much hard graft that he should really reap some reward; it is a gift that has been produced with sweat and effort and as such deserves some kind of payback.[97] Unlike a gift offered by a member of the nobility or gentry but like a product offered by a livery company, a piece of writing reveals the diligence and talent of the supplicant,

---

[95] Maura Nolan, 'Beauty', in *Twenty-First Century Approaches* (see n. 3, above), pp. 207–21 (p. 214).

[96] For a discussion of this passage see Turner, *Chaucerian Conflict*, chap. 4.

[97] We might here be reminded of contemporary discussions about whether or not literary practice could function as 'work'. For a discussion of authors' investment in imagining writing as work in the late fourteenth century, see Kellie Robertson, *The Laborer's Two Bodies: Literary and Legal Productions in Britain 1350–1500* (New York, 2006), pp. 37–50.

functioning as an advertisement, as a demonstration of cultural understanding and of the ability to serve and to work. In the Prologue to the *Testament of Love*, Usk repeatedly calls attention to writing as work, as involving hard labour to make a product. Philosophers, he writes, produced their books 'by a great swetande travayle' (ll. 49–50) and Boethius and other great writers are 'great workmen' (l. 79). His language is often specifically agricultural: he wants his words to 'planten' (l. 6) meaning in his readers' hearts. The great clerks worked 'with theyr sharpe sythes of connyng' (ll. 70–71) and made great piles of hay and crops with which they could feed their readers; they are 'noble repers [...] good workmen and worthy theyr hyer' (ll. 73–74). Writers, he implies, work in God's image as he too is a 'werkman' and 'The crafte of a werkman is shewed in the werke' (ll. 48–49). As well as using agricultural imagery, Usk also places the business of writing on the same plane as militaristic force, comparing his audacious attempt to write a book with grabbing a sword from Hercules, moving Hercules' pillars, pulling up a spear that Alexander could not manage, or trying to conquer France even though Edward III failed to do so (ll. 61–66). We might see these labours as representing the stereotyped work of the first estate; they are chivalric, aristocratic ideas of work, and they bring together classical ideas and the enjoyment of war so typical of aristocratic taste. Usk thus suggests that his own work in writing is as arduous as the work of knights and the work of labourers.[98] Nowhere else in the book is there such a sustained emphasis on the work of the text, and the fact that this opens the *Testament* suggests that it was crucial to Usk to demonstrate his dedication and willingness to labour.[99] Unlike some other contemporary authors, Usk was not struggling with the issue of whether or not it was acceptable to spend one's time thinking and writing; he was only too eager to find another way of spending his time.[100] Instead, he might be attempting to demonstrate his embracing of hard work as a transferable skill, and also to suggest that his agonizing

---

[98] He draws here on various prefatory conventions, which are also apparent in texts such as the *Polychronicon*. See also Ellen E. Martin, 'Chaucer's Ruth: An Exegetical Poetic in the Prologue to the *Legend of Good Women*', *Exemplaria*, 3 (1996), 467–90.

[99] Since the thirteenth-century expansion of bureaucracy, seigneurial administration, and the law, the false work of the king's employees had been a growing cause for complaint. The petition genre, for instance, was largely a response to the potential exploitation of office by civil servants, lawyers, and other kinds of administrators. See Alan Harding, 'Plaints and Bills in the History of English Law, Mainly in the Period 1250–1350', in *Legal History Studies 1972*, ed. by Dafydd Jenkins (Cardiff, 1975), pp. 65–86, especially pp. 66, 71, and Robertson, *Laborer's Two Bodies*, p. 71

[100] See *Written Work: Langland, Labor, and Authorship*, ed. by Steven Justice and Kathryn Kerby-Fulton (Philadelphia, 1997).

labour deserves some acknowledgement.[101] Just as the city's gifts to Richard resulted in Richard's spending extravagantly in the city, so Usk hopes that his production of a book will result in a royal appointment.[102]

Most interestingly, Usk also employs imagery that evokes the work of the city. Love admonishes him: 'A marchaunt that for ones lesynge in the see no more to aventure thynketh, he shal never with aventure come to rychesse' (III. 7. 868–70). Usk here parallels the gains of a merchant with grace. He is possibly echoing the 'Canon's Yeoman's Tale' (ll. 947–50), the most mercantile and urban of all the *Canterbury Tales*. While Chaucer places similar words in a highly equivocal context by putting them in the mouth of a desperate, deluded alchemist, Usk makes the bold merchant and his lifestyle exemplary and admirable by attributing these words to Lady Love. Thus, while Chaucer makes the validity of mercantile ideology doubtful at best, Usk eulogizes the lifestyle of wealthy traders — and this perhaps reveals that at least some of Chaucer's earliest readers interpreted and rewrote his texts in simplifying ways and in ways congenial to their own professional circumstances.[103] We might see in Usk's use of Chaucer early examples of the simplification and domestication of Chaucer's writings that has been noted in fifteenth-century manuscripts, in which the poet is 'socially appropriated for specific educative and commercial goals'.[104]

Usk also uses language that specifically calls to mind his goldsmith associations. Love says, 'Sylver fyned with many heates men knowen for trew, and safely men may trust to the alay in werkynge' (II. 4. 389–90). Since the thirteenth century, the Crown forbade goldsmiths to work silver of a lower standard than sterling. To ensure that their silver wares were of this standard, they were supposed to work in the public streets, not in secret or obscure places.[105] Goldsmiths could test the properties of metals, and they were sometimes called to do this when a buyer

---

[101] Middleton writes that Usk's text 'can only have been an avocation, an alternative and somewhat ostentatious deployment of his marketable abilities, perhaps to advertise their possessor as a man of versatile and useful talents' ('"Perdurable Letters"', p. 100).

[102] Mauss writes about 'the form of the gift, the present generously given even when, in the gesture accompanying the transaction, there is only a polite fiction, formalism, and social deceit, and when really there is obligation and economic self-interest' (Marcel Mauss, *The Gift: The Form and Reason for Exchange in Archaic Societies* (London, 1990), p. 4).

[103] See also Usk's repeated recontextualisations of *Troilus and Criseyde*; in particular he often places Pandarus's words in Love's mouth. I discuss this in *Chaucerian Conflict*, chap. 4.

[104] Lerer, *Chaucer and His Readers*, p. 87.

[105] Reddaway and Walker, *Early History*, p. xxi.

thought he or she had been defrauded. The reference here to testing the silver through heat, and then being able to trust the quality of the metal, is especially interesting now that we know about Usk's goldsmith connections, as he is referring to the technicalities of a trade with which he was very familiar. Crucially, Love is here referring to Usk himself, comparing him to the silver. She suggests that he too, like the silver, has been tested and tried so much that now everyone should know that they can trust him, that he is true. The implication is that he was suspected of being untrue — which of course he was — but has proved himself. This neatly acknowledges his former errors but suggests that they have been put behind him and that they did not affect his essential, true self. Comparing himself to silver also constructs Usk as a product of the Goldsmiths, reminding us that he was patronized and employed by them. But the image works to emphasize Usk's potential courtliness as well as his trade and guild connections; like the pearl it is an image relevant both to the company and to the court. Silver had to be of the same value as the king's money; its point of comparison is coinage. Coins, stamped with the head of the king, replicating his authority, are like the ultimate badged retainers, ciphers for the true authority of the monarch.[106] Usk is no forgery, no traitor; he is the king's true shilling, who may 'safely' be trusted.[107] In other words, he is absolutely ready for a royal appointment.

Like the pearl and the knot, the silver is a metaphor grounded in the products and materials that surrounded Usk in his working life while also bearing ethical connotations. For Usk, steeped in the culture of the Goldsmiths, a world in which commerce and art were inextricably linked, united in the things that the company produced and offered as gifts, these meanings were perhaps not separable. He deserves favour because he can produce a book that is ethical *and* beautiful; his morality and truth should be paid for with silver coins; as an honest servant of the

---

[106] Surely one of the most scandalous aspects of Richard's excessive promotion of Robert de Vere was his granting de Vere the right to strike coins in Ireland, in his patent of 1385.

[107] Strohm discusses the associations between counterfeiting and treason in the late Middle Ages; writing that: 'The traitorous nature of counterfeiting is attested by a long series of treason statutes — from Justinian through Bracton and Glanvill in the thirteenth century to the definitive English statute of 1352 — which agree that counterfeiting is a form of lése majesté', adding that the counterfeit coins are 'impermissably arrogating [the king's] aura or *dignitas* to sanction their otherwise inert matter'. See Paul Strohm, *England's Empty Throne: Usurpation and the Language of Legitimation 1399–1422* (New Haven, 1998), p. 133. Strohm discusses associations between counterfeiting, treason, and heresy throughout Chapter 5, 'Counterfeiters, Lollards, and Lancastrian Unease', pp. 128–52.

king he should be displayed like plate and rewarded with jewels. The holiness of things and the quiddity of art (including books) is fundamental both to Usk's understanding of his world and, more generally, to the livery companies' understanding of theirs. Middleton notes that the skills of producing books are given moral value in the *Testament*;[108] in the same way the art of the goldsmith, the art of communicating through words, and the culture of luxury goods and jewels are embedded in ideas of honesty, integrity, and loyalty in Usk's text.

While the recipients of the city's gifts, including the king, appreciated that they were involved in an economic transaction, it was crucial for such exchanges to be misrecognized (to use Bourdieu's terms). Usk, however, is open about his desire for some return for his service and gifts to his sovereign. At the close of Book I, Love announces, 'And if that Margarite denyeth nowe nat to suffre her vertues shyne to thee wardes with spreadynge beames as farre or farther than if thou were sely in worldly joy, trewly I saye nat els but she is somdele to blame' (I. 10. 1020–22).[109] This reads as a fairly blatant demand for the King's favour — the sunlike warmth of his support should now encompass Usk. Indeed, the language that Usk uses has particular resonance for Richard, who used the badge and image of the sun to represent himself.[110] Richard's attitude to patronage was that its recipients should 'reflect the majesty of kingship through the honours they

---

[108] Middleton writes: 'the bibliophile's, the textworker's, the translator's, and the verbal maker's terms of art are used to signify moral and rhetorical categories and vice versa' ('"Perdurable Letters"', p. 94).

[109] It is highly probable that the word should be 'deyneth' not 'denyeth'; see Shoaf's note to this line in *Testament*.

[110] On Richard's use of the sun as a badge see John Gough Nichols, 'Observations on the Heraldic Devices Discovered on the Effigies of Richard the Second and His Queen in Westminster Abbey, and upon the Mode in Which Those Ornaments Were Executed; Including Some Remarks on the Surname Plantagenet, and on the Ostrich Feathers of the Prince of Wales', *Archaeologica*, 29 (1842), 32–59 (pp. 47, 48). See also Rev. John Webb, 'Translation of a French Metrical History of the Deposition of King Richard the Second, Written by a Contemporary, and Comprising the Period from his Last Expedition into Ireland to his Death; from a MS. Formerly Belonging to Charles of Anjou, Earl of Maine and Mortain; but Now Preserved in the British Museum; Accompanied by Prefatory Observations, Notes, and an Appendix; with a Copy of the Original', *Archaeologica*, 20 (1824), 1–423 (illumination 7 at pp. 74–75, showing the sail of Richard's ship bearing a large sun emblem). See also Staniland, 'Extravagance or Regal Necessity?', p. 92, and Lisa Monnas, 'Fit for a King: Figured Silks Shown in the Wilton Diptych', in *Regal Image* (see n. 10, above), pp. 165–77 (pp. 167, 168, for descriptions of the cloths decorated with suns worn by Richard).

received from it, as satellites around the sun'.[111] Usk, like a good courtier, speaks the language of his king,[112] speaking back to him his own desires to be a sunlike, divinized figure. But he also inserts himself into this fantasy, as one of those who will reflect back Richard's majesty. This book is not really a free gift; there are strings attached, and Usk has expectations that his work (literary and otherwise) will be paid for by patronage ('spreadynge beames'). Usk fully understands the idea that cultural practice is bound up with economic reward, but he does not seem to have taken on board the fact that the crucial element of such exchanges is that their economic character is unacknowledged. Bourdieu writes about the 'production of collective misrecognition' in gifting, in which delay and differentiation between the gift and counter-gift is crucial. He writes: 'Gift exchange is one of the social games that cannot be played unless the players refuse to acknowledge the objective truth of the game.'[113] Usk, however, is quite overtly asking for the King or his party to fulfil their side of the exchange and confer some favours on him, hinting darkly that they will be 'somdele to blame' if they do not. His anxiety echoes through the text: he seems incapable of participating in the fiction of *méconnaissance*.[114] This impatient hastiness is typical of Usk's indiscreet, and ultimately catastrophic, political and textual strategies. Throughout this essay, I have been suggesting that Usk had a similar understanding of culture to that of his guildsman associates, that he and they perceived the cultural world as material, commercial, beautiful, and ostentatious. It seems clear to me that Chaucer did not perceive culture in this way, and did not want to play the game of such a world.[115] Usk did want to play the game but he never really grasped the rules.

[111] Harriss, *Shaping the Nation*, p. 452.

[112] For a discussion of the totalized discourse of the sovereign, see Louise Fradenburg, 'The Manciple's Servant Tongue: Politics and Poetry in *The Canterbury Tales*', *Journal of English Literary History*, 52 (1985), 85–118, especially p. 89.

[113] Pierre Bourdieu, *The Logic of Practice*, trans. by Richard Nice (Cambridge, 1992), pp. 106, 105.

[114] I differ here from Summers, who suggests that Usk's desire for reward remains ambiguous and tacit (*Late-Medieval Prison Writing*, pp. 48–49).

[115] The disarray of Chaucer's texts at his death alone demonstrates his reluctance (or indeed refusal) to use ostentatious cultural production as a commercial or social bargaining chip. Although attributing motives to Chaucer is obviously deeply problematic, Fisher's comment that Chaucer 'was loath during his lifetime to lose control of his materials' does make sense. ('Animadversions', p. 783).

Scribes, Politics, and the 'Appeal'

Usk's Goldsmith affiliations also throw new light on the politics of his earlier text, the *Appeal*, and on his own position in the world that he describes in this document. The *Appeal* foregrounds the Goldsmiths' hall — Usk's workplace and a site of extravagant hospitality and display, as we have seen — as a locus of political agitation. While the *Testament* evokes the ostentatious display culture of London and its livery companies and the complicated ways in which cultural gifts were entwined with labour and reward, the *Appeal* draws a sharp and unromantic picture of the hard-nosed, high-stakes politics in which companies such as the Goldsmiths, Mercers, and Tailors were embroiled. Considering Usk's Goldsmith associates in more detail reveals that they made similar political shifts to him, that his side-switching was not unusual. I suggest below that his difference and his downfall lay in his overenthusiastic commitment to writing and in his too-secure belief in the transparency of cultural production.

Usk turns on his erstwhile masters in the *Appeal*. Singling out the Goldsmiths from other companies, Usk implicates the company as a whole as well as accusing specific individuals. This attack is especially striking now that we know how closely connected Usk had been with the company, and particularly with Adam Bamme, one of the named targets of the *Appeal*. Knowing about Usk's employment by the Goldsmiths makes sense of the repeated references to the guild in the *Appeal*. Usk tells us of being dispatched to Goldsmiths' Hall, of arranging meetings there, of Northampton speaking there, of being sent to Gaunt with two goldsmiths to promote Northampton. It is manifest that Usk's Goldsmith and Northampton connections were crucially bound up together, and that the Goldsmiths' Hall was a natural meeting place for those interested in Northampton's politics. Usk, as an employee of the Goldsmiths must have been a particularly useful messenger and activist for Northampton, with his access to the hall and to its owners.

One of those to whom he had particular access was Adam Bamme. This influential goldsmith acted as renter, warden, and prime warden for the company in the 1370s and, in the 1380s and 1390s, he took high office in the city, serving as alderman, sheriff, MP, and mayor.[116] Bamme was also the principal supplier of goldsmiths' wares to John of Gaunt.[117] In 1383–84, the Goldsmiths' accounts

---

[116] Reddaway and Walker, *Early History*, p. 277.

[117] Nightingale, *Medieval Mercantile*, p. 256. Caroline Barron suggested (in her paper 'Thomas Usk' at the New Chaucer Convention, New York, 27–31 July 2006) that Bamme was the conduit for the connection between Northampton and Gaunt that has puzzled scholars.

record a cluster of payments, to Adam Bamme, Thomas Usk, John Walsh, William Louth, Bartholomew Castre, John Carbonelle, and Thomas Raynham, and also to 'les mynstrales pur chivacher ové le vicecompte' (the minstrels for their riding with the sheriff).[118] It seems probable that this payment refers to the previous year, 1382–83, when Bamme was sheriff. When the Mayor was sworn in, he then rode in procession (on 29 October) from the Guildhall along Cheapside to Westminster, escorted by the recently elected sheriffs, representatives from the guilds, and minstrels (exactly the kind of event that Perkyn leaps out of the shop to enjoy in the 'Cook's Tale').[119] The payment could alternatively refer to the sheriffs' own riding on the 30 September, an event which also involved music and display. Either way, it is clear that Usk was singled out as one of only a handful of men to accompany Bamme. It is also clear that Usk participated in a ceremonial riding, testament to his knowledge of guild culture and civic display and a further example of how the world in which Usk lived consistently linked sociopolitical success to cultural performance and display. All of the others named here either had been or went on to be Warden of the Goldsmiths' company, so they were an important group of people.[120] Seeing Usk in their company reminds us of the level of success that he achieved at this time. It is also likely that Bamme handpicked him to accompany him, and as Usk (unlike the others) was not an important goldsmith, there must have been some reason for this. Perhaps Bamme got to know him through their mutual connection with Northampton; perhaps he himself patronized him and took a special interest in the scribe. If that is the case, his interest was rather badly repaid when Usk named and shamed him in his *Appeal*.

In Usk's *Appeal*, Bamme is mentioned six times. John Northampton, John More, William Essex, and Richard Norbury are marked out as the worst offenders, but Bamme comes next, repeatedly associated with their dark dealings and factional machinations. Usk's first four references to Bamme group him with More, Norbury, and Essex attending meetings, muttering seditiously, and forcing the election of Northampton. Usk emphasises Bamme's perfidious associations, for instance:

[118] *Wardens' Accounts*, pp. 208–09.

[119] See Lancashire, *London Civic Theatre*, pp. 52–54.

[120] Walsh was Warden 1372–73, Louthe 1397–98, 1402–03, Castre 1367–68, 1381–82, Carbonelle 1373–74, 1377–78, 1382–83, 1392–93, 1401–02, Raynham 1356–57, 1367–68, 1370–71, 1374–75, 1380–81.

> Also, a-yeins the forseyde seconde eleccion, [ther] was made mochel ordinance be John More, Richard Norbury, Adam Bamme, William Essex, & many a[lso] mo, & be me Thomas Usk, to make ful [certei]n the comunes atte that day shulde chese the forseyde John Northampton to be mair. (ll. 60–63)

Bamme is characterized as deeply enmeshed in Northampton's circle. Toward the end of the *Appeal*, however, Usk's heart softens toward his associate and colleague, and his final references to Bamme seek to exculpate him, as Usk twice explicitly mitigates Bamme's guilt. He writes that 'Adam Bamme, sithen that he was noght mair, that I wot of, hath noght entremeted hym' (ll. 155–56) — in other words that Bamme has disentangled himself since Northampton lost the mayoralty and has not been fomenting rebellion against Brembre. Usk also favourably compares Bamme with the others, writing that 'truly, Adam Bame was noght so comunly, ne so bysy on thys purpos [& confederaci]es as [wer] the tother' (ll. 169–70). Bamme is thus constructed as a lukewarm supporter of the cause, who backed off and saw the error of his ways. It is possible that Usk realized he could not ignore Bamme's role, or was not allowed to do so, but did what he could to soften his accusations.

Changing sides as Usk did in 1384 was hardly unusual, and Bamme himself is an instructive example here. In the 1370s Bamme and his fellow goldsmith Nicholas Twyford opposed the grocers and fishmongers headed by men such as Exton, Walworth, Philipot, Brembre, and Carlisle, and in 1378 Bamme stood surety for Twyford in the latter's violent stand-off with Brembre.[121] It is unsurprising, then, that in the 1380s Bamme supported Northampton. But it seems that, as Usk's *Appeal* suggests, Bamme lost enthusiasm for the cause when he saw which way the wind was blowing. After Brembre's election, which deprived Northampton of the mayoralty, Northampton's supporters gathered and marched through London. Brembre heard this news while at Sir Richard Waldegrave's house with Walworth, Philipot, and Bamme, his erstwhile opponent.[122] Bamme's new allegiance prospered, and his position was unaffected by Brembre's death. In fact, the deaths of his new friends tended to benefit him, as he ultimately married Philipot's widow and took over some of Brembre's confiscated estates. His marriage, indeed (which probably took place in 1392), demonstrates his position within this group and also secured that position. He became the fourth husband of Margaret Stodeye, descendent of Sir John Gisors, a notable London merchant,

---

[121] Bird, *Turbulent London*, p. 29; Nightingale, *Medieval Mercantile*, p. 256.

[122] Bird, *Turbulent London*, p. 83.

oligarch, and advisor to princes. Margaret's sister Idonia was Brembre's widow. Margaret herself, as Philipot's widow, had great wealth and status, and her connection to Brembre allowed Bamme to gain control of his confiscated Kentish manors.[123] Bamme managed to effect a smooth, effective, highly successful transition from Northampton partisan to heir to Brembre, with seemingly no ill effects. He went on to be mayor twice in the 1390s.

Bamme's example demonstrates that switching sides, and bearing Brembre company as a new intimate in the mid-1380s, did not inevitably have fatal effects. His position was in many ways different from Usk's: Usk was less socially important than Bamme and could thus easily be scapegoated; he was also foolishly overzealous in each cause that he espoused.[124] But, more crucially, Usk made himself vulnerable because he wrote things down. The *Appeal* is only the most obvious example of this. Usk seems never to have just turned up for meetings or to have given vague oral promises; he was always taking notes and committing himself through writing — and he was obliged to do this in order to earn his living. Northampton's use of bills had been a new strategy in London civic politics and must have been successful as Brembre swiftly copied it and issued his own English proclamations.[125] Usk was a scribe specifically employed to write Northampton's bills (*Appeal*, l. 8). In this era, scribes could not claim that they were merely following orders, copying texts out slavishly. The blurred boundary between scriveners and lawyers exemplifies the fact that scriveners were expected to think about the texts that they wrote. The fact that scriveners were sent to the pillory for forgery during this time demonstrates that they were held responsible for their writings.[126] Usk's next textual foray, the production of the *Appeal*, committed him absolutely to his course of action. Not only was it reckless to burn his bridges quite so dramatically but he also, as Strohm writes, 'ceased to be necessary to the Brembre faction *precisely at the moment when he reduced his*

---

[123] Carole Rawcliffe, 'Margaret Stodeye, Lady Philipot (d. 1431)', in *Medieval London Widows, 1300–1500*, ed. by Caroline M. Barron and Anne F. Sutton (London, 1994), pp. 85–98, especially pp. 93–95.

[124] Strohm's comment that in writing the *Testament of Love* Usk 'seized on the genre of *consolatio* in a hectic, transformative, and ultimately destabilizing way' sums up Usk's political and narrative strategies more generally. Strohm, 'Politics and Poetics', p. 111.

[125] Caroline Barron and Laura Wright, 'The London Middle English Guild Certificates of 1388-89', *Nottingham Medieval Studies*, 39 (1995), 108–45 (p. 114, n. 32).

[126] H. T. Riley, *Memorials of London and London Life* (London, 1868), pp. 333–35, 527–29. See also Turner, 'Conflict'.

testimony to writing.[127] Once Usk had written down his case, the writing could stand in for him (as it did, in court) and that writing could be changed (as it was, into the later versions of his *Appeal*). We might also reflect that the version of the *Testament* that we read today may bear witness to the fear that the power of writing can inspire — it seems to have been butchered to remove certain political statements.[128] Gower was, of course, far more circumspect and less vulnerable than Usk in general, but he also managed to maintain control over his work, altering it to fit his changing views and the changing political context.[129] Usk's *Testament*, like his *Appeal*, was at the mercy of politically self-interested readers and editors. In Fredric Jameson's terms, Usk's voice has been partly 'reduced to silence', partly 'reappropriated [...] by the hegemonic culture'.[130]

The scribal role that placed Usk at the intersection of so many cultural and political worlds and opened up opportunities for him to associate with and assist diverse powerful men in London and Westminster also in itself made him an object of suspicion, and an easy target. Being a scribe was a dangerous job in the 1380s; in 1388 many clerks were suspected or punished for their association with documentary culture. Carrying letters, for instance, could be enough to merit punishment; Douglas Biggs has written about the 'unfocused fury' and 'vindictiveness' focused on minor officials and clerks on the part of the Merciless Parliament, adding that this aggression instilled 'great fear among the clerks of the writing offices'.[131] This specific scapegoating of clerkly officials caused Usk's

---

[127] Strohm, *Hochon's Arrow*, p. 158, emphasis his.

[128] Shoaf suggests that 'the part of the manuscript containing Book 3 was deliberately mutilated in order to erase the name of Usk and any possible allusion to Richard II; this mutilation was a Lancastrian agenda, like the obliteration of Richard's portrait from Bodley MS 581 [...] and its motive was the new regime's systematic desire to legitimate itself' (*Testament*, ed. by Shoaf, p. 22). Summers supports this idea (*Late-Medieval Prison Writing*, pp. 51–52).

[129] For Gower's 'rolling revisions', see M. B. Parkes, 'Patterns of Scribal Activity and Revisions of the Text in Early Copies of Works by John Gower', in *New Science Out of Old Books: Studies in Manuscripts and Early Printed Books in Honour of A. I. Doyle*, ed. by Richard Beadle and A. J. Piper (Aldershot, 1995), pp. 81–121, especially pp. 82–84.

[130] Fredric Jameson, *The Political Unconscious: Narrative as a Socially Symbolic Act* (London, 1983), p. 71.

[131] In Chancery, Parliament, and at court too writing was becoming increasingly dangerous. See Douglas Biggs, 'The Appellant and the Clerk: The Assault on Richard II's Friends in Government 1387–89', in *The Reign of Richard II*, ed. by Gwilym Dodd (Stroud, 2000), pp. 57–70, quotations at pp. 65 and 66. He comments on the novelty of condemning to imprisonment or death 'the most insignificant officials within central government' (p. 69).

downfall. When Usk was accused and condemned to death in Parliament, his principal crime was that he had had made 'faux enditementz et atteyndres' (false indictments and attainders).[132] In the same article, John Ripon, another clerk, was accused of carrying 'lettres de credence' (letters of credence) which were then to be used to further a malicious plot against Gloucester and others. Usk and Ripon were clearly held to be responsible for the contents of these documents; their vulnerable position as paid junior employees was not considered. Both men were clerks, condemned for their involvement with documents, and both died for this involvement. One of the most interesting aspects of Usk's career as a professional go-between is his familiarity with diverse kinds of texts and with various cultural environments, but it was this very involvement with writing and its transmission that caused his death. Being a scrivener was a risky business.

Conclusions

In the late fourteenth century, the Goldsmiths were self-consciously constructing themselves as sponsors and producers of culture and hospitality, and their use of writing and regular employment of a clerk helped them to record and to encourage reproduction of what they had done. Owning account books, employing clerks, and self-fashioning through keeping and maintaining records were new aspects of guild life at this time. Like the acquisition of halls, this commitment to writing stabilized and enhanced the position of the great livery companies — they could demonstrate that they had a history (which was written down and could be consulted)[133] as well as a geography (the tangible and impressive hall itself). And indeed, while the golden cups, the badges, the costumes, and even the buildings have vanished almost without trace, many of the written records remain, detailing the extent of the company's cultural world, and (inadvertently) revealing that canonical Ricardian literature was embedded in this world from the time of its production. The literary activities of the scribes employed by the Goldsmiths and their fellow great livery companies reveal to us a new aspect of late-fourteenth-century literary culture; these clerks formed a conduit between the livery companies and the writings of men such as Chaucer and Gower.

---

[132] 'Richard II: Parliament of October, 1385', in *Parliament Rolls*, III, 234.

[133] The great merchants in London also had control over city chronicles and annals; see Meale, '*Libelle*', p. 200.

While these scribes were crucial links in these cultural networks, they were also weak points in the chain, vulnerable to attack and injury. Although writing was increasingly important in the later Middle Ages,[134] it and its practitioners were also increasingly viewed with suspicion, and Usk was never able adequately to protect himself.[135] Usk states a supposed belief in the truth and power of writings through the words of Love in Book I of the *Testament*: 'For bookes written neyther dreden ne shamen ne stryve conne, but onely shewen the entente of the writer and yeve remembraunce to the herer' (I. 2. 235–36). He here claims that books cannot be cowed; they stand forth with the simplicity of truth demonstrating a transparent intent and communicating a writer's meaning directly to the hearer's mind. The philosophical and material naivety of such a position is clear — all the more so if we remember how the text of the *Testament* has been pulled about and altered, possibly cut for political reasons, attributed to Chaucer, and read as a confession of Lollardy.[136] Usk's dubious statement also elides the fact that all too often he wrote what others told him to write, or what he imagined others wanted to hear. Writing was never straightforward or uncompromised for Usk (nor, indeed, is it for anyone). Indeed, his writing was always strategic. The evidence suggests that Usk believed strongly (too strongly, more strongly than others) in the material cultural world in which he lived, a world in which writing was part of a cultural act (alongside the materiality of the book itself and its function as a gift, for instance) and cultural acts were also economic and rooted in exchange. In this world, culture was bonded to work and to commerce: it could help you get ahead. Usk committed himself through texts when others slipped away, hedged their bets, and prevaricated (both Bamme and Chaucer did this successfully, but in different ways). Usk's praise of pearls, his imagining himself as a piece of sterling silver, his overt support for political strategies of gifting, his belief that his texts would win rewards for him, reveal a deep faith in culture as a political tool. Knowing about Usk's affiliation with the livery companies' cultural environment helps us to understand this attitude and provides a window on a world in which things of beauty were firmly and strategically embedded in political and commercial ambition.

Jesus College, Oxford

---

[134] See Michael Clanchy, *From Memory to Written Record: England 1066–1307* (Oxford, 1993).

[135] See Lindenbaum's comments on the 'local climate of hostility to clerkly writing' ('London Texts', p. 291).

[136] See *Testament,* ed. by Shoaf, p. 22, for the way the text has been altered. Thynne attributed the piece to Chaucer in his 1532 edition. For Usk as an apologetic Lollard, see *Chaucerian and Other Pieces*, ed. by Walter W. Skeat (Oxford, 1897), p. xxiv.

Symposium I.

Can You Be a Comparatist in Translation?

This symposium originally took place as a panel program arranged by the Division on Comparative Studies in Medieval Literature and organized by Jeanette Beer for the 122nd Modern Language Association in Philadelphia on 28 December 2006. The informal style of the original panel has been retained.

THE STATE OF THE QUESTION

Jeanette Beer

The question is of course loaded, and no unqualified response will do. Leaving aside for the moment the tendentious question 'What makes the ideal comparatist?' and the impossible question 'What constitutes the perfect translation?' one is bound to answer 'yes' just because it is being done. But what is being done? by whom? to whom? for whom? how? and why? If the answers to any of these questions prove to be problematic, the purist will immediately opt for a negative response to the initial question or, at least, to a reformulation of it to '*Should* you be a comparatist in translation?'

The Modern Language Association provides some useful background information about what is currently being done by American students of comparative literature at the undergraduate level. The 2005 report of the Association of Departments and Programs of Comparative Literature on the undergraduate comparative literature curriculum gives the results of a survey that was administered to the one hundred schools currently granting a B.A. in comparative literature. (The response rate was 40 per cent.) For the curriculum for the major, the most common requirements were 'some type of proficiency in a language other than English (required by 90.5 percent of schools with requirements), courses that focus on literary analysis (90.5 percent), and courses on literary theory (81.0 percent)'.[1] The phrase '*some type of* proficiency' (my emphasis) is vague enough to be disquieting. But the report goes on to say (p. 181) that some three-quarters of schools require advanced proficiency in a language other than English for the major, while 11 per cent require more than one

---

[1] '2005 Report on the Undergraduate Comparative Literature Curriculum', *Profession* (2006), 177–96 (p. 180).

language (plus English) and 80.5 per cent require a literature course taught in a language other than English. And it concludes:

> [T]he foreign (or second-) language component long associated with comparative literature and thus the field's commitment to studying selected texts and cultures in their own words have definitely been preserved. In this way, comparative literature is related to foreign language curricula and is distinct from English or cultural studies curricula, which rarely have substantial language requirements. In English or cultural studies curricula, when foreign language works are assigned, they are generally assigned only in translation, usually without any expectation that students will read the work in the original. (p. 189)

These observations highlight an ongoing debate concerning the administration of comparative literature which became a departmental 'discipline' in the American sixties. The committee calls the NCES's decision to move comparative literature from English Language and Literature/Letters to Foreign Languages, Literatures, and Linguistics 'felicitous, as the new designation better reflects how comparative literature sees and defines itself' (p. 189). But that decision hardly reflects the heterogeneous reality of the situation whether in the United States or worldwide. For example, Comparative Literature does not exist per se in Oxford, and British universities usually offer Modern Languages rather than Comparative Literature because of a probably legitimate objection to literature in translation. There are one or two comparative literature programmes in the newer universities, for example, Sussex, York, and Warwick. In France Pierre Brunel's Institut de littérature comparée springs to mind (Paris IV) as well as several programs in Littérature générale et comparée throughout France, not forgetting the classics-to-contemporary American-style comparative literature program at the American University of Paris. But what's in a name? Chrétien de Troyes, Jean de Meun, Chaucer, Dante, and Petrarch all explored and exploited the relation between Latin and the vernacular. And the medieval giants Curtius, Spitzer, C. S. Lewis, and, more recently, S. S. Prawer were nothing if not comparatist, because the philological method in which they were trained was comparative by nature.

The key issue in our present discussion remains, then, the growing reliance of comparative studies upon translation, concerning which the MLA report concludes:

> While comparative literature programs continue to encourage substantial language study among majors, a significant and probably growing portion of works must be studied in translation. An encouraging finding from the data is that some three-quarters of respondents say that they and their colleagues use translations critically—an encouraging finding, if critical use means more than simply remarking on a translation's critical errors or infelicities. Few programs yet offer (and fewer still require) courses in the theory and

practice of translation; we can hope that such courses will increase steadily in the coming years. (pp. 191–92)

It is clear that the 2006 report aims to be positive and to encourage optimism (note the triple use of 'encourage' in its concluding paragraph!). It also hints at a possible linking of comparative literature to translation studies. And a valid interpretation of the question 'Can you be a comparatist in translation?' although not treated by the panel is 'Can you be a comparatist of translations?'

The report is not all sweetness and light, however. It makes clear that the level of language expertise of the practitioners of comparative literature, whether they be students or teachers, could potentially be troubling for the future of the discipline, and any decline in this level of expertise will have disturbing consequences, not least for comparative literature *medieval*. Currently we are living off our patrimony. And if nothing is done to preserve and renew it, the next generation may know the 'textual past' (as one of the panelists calls it) only through translation.

And what about 2017 and 2027? Can the text survive the multiple dangers posed by its multiple translators and interpreters as they re-create in their own image, so many angels dancing on the head of a pin? A perceptive article by Karine Zbinden on the Bakhtin Circle discusses the 'normative force' of adapting the source-text to a target readership's contemporary contextual knowledge and current preoccupations:

> In addition to making the translated text instantly accessible and marketable [...], it also has the advantage of making the translated text immediately relevant and, perhaps more significantly, of opening up new perspectives in the original work, enriching it, contesting it, revitalizing it.[2]

But the dangers of such 'revitalization' are obvious, and Zbinden includes Caryl Emerson's comment at the same conference that 'Bakhtin studies in the West might have to be entirely revised as better translations of his work become available' (p. 157).

Of course, a masterwork becomes 'canonical' when it continues to say something to successive generations over the centuries. But can the medieval text survive if its interpreters, never having read it, function in total independence of it and are incapable of reading it, let alone assessing the quality of its editions or its translations? Demythologized, detheologized, colonized, postcolonialized,

---

[2] Karine Zbinden, 'The Bakhtin Circle and Translation', *Yearbook of English Studies*, 36.1 (2006), 157–67 (p. 157).

commodified, postmodernized, regendered, queered, psychoanalyzed, and deconstructed, can it, like the lodestar, continue to shine through the mists that successively pass across it, clarifying/obfuscating it? If not, will the 2016 Modern Language Association (then to be called the 'Modern Translation Association') sponsor a panel entitled 'Can You Be a Comparatist of Translations?'

Lady Margaret Hall, and
St Hilda's College, Oxford University

ACTS OF TRANSLATION

Robert M. Stein

Es ist notwendig, den Begriff der Übersetzung in der tiefsten Schicht der Sprachtheorie zu begründen, denn er ist viel zu weittragend und gewaltig, um in irgendeiner Hinsicht nachträglich, wie bisweilen gemeint wird, abgehandelt werden zu können.

(It is important to ground the concept of translation at the deepest level of linguistic theory, because it is much too far-reaching and powerful to treat it in any way as supplementary, as is sometimes thought.)[1]

My first response, when Jeanette Beer asked me the question 'Can you be a comparatist in translation?' was 'you'd better be or you'll be out of a job!' But, of course, this complex question requires a much more complex answer, one which demands that we interrogate all its terms and also the history that both raises the question and of course already has given us the theoretically proper and rhetorically demanded answer — no — that makes my first response a species of cynical irony or a joke.

In 1994 the decennial report of the American Comparative Literature Association was happily titled *Comparative Literature in the Age of Multiculturalism*;[2] the 2004 report was the more edgy *Comparative Literature in an Age of Globalization*.[3] The globalization predominantly in question here concerns the reach of global capital, the clearing away of obstacles political, economic, and cultural to its

---

[1] Walter Benjamin, 'Über Sprache überhaupt und über die Sprache des Menschen', in *Gesammelte Schriften*, ed. by Rolf Tiedemann and Hermann Schweppenhäuser (Frankfurt a.M., 1972), p.151; my translation.

[2] *Comparative Literature in the Age of Multiculturalism*, ed. by Charles Bernheimer (Baltimore, 1995).

[3] *Comparative Literature in an Age of Globalization*, ed. by Haun Saussy (Baltimore, 2006).

deepest penetration, and the consequent redistribution of inequalities within the universalizing realm of globalized financial interchange.[4] The literary reflex of this whole process is the proliferation of 'world literature in translation' anthologies as textbooks for Comparative Literature classes (or for Comp. Lit's evil twin, Cultural Studies). Publishers, themselves ever more swallowed up in international conglomerates, have a great deal at stake in standardizing the university curriculum, making it a predictable field within which to market their anthologies for course adoptions and ever new upgrades.

Would comparative literature be so desirous of global inclusions without the pressures of the global publishing market? I have no intention of side-stepping this question by suggesting that the proper object of comparative literary study is *literaturnost'*, a kind of transnational literariness many of whose particulars can easily migrate from one language to another. In the context of global capitalism, there may be new reasons for comparatists to opt for a kind of strategic essentialism, and identify strongly with the demands for the primacy of the study of language. This demand is a residual formation which once was the property of Eurocentric cultural conservatism; it now may well already be radically oppositional.[5] Comparative literature, that great orphan within the disciplinary structure of our universities, comes naturally to medievalists, the other orphans. For the departmental structures of our universities that often provide only grudging shelter to medievalists are organized directly by the idea of national languages, national literatures, and national history. This disciplinary organization still rests directly on the fundamental, even if now highly contested, assumption of philology: namely, that the essential ethnic characteristics of a nation are embodied most profoundly in the deepest characteristics of its

---

[4] For some brave reflections on the implications of global financial capital and the standardization of the curriculum, see especially Haun Saussy, 'Exquisite Cadavers Stitched from Fresh Nightmares: Of Memes, Hives, and Selfish Genes', in *Comparative Literature in an Age of Globalization*, pp. 3–42,

[5] Cf. Gayatri Chakravorty Spivak, *Death of a Discipline*, Wellek Library Lecture Series at the University of California, Irvine (New York, 2003), p. 9: 'The new step I am proposing [...] would work to make the traditional linguistic sophistication of Comparative Literature supplement Area Studies (and history, anthropology, political theory, and sociology) by approaching the language of the other not only as a "field" language. In the field of literature, we need to move from Anglophony, Lusophony, Teutophony, Francophony, et cetera. We must take the languages of the Southern Hemisphere as active cultural media rather than as objects of cultural study by the sanctioned ignorance of the metropolitan migrant. We cannot dictate a model for this from the offices of the American Comparative Literature Association.'

language. In these linguistic characteristics the truth of the nation progressively realizes itself and becomes most profoundly manifest in its literature and in its law. Philology is thus the sister discipline of the kind of philosophical history that since the time of the early German romantic writers and especially since Hegel sees the formation of the secular state as the highest achievement of human culture.[6] The philological study of the language of literary works and legal texts thus intended to bring the truth of the nation to critical self-consciousness just as romantic philosophy of history saw this same truth embodied in the state. Philology, if you will allow me to say it this way, recapitulates an ontology.

Philology so construed requires the identification of the state with the nation, an imaginary structure that maps political sovereignty onto territories presumed to be ethnically and linguistically homogenous. We have not yet escaped the fact that the study of national literatures emerged during the period of high imperialism. During this period the linguistic and ethnic purity of the European national state was taken to be the sign both of its rationality and its modernity, and it granted Europe its *mission civilisatrice* and authorized its right to rule.

The imperial narrative maintains that the division of the world into ethnically and linguistically bordered national states began in Europe when the 'not yet modern' medieval associations coalesced into the early-modern state, and thence spread by the 'modernizing' and 'civilizing' imperial project to the polyglot, lawless, disorderly world of the darker races, the races 'without history' who needed to be ruled and dragged into modernity.[7] Hence, for medieval literary

---

[6] Erich Auerbach was extremely aware of the debt of his own work to Hegel and German Romanticism as well as to Vico. In the 'Epilegomena to Mimesis', he writes that *Mimesis* would be 'inconceivable in no other tradition than in that of German romanticism and Hegel (in *Mimesis*, trans. by Willard R. Trask (Princeton, 2003), p. 571 (first publ. in German in *Romanische Forschungen*, 65 (1953), pp. 1–18)). It would never have been written without the influences that I experienced in my youth in Germany'. See also the brilliant analysis of the work of Auerbach and its reception in America in Paul Bové, *Intellectuals in Power: A Genealogy of Critical Humanism* (New York, 1986). For the importance of Vico see Edward W. Said, *Beginnings: Intention and Method* (New York, 1975; repr. 1985); Erich Auerbach, 'Giovambattista Vico E L'idea Della Filologia', *Convivium*, 4 (1956), 394–403.

[7] The process is by no means over. The Medieval Academy Annual Conference, Spring 2000, Austin, Texas, devoted a session to examining whether Middle English is a creole. The answer was a definite no — in fact, the answer was a no in thunder — and emotions ran very much higher than one would ever expect to find in response to a panel presentation using quantitative historical linguistic methodology. For further discussion of the relations between medieval studies and its imperial history, see Robert M. Stein, *Reality Fictions: Romance, History, and Governmental Authority, 1025–1180* (Notre Dame, 2006).

studies, the great privilege granted to writing in the European vernaculars: they were presumed to contain the national soul in its most direct manifestation. Indeed, in the birth of national literary studies, the medieval vernaculars occupied the same intellectual slot as Greek and Latin had done in the pan-European humanist curriculum. Thus the sense of the natural alliance between medieval studies and comparative literature, too, is haunted by the imperial ghost bequeathed it by philology. Desiring to seize rationality directly, in the name of a certain universal humanity, and to free the aesthetic consciousness from the shackles of national particularity, comparative literature proceeds like a medieval alchemist, by multiplication of particulars, and preserves national boundaries in the act of comparison even as it would transgress them in theory, and it institutionalizes a certain European cultural hegemony in its discourse even as it disavows both the significance of that discourse and the American exceptionalism that is its global reflex.

But can you be a comparatist in translation? The Italians say, *traduttore traditore*. And all medievalists know that translation is never a one-way street, never merely utilitarian, secondary, a step away from the betrayed original.[8] Translation is a permanent disturbance in the linguistic field.

We cannot, therefore, fail to be comparatists in translation even as we read in multiple languages, for we inhabit our own polyglot milieu in which linguistic transactions across borders never cease even as we study a perhaps even more radically polyglot literary reality. Galbert de Bruges's late-medieval vernacular translator translates the characterization of Baldwin VII, 'adolescens fortissimus', as 'encore jeusne homme tres vaillant' and thus subjects Latin canons of public virtue to chivalric conceptions of feudal honour.[9] The private here changes places with the public sphere. And what if Galbert, presumably Francophone, was

---

[8] The early German romantics, Novalis and Friedrich Schlegel, voice this sense throughout their writings. Walter Benjamin's important preface to his translations of Baudelaire, 'Die Aufgabe der Übersetzer' is perhaps its most well known articulation. But see also his 'Über Sprache überhaupt': 'Seine volle Bedeutung [d.h. der Übersetzung] gewinnt er in der Einsicht, dass jede höhere Sprache (mit Ausnahme des Wortes Gottes) als Übersetzung aller anderen betrachtet werden kann' (The full significance of translation is gained in the insight that each higher language (with the exception of the word of God) can be considered as the translation of all the others), edited by Walter Benjamin, Rolf Tiedemann, and Hermann Schweppenhäuser, in *Gesammelte Schriften*, 1. Aufl. edn, 7 vols (Frankfurt a.M., 1972–89), II, pt 1, 151; my translation.

[9] Galbert de Bruges, *De multro, traditione, et occisione gloriosi Karoli comitis Flandiarum*, ed. by Jeff Rider, Corpus Christianorum Continuatio Mediaevalis, 131 (Turnhout, 1994), pp. 4–5.

thinking 'encore jeusne homme tres vaillant' even as he wrote 'adolescens fortissimus'?

In the extremely complex arena of linguistic interchange, England after 1066, with its shifting privileging of French and Latin as languages of record, and its porous borders among the vernaculars of French, English, Danish, and the Celtic languages of the indigenous population, each language having its own multiplicity of registers, is perhaps more typical of medieval Europe than not. Acts of translation are unavoidable because they are everywhere, from the sphere of high literature to the everyday activities of notarial recording, sermon composition, and the public reading of proclamations.[10] Geoffrey of Monmouth's Latin prose *Historia regum Britanniae*, within one generation, is available in the French octosyllabics of Wace's *Brut*, and the deliberately archaized English of Lawman. And Lawman's archaic alliterative verse is to be found in the same multilingual manuscript, Cotton Caligula A. ix., with the elegantly octosyllabic English rhyme of *The Owl and the Nightingale*, presented in an unmistakably French *mise en page*. Every choice to speak one way is a choice not to speak otherwise; every utterance is not only dialogized internally but haunted by its other.

That the unquestioned confidence in the truth of philology has vanished utterly is a pregnant moment in the history of globalization. At an earlier moment in that history, one dreamed optimistically of another ancestor of comparative literature, a *Weltliteratur*, a huge library of ethnic and national diversities conversing together polyphonically in a multitude of languages that demonstrated the richness of human experience and the vast range of human possibility contained fully in no one national linguistic confines.[11] A revisionary comparative literature stands at a place where its version of the past can no longer imply a preordained future. Yet perhaps the beginnings of its awareness of the multiple perspectives opened by the continuous, fluid, polyglot circulation of

---

[10] For a thorough discussion of postconquest multilinguality see M. T. Clanchy, *From Memory to Written Record: England, 1066–1307* (Cambridge, MA, 1979). See also Robert M. Stein, 'Multilingualism', in *Twenty-First Century Approaches to Literature: Middle English*, ed. by Paul Strohm (Oxford, 2007), pp. 23–27, from which much of this brief essay is adapted.

[11] Contemporary reflections on the Goethean notion of *Weltliteratur* run throughout the most important work of Edward Said. See especially the posthumously published, Edward W. Said, *Humanism and Democratic Criticism*, Columbia Themes in Philosophy (New York, 2004). See also Emily S. Apter, *The Translation Zone: A New Comparative Literature*, Translation/Transnation (Princeton, 2005).

expression and representation in the past might allow it to hear a new and as yet unheard whisper from the world yet to come, to begin to create a knowledge new enough that one cannot know before it has arrived what it might be or where it might lead.

for Jacques Derrida *in memoriam*

Purchase College and Columbia University

TRANSLATING IN THE ZONE

Michelle R. Warren

The question of whether one can practice comparative literature in translation has become for me a matter of pedagogical survival. After spending years teaching French language and literature, I recently began teaching in a comparative literature program — where all of my courses are offered in English with texts available in English (the majority of them translated from other languages). This situation reflects the long-established practice of comparative literature as a discipline in the United States, where the erudite tradition of scholarly multilingualism confronts the narrower linguistic experience of undergraduate students. The same situation occurs in medieval studies: published scholarship reveals deep currents of multilingual learning, while pedagogical practice relies extensively on translations even of Middle English (not to mention Latin, Old French, Welsh, etc.) into Modern English. Indeed, many students experience the Middle Ages solely in translation. But can one be a medievalist in translation? Instinctively, most if not all medievalists would answer *no*: too much labour in learning, too many historical and cultural nuances, too much of the 'medieval' itself would be lost to a medieval studies practised solely in translation. And yet today's multilingual professionals were all once students — and like today's students, most encountered the textual past in translation.

And so instead of answering *no* to comparative literature in translation, I wish to answer an emphatic *yes*. There would be no comparative literature without translation; in fact, comparative literature was born in and from translation. Similarly, medieval studies owes many things to translated texts. Medieval comparative studies are thus doubly freighted with complex translation issues. Of course, accepting translation does not mean licensing all manner of irresponsible pillaging in the misunderstood foreign. Rather, it can structure a theoretically cognizant approach to the linguistic and cultural diversity of literary life in the past and the present (involving both reading and writing, of and about literature).

The challenge for comparative literature is not *whether* to work in translation but *how* — how to press the various artefacts that we take as 'sources' with questions that each is uniquely equipped to answer. Rather than accepting the traditional (modernist) aesthetic that teaches us to value 'originals' over copies, or the postmodern inversion that invites us to prioritize the margins, we can dispense with hierarchical metaphors altogether and instead seek to identify the critical and cultural range of any given textual manifestation — asking certain questions of manuscripts, others of electronic editions ... and others of translations. Just as new media do not displace manuscripts or printed books with greater 'accuracy', the relation between translations and their sources can be rendered more supple and varied: rather than replacing the translation of first experience with the 'original' of professional practice (and which original do we mean: the manuscript? an edition? which edition?), each can serve according to circumstance and question. Translations, like editions, condition the scholarship of medieval studies and comparative literature alike (not to mention the production of medieval literature itself). Without them, there would certainly be no *medieval* comparative literature (and very little medieval literature at all). Integrated into theoretical discourse and our understanding of past and present, translations can ground a comparative literature that deviates from specious quests for origins and originals, that commits instead to more precarious balancing acts among texts in any number of languages. Translations have much to offer cultural criticism when we are imaginative enough to press them with questions they can answer. By demystifying the translated and untranslated artefact alike, we also critically resist the imperialist overtones of insisting on only 'pure', 'untainted' texts.[1]

To structure some further thoughts on comparative literature in translation, I would like to draw on some of the arguments of Emily Apter's recent book *The Translation Zone*.[2] Apter's book joins a broader trend of calls to reinvigorate comparative literature by placing it in dialogue with translation studies.[3] Apter

[1] This paragraph adapts for translation my arguments in 'Post-Philology', *Postcolonial Moves: Medieval through Modern*, ed. by Patricia Clare Ingham and Michelle R. Warren (New York, 2003), pp. 19–45.

[2] Emily Apter, *The Translation Zone: A New Comparative Literature* (Princeton, 2006).

[3] *Comparative Literature in the Age of Multiculturalism*, ed. by Charles Bernheimer (Baltimore, 1995); *Comparative Literature in the Age of Globalization*, ed. by Haun Saussy (Baltimore, 2006);

meditates on the roles of translation in the twentieth-century history of comparative literature and also in the discipline's twenty-first century future. While Apter's studies of contemporary global translation may not bear directly on medieval comparative literature, her attention to the foundational figures Leo Spitzer and Erich Auerbach make portions of her arguments particularly pertinent to medieval studies. Spitzer and Auerbach both published influential studies of individual works of medieval literature from throughout the European tradition, while demonstrating the fundamental roles of linguistics in literary study.[4]

In relation to the history of comparative literature, Apter looks most closely at the experiences of Spitzer in Turkey. She argues that despite vigorous claims to the contrary, comparative literature as conceived by Spitzer included translation from the beginning. Apter hinges this argument ultimately on Spitzer's reflections on learning Turkish, published in Turkish in the journal *Varlig* in 1934. Spitzer discerned in the grammatical sequencing of Turkish, which marks what is happening as it happens, what Apter paraphrases as 'a habit of self-questioning that initiated an othering of self within subjectivity'; the term *gibi* 'signaled the speaker's loss of conviction in his own words'. Apter then quotes Spitzer in English translation: 'Words no longer signify a definite event but carry the ambiguity of comparison within them.' In Apter's interpretation, '*gibi* [...] called attention to how each word internalizes comparability'.[5] Spitzer thus identifies how comparison enters language at the lexical level. By pluralizing even monolingual expression, Spitzer's comments open a place for a translational definition of philology. Apter goes on to compare Spitzer's reflections on Turkish with Said's on Arabic.[6] Similarly to Spitzer, Said finds the aporia of

---

Gayatri Chakravorty Spivak, *Death of a Discipline* (New York, 2003); *Nation, Language, and the Ethics of Translation*, ed. by Sandra Bermann and Michael Wood (Princeton, 2005); David Damrosch, *What Is World Literature?* (Princeton, 2003).

[4] Geoffrey Green, *Literary Criticism and the Structures of History: Erich Auerbach and Leo Spitzer* (Lincoln, 1982); *Literary History and the Challenge of Philology: The Legacy of Erich Auerbach*, ed. by Seth Lerer (Stanford, 1996); Paul Zumthor, 'Erich Auerbach, ou l'éloge de la philologie', *Littérature*, 5 (1972), 107–16; William Calin, 'Makers of the Middle Ages: Leo Spitzer', *Journal of Medieval and Early Modern Studies*, 27 (1997), 495–506. And both, of course, taught in Istanbul: see Azade Seyhan, 'German Academic Exiles in Istanbul: Translation as the *Bildung* of the Other', in *Nation, Language, and the Ethics of Translation* (see n. 3, above), pp. 274–88 (my thanks to Robert Stein for bringing this article to my attention).

[5] Apter, *The Translation Zone*, pp. 248–49.

[6] Edward Said, *Humanism and Democratic Criticism* (New York, 2004), pp. 57–84.

comparison in the 'space of words'; as such, according to Apter, 'Saidian-Spitzerian philology portends the advent of a translational humanism that assumes the disciplinary challenges posed by Turkish and Arabic in their respective circumstances of institutional exile.'[7] In comparative literature's earliest and most recent moments, then, individual words themselves bring translational logic into literary interpretation. Through the fractured multilingualism wrought by exile, comparative literature opens paths toward various kinds of translational multiculturalism.

I would argue further that Spitzer's explicit discussions of method also rely on translational models, even as they proclaim their commitments to 'original' sources. Spitzer clearly states his 'hallowed principle' of nontranslation, his 'plurilingual dogma',[8] in *Linguistics and Literary History*:

> The frequent occurrence, in my text, of quotations in the original foreign language (or languages) may prove a difficulty for the English reader. But since it is my purpose to take the word (and the wording) of the poets seriously, and since the convincingness and rigor of my stylistic conclusions depends entirely upon the minute linguistic detail of the original texts, it was impossible to offer translations.[9]

According to Apter, Spitzer's approach makes language acquisition a categorical imperative of *translatio studii*.[10] Spitzer's reflections on his own experience of learning to communicate in English in the United States in the preface to *Linguistics and Literary History*, however, emphasize the *translatio* dimension above all else:

> It is one of the benefits falling to the lot of the emigrant scholar that, however much his outward activity may be curtailed in the new country in comparison with his former situation, his inner activity is bound to be immensely enhanced and intensified: instead of writing as he pleases [...] he must, while trying to preserve his own idea of scholarship, continually count with his new audience, bearing in mind not only the conventional requirements but also those innermost strivings of the nation (inasmuch as it is given to him to feel them) which, opposed to his nature as they may have seemed to him in the beginning, tend imperceptibly to become a second nature to him—indeed, to shine by contrast his first nature in the clearest light. And, by so doing, he comes to feel enriched and to find that he has attained peace and happiness.[11]

---

[7] Apter, *The Translation Zone*, p. 249.

[8] Apter, *The Translation Zone*, pp. 61, 62.

[9] Leo Spitzer, *Linguistics and Literary History: Essays in Stylistics* (Princeton, 1948), p. 38, n. 16.

[10] Apter, *The Translation Zone*, p. 62.

[11] Spitzer, *Linguistics and Literary History*, pp. v–vi.

Here, in a tour de force of Germanic syntax, Spitzer sings the praises of the translational experience on all levels — geographic displacement, intercultural communication, multilingual expression, inner subjectivity. Comparative literature becomes nothing less than the path to blissful fulfilment. The happy and successful critic learns to love *two* languages and cultures, and from the comparison discovers the 'true nature' of what he thought he knew already.

Spitzer's overt commitment to the untranslated source, however, seems unwavering. In the conclusion of one of his last lectures, 'Development of a Method', he articulates a vision of multilingual experience that contrasts rather sharply with the comparative ecstasies expressed above:

> La filologia è l'*amore* per lavori scritti in una *lingua* particolare. E si i metodi di un critico devono essere applicabili ad opera in tutte le lingue, affinchè la critica convinca è necessario che, per lo meno *nel momento* in cui egli commenta un poema, ami *questa* lingua e *questo* poema più di qualsiasi altra cosa al mondo.[12]

> (Philology is the *love* for works written in a particular *language*. And if the methods of a critic must be applicable to works in all languages, in order that criticism be convincing, the critic, at least *at the moment* when he is discussing the poem, must love *that* language and *that* poem more than anything else in the world.)

Spitzer here affirms that convincing criticism depends on a monolingual mind-set — on the critic's ability to block out thoughts of comparison. As a critical ideal, this method imagines the critic relating to one language at a time (without acknowledgment, interference, or use of any other language); it nearly denies the possibility of comparative thought. At the very least, it marks comparison as an inferior mode of criticism. Apter concludes that Spitzer's 'credo of linguistic serial monogamy' deeply disturbs 'monolingual complacency' and its imperialist overtones; instead, Spitzer envisages a transnational humanism grounded in multilingualism.[13]

While the serial monolingual does engage with multiple languages, this approach entails some of the same risks as traditional monolingualism: an ethical stance against translation denies the possibility of communication across languages and cultures. As Apter argues elsewhere (not in relation to Spitzer), the denial of translational communication can lead to a 'false piety' of respect for the

---

[12] Spitzer, 'Sviluppo di un metodo', *Cultura neolatina*, 20 (1960), 109–28 (p.128); translated (with slightly different punctuation) in 'Development of a Method', in *Leo Spitzer: Representative Essays*, trans. by Eileen Reeves, ed. by Alban K. Forcione, Herbert Lindenberger, and Madeline Sutherland (Stanford, 1988), pp. 421–48 (p. 448).

[13] Apter, *The Translation Zone*, pp. 61, 62, 64.

untranslatable other — and thereby authorize an ignorance that also sustains imperialist complacency.[14] Spitzer's rejection of translation can thus lead to a linguistic politics as damaging as monolingualism. Reacting to this danger, Gayatri Spivak calls for a 'politics of translation', an ethical and aesthetic encounter with the 'other in translation'.[15] Spivak and Spitzer both address the places of language in subjectivity and politics, but from nearly opposite stances on translation. Ultimately, though, Spitzer's method implies (even as it denies) a translational engagement as fundamental as Spivak's. In this sense, Spitzerian and Spivakian translation can actually mediate between the extremes of belief in fully transparent translation and the impossibility of translation at all.

If translation has always already been the basis of comparative literature, as Apter argues, it also provides the basis for a radical new 'future'. The (hidden) operations of translation in the disciplinary history of comparative literature lead Apter to propose translation as the basis for a new comparative literature, fit for globalized communications in which linguistic understanding can mean the difference between life and death, peace and war. The principal benefit of this concept is that it decouples languages from the nations that bear their names, and vice versa: 'In naming a translational process constitutive of its disciplinary nomination comparative literature breaks the isomorphic fit between the name of a nation and the name of a language.' The conflation of languages and nations leads to power plays between languages that serve as proxy for political rivalries. By contrast, Apter proposes: 'A new comparative literature would acknowledge this jockeying for power and respect in the field of language. A new comparative literature seeks to be the name of language worlds characterized by linguistic multiplicity and phantom inter-nations.'[16] This approach is especially apt for medieval comparative studies, where the 'isomorphic fit' between languages and 'nations' is especially deforming — and also especially entrenched in disciplinary formations. Medievalist scholars, like their counterparts in more recent periods, generally work in institutions that define literary departments or units according to language names that are also nations — nations that do not define the literatures that may be expressed in the medieval forms of those languages.

---

[14] Apter, *The Translation Zone*, p. 91.

[15] Spivak, *Death of a Discipline*, pp. 18–19. Also (among others): Spivak, *Outside In the Teaching Machine* (New York, 1993), chap. 9, 'The Politics of Translation', pp. 179–200, and Spivak, 'Translating into English', in *Nation, Language, and the Ethics of Translation* (see n. 3, above), pp. 93–110.

[16] Apter, *The Translation Zone*, pp. 243, 244–45.

Placing translation studies in close dialogue with comparative literature, grounding comparative literature in translation, has the potential to expose the translational processes involved even in monolingual communication. This is the effect of Jacques Derrida's argument in *Le monolinguisme de l'autre*. As Apter summarizes it:

> Derrida's aporia deconstructs the nationalist nominalism of language names by locating an always-prior other within monolingual diction. The aporia loosens the national anchor from the language name, wedging a politics of the subject between the name of a nation and the name of a language.[17]

A translational comparative literature, in other words, challenges the putative monolingualism of national literatures (for example, the notion that all 'English' literature is in the same language). The effects of this approach touch all aspects of comparative literature, from teaching to professional research. What methods and theories of translation are at work in the monolingual classroom? How do these shape the kinds of interpretations considered convincing, or even considered possible? What does it mean to consider the reader a multilingual subject? If talking about even single-language literature means talking about translation, then how can we bring the dynamics of translation theory and practice to bear upon the task of vivifying medieval literature for new generations of students and future scholars? These readers might be native speakers of one of the Englishes wrought by anglophone globalization. Or they might come to English as non-native speakers or have more than one 'native' language. Whatever the case may be, the place of translation in modern daily life, in academic life, and in the historic life of medieval writers can all provide fruitful points of comparison.[18]

Translation ultimately offers numerous opportunities for a new medieval comparative literature. First of all, no one has a direct, 'native' relation to medieval languages and literatures (no matter how close to medieval some modern forms might be). Multilingualism (even if it is a variety of modern English in contact with a variety of Middle English) is inherent to any critical interpretation. Secondly, we can see how 'serial monolingualism' acts as a cover for multiple acts of invisible translation. Once we are aware of this phenomenon, we can work to make translation visible in the most secret corners of our

---

[17] Apter, *The Translation Zone*, p. 256. Jacques Derrida, *Le monolinguisme de l'autre, ou la prothèse d'origine* (Paris, 1996).

[18] I have developed this idea in my article 'Translation', in *Oxford Twenty-First Century Approaches to Literature: Middle English*, ed. by Paul Strohm (Oxford, 2007), pp. 51–67.

scholarship and pedagogy. The unspoken history of many medievalists is a primal encounter in translation, followed at some point by the discovery of translation itself. The very corpus of 'medieval literature' offered to students depends greatly on the market forces that determine the availability of editions and translations. 'French medievalists', for example, encounter the Middle Ages of the Modern French translations, while 'English' and 'comparative' medievalists read a somewhat different corpus of 'French' literature in English translations. The scholarly imaginations of tomorrow's professionals are being shaped by the pedagogical possibilities of today. By embracing the many ways in which we are comparing whenever we are translating, and translating whenever we are comparing (and doing both at once whenever we are talking the Middle Ages), we can strive to make those imaginations more vivid.

Dartmouth College

Translating Theory

Sarah Kay

I have not been long in the United States, although I am familiar with the recent development of programmes in comparative literature (= literature in translation) in the United Kingdom. My take on this topic comes from my interest in modern theory, if that is what it must be called, and from the assumption that departments or programmes of comparative literature are homes of theory.

Theory is powerful and empowering because it enables the making of connections and comparisons between what might have been thought to be unconnected. It is a tool of translation, if you will, that makes it possible to relate (transfer) between texts and find ways of making them communicate with one another. In fact the idea that comparison is in some ways an act of translation is something which theoretical thinkers themselves have been increasingly addressing.

Given their importance to comparative literature programs, theoretical texts themselves are often used in translation, and there is an inevitable risk involved in relying on such translations, which are very divergent in quality. There are some noted translators who were specialists on the texts they translated such as Caryl Emerson on Bakhtin, Annette Lavers on Barthes, Spivak on Derrida, and Heller-Roazen on Agamben;[1] several books of Lacan's Seminar (I and XX, for

---

[1] Mikhail M. Bakhtin, *The Dialogic Imagination: Four Essays* [*Voprosy literatury i esthetiki*], ed. by Michael Holquist, trans. by Caryl Emerson (Austin, 1981); Roland Barthes, *Le Degré zéro de l'écriture suivi d' Eléments de sémiologie* (Paris, 1953), trans. by Annette Lavers and Colin Smith, *Writing Degree Zero* and *Elements of Semiology* (both London, 1967); Roland Barthes, *Mythologies* (Paris, 1957), selected and trans. by Annette Lavers, *Mythologies* (London, 1972); Jacques Derrida, *De la grammatologie* (Paris, 1967), trans. by Gayatri Chakravorty Spivak, *Of Grammatology*

example) were also translated by noted experts on Lacan.[2] Such translations are excellent, and in the case of Bakhtin, since I don't read Russian, I am grateful for them and moreover not in a position to be sniffy. But when one is well versed in the language and the thinkers concerned, it becomes obvious that many published translations of theoretical texts that have been commissioned to meet a market need in fact frustrate the intellectual purpose which they ought to serve. Among the poorest translations I have encountered are some in standard use, notably a lot of Kristeva and some Lacan (the *Ecrits*, impenetrable enough in French, are worse in Sheridan's English).[3] For example, in Kristeva's *Histoires d'amour*, the 'grand chant courtois' is rendered by 'grand courtly narrative'; more importantly Kristeva's thought is often rendered unintelligible. It may be that some of the antagonism to theoretical writers as 'obscurantist' is a result of the prevailing translations, which is not to say that the originals are a breeze, but just that basic things like syntax and the signposting of the argument are clearer in the original texts. In the Derrida affair that rocked Cambridge in the late 1980s, most of those opposed to awarding the distinguished French philosopher an honorary degree were people who, if they had read his work at all, had read it in English.

I'd be interested to know whether others share my experience, and if so whether we can do anything to change attitudes to translation? I have noticed that US publishers of academic books not only want every foreign language to be rendered into English, but they also prefer scholars to use published translations

(Baltimore, 1976); Giorgio Agamben, *Categorie italiane: Studi di poetica* (Venezia, 1996), trans. by Daniel Heller-Roazen, *The End of the Poem: Studies in Poetics* (Stanford, 1999); Giorgio Agamben, *Homo sacer: Il potere sovrano e la nuda vita* (Turin, 1995), trans. by Daniel Heller-Roazen, *Homo Sacer: Sovereign Power and Bare Life* (Stanford, 1998); Giorgio Agamben, *Quel que resta di Auschwitz: L'archivio e il testimone* (Turin, 1998), trans. by Daniel Heller-Roazen, *Remnants of Auschwitz: The Witness and the Archive* (New York, 2002).

[2] Jacques Lacan, *Le Séminaire de Jacques Lacan*, ed. by Jacques Alain Miller (Paris, 1973–); *Livre I: Les Ecrits techniques de Freud; 1953–4* (1975), trans. by John Forrester, *Freud's Papers on Technique* (New York, 1988); *Livre XX: Encore: 1972–3* (Paris, 1975), trans. by Bruce Fink, *Book XX: Encore; On Feminine Sexuality, the Limits of Love and Knowledge* (London, 1998).

[3] Jacques Lacan, *Ecrits* (Paris, 1966), trans. by Alan Sheridan, *Ecrits: A Selection* (London, 1977); Julia Kristeva, *Histoires d'amour* (Paris, 1983), trans. by Leon S. Roudiez, *Tales of Love* (New York, 1987); Julia Kristeva, *Pouvoirs de l'horreur. Essai sur l'abjection* (Paris, 1980), trans. by Leon S. Roudiez, *Powers of Horror: An Essay on Abjection* (New York, 1989); Kristeva, *Soleil noir: Dépression et mélancolie* (Paris, 1987), trans. by Leon S. Roudiez, *Black Sun: Depression and Melancholia* (New York, 1989).

of the works they cite wherever possible (Why do they do this? Is this a closed shop?). I have always provided my own translations of what we are pleased to call 'primary texts' and increasingly I have also begun translating my quotations from critical and theoretical texts even where published translations exist. We are also in a position to inflect attitudes in academic life, where it is rare for senior figures to involve themselves in translation. My ambition in retirement is to translate a Lacan seminar, but I don't think I could justify to myself doing such work now — yet why not? Because I know that in the United Kingdom this would not have been rewarded. Are our attitudes right? Maybe the United States is different?

Of course, even when real specialists take control of translation the problems don't go away. The sheer difficulty of many of the texts and their rootedness in a particular language with its particular language games hamper the translator. The translation can become burdened with notes if it is to retain any contact with the dimensions of thought in the original, and this can also make it very unwieldy and difficult to use — e.g., Derrida's *La Carte postale*, which operates on a series of puns.[4] The choices translators make in the face of difficulty can be stigmatized as betraying *parti-pris*; this is notoriously the case with the Standard Edition of Freud by a team of British analysts overseen by James Strachey.[5] Not despite being professionally involved in psychoanalysis, but precisely because they were, Strachey's team sought to render Freud's vocabulary more scientific, using terms such as *id, ego* and *superego, instinct,* and *cathect* for Freud's far more vernacular usage. (French translations of Freud are also much criticized, but the German title which is rendered in English as 'Instincts and Their Vicissitudes' is a lot closer in tone in the French 'Les pulsions et leurs détours' to the original German 'Die Triebe und ihre Umwandlungen'.)

The point is not one to labour; we all know about the pitfalls of translation. The problem with theoretical texts, though, is that they tend to be regarded as belonging in a different category from literary ones (everyone acknowledges the difficulty of literary translation), a category that permits being used *as tools*. Yet as these translation difficulties attest, theoretical texts cannot just be a transparent medium of communication between other cultural works; if anything they are

[4] Jacques Derrida, *La Carte postale: De Socrate à Freud et au-delà* (Paris, 1980), trans. by Alan Bass, *The Postcard: From Socrates to Freud and Beyond* (Chicago, 1987).

[5] Sigmund Freud, *Gesammelter Werke, chronologisch geordnet*, ed. by Marie Bonaparte, Anna Freud, Edward Bibring, and Ernst Kris, 17 vols (London, 1940–52), trans. under the editorship of James Strachey, *The Standard Edition of the Complete Psychological Works of Sigmund Freud*, 24 vols (London, 1953–74).

more densely worked than some of the texts in conjunction with which they are used — as when Lacan is read together with B movies, an imbalance Žižek loves to exploit. The tendency to see theory as a tool bespeaks the desire to reduce it to the status of method. In France, although it is the home of theory, medieval studies, insofar as it is theorized at all, most commonly still uses some form of structuralism, precisely because this allows itself to be used as method. What I mean by the difference between theory and method is that once elaborated, the method is transparent and repeatable. This is what theoretical works, especially in translation, are not. Being a comparatist in translation, if it means using theory as a tool, might then mean losing precisely the capacity to compare what one was looking for in favour of reduction to a misleading sameness.

As I said at the beginning, translation between languages and between cultures has been a major theme of what we call theory in recent years, and this as a result of theoretical attention to singularity, difference, and diversity. There are two fundamental axes to attend to here: the rekindling of interest in universality; and developments in the idea of relationship *to*. Theory remains the basis of communication between texts, whether you think in terms of particulars and universals or in terms of ethical response. So although translating theoretical texts remains impossible, it is necessary. It's just we need to be aware of this when — if we have to — we use theory in translation.

Princeton University

COMPARATISTS IN TRANSLATION:
A PREMODERN EXAMPLE

Marina Brownlee

The question posed by this session could not be more timely. When I walk into a Barnes and Noble and, amid myriad aisles of bookshelves, spot one small shelf labelled 'untranslated literature', I feel both amused and depressed. The implicit assumption is that a translation achieves total fidelity to the original text — which is obviously, problematic. We live in the expository 'information age' where the word *literature* makes many people uneasy. It has become the 'l-word' as reflected in the bookstores where the rubric 'literature' is frequently effaced or, to make it more palatable, included in the label 'fiction and literature'.

I do not have time here to linger on these fascinating labels and the paradigm shifts they entail, but I would like instead to offer some thoughts on why I would answer 'yes' to the question of whether you can be a comparatist in translation. 'Yes', that is, to the degree that you have a reading knowledge of the texts and languages being compared. Indeed, the study of translation can teach us a lot about the most intensely debated areas of exploration that occupy the academy these days: cultural identity, periodization, subaltern and gender studies, media studies, text and image — you name it.

The role of ideology in translation is paramount — whether we are thinking of the explicitly ideological *translatio studii et imperii* model or of the implicit — yet powerful — political statement made by *aljamiado* works (Romance language texts written in Arabic or Hebrew alphabets). In working with translations, we need to consider whether they are construed as instrumental or hermeneutic — as aspiring to offer a faithful linguistic reproduction of the meaning of the original, or as aiming instead to convey social contexts and effects. Questions we might ask are whether the translation is designed for readers who do not understand the original (or not), whether words (lexical fidelity) or the overall purpose of the original (or both) are the issue, and whether the translation is produced within the same time period as the original. If not, then Benjamin's notion of the 'afterlife' seems useful.

The text I would like to consider briefly here defies the exclusionary categories as either instrumental or hermeneutic — functioning as both. The Italian *Historia de Isabella et Aurelio* (1521) presents itself as a translation by Lelio Aletiphilo of Juan de Flores's Spanish *Grisel y Mirabella* (dating from the 1480s). 'Aletiphilo' — a composite of *philos* (lover) and *alethia* (truth) is a pseudonym used by several writers in Italy, France, Germany, Holland, and Belgium, and in the seventeenth century it was also the name of a society, the Academia degli Aletiphili. This Italian translation of the Spanish work is of interest, among other reasons, because it was one of the most widely read novels in Europe: with French, German, English, and Polish versions, as well as numerous bi-, tri- and quadrilingual editions being produced. The earliest of five quadrilingual editions (published in Antwerp, in 1556, includes French, Italian, Spanish, and English in four parallel columns printed on facing pages.[1]

Of the many translations that appeared, none includes the name of a translator. Though this omission might incline us to assume that whoever rendered the Spanish into Italian chose anonymity because he viewed his labour as an uncreative, mechanical transference of vocabulary words from one idiom into another, the enigmatic identity of 'Aletiphilo' can be interpreted as protection from attacks by misogynists and/or misandrists.

The story of both the Italian text and its Spanish predecessor is a tragic tale of love between a young knight and a princess (tyrannized by her overly protective father — the King of Scotland, who is reluctant to marry off his only child). As a result of this royal parental oppression, the couple enters into a relationship and is discovered *in flagrante delicto*. The King has both Aurelio and Isabella tortured and interrogated in order to ascertain who initiated the affair, intending thereby to identify the guiltier party. Once determined, the more guilty lover will die, and the other will be exiled for life — in accord with the Law of Scotland.

Given that Isabella and Aurelio each claim responsibility for the greater guilt, the King appoints judges who choose one maiden and one gentleman to debate — in general terms — whether men or women are more at fault in seduction. Hortensia (an ancient Roman heroine *c.* 50 BC — found also in the *Champion*

---

[1] *Histoire de Aurelio et Isabelle* (Antwerp, 1556).

des dames) argues in defense of women, while Afranio, that of men. The change of name from Torrellas (in the original Spanish text) to Afranio is significant. For while Torrellas was a notorious misogynist poet, whose scurrilous poetry in Castilian and Catalan survives to this day, Afranio is not a historical figure at all. He is, rather, just an average phallocrat.

The consequences of the translator's choice here is serious, indeed, for by substituting Afranio for Torrellas the debate on gender is inadvertently problematized in two different ways: First, by replacing Torrellas with an invented debater who makes the usual misogynistic points, his death seems unwarranted. While Torrellas's notoriety made him worthy of punishment, Afranio does not deserve the slow torture and death leading to the wearing of pendants containing his ashes by the enraged females who kill him. Presumably the Italian translator was unaware of Torrellas's historical — and heavily gender-inflected — existence.

An additional — yet different — type of distortion arises from the replacement of the historically real Iberian poet Torrellas by the fictional Italian Afranio. Namely, Aletiphilo has Afranio repeat the same words as Torrellas, but he does not understand their context. This is why Aletiphilo speaks somewhat disparagingly of the Spanish text as being 'obscure'. Torrellas's 'obras' are his poems, but the Italian translates *obras* as 'opere'—the 'opere' in question being ambiguous. The translators of the work into French and English choose to eliminate the ambiguity by turning the 'opere' into 'oeuvres' and 'deeds' — i.e., his exploits as a seducer, not as author. The 1556 Antwerp edition spells it out: 'estoit en oeuvres amoureuses grand entrepreneur'. Other references are made to Afranio's books (e.g., 'Gia altra volta dissi in uno mio libro'), which seem cryptic, since no information is given regarding the nature of any books he had allegedly produced. Here too, Aletiphilo's ignorance of Torrellas's reputation has a notable impact on his text, minimizing the pro-feminist thrust of Flores's original. Nonetheless, this unaccountable attribution is translated into the other languages as well.

Paradoxically, though the Italian translation distorts the gender-based message in such a way as to subvert Flores's novel and create inconsistencies, it is the Italian version that is overwhelmingly favoured by European readers — with fifty of the fifty-six known editions being of Aletiphilo's translation. As such, Aletiphilo offers a hermeneutic translation that illustrates the Benjaminian 'afterlife' by replacing the notorious fifteenth-century Iberian poet with a typical sixteenth-century Italian male — thereby updating the text for his contemporary Italian readers, making the gender-debate more relevant. At the same time, the quadrilingual edition offers a prime example of instrumental translation, with four parallel columns aspiring to precise linguistic equivalence. This edition was designed as a manual for language instruction.[2]

Whatever the purpose of a translation, it is irreducibly different from the production of literature. Though the *Historia* offers us a premodern example of some of the intricacies that the act of translation involves, the same opportunities and potential pitfalls are afforded by the translation of later texts as well. You can be a comparatist in translation. Whether we evaluate the relative semantic fidelity of an instrumental translation to the original, or explore the social contexts of a hermeneutic one, there are undeniable intellectual and pedagogical benefits to be gained from being a comparatist in translation.

Princeton University

---

[2] For further discussion of the *Historia* and its dissemination, see Barbara Matulka, *The Novels of Juan de Flores and Their European Diffusion* (New York, 1931), pp. 169–78.

SCANDALS OF TRANSLATION, PRAGMATICS OF DESIRE

David Townsend

The more often I've asked myself, 'Can you be a comparatist in translation?' the deeper my perplexity. For the question we've set ourselves is at once insoluble and deliberately, provocatively coarse-grained, a three-way train-wreck of quodlibet, koan, and klots kashe, whose answer is both 'obviously no', and at once a self-evident, perhaps even impatiently delivered, 'yes, of course'. My anxiety probably stems not so much from the question itself as from my inability to settle another that remains prior: to what discursive community do I address my answer, and to what grounding assumptions of that community must I appeal for my answer to be either meaningful or usefully received? If I were to translate the question into the language I spend much of my classroom time teaching, I'd insert an interrogative particle to cue an expected response: whatever the intention behind the question, I suspect you are waiting for Answer No. 1, 'obviously, no', if only on grounds of institutional exigency, since without the credential of competence in multiple medieval languages, many of us would be out of a job. So I've translated the question before I've translated it, and thus already instantiated a commonplace of translation theory, elaborated for example at some length by George Steiner.[1] But in acknowledging that commonplace — to wit, that every hermeneutic act is translation of a sort before the question of interlingual transposition might ever arise — I arrive, paradoxically, at the answer 'Yes, of course'. And yet even so, such a comprehensive a priori observation about the nature of translation might run the risk of shutting down conversation rather than opening it up.

---

[1] George Steiner, *After Babel: Aspects of Language and Translation*, 2nd edn (Oxford, 1992).

My anxiety also reflects a dynamic tension in medieval translation practice itself, between translation as grammatical exercise and as rhetorical enterprise, a dialectic that, as Rita Copeland points out,[2] subtends the venerable but analytically less productive topos of fidelity to the letter versus fidelity to sense. In this respect, my inability to understand the question, without imagining a community of hearers to whom I might address myself, distantly echoes Ælfric's protestation that he's had it with biblical translation, since he can translate only the letter but not the interpretive matrix around the text that guarantees its orthodox meaning — which is to say, he cannot assure the reception of his translation by a hermeneutic community steeped in Augustinian reading practices inextricably connected in his mind to Latinity.[3]

So in my translation, I'd have to find a way to imply that the negative particle — now the questions reads, 'You can't be a comparatist in translation, can you?' — should be taken disingenuously, included in order to invite finer distinctions that allow us to answer 'yes' without descending into tautology, and without entirely undermining the justification for our own profession. How, then, to translate the question so as both to imply an ostensibly expected negative response and at the same time to encourage resistance to that expectation? Could I translate the question's seven words, along with the implicit contexts that seem essential to me if it's to have real meaning and import, in less than a hundred? And then, how outraged, or at least hijacked, would you feel if I tried to pass off my solipsistic rendition as a substitute for the original question?

Lawrence Venuti has pointed out that the scandals of translation are multiple and necessary to the maintenance of pervasive academic, social, and legal regimens of knowledge and discursive power.[4] But some scandals, however much we may need them, have worn thin in 2007. How scandalized at this point can we possibly remain that in translation we transgress some bounded stability of the text? How could we possibly protest that by abjuring translation we might hope to produce readings definitive once for all, by attending instead to the

---

[2] Rita Copeland, *Rhetoric, Hermeneutics and Translation in the Middle Ages: Academic Traditions and Vernacular Texts* (Cambridge, 1991), pp. 9–36.

[3] *The Old English Version of the Heptateuch*, ed. by S. J. Crawford, Early English Text Society, o.s. 166 (London, 1922), pp. 76–77; for a discussion of Ælfric's anxieties about his inability to control the reception dynamics of his translation, see also Robert Stanton, *The Culture of Translatio in Anglo-Saxon England* (Cambridge, 2002), pp. 131–41.

[4] Lawrence Venuti, *The Scandals of Translation: Toward an Ethics of Difference* (London, 1998).

integrity of the originals? We sawed those limbs off the tree far too long ago to imagine that we might still venture out on them.

Yet surely among the scandals of translation on which we can continue to rely is this: that I'd presume to exhibit what is private in my reception of a text, or in my imagination of a larger community that receives it, as itself an object for others' attention. We all translate intralingually as we read. But should I not then, as a good comparatist, translate that idiosyncratic experience — an experience permeated with the pleasure of the text, desire for the text — into a less directly erotic key? Should I not have the professional tact to repress those aspects of my response peculiar to my own specular relation to the text by instead fetishizing its alterity? A feminist critique like Lori Chamberlain's addresses the gendered conceptualization of translation as a site of power relations — among text, translator, author, reader.[5] While I may find that critique convincing, useful, and politically worthy, I wish in my decadence that I had a more elaborate language for the complex, productive indeterminacies of the erotics of translation — not in order to resolve the undecidable longing and pleasure of translation into analytic clarity, but to celebrate it as the grounding condition of interpretive experience's enrichment and depth.

A friend once told me that a rabbi with whom she'd studied said, 'Trying to read the Torah without knowing Hebrew is like trying to kiss the bride through a veil. Trying to read the Talmud without knowing Hebrew is like trying to kiss the bride through a thick wall.' But some of us are into that. *I kiss thy stones, O wall.*

If translation in the narrow sense is indeed a specialized instance of our general hermeneutic condition — the re-encoding of meaning in the target language, without the security of appeal to any stable substrate — then I approach every text in the first instance with a specular delight in recognition (and misrecognition) of what's homologous with my own semiotic repertoire. To engage in this process at a social level may be colonizing, or patriarchal, or else may resist colonization or patriarchy — a central concern of Robert Stein's remarks; but to engage in it at the level of desire is in this primary instance homoerotic, and as all interpretation is driven at some level by desire, whether acknowledged or not, all interpretation is therefore at one of its poles homoerotic.

At the same time, interpretation depends on the irreduceable alterity of the source, which can't be fully internalized: if it is, desire collapses and our attention

---

[5] Lori Chamberlain, 'Gender and the Metaphorics of Translation', *Signs*, 13 (1988), 454–72.

turns elsewhere. At this pole, all interpretation requires continuous return to the text, there to confront continuous (and equally eroticized) reminders that the text remains provocatively alien. My most narcissistic investment in the text sooner or later runs up against the fact that the text surprises by its strangeness, its failure to function as an adequate mirror of myself. And I want it to surprise me thus. To engage in the hermeneutic enterprise is to desire the other, and at this pole, all interpretation is heteroerotic. Thus we go on needing the original unendingly, as much if we kiss the bride through the wall as if it's square on the unglossed lips.

An interlingual translation of a literary work is the direct trace of another's hermeneutic desire, and so of the complex, subtle, shifting accommodation of homoerotic and heteroerotic elements in the playing out of that desire. It's not simply that I subconsciously negotiate those accommodations within my own reading practice. They're mirrored back to me in the fact that I confront the messy, self-contradictory desire of a third, that my desire is bound up with the desire of another that may or may not at any given moment reflect my own, spur on my own, shape my own — or perhaps even itself become the object of my own.

To use a translation is to consent that the desire of a third should intervene in the experience and expression of one's own hermeneutic desire. It's like inviting a trick with an exceptionally forceful personality into a threesome. Or if you have no choice, maybe it's like being the trick, knowing the only way circumstances will allow you to connect with the one you're really interested in is to accept the arrangement. Sustaining a *menage à trois* is always a challenge, and satisfaction depends on the ongoing possibility of renegotiation. How do you put the translator in his or her place? What place would you like to put him in? Is he, in fact, servant of the text, a pushy, exhibitionistic bottom who insists at every juncture that you pay attention to his experience? *Bless thee, Bottom, thou art translated.* Is she a top who handcuffs the text and brings out a side of it that you've never noticed before? Or are you the one in restraints, watching text and translator go at it in ways that you find sometimes exciting, sometimes repellent, sometimes a little dull and can we just please get on with it? How do you play with the power you've given this third over the hermeneutic exchange? How do you simultaneously destabilize that power?

And how as a translator do you take on that role and put it off? How do you assume the power your gentle reader consents that you hold, and how do you remind your gentle reader that this goes on being a game that can be called off? How do you wield that power for your reader's good, and his pleasure, and not for his ill? One answer echoes Michelle Warren's emphasis on the ethical obligation to translate so as to call attention to the translatedness of the translation — so as to keep the reader focused on the tension between the transparency and the opacity of one's translation practice. Venuti would call this a 'minoritizing' practice of the craft. Medieval translation minoritizes itself continuously, it seems to me, most obviously and thematically — though often disingenuously — in highly adaptive practices (Copeland's 'secondary translation') like that of Chaucer in *Troilus and Criseyde*; but also in a less ostensibly self-conscious text like the Old English *Apollonius of Tyre*, where, for example, the incest riddle on which the first part of the plot hinges is given first in Latin and only thereafter questionably translated.[6] (The Old English *Apollonius* is further noteworthy for a practice whose idiomatic but usually close rendition of the Latin source belies the radically transformed cultural context into which the translation inserts itself.)[7]

To conclude: how does this return us to our original question? If any of this riff has validity, or interest, then one reason we'd want to be comparatists in translation — for, of course, we already are, all the time, reading works translated out of languages we don't know, or don't know well; teaching undergraduates; reading texts in the original when we know full well that the competencies with which we receive them bear finally indefinable relation to those of any other reader, well-read native speaker or not — the reason we'd want to be, that we'd embrace this necessary condition of who we are as readers, is that we become more palpably aware of the nature of our own hermeneutic desire as we confront the desire of another — sometimes mirroring our own, sometimes radically distinct from our own — weaving its way past lost Athenians, rude mechanicals, and fairies mixing it up with donkeys, through a dark, sexy forest of sameness and alterity.

University of Toronto

---

[6] *The Old English 'Apollonius of Tyre'*, ed. by Peter Goolden (London, 1958), p. 6.

[7] I've elsewhere addressed the dynamics of this transposition into a radically alien cultural context in 'Naked Truth of the King's Affection in the Old English *Apollonius of Tyre*', *Journal of Medieval and Early Modern Studies*, 24 (2004), 173–95.

Symposium II.

Medieval(isms)

WHAT IS HAPPENING TO THE MIDDLE AGES?

Thomas A. Prendergast and Stephanie Trigg

T he distinction between the twinned disciplines of medievalism studies and more traditional medieval studies is perfectly evident to all those who work within those two fields but almost completely opaque to those outside them. For most scholars in these areas, the distinction between the historically real Middle Ages and the post-medieval re-creation of them is not only an epistemological and ontological issue, but also an important disciplinary and pedagogical principle. We are far from wanting to run these two things together indiscriminately, but we do think there might be lessons to learn from the fact that for most outsiders, the distinction is barely meaningful.

Current trends in medievalism studies are still dominated by the critical framework established by Umberto Eco, and his oft-cited insistence that we need to distinguish between competing or variant representations of the Middle Ages: '[E]very time one speaks of a dream of the Middle Ages, one should first ask which Middle Ages one is dreaming of.'[1] Eco combines his exhortation with an injunction that we choose from his list of 'ten little middle ages'. To ignore his list is to fail to do our 'moral and cultural duty'. He expands on what this means when he says that 'to say openly which of the above ten types we are referring to means to say who we are and what we dream of'.[2] To fail to engage in Eco's taxonomy is, presumably, to conceal who we are and what our dreams are for ourselves as well as other people. Behind Eco's seemingly audacious claim is a healthy suspicion of the use of the medieval — a belief that the ideological history of the medieval (what he calls at one point the new Aryanism)

---

[1] Umberto Eco, 'Dreaming of the Middle Ages', in *Faith in Fakes: Essays*, trans. by William Weaver (London, 1986), p. 68.

[2] Eco, 'Dreaming of the Middle Ages', p. 72.

necessitates an openness that is only fulfilled if we know precisely, even before we speak of the Middle Ages, what we mean by the term.

While we are profoundly sympathetic with Eco's political concerns, we believe that his list has had a stultifying effect on the study of the Middle Ages both because it has encouraged the field of medievalism to engage in a kind of criticism that is largely taxonomic and because it has perpetuated the split between understandings of medieval and medievalism. The concerns, of course, are not separate. Number eight on Eco's list of 'ten little middle ages' is 'the middle ages of *philological construction* [...] which help us [...] to criticize all the other Middle Ages that one time or another arouse our enthusiasm'.[3] By separating and, frankly, privileging this Middle Ages even while including it in his list, Eco assumes that the Middle Ages themselves are stable, while different variable and partial elements of medieval culture are emphasized by different groups of game players, fiction writers, filmmakers, and so on. In a single move, he also licenses the academic critique, on the grounds of historical accuracy, of the medievalism offered by those groups.

The popularity of Eco's title, 'Dreaming the Middle Ages', however, as it is echoed in the many subsequent variations on 'making', 'remaking', 'inventing', and 'reinventing' the Middle Ages, gestures toward a rather more active sense that the Middle Ages are always in process of being remade. We wish to take all these movements further but to focus critical attention less on the particular representation of the Middle Ages, or the distinction between medieval and early modern, and more on the broader conceptualization of the medieval *in its relation to* any given present. How do we still recognize and produce the medieval? What are the discursive, institutional and political effects of these various acts of medievalization, whenever they take place, and to whatever end, whether scholarly, imaginative, or strategic?

We see the action of 'medievalizing' as a productive act, in the Foucauldian sense. Naming something as medieval, or setting it firmly in the past in a regressive or abject relationship to the present, produces a powerful spiral of pleasure and familiarity of cultural reference, even as it also produces an increasingly narrow understanding of the medieval as the object of general knowledge. To medievalize is a powerful strategy of claiming cultural authority over a cultural, historical, or ideological mode that becomes most recognizable at the moment of its own supercession. Things appear to become medieval, then, when it becomes possible — and perhaps desirable — to leave them behind. The necessary corollary,

---

[3] Eco, 'Dreaming of the Middle Ages', p. 71.

however, is that having left the Middle Ages behind, we can always return to them. Moreover, they can always return to us, whether in dreamy, embroidered, and idealized form (the medieval as romance), or as the abjected dark other to modernity (the medieval as gothic), or indeed in other variations made increasingly possible through postmodernist recombination and play. This possibility of return is the enduring legacy of King Arthur, as *rex quondam et futurus*, and one reason, perhaps, for his enduring popularity as a figure of medievalization: the mystery surrounding his death and the prophecy of his return promises a rich source for reinvention, and a powerful trope for marking the end of an era — 'the one brief shining moment' — that is, however, never truly ended beyond hope of recovery, never truly closed over or buried. The pre-eminent figure of the pastness of the medieval, King Arthur is also its most frequent revenant, medievalized over and over again.

The opposition between medieval and modern is not always bound to the historical periods we customarily associate with it. Variations of the 'medieval' can indeed be produced by more or less conscious acts of historicization. In our more Foucauldian sense of the word, the practice of medievalizing exists as a kind of reflex to the past, producing a dynamic and flexible relationship between present and past. In these relationships, the past can be ennobled, or abjected; it is rarely neutral, or subtly modulated. In recent commentary, one of the most powerful discussions of this dynamic is Carolyn Dinshaw's analysis of the surprising and sudden currency of Quentin Tarantino's 'getting medieval' as a condensation of a whole series of abjected others, such as 'sodomy, sadomasochism, southerners' (her perspective is irreducibly American). As Dinshaw comments, 'The medieval [...] is the space of the rejects — really, the abjects — of this world.'[4] We might even go so far as to suggest that for Western culture, the problem of medievalization is the problem of historicism *tout court*. The construction of the Middle Ages by the Renaissance is the first major installment of European historiography: the self-conscious construction of a relationship with the past that is founded in the recovery of that past. These influential processes produce a relationship between past and present that foregrounds the question of the *use* of the past in the present. Once the Middle Ages are identified as over, as belonging to the past, they can be safely recuperated — revived or reviled — and relationships of affinity or abjection formulated.

[4] Carolyn Dinshaw, *Getting Medieval: Sexualities and Communities, Pre- and Postmodern* (Durham, 1999), p. 186.

Within the discourses, policies, and practices of modern nationhood and democratic statehood, the 'medieval' is frequently used as a code for all that is not relevant to the 'modern', not just in terms of aggressive foreign policies but in the relentless modernizing of domestic policy. We are, for instance, familiar with the construction of Islamic regimes being described as 'medieval' in order to characterize their totalitarian regimes as feudal, as oppressive to women, and as driven by religious fundamentalism.

A very stable opposition and contrast between past and present, medieval and modern, is readily invoked by nonspecialist writers and commentators, whether in the service of a reforming or revolutionary ideal. The 'medieval' can signify a conservative ideal of social harmony and racial homogeneity to which we should return, or it can signify an archaic mode of social repression which we should colonize and conquer, or it can signify simply the 'not-modern'.

The relationship between medieval and modern is far more complex than this,[5] but we are concerned principally with the general, or popular, conception of the relationship, and the effects of this black-and-white opposition on the disciplines of medieval and medievalism studies. For example, when a simple relationship of alterity is the dominant structure of the relation between medieval and modern it is the easiest thing in the world to dismiss the 'medieval' as the opposite of all that is useful to a modern university, a library, or a nation, on the simple grounds that the medieval has no place in the modern. Under pressure to fund expensive research into nanotechnology, genetics, or the prevention of global influenza, medieval studies seems an obvious target as the weakest link, the least modern, the least useful, the least relevant part of the humanities clamouring for government funding. Again, little of this is new to humanities scholars — Dinshaw's critique of US right-wing objections to various National Endowment for the Humanities–funded seminars on gender and sexuality makes a crucial intervention here — but we argue that our response to such utilitarian prioritizations represents one of the greatest challenges for our discipline.

Within the academic field, we frequently find a deep structural affirmation that medieval studies is valuable precisely because it is *not* relevant. We do not need to invoke the full force of the 'rancid solipsistic pit' into which D. W. Robertson threatened we would fall if we insisted on bringing our modern presuppositions to our reading of medieval texts, to agree that part of what we treasure about

---

[5] See for example, Bruce Holsinger, *Neomedievalism, Neoconservatism, and the War on Terror* (Chicago, 2007).

medieval culture is its radical alterity, and the play of difference and similarity between medieval and modern culture. To argue for the relevance of the medieval as the simple point of origin of modernity would be equally simplistic and regressive. We need to distinguish, too, between 'relevance' and 'similarity': the relationships between medieval, modern, and indeed postmodern constitute a rich and complex area of study in their own right and are barely reducible to the simple oppositions voiced by government and research-funding agencies.

At the same time, however, in the critical writings of many medieval scholars, the notion of 'relevance' is often seen as a threat to what Nicholas Watson calls 'the magic garden' of medieval studies — a contemporary medievalism that will uproot the carefully tended garden and force medievalists to leave their *hortus conclusus*.[6] This anxiety has been exacerbated in the last decade or so in the context of the extraordinary resurgence of interest in the medieval and the pseudo-medieval amongst fiction writers and filmmakers. As long as 'medievalism' meant studying Spenser, Tennyson, Morris, and Ruskin, even T. H. White and Tolkien, scholars could remain within the relatively safe territory of high culture and Renaissance, Victorian or high modernist cultural theory, or the respectable safety of Arthurian tradition, or the biographical study of one of their own forebears. But now that 'medievalism' means engaging with the fantastically free and inventive products of popular culture, it means venturing into quite a different disciplinary formation altogether; namely, the field of cultural studies. How else can we take proper account of the intersections between medievalism and mass culture exemplified by television shows, role-playing games, and advertising? Or the productive interplay between medievalism and the gothic in the current fashion for paganism? How else can we analyse the significance of medievalist subcultures like gaming groups and the Society for Creative Anachronism?

For if we concede that medieval studies have any relevance to the modern age (and many medieval scholars do in fact freely argue for such relevance), this might force us to engage in discussions of the particularities of those relationships. It might not be enough just to say, then, that the medieval period is important in its own right, that its buildings, music, art, and literature are still enjoyed and treasured by Western society, or that medieval culture exerted a powerful influence on modernity. We might have to engage in public dialogue and publish outside our own favoured journals and presses. We might have to become public intellectuals like Umberto Eco. Perhaps even more worrying, we might have to

---

[6] Nicholas Watson, 'Desire for the Past', *Studies in the Age of Chaucer*, 21 (1999), 59–97 (p. 92).

read contemporary medievalist fantasy fiction and take it seriously, or we might have to dress up in a velvet robe, weave our own baskets, or fight each other with rattan swords before an audience of enthusiasts. Worst of all, we might end up blurring the distinction between the medieval and the medievalistic that we have disciplined ourselves to making and remaking, over and over again.

It is this notion of discipline in its most controlling sense that we find most disturbing, for it indicates a totalizing, even totalitarian, desire to control the extent to which the field is defined. We overdramatize the case, perhaps, but Watson's metaphor of the 'garden' draws attention to a certain medieval prejudice against 'medievalistic' representations of the Middle Ages that (despite the habitual denial of this prejudice) continues to colour approaches to the *medium aevum*. Part of the reason for the reflexive reaction against medievalism has to do with what might be called less the garden, than the plot of medieval studies. By invoking the notion of plot we mean to invoke the idea that medieval studies has a kind of narrative that informs the hermeneutic choices that we as medievalists have made. But we also mean to be provocative and suggest that we might take the word in the sense of conspiracy. We do not mean to suggest that this plot operates along the classical Freudian lines of paranoid subject versus controlling authority. Instead we invoke the idea of 'a cover up' in which the study of the medieval often leads to a cyclic repression of all that is medievalistic.

Perhaps the most apparent example of this cover up is the term *medievalism* itself. As it is applied to postmedieval recuperations of the medieval, the term separates and abjects the academic study of medievalism in order to retain the 'purity' of medieval studies. Part of the reason for this abjection has much to do with the origin of the 'discipline'. As Lee Patterson notes, the operative term when talking about the recuperation of the medieval in medieval studies was labour: '[T]his work was accomplished through a laborious attention to detail, polyglot inclusiveness, and mastery of accurate techniques of recovery and restoration — through, that is, those procedures and values that successfully transformed the study of medieval literature from uncritical amateurism into a scientific profession.'[7] Labour, mastery, and professionalism displaced uncritical amateurism in an effort to legitimate the emergence of medieval studies. This positivistic method enabled scholars to separate themselves from the popular ideas of the medieval that seemingly confused the field and to legitimate the academic

---

[7] Lee Patterson, *Negotiating the Past: The Historical Understanding of Medieval Literature* (Madison, 1987), p. 15.

study of the medieval as the preserve of specialists.[8] Medieval studies thus
characterized itself as an academic discipline in the full and foundational sense of
that word. In order to be a medievalist one could not simply be a general reader
— one had to have the learning and training to be part of the discipline.[9] It was
crucial that medieval studies insisted on this discipline if it was to survive. For if
there was no mastery to strive for, then there could be no master class of scholars
who disseminated this cultural capital. In terms already sketched out by John
Guillory (though in a different context), the difficulty in understanding medieval
texts had to be maintained in the face of the popular medievalistic reception of
such texts. Hence popular recuperations of the medieval necessarily became
misunderstandings — a kind of afterbirth which maintained only an attenuated
relationship to the real work of medieval studies.

The disciplining of medieval studies coexisted with the great florescence of
what has been termed 'romantic medievalism'. During the nineteenth century
figures such as Gaston Paris and Viollet-le Duc both used what Kathleen Biddick
has called 'isolating methodologies' in order to 'imagine a coherent inside to the
discipline of medieval studies',[10] while in England Walter W. Skeat and Henry
Bradshaw established what one scholar has termed the 'Modern Age' of Chaucer
scholarship.[11] This modernization would continue and with it would seemingly
come the eclipse of the romantic medievalism of William Morris and John
Ruskin. The received narrative suggests that as a formalist sensibility of art took
hold (encouraged by the Bloomsbury Group), earlier versions of a functionalist
medievalism were eclipsed — and completely abandoned during the First World
War.[12] In fact, of course, no such thing happened. As Michael Saler and others have
argued, the disciples of Morris continued to advance the cause of medievalism in

---

[8] Kathleen Biddick cites the examples of Gaston Paris, Viollet-le-Duc, and Bishop Stubbs
(*The Shock of Medievalism* (Durham, 1998), pp. 1–2).

[9] For a modern example of this split between the professional and the popular that involves
an encounter with a medieval text, see Stephanie Trigg, *Congenial Souls* (Minneapolis, 2002), p.
13.

[10] Biddick, *The Shock of Medievalism,* p. 2.

[11] A. S. G. Edwards, 'Walter Skeat (1835–1912)', in *Editing Chaucer: The Great Tradition*
(Norman, OK, 1984), p. 171.

[12] See the bibliography of this received idea in Michael T. Saler, *The Avant-Garde in Interwar
England* (Oxford, 1999), p. 178, n. 3.

the interwar period, 'reconciling Morris's medieval utopian vision *A Dream of John Ball* (1888) with the economic dream of John Bull'.[13]

So why does the received narrative about the modern eclipse of medievalism continue to hold sway? It is almost as if the critical genealogy reinstantiates the split between modern and premodern that so irks medievalists. The marginalization of medievalism is a curious re-enactment of the marginalization that was once practised by classical studies on English literary studies. Moreover, if medieval studies is currently still in danger of being marginalized, we can certainly understand the institutional pleasures of being, ourselves, the marginalizers, as we consistently relegate medievalism to the margins of the real. After all, it is easy (and pleasant) to abject medievalism as the false Other of the medieval real, to show how most invocations of the medieval in fields such as literature, architecture, visual arts, cinema, and ritual practice of various kinds perform a kind of misrecognition of the medieval. But what if we ourselves have also misrecognized it? What if, in the light of many recent studies, we are progressively blurring the distinction between late medieval and early modern? What if we no longer see the 'medieval' as a discrete epistemic formation?

The persistent rationale for this narrative of recognition and abjection is, as Patterson has suggested, labour. And if we return to the metaphor of the garden we find that even as the garden has been defined as the *locus amoenus*, medievalists have been particularly attentive to how much labour has been put into maintaining this pleasurable plot. The reception of a text that is preoccupied with agricultural labour might be instructive here. In a moment of almost overdetermined labour, the eponymous hero of *Piers Plowman* says that he will 'swynke and swete and sowe [...] And [ek] labour[e]' to keep the Church from 'wastours' (6. 26–28).[14] Anne Middleton argues that this notion of labour extends to the production of the poem itself, claiming that 'the argument Langland projects [...] is that Will's enterprise, and hence the poet's, was not "idle" talk, fable, or fantasy, but in some socially significant and spiritually valuable sense "real" work'.[15] Middleton further asserts that there is a sense in which the poem was not isolated in its call to work. Rather, it encoded what had increasingly been an expectation on the part of larger society. No longer

[13] Saler, *Avant-Garde*, p. 13.

[14] William Langland, *The Vision of Piers Plowman: A Critical Edition of the B-Text Based on Trinity College Cambridge MS B. 15. 17*, ed. by A. V. C. Schmidt (New York, 1978), p. 66.

[15] Anne Middleton, 'Acts of Vagrancy: The C Version 'Autobiography' and the Statute of 1388', in *Written Work: Langland, Labor and Authorship*, ed. by Steven Justice and Kathryn Kerby-Fulton (Philadelphia, 1997), p. 280.

could the *literati* depend on their activities being seen as a '"louable" exemption from, or obverse of, the laborious'.[16] Rather they were expected to '"work" for the community's good'.[17] Finally, though she does not expand on this assertion, she implies that this ethic of labour is no relic of the fourteenth century but continues to haunt scholars in the arts and humanities. In other words, what is important about *Piers Plowman* is not only that it is about labour, or even about the labour of its own production, but that its own recuperation legitimates our identity as scholars, precisely because we must labour to recuperate it.

On the other hand Arthur, that dangerous exemplar of medievalism, is the medieval figure everyone 'knows' about; the most obvious face of medievalism, and thus the point where the line between medieval and medievalism is most dangerously blurred. In the area of the medieval academy, Arthurian studies involve the interdisciplinary challenges of archaeology, textual criticism, source study, literary criticism, and historical study. But in the area of medievalism, Arthurian studies quickly bring us out of the medieval into the Renaissance, to Spenser, to Purcell, to Tennyson, to Twain, and Monty Python, into science fiction, children's fiction, and myriad novelistic and cinematic retellings, to say nothing of the easy allusions of television, comedy, cartoons and advertising. In this world almost anything goes. As the most egregious example, *First Knight,* shows, Lancelot and Guinevere need not be parted by death, but can go on and rule the kingdom with Arthur's dying blessing. Such moments exemplify the deep problem of the economy of medievalism. Just as Lancelot and Guinevere never have to 'pay' for their sin, so too one does not need to expend labour in order to recover this vision of Arthur.

One of the great lessons of *Piers Plowman*, on the other hand, is 'redde quod debes' (pay back what you owe) (19. 188). If Langland ends his poem by suggesting that Conscience must 'gradde after Grace' (20. 387), *Piers Plowman* is nonetheless a poem that is obsessed with payment, sacrifice, and labour.[18] Yet the lesson of Piers (that labour is necessary for redemption) is only marginally applied to our own genealogy of labour over 'the medieval'. Despite our certainty (in this post-Foucauldian moment) that to understand any cultural formation we must acknowledge its genealogy, medievalists remain reluctant to own the medievalism of their forebears. For instance, Patterson's narration of the development of

---

[16] Middleton, 'Acts of Vagrancy', p. 280.

[17] Middleton, 'Acts of Vagrancy', p. 280.

[18] The sacrifices of both Saul and Abraham, for instance, both prefigure the ultimate sacrifice of Christ (12. 116; 16. 243).

Chaucer studies, particularly his discussion of New Criticism and Exegetics has been enormously useful. Yet even at the moment of the narration of the interplay of these forces, names like William Morris and Dante Gabriel Rossetti are pushed into the past — a kind of ancient history, a prescholarly world beyond which we have thankfully advanced. The profession has been able to see only its own ephebes, in Harold Bloom's term, not those who never sought to play in its garden.[19] The rich traditions of nineteenth-century medievalism, its desire to re-enter what it saw as the imaginative and physical space of the medieval in its literature, architecture, visual imagery, and design, even its social structures, play no part in these narratives.

A similar phenomenon is observed in the anthology edited by Bloch and Nichols, *Medievalism and the Modernist Temper*, and what Aranye Fradenburg calls its 'evil twin', Norman Cantor's *Inventing the Middle Ages*, which articulated and critiqued the traditions of late-nineteenth- and early-twentieth-century medieval studies and the patriarchal figures who dominated them.[20] The preoccupation with genealogies, in the old-fashioned sense of traditional inheritance and Oedipal struggle, is the dominant interest here. Such texts often seem to examine the way medieval studies polices itself as a discipline, but they themselves also attempt to set the *cordon sanitaire* around the garden firmly in place. The reality is that such boundaries are themselves vexed.

The split between labour and pleasure is at the heart of the paradox of the medieval/medievalism split. Contemporary medievalism is now tarred by the same brush that in conservative circles continues to dismiss cultural studies as mere chat about television, cinema, and the Internet; that is, the accusation that there is too much pleasure, too little work in its study. Perhaps surprisingly, the relationship between labour and pleasure turns out to be an important feature of many other versions of medievalism, too, though the lines are often drawn differently. We need think only of William Morris's desire to recapture both the beauty and the labour of the medieval or preindustrial ethos. Handwoven tapestries and turned chairs are not only things of beauty in their own right; they

---

[19] For an intriguing reflection on the view from 'outside' the castle of medieval studies, from the perspective of those concerned more with the imaginative re-creation of the Middle Ages, see Adina Hamilton, 'A New Sort of Castle in the Air: Medievalist Communities in Contemporary Australia', in *Medievalism and the Gothic in Australian Culture*, ed. by Stephanie Trigg (Turnhout, 2005; Melbourne, 2006), pp. 205–22.

[20] See L. O. Aranye Fradenburg, *Sacrifice Your Love: Psychoanalysis, Historicism, Chaucer* (Minneapolis, 2002), p. 66.

also embody an intimate relationship between labourer and materials, between art and craft. The labouring process, the slow work of the hands, is what is prized here. It is an ethos that has been embraced by many medieval revivalists who produce their own costumes, armour, food, furnishings, and even more substantial building projects. Some are willing to use sewing machines and angle grinders; others insist on the virtues of hand-stitching and traditional methods of metalwork in the service of serious play. The difficulty of the labour is precisely the point, a contrast from the heavily mechanized and disembodied everyday labour at the computer terminal. Many members of the Society for Creative Anachronism, it turns out, are involved in the computer industry as programmers. 'Play' or 'gaming' with an adopted *alter ego* constitutes a welcome release into a world carefully distinguished from the mundane, even though it often involves a degree of 'work' in historical research that is barely acknowledged by the academies of medieval studies (or it if is acknowledged, it is quickly dismissed as amateurism). A similar escapism is shared by those who play in company, wearing medieval 'garb' and take part in tournaments, and those who play tabletop games or online role-playing games. Such gamers distinguish their play from the mundane world of work in capitalist enterprise, allowing the imagination to play — or work — across a range of historically inspired or fantastic scenarios. The careful distinctions and taxonomies of many versions of medieval studies start to unravel at dizzying speeds.

Work, then, can be a relative term.[21] But this is just our point. Everyone thinks that they know who Arthur is and so he becomes an exemplar of *otium* — the easy medievalism of Sidney Lanier, Marion Zimmer Bradley, and Hollywood. In Freudian terms, it is medievalists' attempts to avoid the unpleasure of a lack of work that leads us to abject Arthurian studies as a whole. There is more than a hint of death here. For without work, there is nothing to justify our existence as academics. It is as if we have found ourselves in a garden and been embarrassed by the evident lack of labour required to enjoy it. We have been trained to curse this garden as false — a seemingly pleasurable place that will only breed sloth and ultimately death. The 'real' medieval garden can therefore be understood as one that requires work and guarantees life. Yet, as in the *Roman de la Rose*, it is all the same garden. There is no need to invest in a labourious procedure of policing a spurious border or creating enclosures in order to justify the pleasure that we take

---

[21] The reality, if one can speak of such a thing, is that Arthur's recuperation requires an enormous amount of learning and labour. See, for instance, Michelle R. Warren's fine *History on the Edge: Excaliber and the Borders of Britain, 1100–1300* (Minneapolis, 2000).

in things medieval. It is simply necessary to understand that there is more than one form of labour in the garden and thus that there will be more than one tool required to carry out the tending of that garden.

One of the reasons why there has been so much interest in the transition from medieval to postmedieval is that this historical moment has seemed foundational to the formation of the modern subject, who thus emerges as capable of both forgetting *and* remembering the past. Yet this simultaneous movement also characterizes the relationship that medieval men and women were able to have with their past. The medieval pilgrim, for example, was supposedly able to have a kind of direct access to the past via the medieval residue of historicity par excellence, the relic. A compelling example from the Middle English *Life of St Kenelm* combines the notion of relic, text, and medievalism. As the pope is celebrating Mass in St Peter's, a dove descends from heaven and delivers a piece of paper upon which is a couplet written in 'pur' English. This piece of verse, which reveals the location of the saint's body in England, is written in Late Old English. It is, as the *Life* says, held to be 'a gret relic, as ȝeot it is also'.[22] In the internal logic of the story, the essence of the relic resides in the fact that it comes from heaven, written in shining letters in a language that the pope does not understand. But for the medieval reader of the story the relic is a medievalistic residue which must be authentic precisely because it is written in an earlier form of the language — purportedly the Old English of Kenelm's England (*c.* 821). The relic exists 'ȝeot' in material form and the antiquity of its lexical form both attests to its authenticity and connects the reader to the miraculous production of its writing. Our point here is that as hagiography and historiography were indistinctly differentiated, the medievalism of the relic could collapse time and allow the viewer, or in this case the reader, to join with the past.

The attitude toward these relics was not completely uncritical, of course. As Peter Marshall has pointed out, even as medieval pilgrims piously made their pilgrimages to shrines at Walsingham and Canterbury they understood all too well that 'ostensibly sacred things might be fakes'.[23] The journeys often occasioned a kind of suspension of disbelief, or a kind of contradictory consciousness in which they knew that what they were viewing could be false but were able to

---

[22] *The South English Legendary*, ed. by C. D'Evelyn and A. J. Mill, Early English Text Society, o.s. 235–36, 2 vols (Oxford, 1956), I, 288. But see James Earl's treatment in 'Typology and Iconographic Style in Medieval Hagiography', *Studies in Literary Imagination*, 8.1 (1975), 11–12.

[23] Peter Marshall, 'Forgery and Miracles in the Reign of Henry VIII', *Past and Present*, 178 (2003), 39–73 (p. 41).

forget such doubts in the presence of the 'holy' object. It was the genius of late reformers to exploit these doubts about the material remains of the medieval (and earlier), thus short-circuiting the ability of the traveller to equate physical distance with historical distance. These reformers focused not so much on the ability of relics to connect men and women with the sacred past (though this was undoubtedly their goal) as on the *already accepted fact* that many of these remains were inauthentic. Crucially, however, they did not dismiss all relics as false. In 1536, for instance, the reforming bishop of Salisbury, Nicholas Shaxton, promised that after all relics in his jurisdiction were delivered to him 'those [relics] that be esteemed and judged to be undoubtedly true relics, ye shall not fail at convenable time to have again'.[24] What reformers banked upon, then, was the idea that people would forget what they already knew (that many relics were false) so that false relics (like the infamous Rood of Boxley) could stand in synecdochical relationship to all relics. In a sense, the relic trade — the ultimate form of medievalism in that it helped modern things 'pass' as old — was now transformed into a weapon against the medieval. The reforming response to relics was, in turn, to make manifest their medievalness, in their abjectness, their falseness, and their revelation of a backward-thinking mind.

This moment is crucial because it signals not only an important move in the religious history of England, but also a transformation in the way history is perceived. Reformers here cast the medieval as always medievalizing — always a re-creation, always a restoration and hence false. When, for instance, reformers came to question the white liquid that was said to be the Virgin's milk at Walsingham, they pressed the former sexton about whether he had 'renewed the liquid when it seemed likely to dry up'.[25] The suspicion is that behind that which 'remains' lies human agency to restore or renew that remainder. Relics in this way of thinking become a kind of manmade parody of the supernatural. The medieval is collapsed with medievalism and in this collapse comes the abjection of both.

Perversely, the history of the medieval continues to narrate the collapse of medieval and medievalism even as it insists on their differentiation. One of the better examples of this process is what might be termed a secular relic: the Round Table. John Hines draws attention to the thirteenth-century Round Table at Winchester Castle as a 'icon' of medieval medievalism, the desire to revive the

---

[24] Qtd in Marshall, 'Forgery and Miracles', p. 58.

[25] Marshall, 'Forgery and Miracles', p. 52.

days and the spirit of King Arthur by Edward I.[26] Yet the first recorded mention
of the Winchester Table (John Hardyng's 1464 revision of his verse chronicle)
misremembers the table as the original table at which Arthur and his knights sat:
'The Round Table at Wynchestre beganne | And ther it ende and ther it hangeth
yet.'[27] Hardyng was not alone. Some twenty years later when approached to print
Thomas Malory's romance about Arthur, William Caxton famously tells us that
he initially objected because 'dyuers men holde oppynyon that there was no suche
Arthur'.[28] That which purportedly convinces him to go forward with the Malory
project was not just Arthur's 'sepulture in the monastery of Glastyngburye' or
'Gauwayns skulle [...] in the castel of Dover', but 'at Wynchestre, The Rounde
Table'.[29] Despite pronounced doubts about Arthur's historicity in the sixteenth
century the antiquary John Leland continued to support the veracity of the
Winchester Table in 1544.[30]

   This confusion of the historicity of Arthur and the historicity of relics that
point back to Arthur suggests why it is so difficult to unravel the connection of
the medieval and the medievalistic. Often, even if the historical veracity of the
thing being proved is accepted as true, the relics that point back to the veracious
thing are themselves false — even if they were created as a kind of medievalistic
simulacrum. Worse yet, the attempt to make them appear more medieval often
results in their appearance being less convincing — a situation that the historian
and antiquary Paulo Giovio found himself in when writing about the Round
Table a few years after Leland. He at once asserts that the table is still 'reverently
preserved in the town of Winchester', but then complains that the recent
restoration of the table (it was repainted *c.* 1516) has made it look 'as if it is a
fake'.[31] In this hall of mirrors the dichotomies of original and fake, appearance and
reality, and medieval and modern become unmoored. The table that was created

---

[26] John Hines, *Voices in the Past: English Literature and Archaeology* (Cambridge, 2004), p. 107.

[27] Qtd in Martin Biddle, *King Arthur's Round Table* (Rochester, 2000), p. 393. The quotation is from BL Harleian MS 661, fol. 55[r-v]. As Martin Biddle points out, this assertion about the Winchester Round Table suggests that Hardyng must have heard about or seen the table between the first version of his chronicle and the revised version.

[28] *Caxton's Malory*, ed. by James W. Spisak (Berkeley and Los Angeles, 1983), pp. 1–2.

[29] *Caxton's Malory*, pp. 1–2.

[30] John Leland, *Assertio inclytissimi Arturi* (London, 1544).

[31] The phrase he uses is 'ueluti suspecta fide'; qtd in Biddle, *King Arthur's Round Table*, p. 405. For the date of the repainting see Biddle, *King Arthur's Round Table*, pp. 423–24; 432–45.

as a likeness has been misremembered as the thing itself. The attempt to 'restore' the table to its 'original' state has led to its looking as if it is not the original thing. It is the repainting, the process by which the table was made to look more like itself, that is the issue. The logic behind this medievalistic attempt at restoration can be located in the ways in which Giovo frames his complaint. He says that after the restoration, the table had 'lost a great part of its dignity' (magnam partem dignitatis amiserat) — a curious comment until we realize that *dignitas* is also used to describe the supernatural part of the relic.[32] It is that thing, the indescribable portion, that (like the dignity of the king) never dies ('dignitas non moritur'). This *dignitas* does not reside in the thing itself, but describes that which we attribute to the thing because we believe it genuine. On the analogy of the religious relic, the rejection of medievalism is an attempt to forestall the ability of a credulous pilgrim to imbue this *dignitas* into the fake, by suggesting that the very idea of *dignitas* is medieval and medievalistic, hence is itself false.

These examples suggest that the distinctions between the medieval and the modern, and between traditional medieval studies as the primary discipline and medievalism as its secondary, derivative offshoot are both ideologically rich and intellectually shortsighted. Moreover, they show that conventional distinctions between the medieval, the modern, and the postmodern do not always answer to the particularities of either medieval or early-modern historiography, or to the political needs of successive eras, from the medieval period to the present. In order to write the history, the present and the future of the medieval, we must engage in a systematic investigation of the genealogy of these categories and divisions, and recollect along the way that the remains of the medieval always have a contemporary plot.

College of Wooster

University of Melbourne

---

[32] Qtd in Biddle, *King Arthur's Round Table*, p. 405.

ARE WE HAVING FUN YET?
A RESPONSE TO PRENDERGAST AND TRIGG

Carolyn Dinshaw

I read Thomas Prendergast and Stephanie Trigg's essay while in my part-time home in the Catskills, a mountainous region in upstate New York.[1] I can imagine few better settings for taking in their argument, especially their point that the distinctions privileging medieval studies over medievalism, medievalists over antiquarians, Prendergast and Trigg maintain, boil down to anxious disciplinary preferences for work over pleasure. In this remote, some say even magical, place I engaged with the ongoing life of the past, spurred on by the essay, and began to imagine a more inclusive, a more pleasurable field of study. I must say that work, indeed, has rarely felt so playful.

The Catskills provide the perfect locale for such theorizing and imagining. Not only the beauties but also the strange temporalities of the area are legendary: if you believe the story by Washington Irving, published in 1819 and taken 'so seriously' in the region 'that they [i.e., Irving's legends] became a part of almost every historical account thereafter', Rip van Winkle slept for twenty years one night in these hills, enchanted by ancient Dutch spirits.[2] Irving, an American

---

[1] This response had its genesis in the panel 'What Is Happening to the Middle Ages?' at the New Chaucer Society Conference, New York, July 2006, where I presented a response to papers by Stephanie Trigg, Philip Thiel, and James Simpson. Thanks to all the panelists for their stimulating work.

[2] Raymond O'Brien in *American Sublime*, qtd by Judith Richardson, *Possessions: The History and Uses of Haunting in the Hudson Valley* (Cambridge, MA, 2003), p. 66. Richardson observes that this mountainous region was 'historically a place of rapid change and development' (p. 3), and abandoned ruins of such rapidity still assert their own time lines in the postindustrial landscape. I note, too, that the Catskills area provides a pleasant retreat for me and other privileged urbanites

writer who eventually made his home in the Hudson Valley region of the Catskill mountain range, was in fact a dedicated reader of English medieval literature, an Anglophile and enthusiastic antiquarian. Prendergast and Trigg's essay inspires me to take seriously not only the temporal weirdness of 'Rip van Winkle' but also the medieval re-enactments and longings of Geoffrey Crayon, the narratorial voice of Irving's *Sketch-Book of Geoffrey Crayon* in which 'Rip van Winkle' and numerous other short pieces appear.

Nonlinear, nonprogressive temporalities have always been a fact of life for medievalists, and such 'new times', to use Homi Bhabha's convenient if somewhat misleading term, have become urgent of late in the context of medievalists' deployments of post-structuralist and postcolonial theories.[3] Indeed, ease with the collapse of linear times and periodizations, and openness to 'new' (if old) ones, enable and underwrite Prendergast and Trigg's analysis here. But a similarly serious stake in what we medievalists have heretofore shrugged off as 'medievalistic' — costume fairs, theme restaurants, novels, movies, video games — has been harder for us to imagine. Medievalism is not as easy to assimilate to our received disciplinary practices, Prendergast and Trigg contend, because it looks too trivial and easy (not to mention delightful) to us, while we are highly trained labourers in our sombre vineyard of scholarship. But Prendergast and Trigg challenge us to acknowledge the vital connections between and among temporal practices recorded in our medieval texts, our own scholarly activities, and popular medievalistic endeavours. They argue that 'the "medieval" is continually in process of becoming', which means not only that we constantly shift and revise our ideas of the Middle Ages with new information and analyses about the past, but also that the medieval is always being produced in relation to the present, 'any given present', and that the problems of relevance and use of the past are thus foregrounded in the process they call 'medievalization'.

---

but the local economies, at least in Sullivan County, are far from robust. For my general orientation to Washington Irving, in addition to Richardson's work and Warner's, cited below, I have relied on Susan Manning's helpful introduction to *The Sketch-Book of Geoffrey Crayon, Gent.* (Oxford, 1996). References to this edition appear parenthetically in the text.

[3] I have commented on the usefulness and the shortcomings of Bhabha's approach in *Getting Medieval: Sexualities and Communities, Pre- and Postmodern* (Durham, 1999), pp. 16–21. For a sampler of medievalists working on temporal issues in theoretically informed frameworks, see Paul Strohm, *Theory and the Premodern Text* (Minneapolis, 2000); Jeffrey J. Cohen, *Medieval Identity Machines* (Minneapolis, 2003); and Kathleen Biddick, *The Typological Imaginary: Circumcision, Technology, History* (Philadelphia, 2003).

In my remarks here I am inspired by Prendergast and Trigg to undertake some serious play, engaging their discussion from my couch before the fire in this charmed place. I look closely at the perennially delightful short story, 'Rip van Winkle', with a hunch that this unlikely source (indeed, a medievalist might snort, what is easier to read and therefore less inconsequential than an American short story?) can be seen to animate the temporal principles informing Prendergast and Trigg's article and can help expand thinking about our anxious discipline along the lines these authors open up. Then I turn to 'A Royal Poet' in the *Sketch-Book*, which, unlike Rip's story, at least nominally has something to do with the Middle Ages: the poet of the title is James I of Scotland, his poem is the *Kingis Quaire*, and the narrative of this short piece follows Geoffrey Crayon's highly romanticized account of his visit to Windsor Castle. 'A Royal Poet', even as it traces Crayon's nostalgic longings, offers surprising reassurance to the card-carrying medievalist — like myself in another mood, when I'm not sequestered here in my rural retreat — who might worry about the dissolution of her professional self if medievalism, with its blatant pleasures, not to mention flowing velvet robes, gets too close.

Rip van Winkle and Medieval Studies

Washington Irving's famous story introduces Rip van Winkle, living in a village on the Hudson River and roaming happily throughout the mountainous area. Beloved of his fellow villagers, he shirks familial duties and his wife's nagging to attend to any other household's needs but his own, to wander, and to play. Walking deep into the woods one afternoon, he indulges his passion for shooting squirrels, thus successfully avoiding Dame van Winkle and his own domestic obligations. The rest is, as they say, history: as evening starts to fall on his little hunting adventure, Rip hears his name cried out in the twilight air; he sees a stranger, dressed quaintly, carrying a keg up a steep mountainside; he helps the 'old man of the glen' (p. 40), and together they approach a 'a company of odd-looking personages playing at nine-pins' (p. 39). The group is solemn and mysterious, and Rip is puzzled by them. They partake of the liquor of the keg, and so does Rip, whose senses are gradually overpowered. He wakes up later, stiff in the joints, to find his dog gone, his gun oddly aged, and his beard grown a foot long.

Overnight, it seems, Rip has become a walking anachronism: everything, including his own body, has aged considerably, but he is cognizant of only one night's passing. Rip descends the mountain he knows so well but does not recognize much of his village, so 'altered' it is (p. 42); the villagers don't recognize him either, and the whole experience becomes more and more alarming until it provokes an out and out 'identity crisis', as Michael Warner puts it in an article to which I am deeply indebted here.[4] Soon, though, the temporal basics and his identity are re-established, and Rip, the fittingness of whose name is now clear, settles back into life around a two-decade lapse. His wife has died and he can finally live as the bachelor, idle and revered, he always psychically was, 'one of the patriarchs of the village' (p. 47) with its traditions and lore.

So time has passed, but Rip, asleep, did not experience it. There was virtually no duration at all to those twenty years. Rip has become history — he is called 'a chronicle of the old times "before the war"' (p. 47) — but his 'historical consciousness' was achieved without 'inhabiting time', in Warner's terms.[5] Rip is the very embodiment of temporal heterogeneity, at once in and out of time; he has a 'long grizzled beard' (p. 43) and rheumatic joints, and he hobbles along at a slowed down pace (p. 41), but his consciousness does not include the process of aging during those twenty years. He prefers younger people to 'his former cronies [...] all rather the worse for the wear and tear of time' (p. 47), which Rip did not, after all, experience.

Neither did he experience the Revolution. That great rupture in the narrative of American origins, through which he slept, seems to Rip after the fact to be nothing but a matter of minor adjustments. As Rip makes his way back to his village after the twenty-year night, he recognizes the sign outside his favourite inn: the face on it was the same — it was King George's — but the colour of the coat had been changed from red to blue and buff, and 'GENERAL WASHINGTON' had been painted underneath. The permanent deposition of his wife's tyrannical rule brings him joy, however, and he happily resumes the old habits formerly begrudged him (p. 47), occupying 'his place once more on the bench at the inn door' (p. 47).

It's a fascinating tale of time and history, of temporal multiplicity and anachronism, very suggestive about lived, or, better, living relations between past and present, which Prendergast and Trigg see as crucial to medieval studies. We can see in this story the very process of 'medievalization' Prendergast and Trigg identify and discuss — the first instance of which 'invoked' the Middle Ages from the perspective of 'the Renaissance', and which continues to construct the

---

[4] Michael Warner, 'Irving's Posterity', *ELH*, 67 (2000), 773–99 (p. 787).

[5] Warner, 'Irving's Posterity', referring to Irving here, p. 790.

medieval even now. In Irving's story medievalizing happens as a particular manifestation of 'revolutionary consciousness', to use James Simpson's term.[6] Among the Catskill villagers the rupture of the American Revolution isolates creatures like bearded Rip with his rusty gun as alien and outdated. In Rip's befuddlement and panic we get a sense of how it *feels* to be medievalized: in this case it feels very, very wrong, eventually threatening Rip's very being: 'I'm not myself — I'm somebody else [...] I can't tell what's my name, or who I am!' (p. 45). But medievalization is just part of the story in this village: Rip himself feels continuity, not rupture, and his experiential continuities render the 'historical ruptures' of revolution and 'modernity' nugatory, as Warner has demonstrated.[7] As every historian knows and as 'Rip van Winkle' works out in narrative, a revolution does not necessarily or evenly across a population produce a rupture in experience. Moreover, Prendergast and Trigg's analysis opens up the intriguing prospect that something or someone being medievalized can resist or push back against that process of medievalization.

Of course, there *is* a temporal gap or discontinuity in Rip's being; he simply lives with it, or it lives with him, unconcerned as he is with what exactly happened or what 'the changes of states and empires' (p. 47) might mean. A medieval studies attuned to time as a lived phenomenon will accomodate, indeed explore, the fact that chronology, the time line of events, clock time, do not tell us everything — or, in many cases, even very much — about lived experience. Lives do not always proceed tidily as linear narratives; they may be experienced progressively despite chronological gaps, as in Rip's case, or they may be experientially punctuated by holes, lapses, blackouts. Moreover, as Rip's world attests, different people can experience totally different temporalities in the same present moment: not only is time not a smooth stream, but it is also not the same for everyone. As Ernst Bloch, one of the most interesting theorists of asynchrony, writes:

> Not all people exist in the same Now. They do so only externally, through the fact that they can be seen today. But they are thereby not yet living at the same time with the others.[8]

---

[6] James Simpson, 'Diachronic History and the Shortcomings of Medieval Studies', *Reading the Medieval in Early Modern England*, ed. by David Matthews and Gordon McMullan (Cambridge, 2007).

[7] Warner, 'Irving's Posterity', p. 790.

[8] Ernst Bloch, *Heritage of Our Times*, trans. by Neville and Stephen Plaice (Berkeley and Los Angeles, 1991), p. 97. I was first alerted to this passage by Vincent Geoghegan, *Ernst Bloch* (London, 1996), p. 39.

Medieval studies must be capacious enough to encourage us to reckon thoroughly with such heterogeneities of temporal apprehension and the implications (historical, disciplinary) thereof — the felt experience of time, be it the time of medieval merchants, clerics, or labourers (made famous by Jacques Le Goff), or mystics, or scholars, or members of the Society for Creative Anachronism.[9]

Prendergast and Trigg point to a whole range of cultural productions ignored or scorned by medievalists unwilling to explore the consequences that 'medieval studies have any relevance to the modern age'. Moreover, there's another — perhaps related — realm that causes similar medievalist reactions: the realm of the spiritual, of belief, of faith. Temporal heterogeneity is in fact a hallmark of Christianity, with its enormous influence over medieval lives, and a temporally expansive medieval studies needs to take faith, and more broadly the supernatural, to be taken seriously. The supernatural — ancient Dutch spirits in their 'quaint' dress; ghosts; the divine — can emerge into view at any moment and can transform one's sense of causality, history, and time. Faith, moreover, does not merely oppose the rational; 'faith of a kind' is in fact the ground of all interpretation, as James Simpson puts it. Interpretation is like religion, Simpson argues, in that it 'demands' an 'exercise of faith' in order to begin.[10] Furthermore, interpretation is an asynchronous or temporally heterogeneous activity: when I read Margery Kempe's *Book*, I encounter her words in a hermeneutical Now in which medieval past meets twenty-first-century present. The peculiar temporality of interpretation — the time of hermeneutic contact — is out of linear time.[11] In view of such inevitable hermeneutic conditions, medieval studies is not — and we must not pretend that it is — so entirely separate from the spiritual phenomena it discusses. Prendergast and Trigg show how sixteenth-century reformers equated the Middle Ages with credulity and fakery in their

[9] Jacques Le Goff, *Time, Work, and Culture in the Middle Ages*, trans. by Arthur Goldhammer (Chicago, 1980).

[10] James Simpson, 'Faith and Hermeneutics: Pragmatism versus Pragmatism', *Journal of Medieval and Early Modern Studies*, 33 (2003), 215–39 (pp. 215, 229).

[11] See Dipesh Chakrabarty, 'Minority Histories and Subaltern Pasts', in *Provincializing Europe: Postcolonial Thought and Historical Difference* (Princeton, 2000), pp. 97–113, which has informed my thinking about hermeneutics and the supernatural here. On hermeneutics see also Jeffrey J. Kripal, *Roads of Excess, Palaces of Wisdom: Eroticism and Reflexivity in the Study of Mysticism* (Chicago, 2001).

reformist approach to relics. But we would do well to explore the significance of possible conjunctions between faith, on the one hand, and the topics and methods of our scholarly investigations, on the other.

One final aspect of the temporal heterogeneity of 'Rip van Winkle' has a bearing on possibilities for a renovated medieval studies: this particular wrinkle in time occurs outside the bounds of the normative, reproductive family. Rip distances himself from family life, and his outsider-ness is expressed temporally, in the queer time of a night that is twenty years long. If sequential, linear time and narrative are understood as linked to reproduction and generation, forming what Warner calls 'repronarrative', Rip's story provides a glimpse outside such a framework.[12] And though Irving backs away from this vision, as Warner compellingly demonstrates, even the brief sighting is challenging to received ideas of social structure.[13] Contrast this with the movie Prendergast and Trigg cite for its 'egregious' exemplification of the 'deep problem of the economy of 'medievalism'': *First Knight*. As they point out, Lancelot and Guinevere 'need not be parted by death, but can go on and rule the kingdom with Arthur's dying blessing'. Times collapse (indeed, a critic called Richard Gere's Lancelot 'a walking anachronism') yet heterosexuality sallies forth unperturbed.[14] But in order to expand our notions of social possibilities in and across time, medieval studies renovated in ways Prendergast and Trigg suggest must include — indeed, must prioritize — the investigation of temporal phenomena that are not structured by a conventional reproductive imperative.[15]

[12] Warner, 'Irving's Posterity', p. 786.

[13] Warner, 'Irving's Posterity', pp. 787–88. Warner comments on the story's 'frank misogyny' (p. 784) and suggests ways that misogyny functions in the patriarchal structures of Irving's literary endeavours. Judith Fetterley's groundbreaking feminist analysis of 'Rip van Winkle' in her *Resisting Reader: A Feminist Approach to American Fiction* (Bloomington, 1978) is crucial to any discussion of the story's misogyny.

[14] Janet Maslin, 'The Tale of Camelot, Now Color Coordinated', *New York Times*, 7 July 1995, <http://movies2.nytimes.com/mem/movies/review.html?_r=1&res=990CEFDC1631F93 4A35754C0A963958260&oref=slogin> (accessed 20 May 2007).

[15] Simpson analyses the imaginative communication between living and dead as a living communion 'between friends and family, across the boundary of death' in Thomas More's *Supplication of Souls* (1529), in 'Diachronic History'; in *Getting Medieval* I have discussed affective relations across time as resources for community.

Geoffrey Crayon and Creative Anachronism

Prendergast and Trigg examine the suspicions harboured by scholarly medievalists toward popular medievalisms, particularly their worry that these medievalisms do not offer difficulty enough to sustain professors — or, more to the point, professions. We can extrapolate further from their analysis: medievalists may well suspect that it is not only easy to give in to desire for the past but unethical: with desire let loose, one will inevitably re-create a past that is but one's own reflection, idealized or abjected. Thus medievalisms violate not only the medievalist's work ethic, but also medievalists' sense of the integrity of the past. Irving's 'A Royal Poet' offers unexpected reassurance to medievalists on this score. Sentimental antiquarian reverie though it is, the piece nonetheless suggests that the past retains its otherness even though deep desire and labour enough have been expended in its present re-creation.

Washington Irving's Geoffrey Crayon is his fictionalized self — an unmarried New Yorker who reads and visits monuments of British literature and culture, and produces 'sketches' of them. For Crayon, crossing geographical boundaries entails crossing temporal boundaries as well; for him the contrast between America and Europe can be graphed on a timeline: 'My native country was full of youthful promise: Europe was rich in the accumulated treasures of age' (p. 12). The tone is satiric and mockingly self-deprecating ('I will visit this land of wonders, thought I, and see the gigantic race from which I am degenerated') but such self-conscious belatedness proves a guiding light through the book (p. 12).

The very name 'Geoffrey Crayon' reflects the Chaucerian-ness of this narratorial stance, which extends from belatedness to outsider status in love. As Michael Warner argues, not only did national difference from England prove a bounteous source of Irving's 'antihistorical rhetoric of anachronism' but so also did his bachelorhood.[16] Crayon is radically unattached, as the *Sketch-Book*'s epigraph from Burton announces: 'I have no wife nor children, good or bad, to provide for. A mere spectator of other men's fortunes and adventures, and how they play their parts', he is distanced from all, and that isolation proves both a motive of his chosen literary genre — the 'sketch', record of a 'vagrant inclination' (p. 13) — as well as the psychic core of his nostalgia and felt sense of anachronism.[17]

---

[16] Warner, 'Irving's Posterity', p. 776.

[17] Warner, 'Irving's Posterity', p. 774.

In 'A Royal Poet', Crayon recalls his visit to Windsor Castle, where James was imprisoned before he became king of Scotland. Geoffrey has read James's poem, the *Kingis Quaire*, and found it remarkable; he gives a leisurely, appreciative account of it, including its bookish, Chaucerian beginning in which insomniac James (the opposite of epic sleeper Rip van Winkle) picks up the *Boece* to wile away the long night. But Crayon is most interested in the elements of James's poem that touch upon his captivity. Self-professed idler and 'vagrant bachelor', distanced from institutional power or the bosom of a wife, Crayon finds in James's poem the inspiring message of aristocratic fortitude in the face of adversity and an expression of the highly romantic love of a lady. As do olden times in general, the *Kingis Quaire* provides Geoffrey Crayon a corrective to his present day; the past is where an old bachelor can begin to feel whole.

Indeed, the chronic movement of loss and desolation has been halted by means of poetry. Poetry has converted the negative effects on Windsor Castle of time into 'charm':

> Time, which delights to obliterate the sterner memorials of human pride, seems to have passed lightly over this little scene of poetry and love, and to have withheld his desolating hand. Several centuries have gone by, yet the garden still flourishes at the foot of the tower. It occupies what was once the moat of the keep; and though some parts have been separated by dividing walls, yet others have still their arbors and shaded walks, as in the days of James, and the whole is sheltered, blooming, and retired. (p. 86)

The charmed spot inspires 'poetical devotion', a contemplative 'musing over the romantic loves of the Lady Jane and the Royal Poet of Scotland' (p. 87) that moves toward union with the departed spirits. Geoffrey walks where James walked and feels the 'voluptuous vernal' weather that James felt, in 'the same genial and joyous month' as that in which James wrote his poem (pp. 75, 85). The sight of a suit of armour, 'richly gilt and embellished, as if to figure in the tournay, brought the image of the gallant and romantic prince vividly before my imagination' (p. 85).

Geoffrey is absorbed in imaginative re-enactment. That is, he is *almost* absorbed. 'I paced the deserted chambers where he had composed his poem; I leaned upon the window, and endeavored to persuade myself it was the very one where he had been visited by his vision; I looked out upon the spot where he had first seen the Lady Jane' (p. 85). Between the pacing of the chambers and the gaze upon the spot Geoffrey must work to convince himself of authenticity, presence, identity, union. The statement of the effort of self-persuasion opens a suggestion of failure: *I endeavored to persuade myself*, I laboured, but I couldn't after all believe that the future king and I were so proximate, that he and I could be one.

The acknowledgment of distance within Geoffrey's elaborate re-enactment at Windsor attests to something of ineradicable alienness: the past, revealed in this brief moment, retains its otherness. Despite the nostalgic framework, despite the subjective anachronism Irving has created in the character of Geoffrey Crayon, something about that past resists absorption.

If its use of the past as ideal mirror is cloying, 'A Royal Poet' at last reassures us of a firm subject/object relation, an epistemological condition finally familiar to and comfortable for scholars. The work is gently nostalgic; Crayon has no mystical experience at Windsor Castle. In fact, his perception of difference foreshadows the failure of imperial control that Irving senses in his later works.[18] That little distance between self and other, and the labour necessary to attempt to cross it, assure us that a distinction between the medieval and the medievalistic really does obtain, and thus what we understand as the past's own intransigence makes an ethical relation to it possible. Prendergast and Trigg point to the elision of 'the rich traditions of nineteenth-century medievalism' in our discipline's genealogical narratives, elisions made because that medievalism does not fit into 'our own genealogy of labor over "the medieval"', but the Irving of 'A Royal Poet' is not so threatening, after all, for at least this American medievalist to assume as her forebear.

(Jury) Duty and Pleasure

In the hub of urban labour in lower Manhattan, far away from my upstate retreat, I sat recently in the New York County Court House, diligently doing jury duty. I watched an orientation video on the evolution of the justice system in the West, from which I learned that justice has apparently reached its zenith in the US jury system. In demonstrating this, the video contrasted the modern American way with — you guessed it — the medieval system of the ordeal. I was only half-watching, so my details are sketchy at best, but there it was, as if to prove the ubiquity of the medievalizing phenomenon Prendergast and Trigg analyze: the Middle Ages in gruesome re-enactment, all mucky and guttural. Prendergast and Trigg are onto something that is so utterly familiar to me that I don't even pause over many instances I see. But their essay prompts me to

---

[18] See José F. Buscaglia-Salgado, *Undoing Empire: Race and Nation in the Mulatto Caribbean* (Minneapolis, 2003), chap. 1, 'Tales of the Alhambra: Washington Irving and the Immaculate Conception of America', especially p. 27. Thanks to Jeffrey Cohen for this reference.

regard such phenomena afresh with the sense that our discipline of medieval studies might actually be changed by attention to them. This is an immensely liberating prospect: as it turns out, I can accommodate Geoffrey Crayon's syrupy encomium to 'A Royal Poet' to a scholarly framework, but I remain interested in what might threaten the boundaries between scholarly medieval studies and medievalism, or further down that road, between labour and pleasure, between past and present, between object and subject, between not-me and me. Not knowing exactly where all that could lead, I'm nonetheless willing to go there — are we having fun yet? — and if others as well take up the challenge, medieval studies could in fact shift on its axis, never to be quite the same.

New York University

Analytical Survey

THE HISTORY OF THE BOOK

Alexandra Gillespie

In July 2006, Jonathan E. Rose sent an e-mail to the listserv for the Society for the History of Authorship, Reading, and Publishing (SHARP): it had the subject line 'Book History Still Smokin'" and it directed members' attention to an article in the *Chronicle of Higher Education*, January 2006. There, Jennifer Howard announced that the history of the book was 'hot type': the hottest topic in English literary studies. It had attracted the greatest number of, and the most animated, discussions at the 2006 meeting of the Modern Language Association; it was the matter over which the junior academics who impressed the 2006 MLA hiring committees cut their scholarly teeth. According to another *Chronicle* article, such interest in the book is inevitable: we live in a digital age and we must 'prepare students to be discerning users of, and contributors to, all media'.[1] Publishers as well as pedagogues are on side: Howard cites the opinion of the Humanities Editor of Oxford University Press (USA) that work on books, archives, and 'an interest in print culture' is the 'main trend' in publication in the field of literary scholarship. A quick glance at some publishers' lists bears this out: Blackwell has just come out with a companion volume on book history;[2] Routledge produced a book history *Reader* in 2004, a short introduction to book history in 2005, and a second, revised and updated edition of the *Reader* in 2006;[3]

---

[1] Howard, 'At the MLA'; Tenner, 'The Prestigious Inconvenience of Print'. I say no more about the impact of digital technologies on the history of the book below; *Electronic Text*, ed. by Sutherland, is a useful introduction. For full citations of the sources listed throughout, see my bibliography, pp. 279–86, below.

[2] *A Companion to the History of the Book*, ed. by Eliot and Rose (in press at time of writing).

[3] Finkelstein and McCleery, *An Introduction to Book History*, and *The Book History Reader*, ed. by Finkelstein and McCleery.

new volumes from the *Cambridge History of the Book in Britain* series are keenly anticipated;[4] Oxford University Press, too, has a *Companion to the Book*.[5] Penn Press has established a series in 'Material Texts' which publishes the sort of monographs and volumes familiar from the lists of most prestigious academic presses in the last few years — for instance *Bibliography and the Book Trades: Studies in the Print Culture of Early New England,* and *American Literature and the Culture of Reprinting, 1834–1853*.[6] *Book History,* the flagship journal for SHARP, is widely subscribed. The success of SHARP itself indicates that the topic is even hotter than just these Anglo-American examples suggest. SHARP was founded in 1991 in order to coordinate the work and concerns of book historians globally; it includes scholars working on the history of the book in over twenty countries. There are projects and published and projected volumes on the history of the book in Australia and New Zealand; the most recent title of the University of Toronto Press's Book History series is *The History of the Book in Canada: Volume III, 1918–1980*.[7] National projects and institutes for the study of book history in continental Europe — for instance, the collaborative *Livre et société dans la France du XVIIIᵉ siècle*[8] or the work of the Arbeitskreis für Geschichte des Buchwesens in Germany, founded in the late 1970s — predate and to some extent shape all others.

It is customary to start an essay such as this by noting that what follows will be incomplete. Here the point seems a little redundant. No survey of work done lately in the field of book history can hope to be comprehensive, for, as Howard observes, the term *book history* describes a great proportion of all the recent work in the field of literary studies. Moreover, her observation comes hot on the heels of Robert Darnton's that the history of books is 'interdisciplinarity run riot'.[9] Just as book history accommodates all sorts of material forms for texts — bound codices; scrolls; scores; epigraphic inscriptions; sound recordings; and e-texts — so does the history of the book accommodate all kinds of academic activity: literary studies but also social history, sociology, cultural studies, communications

---

[4] For instance *The Cambridge History of the Book in Britain,* II: *1100–1400,* ed. by Morgan and Thomson, and *The Cambridge History of the Book in Britain,* V: *1695–1830,* ed. by Suarez and Turner.

[5] *The Oxford Companion to the Book,* ed. by Woudhuysen and Suarez (in press).

[6] *Bibliography and the Book Trades,* ed. by Amory and Hall; McGill, *American Literature.*

[7] *The History of the Book in Canada,* ed. by Gerson and Michon.

[8] Bollème, *Livre et société.*

[9] In his famous 1983 essay 'What Is the History of Books?', p. 5.

theory, the history of technology including digital technologies, antiquarian book collecting, library and archival science, publishing history and book trade economics, theories of text, and practices of textual editing.

I want to start my survey (which will be replete with 'my' opinions; I do not aim for objectivity here) with a disclaimer about scope for the usual reasons, but also because the impression of a field that is burgeoning, flourishing, riotous, crammed with people, full of projects and publications, and above all 'hot' is useful to me. It is one purpose of this survey to suggest that some of this energy is missing from, and might be useful to, the study of medieval books. But the discussion will also consider the following paradox. An interdisciplinary riot described, categorized, and labeled 'the history of books' is also riot disciplined, made subject to what Pierre Bourdieu calls the 'dominant definition', the 'norms and sanctions' of the academic 'field'.[10] The paradox is also a problem. What is hot is not *cool* anymore: its energy is dissipating; it is the cool thing discovered, which, according to the theory of cool, causes cool to move on.[11] The hot is always somewhat belated — there is no more chance of its heating up in the future. Rose makes this point inadvertently in the message to the SHARP listserv with which my discussion began. Howard's was not the first *Chronicle* article to identify the trend in book history; apparently the same thing was written about the field in 1993.[12] Here is Rose's response: '[Y]es, I know, the Chronicle said we were hot 15 [*sic*] years ago — so I guess you could say we're the Mick Jagger of academia.' You could surmise from this that the field is 'hot' — or else, with all respect to Mr Jagger, you could say that the history of the book is getting a little long in the tooth.

The hot/cool distinction provides a further way to think about the status of book history, since it can be likened to one of Marshall McLuhan's famous descriptions of books themselves. In *Understanding Media*, McLuhan argues that the 'word', recorded in writing and especially in print, is 'hot', because it is crammed with data and 'high definition'.[13] It leaves few 'cool' gaps for the reader to fill in, but explains itself in ways that much oral and digital discourse does not (you are not told as much by the words you hear during a telephone call as you are

[10] Bourdieu, *The Field of Cultural Production*, pp. 77–80.

[11] On what is and then is not cool, see Gladwell, 'The Coolhunt'.

[12] Winkler, 'In Electronic Age'.

[13] McLuhan, *Understanding Media*, pp. 22–23.

by the words in this neatly and conventionally arranged book). The 'hot' history of the book is certainly 'high definition'. Darnton's 1983 article; the volume on *Needs and Opportunities in Book History* produced by the American Antiquarian Society in 1987;[14] the introduction to the first issue of the journal *Book History*;[15] Edward L. Bishop's entry on 'Book History' in the second edition of the *Johns Hopkins Guide to Literary Theory and Criticism*; Cyndia Clegg's 'History of the Book: An Undisciplined Discipline?'; Jean Shelley Rubin's 'What Is the History of the History of Books?'; the introductory comments and the short guide compiled by McLeery and Finkelstein for the Routledge *Reader*;[16] Leslie Howsam's *Old Books and New Histories: An Orientation to Studies in Book and Print Culture*; essays by Leah Price and Seth Lerer in their 2006 special issue of *PMLA* on book history;[17] the opening chapter of Joseph A. Dane's *The Myth of Print Culture* — each of these defines book history. Each assumes and produces the coherence that constitutes a 'university sub-field', a 'site of struggles in which what is at stake is the power to impose [...] dominant definition' and so to claim the 'monopoly of the power to consecrate producers or products'.[18] Howard identifies the sort of agents 'with the power to consecrate' book history as a field in her *Chronicle* article: they are members of hiring committees, commissioning editors, and the hirable writers of academic work that they commission. There are new signs of this process of consecration. When Darnton described the field in 1983, he noted that the history of the book did not have its own 'generation of Ph.D.s'.[19] There are PhDs now — emerging from the collaborative programme in 'Book History and Print Culture' at the University of Toronto, for instance. There are societies; book series; MLA sessions; and any number of survey articles to which an aspiring book historian may refer. 'The history of books' thus 'shows how a field of knowledge can take on a distinct scholarly identity.' It begins with the cool 'glint' that Darnton says he can recognize in the eyes of like-minded

---

[14] *Needs and Opportunities*, ed. by Hall and Hench.

[15] Rose and Greenspan 'An Introduction to *Book History*'.

[16] Finkelstein and McCleery, *An Introduction to Book History*, and *The Book History Reader*, ed. by Finkelstein and McCleery.

[17] Price, 'Introduction: Reading Matter', and Lerer, 'Epilogue: Falling Asleep over the History of the Book'.

[18] Bourdieu, *The Field of Cultural Production*, p. 78.

[19] Darnton, 'What Is the History of Books?', p. 4.

scholars.[20] A couple of decades later, it has closed the gaps between those scholars: it is the sort of club that is suspiciously happy to have anybody as member.

I am making the point that Leah Price makes when she says 'so far, so triumphalist' — and then suggests that 'the history of the book' might need some redirection.[21] It is the mock-serious point that David Finkelstein made when he introduced the Routledge *Reader* to a group of Toronto Book History and Print Culture students in 2005 and predicted that the volume would bring about the field's demise. Soon scholars everywhere will be bored by 'book history' — that tedious course they had to take at graduate school, its orthodoxies bound up in a cheap paperback reader. What is the book historian to do with these feelings of belatedness, this sense that book history is no longer *cool*? And why situate the study of medieval books in the midst of such a field, if book historians can already see the end (that is, the distinctive purpose and the pending irrelevance) of all of their endeavours?

In what follows, my answer to the first of these questions is also meant to be an answer to the second. The prevailing concern of the highly defined field of book history is, I will argue, cultural history. The hottest of the hot topics taken on by students of book history are those interested in the human contexts for the production and reception of texts. Ralph Hanna III argues that this is the 'cultural move' that premodern book history is missing, and I agree:[22] the first and second parts of my survey are devoted to unpacking the assumptions about book history and the study of medieval books implicit in these statements. The third part of the discussion scores points off a large and rather slow-moving target: 'print culture'. On the one hand, scholars of medieval texts might borrow from the riotous and attention-grabbing energy of the field of book history; on the other hand, book history's most energetic practitioners might notice that the word *book* does not map onto the word *print* as precisely as is usually supposed. Of course, the 'manuscript' is a matter of great interest to scholars of the post-print world, who never cease to be amazed that people continued to write with their hands after Gutenberg cast the first type. I am arguing something different here: that the medieval book comprises some of the 'coolest' gaps in this crowded field; that it proffers new answers to some of the field's most important questions. For

[20] Darnton, 'What Is the History of Books?', pp. 3, 4.

[21] Price, 'Introduction: Reading Matter', p. 9.

[22] Hanna, 'Middle English Manuscripts', p. 248.

instance, what exactly is it about 'print' culture that makes it a 'culture' — or more than just, to quote Joseph A. Dane, 'a pair of words'?[23]

But I am mindful that this approach makes the medieval book an answer to questions about modernity, and while, in doing so, it addresses the impoverishing effects of periodization, I am reluctant to argue that all books and moments and cultures are the same, or that work on medieval manuscripts offers nothing particular, nothing unique, to the field of book history. The fourth part of the survey argues that the medieval book might provide more than new answers to some slightly tired questions about printing: it might be a basis upon which scholars can think again about the field of book history itself. The most obvious gap in a history of books that has become a history of human culture is books themselves. Dane argues this: so do Thomas R. Adams and Nicolas Barker and more recently David L. Vander Meulen.[24] I will argue it again — by considering the book in terms of its productive presence instead of regarding the book as a self-professedly 'boring' way to approach the — finally irrecoverable — past (part of the discussion will be about what David Kastan first described, ironically, as the 'New Boredom' in literary studies). I will argue that this approach — interest in the 'forms' of the book — is not a way to resist, but rather is a new way to respond to D. F. McKenzie's imperative that the scholar recover 'the human presence in any recorded text'.[25] And I will argue that, in what Hanna and many other medieval scholars have described as its opacity, its thickly meaningful particularity, in its blurring of the boundary between the word and its material form, and as the object of very close and formal scholarly inquiry, the medieval book may be the invigorating new beginning that the history of the book needs.

What Is the History of Books?

The question posed by Darnton's 1983 article can be answered negatively. Book history is *not* just a variety of intellectual activities related to books. It does not, therefore, 'dat[e] from the scholarship of the Renaissance, if not earlier', as Darnton claims,[26] no matter how many times this rather vague point is made in

[23] Dane, *The Myth of Print Culture*, p. 17.

[24] Adams and Barker, 'A New Model for the Study of the Book'; Vander Meulen, 'How to Read Book History'.

[25] McKenzie, *Bibliography and the Sociology of Texts*, p. 29.

[26] Darnton, 'What Is the History of Books?', p. 4.

other surveys — for instance by Price: 'Bibliography, palaeography, and editing have been central to scholarship (and not just literary scholarship) since at least the fifteenth century'.[27] All that such statements suggest is that even nuanced narratives about the field need an originary moment, a way to show that the habit of messing about with old books does not begin with *us*. Instead, book history begins in the past — here with the Italian humanists' work to find and edit manuscripts of classical texts. Since suggesting that everything began in the Renaissance is grist for a medievalist's mill, it might be worth noting that it is possible to locate the beginnings of book history earlier, with Richard de Bury's history of book collection and care in the *Philobiblon*,[28] or with Jerome, who worried at the text of the Vulgate amid the piles of Latin, Greek, and Hebrew manuscripts he had collected, and wrote eloquently to Damasus about the problem of scribal corruption and exemplar poverty.[29] Why not go further? Perhaps the history of the book begins when Horace and Martial write so self-consciously about the books and rolls that will bear the imperfect forms of their texts to posterity.[30] Or perhaps the first book historians were more self-conscious and more systematic than were any of these writers or bookmen. Book history could have its origins with exercises in diplomatics and palaeography: with Jean Mabillon's *De re diplomatica* of 1681, which is the first effort to lay out the principles by which diplomatic inquiry into the authenticity of charters should proceed; with Bernard de Montfaucon's 1708 *Paleographia*, which extends and refines Mabillon's work into scientific system for the analysis of scribal hands.[31] It could be traced to the guidelines the study of books and book collections and for collecting itself found in Thomas Frognall Dibdin's *Bibliographical Decameron* (1817). By the mid-eighteenth century, Christian and humanist textual criticism was also increasingly self-aware: consider Johann Albrecht Bengel's invention of the rule *lectio difficilior* in the commentary to his edition of the New Testament of 1734, for instance.[32]

---

[27] Price, 'Introduction: Reading Matter', p. 9.

[28] See *The Love of Books: The Philobiblon of Richard de Bury*, ed. and trans. by Thomas.

[29] De Hamel, *The Book*, pp. 12–28.

[30] For a discussion of the bibliographical awareness of classical writers see Roman, 'The Representation of Literary Materiality'.

[31] See the surveys of Boyle, *Medieval Latin Palaeography*, and Petrucci, *Prima Lezione di Paleografia*.

[32] See Vincent, *A History of the Textual Criticism*; for more on the history of textual criticism, see Greetham, *Textual Scholarship*.

Or perhaps the history of books waits until the moment when these two traditions — study of the forms of books, their production and survival, and study of the text borne by the book — merge in a fully articulated way in the twentieth-century 'New Bibliography' associated with A. W. Pollard, W. W. Greg, R. B. McKerrow, Fredson Bowers, and Thomas Tanselle.[33] The goal of the New Bibliography was editorial: 'to present the text [...] in the form in which we may suppose that it would have stood in fair copy, made by the author himself, of the work as he finally intended it.'[34] In practice this required the formal analysis of emendations and errors, print shop practice and compositorial technique, manuscript sources and paratextual material — in short, the study of books. The New Bibliography produced textbooks, such as Bowers's *Principles of Bibliographical Description*, McKerrow's *An Introduction to Bibliography for Literary Students*, or Gaskell's *A New Introduction to Bibliography*. It also produced taxonomies. In a 1977 essay, Terry Belanger divvies up the field into enumerative bibliography (the cataloguing of books) and analytical (the study of books as objects and analysis of the mode of their production). Analytical bibliography is textual (the relationship between a text in a book and a putative authorial original), historical (study of the contexts for book production), and descriptive (formulaic accounts of a book's form).[35] New Bibliography has also produced, lately, dissent: in Jerome McGann's account of final intention as an effect of collaborative social processes;[36] and in the publications of Randall McLeod, which argue in maddeningly playful ways that the meaning of a text is fully instantiated in its material form — that it should be studied in that form, and not edited at all.[37]

By the time that an account of the origins of book history reaches both the New Bibliography and challenges to its aims, it is in messy territory. McCleery and Finkelstein include some of the work of Jerome McGann in their *Reader* — but exclude the Greg-McKerrow-Bowers-Tanselle tradition that contextualizes McGann's polemic. Most other commentaries — that of Bishop in the *Johns*

---

[33] For the women missing from this well-known lineage, see Maguire, 'How Many Children Had Alice Walker?'

[34] Greg, *The Editorial Problem in Shakespeare*, p. x.

[35] Belanger, 'Descriptive Bibliography'.

[36] McGann, *A Critique of Modern Textual Criticism* and *The Textual Condition*.

[37] McLeod, 'UN-Editing Shak-Speare'.

Hopkins Guide for instance[38] — mention the New Bibliography as a school of early-twentieth-century thought, one that gives rise to but is superceded by 'book history'. Darnton himself suggests that the question New Bibliographers ask — 'What were Shakespeare's original texts?' — is one of the threads that make up the texture of book history, but that book history is something else. It is the 'convergence' of this question with other questions asked by book collectors, librarians, book conservators, students of literacy, learning, and popular culture. It is the 'convergence' of all of the procedures and approaches and histories just described, from which medieval manuscript studies are not necessarily to be excluded, although Darnton says that 'manuscript books will have to be considered elsewhere'.

The question 'what is the history of books?' emerges as this messiness is charted and defined in a particular way — not as 'palaeography' or 'New Bibliography' and certainly not as 'manuscript studies' (which always happen elsewhere) but as 'the history of books'. It emerges because a question like Darnton's, and his narrative of 'convergence', are deemed interesting, tested, challenged, feted, anthologized, repeated, and forgotten, and in the process transformed into what Bourdieu calls a 'dominant definition' of the field. This definition is never perfectly finished or stable; it constructs an idea of external sanction in hazy accounts of its origin; ultimately it sanctions itself. For instance, if it has become conventional for the chroniclers of book history's disciplinary development to nod to 'the Renaissance', it is even more conventional for them to make a statement that follows Darnton along these lines: 'The new book historians brought the subject within the range of themes studied by the 'Annales school' of socioeconomic history.'[39] The *Annales* school is so-called after the body of historical writing associated in the 1950s with the French scholarly journal *Annales d'histoire économique et sociale*, whose contributors' historiographical approach was of the 'large-scale cultural' variety and employed the tools of sociological and statistical analysis. History is not, the school's adherents insist, the doings of a political, social, or intellectual elite, but the experiences of an ordinary majority, which can be discovered from the myriad material traces of their unexceptional existences. These traces include books (they must, because books tend to survive in greater numbers than any other historical artefacts). The work of Lucien Paul Victor Lefebvre and Henri-Jean Martin was important to

[38] Bishop, 'Book History'.
[39] Darnton, 'What Is the History of Books?', pp. 3, 7, 4.

this historiographical tradition, and their best-known publication, *L'Apparition du Livre*, published in English as *The Coming of the Book: The Impact of Print 1450–1800*, founded the French field *histoire du livre*. Lefebvre and Martin test statistical and sociological methods — twenty million incunables are counted and their 'impact' described in the broadest possible terms — and develops a basis from Darnton's own project can proceed.

More than twenty years later, Leslie Howsam's *Old Books and New Histories* reshapes but also reiterates this account of the field. 'Like social class' she writes, 'the book is not so much a category as a process: books happen; they happen to people who read, reproduce, disseminate, and compose them; and they happen to be significant. *The book* can be a force for change and *the history of the book* documents that change.'[40] The common ground between Darnton's, Howsam's, and all other attempts to establish and even disrupt the norms of the discipline of book history, is the assumption that those norms produce 'a human story' from a 'tale of books'.[41] This is why McGann, who is a textual bibliographer, and who positions himself not in relation to book history but against the New Bibliography, makes it into the Routledge *Book History Reader* when Greg or Tanselle and even McLeod do not. New Bibliography is concerned with the text as a witness to final authorial intention. McLeod writes about the way that books and texts stake their claims to meaning largely on their own terms[42] — some of his most recent work concerns the accidental forms left by bearing type for instance. McGann by contrast insists that the only way to get around the formalism or 'romantic hermeneutics' of such approaches, in which the text is conceived in its own linguistic and/or bibliographical conditions, is 'by socializing the study of texts at the most radical levels' by recognizing that 'of course all texts' are 'like all other things human'.[43] Books have a history, become significant, as index to 'change', which is not to do with books: it has to do with people.

The claim that book history is a human story about books totalizes some extremely diverse scholarly work: let me briefly categorize some of this diversity and include representative titles that will not appear elsewhere in the discussion. Book history is in a very large part, especially recently, a history of readers and reading, for it is they who change books, and are changed by them. The work of

[40] Howsam, *Old Books and New Histories*, p. 5.

[41] Lerer, 'Epilogue: Falling Asleep Over the History of the Book', p. 230.

[42] McLeod, 'UN-Editing Shak-Speare'.

[43] McGann, *The Textual Condition*, pp. 12–13.

Roger Chartier on readerly 'appropriation' and bookish 'mediation' of reading has been especially influential.[44] Reading is the subject of many more specific studies: Kate Flint's *The Woman Reader, 1837–1914*; Anthony Grafton's work on 'The Humanist as Reader'; Elizabeth McHenry's *Forgotten Readers*, which considers the 'lost history' African American literary societies; Heather Jackson's work on *Marginalia*. Interest in authors has not diminished as a result: book history is involved in finding answers to Michel Foucault's essay 'What Is an Author?' — as in Mark Rose's work on *Authors and Owners: The Invention of Copyright* or Juliet Gardiner's brilliant account of the uses found for authors' names in the mass marketing of textual products in the 1990s.[45]

Book history is to a significant extent, as Howard argues in the 2006 *Chronicle* article, an aspect of literary studies: it is a short hop from the New Historicist or cultural materialist critical 'turn' of the 1980s, which relocated the production of literary meaning in historical settings, to the turn that reads the book as a force for change in human society in those same settings.[46] As in the New Historicism, much important work has been done on Renaissance texts — think of Jeff Masten's *Textual Intercourse: Collaboration, Authorship, and Sexualities in Renaissance Drama*; Douglas Brooks's *From Playhouse to Printing House*; and Joseph Loewenstein's brilliant work on Ben Jonson, print and 'possessive authorship'.[47] Historians whose work overlaps with the work of book history are attuned to questions about social and cultural history that define the field. James Raven's *The Business of Books* is a superb survey of the commercialization of the book trade and a social history of the novel; James Secord's *Victorian Sensation: The Extraordinary Publication, Reception and Secret Authorship of 'Vestiges of the Natural History of Creation'* describes the furor surrounding publication of a scientific book and its relation to the emerging industrial economy of print. In American historical studies, the comments of Michael Denning, *Mechanic Accents: Dime Novels and Working-Class Culture in America* are characteristic. Much of the work in this part of the field is on real books, and real readers' testimony, but this empirical work is considered 'antiquarian' unless addressed to 'cultural history and cultural criticism'.[48]

---

[44] Chartier, 'Frenchness in the History of the Book' and *The Order of Books*.

[45] Gardiner, 'Recuperating the Author'.

[46] See *The New Historicism*, ed. by Veeser, on New Historicism.

[47] Loewenstein, *The Author's Due* and *Ben Jonson and Possessive Authorship*.

[48] Denning, *Mechanic Accents*, p. 263.

The descriptive function of analytical and descriptive bibliography has not been wholly lost from this cultural history of books. Gérard Genette's *Paratexts: Thresholds of Interpretation* has turned attention to title pages and finding devices, prefaces, advertisements, imprints, jacket blurbs, and illustrations alongside texts. Genette's ideas have been taken up and 'socialized' by book historians. Paratexts, especially the prefaces to early editions, are the stuff of Wendy Wall's *Imprint of Gender*, for instance, which describes the negotiation of anxieties and desires respecting class and gender in early-modern paratexual space. There continues to be work, like McLeod's, or Robert Bringhurst's on typography,[49] that is differently oriented — toward ways of thinking about the capacity of each mark in a book to create and disrupt its own systems of meaning. But the field of book history is one in which the significance of such work must be explained away, made a part of a story about how people need, use, make, and change texts.

What Is the History of Manuscript Books?

The particularly human story that is book history stops at the study of premodern books. There is, of course, much lively, informative, important work on medieval manuscripts and other nonbook forms for medieval texts. Any survey of this work will, at times, sound similar to a survey of work in the field of book history. Middle English manuscript studies, for instance, were for much of the twentieth century driven by the desire for authorial beginnings for texts and authoritative endings to the process of editing. By the end of the century, such studies were both distrustful of the validity of these procedures and findings — think of Anne Hudson's sceptical account of the uses of stemmatics in *Crux and Controversy* — and interested in the study of books for their own sake. A. I. Doyle's work was groundbreaking in the latter regard: his unpublished 1953 Cambridge PhD thesis is still compulsory reading for any scholar interested in the material dissemination of Middle English texts. Derek Pearsall also contributed a great deal to the development of the field of Middle English manuscript studies. He oversaw innovative work while at the University of York in the 1980s: that of Julia Boffey on the courtly lyric in all its manuscript variety (published 1985) and John Thompson on the Thornton manuscript (published 1987), for instance.[50] Since

---

[49] Bringhurst, *The Elements of Typographic Style*.

[50] Boffey, *Manuscripts of English Courtly Love Lyrics*; Thompson, *Robert Thornton and the London Thornton Manuscript*.

the 1980s, as Pearsall argues in his article 'Value/s of Manuscript Study: A Personal Retrospect', the study of medieval books has burgeoned. But I would make a bold claim about this trend. Beyond the observation that manuscripts have become interesting for their own sake; beyond a loosely shared palaeographical and descriptive methodology (for which there is nothing like the systematic explication of printed book description found in textbooks by Bowers and Gaskell);[51] beyond frameworks for analysis developed internally within discussions, no disciplinary structure is apparent that might suggest that all sorts of medieval manuscript studies are a 'field' or are 'hot' in the way that the history of the book is.

I do not mean to be *too* bold, so let me qualify that statement immediately. First, many distinguished codicologists have endeavoured to lay out procedures for manuscript studies — in Middle English studies, Ralph Hanna III, most obviously and successfully, especially in his work on booklets, vernacularity, exemplar poverty, and the localization of production and meaning in manuscript books, but also Kathryn Kerby-Fulton and Seth Lerer on the relationship between scribal and authorial work; Simon Horobin on scribal dialect; and Linne R. Mooney building on Doyle and Malcolm Parkes's work on professional scribes and scribal hands.[52] In all of their publications, A. S. G. Edwards and Julia Boffey employ a rigorous and cautious methodology in which evidence from manuscripts and also early printed books reveals the complexity of the cultures in which medieval texts subsisted.[53] There has been invigorating work on 'whole' books, in which the manuscript — Vernon or Harley — is considered a meaning-constitutive unit.[54] A scribe, John Shirley, warrants a book-length study by Margaret Connolly; the scribe-author John Capgrave warrants another by Peter Lucas.[55] A large number of studies consider medieval reading practices, especially in interpenetrating lay and clerical contexts, and especially as these involve women; Brian Stock's theories about textual communities are often central to

---

[51] I understand that Ralph Hanna III and Richard Beadle are preparing a textbook of this kind for medieval English manuscript studies, for Cambridge University Press.

[52] Hanna, 'Miscellaneity and Vernacularity', *Pursuing History*; Kerby-Fulton, 'Langland and the Bibliographic Ego' and *Books Under Suspicion*; Lerer, *Chaucer and His Readers*; Horobin, *The Language of the Chaucer Tradition*; Mooney, 'Professional Scribes?' and 'Chaucer's Scribe'; Doyle and Parkes, 'The Production of Copies'.

[53] Consider, for instance, their painstaking work on *A New Index of Middle English Verse*.

[54] Pearsall, *Studies in the Vernon Manuscript*; Fein, *Studies in the Harley Manuscript*.

[55] Connolly, *John Shirley,* and Lucas, *From Author to Audience.*

these studies.[56] Interesting work on the editing of medieval texts continues — see Siân Echard and Stephen Partridge's *Book Unbound* for instance.[57] Orietta da Rold, Mary Swan, and Elaine Treharne's project at Leicester makes manuscripts pivotal to any approach to the textual culture of the transitional period after the Norman invasion; Treharne and others have contributed important work on books before 1066 too.[58] Martha Driver's studies of the illustration of manuscripts and printed books worry cleverly at the boundaries and transition between manuscript and print, as does work on French manuscripts and early editions by Cynthia Brown.[59]

Brown suggests a second and overlapping reason for me to qualify my claim; scholarship on late-medieval French books lies at another boundary, that of the English tradition within which I work. The bias of this discussion throughout is toward English-language studies and frequently English-language books. To some extent this is consistent with the bias of discussions of the 'hot' topic of book history.[60] But it does become especially problematic in the interdisciplinary context of medieval studies. There is a long and rich palaeographical tradition in that context, one focused primarily upon Latin textual culture. Consider, for instance, Albert Derolez's important new guide to *Gothic Palaeography,* which is meant, Derolez states at the outset, to serve as a rejoinder to the assumption — implicit in much work on medieval manuscripts — that knowledge about Gothic books cannot be shared by those who study them; it can only be absorbed from the surfaces of manuscripts themselves, from a sort of monastic commitment to a life's contemplation of the parchment page.

There is also a limit to any discussion of manuscript studies that makes only brief reference to decades of work on the continent to define medieval codicology in new methodological and theoretical terms. This work includes that of Léon Gilissen, *Prolégomènes à la codicologie,* and Bernard Cerquiglini's *Éloge de la*

---

[56] Stock, *The Implications of Literacy.* See Wogan-Browne, 'Analytical Survey 5', for a survey of recent work on medieval female reading communities.

[57] See also Dagenais, 'That Bothersome Residue', on the text and its physical 'residue'.

[58] See for instance *Anglo-Saxon Manuscripts,* ed. by Richards, and important theoretical work in Foys, *Virtually Anglo-Saxon.*

[59] Da Rold, Swan, and Treharne, 'The Production and Use of English Manuscripts'; Driver, *The Image in Print;* Brown, *Poets, Patrons, and Printers.*

[60] A survey of recent work in medieval history or music might tell a different story again — starting, perhaps, with Clanchy, *From Memory to Written Record;* and Huglo, 'Codicologie et musicologie'.

variant; it is best known to scholars of the English tradition as the 'New Philology', as articulated by Stephen Nichols: 'I want to consider the medieval artifact itself, the manuscript as an historical document whose materiality constitutes precisely what the ideal texts cannot be [...] a medieval event.'[61] Andrew Taylor locates himself within this tradition; he argues with verve against the narrow focus of much work on medieval English books, and in favour of a less cautious, more imaginative, multilingual, and culturally situated approach to manuscripts (I think especially of his provocative and useful chapter on the 'Manuscript as Fetish' in *Textual Situations*.)

But having compiled this obviously incomplete list, I stand by my initial position: even together — *especially* together — these disparate studies do not constitute, or have not been taken up or even resisted as some sort of coherent approach to study of the book. Leaf through issues of journals that deal with Latin and continental books, including *Scriptorium*; *Quaerendo*; and *Revue d'histoire des textes*; or through *Studies in the Age of Chaucer*; *Speculum*; *English Manuscript Studies*; *The Journal of the Early Book Society*, *The Library*, and *Studies in Bibliography*, and you will find plenty of work on medieval books, but scant evidence of a fully articulated, debated, and above all, *converging* definition of scholarly practice, and even less evidence that there is a relationship between medievalists' work and 'the history of books' as that field is defined here. The impression remains the one given by the introduction to the ground-breaking collection edited by Pearsall and Jeremy Griffiths in 1989, *Book Production and Publishing in England 1375–1475*: 'In the present state of scholarship, any book on publishing and book-production in England in the century before the introduction of printing is bound to be limited in its ambitions, tentative in its statements, and, to some extent or in some ways, premature.'[62] Study of the medieval book, I suggest, is still *cool*, the preserve of those who are happy with the tentative and premature, with exclusive clubs and the attractive glint in a fellow-initiate's eye.

Actually, this claim is not really bold at all, because I am not the first to make it. It is, in some part, Taylor's case for the significance of his work in *Textual Situations*. And in the introduction to their volume of essays, *Imagining the Book*, Steven Kelly and John Thompson describe it as the problem that they, and before them Hanna, detect within manuscript studies: 'If, says Hanna, medieval book

---

[61] Nichols, 'Philology and its Discontents', p. 117; see also Nichols, 'Introduction: Philology in a Manuscript Culture', and Kay's extremely helpful survey article, 'Analytical Survey 3'.

[62] *Book Production*, ed. by Griffiths and Pearsall, p. 1.

history has a highly finessed arsenal of *skills* for examining the material conditions under which manuscript books were made and disseminated, it has yet to develop *generalizable methods* for achieving what he declares is its "ultimate goal", the "contribution to large-scale cultural history".[63] The history of all sorts of books can be written in all sorts of ways, but not all book histories are created equal — some modes of inquiry are dominant. The dominant mode in book history is one that addresses a large question about the relationship between the material conditions for the production and dissemination of texts, and the society that produces and is shaped by those texts. Hanna suggests that this is the missing generalizable method, 'the cultural move' which is 'the ultimate question manuscript studies needs to face'.[64] Scholars of medieval manuscripts need to develop their own disciplinary structures if they are to make this move, and marry discreet and narrowly focused studies, technical skills, and singular theoretical approaches. What the history of the book offers to that process is an already vigorous cultural account of books; a field akin and potentially enriching to the medieval book historian's own; and a way to forestall the charge that the medieval manuscript is not a part of a larger conversation about books because its students are unwilling or unable to confront 'the demands of contemporary intellectual life'.[65]

What Is Print Culture?

If manuscript scholars engage only occasionally with the broader field, the inverse is also true: book history, as a field, pays little attention to medieval studies. This probably has as much to do with attitudes to the Middle Ages as it has to do with intellectual approaches to medieval culture (which is one of Lee Patterson's points when he discusses the 'enclave' of medieval literary studies in the article just quoted). Perhaps it is unsurprising that students of manuscripts have not adopted book history's disciplinary aims, since work done on medieval books apparently has no place in the history of the book. Howsam explains how this is so: 'for those whose interest focuses on post-Gutenberg periods in the west the compelling

---

[63] Kelly and Thompson, *Imagining the Book*, pp. 8–9, citing Hanna, 'Middle English Books' (my emphasis).

[64] Hanna, 'Middle English Manuscripts', p. 248.

[65] Patterson, 'On the Margin', p. 87.

term' is not 'book history' at all, but 'print culture'.[66] According to Darnton, the history of the book 'might even be called the social and cultural history of communication by print, if that were not such a mouthful'.[67] In Lefebvre and Martin there is no need to read past the English title: *The Coming of the Book* is *The Impact of Printing*. Book history, that is, is not just the study of the culture in which books, those human things, are made and made meaningful: it is the study of the 'print culture' in which this happens.

We may chafe at this, but it is consistent with usage of the word *book* itself, as the *OED* explains. 'Book', sense 3c, is a 'literary composition' with this qualification: 'It is not now usual to call a (modern) literary composition in manuscript a 'book', unless we think of its printing as a thing to follow in due course.' So, if I say I am writing a book, while it might never be printed, I would not say it was a 'book' if I could not, at least, imagine its printing. At some point in the past my book became 'modern': and when it did, it was not any longer just any old book; my book became 'modern' at the moment that it stopped being a 'manuscript' (the work of my hand, written or typed — see *OED*, sense 3c).

'We', medievalists, already know this story. It is the story whereby the modern is defined *as* modern, and in which this circular definition relies on the rejection of all evidence of continuity between the modern and what came before it: the premodern, the medieval, and everything pertaining to it, including its books. It would be possible to argue that the printing press and its products were, like manuscripts, medieval as well as modern technologies, relevant to both periods, located on either side of the boundary that we (and past cultures) have invented between them. But scholarly attitudes — like the uses modernity has found for the word *book* itself — preclude this possibility. It was *against* a medieval manuscript culture that print, in Elizabeth Eisenstein's famous formulation, enacted its 'revolution'.[68] If print culture, according to Arthur F. Marotti and Michael D. Bristol, 'democratically opened up texts to potentially broad and heterogeneous readerships' so that 'knowledge was liberated from the control of a social (and academic) literate elite for an increasingly literate general populace whose access to texts entailed politically charged rights of interpretation and use';[69] if print made the values of modernity, its literacies, knowledge, democracy,

---

[66] Howsam, *Old Books and New Histories*, p. 5.

[67] Darnton, "What Is the History of Books?', p. 3.

[68] Eisenstein, '*AHR Forum*'.

[69] *Print, Manuscript, Performance*, ed. by Marotti and Bristol, p. 5.

rights, and heterogeneity; or even if it was more ambiguous in its effects than this, if it made for less positive change, or effected change in complex and radically contingent ways — it always did so at the expense of the manuscript.

The study of 'print culture' as an aspect of modernity, a part of that sum of real change and persuasive fiction that constitutes the 'modern' is useful. We need to consider the nature of change if we are to achieve what Fredric Jameson describes as 'some general sense of a cultural dominant'[70] — if we are to avoid falling back on some weak idea of history as random difference. 'Print culture' is forged as and because it forgets earlier ways — some identical, some extremely different — of thinking about, and so making and using books. But it is my contention in this section of the survey that most historians of printing and modern books, even those scholars who ascribe a kind of chimerical status and a process of human invention to the idea of 'print culture', adopt the fictions about printing and modernity that they claim it is their business to interrogate, precisely because they are either uninterested by or ill-informed about that part of the story of 'print culture' that involves the preprint, premodern book. If the history of the book has become a little too close for comfort, then here is an opening: what studies of medieval books suggest — whether together they constitute a field or not — is that yoking the terms *book history* and *print culture* impoverishes the study of both.

It was Marshall McLuhan who popularized the term *print culture* in *The Gutenberg Galaxy*;[71] his work describes, in stimulating rather than precise ways, his sense that printing, like 'alphabetization', changed human consciousness. In this thesis he was followed by Walter J. Ong, who in *Orality and Literacy* argues that the history of communication properly proceeds by analysis of the cognitive effects of technological change — first writing, then print, now digitization. He also argues that writing's 'technologizing of the word' was the most drastic of these three technologies, for '[i]t initiated what print and computers only continue' — and if 'print suggests that words are things' it does so in the same essential ways that writing does (by detaching discourse from its producers) but to a different extent and thus with different effects.[72]

Ong thus obviates aspects of McLuhan's argument as he develops others: he does not adopt McLuhan's tendency to make claims about the importance of the

---

[70] Jameson, *Postmodernism*, p. 6.

[71] McLuhan, *The Gutenberg Galaxy*, p. 28.

[72] Ong, *Orality and Literacy*, pp. 82, 118.

technologies of preprint culture but to focus his attention on a postprint world. It seems to me that if someone is to be held responsible for turning McLuhan's disinterest in the culture that came before Gutenburg into the habit of a whole field, it must be Elizabeth Eisenstein. In her 1979 study, *The Printing Press as an Agent of Change*, Eisenstein makes a stronger argument than either McLuhan (who serves as her starting point) or Ong (who follows her in his work on print) for a printing 'revolution'. She does so by adding specificity to the claim that printing continued or extended the changes wrought by literacy itself. She argues that there was an abrupt increase in the number of books as the hours needed for their manufacture declined, and because the press was a commercial success that depended on mass production and wide advertisement rather than individual transactions and coterie culture. She demonstrates that mass production could itself be called revolutionary: more books, in and of themselves, produced change. Mass-produced texts could, for instance, be compared, corrected, and fixed in multiple printed copies. And the production of stable, standardized texts in a large-scale, speculative, and more profitable book trade meant that more knowledge — scientific, theological, political — was more widely disseminated in more reliable forms. The result? A Renaissance in literary culture; reformation of religion; the rise of scientific and democratic culture — and so the advance of 'Western civilization', which, as Eisenstein has lately admitted, is 'currently unfashionable' as a unit of study.[73]

Triumphalist histories of technologically determined progress are indeed out of fashion, and Eisenstein's has lately given rise to a major school of contrary thought. In his monumental study of *The Nature of the Book*, and in a printed exchange with Eisenstein in *American Historical Review* in 2002, Johns rejects the idea of a 'technological order of reality' outright.[74] His is book history as McGann's is textual criticism; it is radically socialized. In Johns's work, the book and the mechanisms for its production and distribution have meaning only in various contexts for their cultural appropriation. For instance, the printed text is reliable, 'fixed' because, by tremendous effort, printers and consumers laboured very hard to imagine and then construe it in this way. We must not attribute 'to printed books themselves attributes of credibility and persuasion that actually took much work to maintain'.[75] The gap between this and Eisenstein's argument

---

[73] Eisenstein, '*AHR Forum*', p. 88.

[74] Johns, '*AHR Forum*'; Johns, *The Nature of the Book*, p. 2.

[75] Johns, *The Nature of the Book*, p. 18.

is narrow — as Johns himself suggests. Johns accepts that with printing came changes of the sort Eisenstein describes: but in his argument agency for that change is dispersed. Change is made possible by processes of human invention that do not stop with machines; that are contingent rather than inevitable (as, I would add, the different uses found for printing in medieval Islam or Asia suggest);[76] and not necessarily 'civilizing', unless you already assume that civilization, like 'print culture' itself, is just one of the ways that Western culture is imagined and arranged.

But if Johns — and many other book historians active in the field — are correct that the bibliographical 'order of reality' is human rather than mechanical, it is difficult to see how the history of *books* is also, in any meaningful way, 'print culture' — for surely human beings worked to make an order of reality in all sorts of technological conditions before Gutenberg invented movable type. They certainly worked to make texts credible and persuasive: think, for instance, of A. J. Minnis's work on that notion of authority and those ideas about authors expressed in the context and the books of twelfth-century medieval scholastic culture.[77] Thus, when the scholar Harold Love defines 'print culture' as a noetic world constructed through print (including, but not limited to, trust in the forms of knowledge); the industrial conditions of print production and distribution; and the social relationship of reading and information management in the context of print[78] he simply begs the question — for the underlying assumption is that there is a noetic, industrial, and social meaning for the book that is specific to 'print'. Is it not at least possible that the 'world', the 'conditions', the 'relationships' that here define 'print culture' have nothing to do with printing? The difficulty in answering that question lies in distinguishing one part of a matrix of cultural meaning from another. The risk in not answering that question, however, is that the discussion of 'print culture' ceases to be a history of the 'book' and becomes, rather weakly, a history of 'culture', in which printing seems to have some particular role, but a role that is never persuasively described. The way to avert this is to answer the question: what does print do that other writing technologies do not do? The solution is to make printing a part of the story, but no longer the whole story, of the history of the *book*.

---

[76] See relevant contributions to the section 'The Book beyond the West', in *A Companion to the History of the Book*, ed. by Eliot and Rose.

[77] Minnis, *Medieval Theory of Authorship*.

[78] Love, 'Early Modern Print Culture', p. 46.

While I think that in their brilliant studies of that tradition of early-modern manuscript production — including commercial production — that continued after the advent of printing, Love, and Arthur Marotti, Peter Beal, and Henry Woudhuysen, go some way toward making this argument, I do not think they go far enough. They have enabled scholars of print culture to arrive at some sensible conclusions: 'Print did not replace manuscript circulation or production: as is the case today, the new technology supplemented earlier ones, partially or largely replacing them for some functions, reinforcing them for others.'[79] But 'print' is still the beginning of this way of thinking about books — the context that makes manuscript circulation interesting. At its most extreme, the discussion of manuscripts in terms of print becomes the position taken by Peter Stallybrass in a forthcoming book that printing *invented* the manuscript. Before printing, he suggests (at least in the version of his argument, as I understand it, presented at the Toronto Centre for the Book, 2007) who could have compelled the sort of literacy that was made compulsory by bureaucratic forms? Who would have thought to buy an empty book for personal use? How could anyone raise significant sums by the sale of blank indulgences? Or vest a written document with the authority vested in the hands of its writers? Indeed, who could have conceived of the manuscript — a word first recorded in English a century or so after printing? The problem with this is that it muddles two quite different processes: the process whereby modernity defines itself as a print culture and 'invents' the print/manuscript distinction as a way of thinking about books; and the process whereby writing became important to culture, which process was changed by, but also independent of print. The rise of a medieval bureaucracy and economy based on written records; dependent on a new class of clerks and scriveners; using documents for revenue gathering — thousands of indulgences for instance;[80] and in which the much-contested authority for utterance was vested more and more in writing itself (signatures, the hands of notaries) is discussed in Michael Clanchy's *From Memory to Written Record: England 1066–1307.* The *MED* tells us that the word *book,* by the turn of the fifteenth century, could refer to those blank books, distinct from 'rolls', in which bailiffs or merchants, students, all manner of folk kept notes and records. Paper and

---

[79] Barnard, 'Introduction', p. 1.

[80] Clanchy discusses government rather than ecclesiastical bureaucracy: for some of the literature on the centrality of indulgences to medieval religious culture in the preprint period, see *Promissory Notes*, ed. by Swanson.

parchment 'quaiers', meaning gatherings of sheets imported or sold, were usually unbound. But a blank page folded or unfolded, bound or not, is a still a 'book' in the Middle Ages, and its blankness anticipates writing just as blankness does after the advent of print. Printing did not invent the manuscript. On the contrary, as these examples suggest, the assumptions, anxieties, changes, and exigencies of a manuscript culture were a reason for and a way to understand the invention of print. The question that remains is just how printing transformed — how it expanded and intensified, for instance — the bookish culture that gave it shape. The history that remains to be written is not about 'print culture'; it is very precisely a history of the book, in its printed and manuscript forms, in modern and premodern contexts.

My argument therefore departs from the arguments made by many of those who study postprint manuscripts. It is closer to David McKitterick's argument that there is continuity between late-medieval manuscript production and print, because printed books and manuscripts both 'depended on a visual sleight of hand in which most of the slippery manufacture was concealed' so that 'the most arresting quality of the printed word and image' is not fixity, but the fact that, like other recorded marks, 'they are simultaneously fixed, and yet endlessly mobile'.[81] My argument is that the history of the book might be written in newly illuminating ways if written about books (fixed, endlessly mobile), rather than about printing. This would reveal more about 'print culture' that any print-centric history could.

Some strung-together examples might lend weight to this claim. Alexandra Halasz's is a compelling account of the emergence, from the sixteenth to eighteenth century, of an increasingly abstract English 'marketplace for print'. But when Halasz writes that print's commercial energies in this way loosened texts from traditional centres of writing, and so authority — 'university, Crown, and Church', she falters.[82] The move from 'traditional centres' to commercial ones took place much earlier in England: in the streets of thirteenth-century Oxford, the Inns of Court by Westminster, and the artisanal and mercantile guilds of fourteenth-century London.[83] This does not undermine Halasz's case. It simply demonstrates that her argument is not about print, but about socioeconomic,

[81] McKitterick, *Print, Manuscript and the Search for Order*, pp. 118, 222.

[82] Halasz, *The Marketplace of Print*, p. 4.

[83] See Doyle and Parkes, 'The Production of Copies of the *Canterbury Tales*; Christianson, *A Directory of London Stationers*; and Blayney, *The Stationers' Company*.

technological, and cultural changes that measure the distance between two quite different marketplaces for books.

Consider other claims about the distinctive features of print culture. The trade in printed books was international, some scholars note. 'Books were imported from all over Europe. But even by the end of the seventeenth century books in English or printed in Britain could provide only a limited proportion of those needed by a serious reader', writes John Barnard in the fourth volume of the *Cambridge History of the Book in Britain*.[84] But the routes of that trade were well established by the time that Richard de Bury could refer to his continental stationers in the fourteenth-century *Philobiblon*; it is hard to see why in the third volume of the *Cambridge History*, meant to deal with the transition from manuscript to print (1400–1557), two chapters were devoted to tracing the movement of incunables from Europe to England, but so little thought was given to the question of whether this was a matter of change or continuity with manuscript culture.[85] Jan-Dirk Müller, like Marotti and Bristol, argues that cultural heterogeneity is an effect of print, because 'effective control of all production sites [...] was far beyond the capabilities of any political institutions of the time'[86] — the argument is a version of Eisenstein's that printing was the basis for religious reformation. But how is this to be reconciled with the argument of Kathryn Kerby-Fulton in *Books Under Suspicion* that the measures of censorship were less possible in Europe before the press? Print is, famously, the ground of Jürgen Habermas's idea of a public sphere — a knowledgeable, disinterested citizenry loyal to reason and the common good[87] — and of Benedict Anderson's revision of this argument (the public is partial and self-interested) in *Imagined Communities*. In each, the public is conceived in the context of the wide dissemination of printed discourse. Could we modify this not only by reference to the debate about the 'public sphere' of fifteenth-century England,[88] but also with Scase's work on the materials of medieval political dissent or Vincent Gillespie's suggestive account of the spread of edicts of the thirteenth-century Lateran Councils and Archbishop Pecham's English syllabus in the books and

---

[84] Barnard, 'Introduction', p. 6.

[85] Ford, 'Importation of Printed Books'; Needham, 'The Customs Rolls'.

[86] Müller, 'The Body of the Book', p. 34.

[87] Habermas, *The Structural Transformation*.

[88] Lawton, 'Dullness and the Fifteenth Century'; Nolan, *John Lydgate and the Making of Public Culture*.

preaching of English clerics?[89] It seems likely that printed books reached more widely, more deeply into communities than could the oral and manuscript forms of medieval texts. Print historians, confronted by evidence that many of the so-called effects of print predates printing, invariably fall back on this argument.[90] But the work of William St Clair on the static real price of most books from the advent of print to the Romantic period, and Roger Chartier's observation that literacy levels barely changed in rural areas for centuries after printing belie even arguments about scale.[91] There may have been more books, but the impact of print has always been inextricable from the social conditions for the reception of books, which did not necessarily change as and when technology did. That is, historical changes may have something, but they do not have everything, to do with print. Nation, polity, 'public', and the extraordinarily pervasive notion of the individual's place in Western Christendom — these were forged in a variety of preprint textual cultures, and are worth studying in those terms.[92]

What Is a Book?

But to propose that it is the medieval book historian's job to point out that manuscripts are missing from the story of print culture may be to propose something all-too familiar. Medieval studies: the perennial wallflower at the party that the Academy keeps throwing for modernity — always whispering in the handsome early-modernist's ear, never getting a dance.[93] I do not propose this. The study of the medieval book can be a useful corrective to the most unreflective work on print culture: it might in this way address a gap in the field of book history as it is currently constituted. But since printing proves, through the examples just listed, to be an interesting technology but not one sufficiently interesting to define a field, it is perhaps more useful to consider the place of the

---

[89] Scase, 'Imagining Alternatives to the Book'; Gillespie, 'Vernacular Books of Religion'.

[90] See Eisenstein's preface to the abridged version of her famous study, *The Printing Revolution*.

[91] St Clair, *The Reading Nation*; Chartier, 'The Practical Impact of Writing'.

[92] Such inquiry is not foreign to the field: Walsham moves with effortless elegance between script and print, the medieval and early modern (see her 'Introduction: Script, Print and History'), as does much of Chartier's scholarship. The new Blackwell *Companion*, ed. by Eliot and Rose, unusually, promises to deal comprehensively with both manuscript and print.

[93] See Aers, 'A Whisper in the Ear of Early Modernists'.

medieval book at that field's definitional limits. It was my contention in the first part of this discussion that book history currently defines itself as human or cultural history. It is my contention in this section that what is missing from this definition of the field is enough thought about what it is to write a cultural or human history of the book itself.

Let me start to substantiate this claim with Chartier, who begins *The Order of Books* by reflecting that reading is 'of the order of the ephemeral'; it 'only rarely leaves traces'.[94] His comments are a reflection on a quotation from Michel de Certeau's *Practice of Everyday Life*, which forms the epigraph to his chapter:

> Far from being writers — founders of their own place, heirs of the peasants of earlier ages now working on the soil of language, diggers of wells and builders of houses — readers are travellers: they move across lands belonging to someone else, like nomads poaching their way across fields they did not write, despoiling the wealth of Egypt to enjoy it themselves. Writing accumulates, stocks up, resists time by the establishment of place and multiplies its production through the expansionism of reproduction. Reading takes no measures against the erosion of time (one forgets oneself and also forgets), it does not keep what it acquires, or it does so poorly, and each of the places through which it passes is the repetition of a lost paradise.[95]

Perhaps the passage is compelling for Chartier (and many others who cite it) not just because it describes human encounters with books, but because it gives a familiar shape to the dominant mode of inquiry in the field of book history. The ground for de Certeau's metaphorical mode here is ground itself — land, described in Western, Christian, pre-agrarian, feudal, and capitalist terms. This land is 'the soil of language'; the field is the page, everywhere marked by change and decay, the traces of the 'erosion' that constitutes the postlapsarian condition. Land is all that is there, in the place of some 'lost paradise' in which goodness and meaning are endless, perfect, and immutable. Writers, de Certeau argues, *create* something out of lack; they erect wordy edifices upon hard and barely yielding ground. And then these writers, reconceived as the producers of books as well as texts, use 'the expansionism of reproduction' to maximize their gain. Readers do nothing so productive; at least that is not how de Certeau believes that they imagine their experience. Instead they imagine, again and again, that knowledge, meaning, 'paradise' is within their grasp, and then discover, repeatedly, through the inevitable 'erosion of time', that solid ground is something they cannot possess.

---

[94] Chartier, *The Order of Books*, p. 1.

[95] De Certeau, *The Practice of Everyday Life*, p. 174.

But what *is* in readers' grasp in this way of describing textual culture is precisely what they 'forget': the books that they are reading, those things that can be piled up against the vagaries of a mutable world. Reading, Chartier tells us, belongs to the order of the ephemeral. This is true if you forget that the thing you are reading is there, as words on a page. If you recall this, then reading is involved in the same productive response to lack or absence that writing is. Reading is a way to make something; it always leaves traces; those traces are the forms of whatever is read. To cite a discussion concerned with 'New Formalism' in literary studies (to which I will return below), '[r]eading [...] quite simply produces the basic materials that form the subject matter of even the most historical of investigations.'[96]

The last section of this discussion unfolds from this point. Book history not only accommodates the study of readers, but it is itself a particular reading of culture. Not always, but not infrequently, this reading dislodges books themselves from the central place they might occupy in book historical narratives. My argument is that the book, in at least some historicized accounts of its importance and meaning, is not the evidence with which the historian works to produce an account of the past, but a sort of substitute for that past. This distinction is a fine one, but it describes, in the slightly counterintuitive terms in which the problem arises, the difference between an approach to the material survival of the past that seeks to understand the formal values of that material, and so focuses attention on the complex, even contradictory ways in which readings of texts and other cultural artefacts produce history, and an approach that latches onto material evidence as if it simply solves the problem of the past's ephemerality (the fact that it is always 'lost'). In the latter approach, the book becomes a strange sort of absence: because the concern is less with books than with the cultures that they represent in apparently uncomplicated terms.

Consider what one book historian, Zachary Lesser, has to say in his study *Renaissance Drama and the Politics of Publication*. What we have always wanted to know is 'What did these plays mean in these editions, in these specific historical moments, to these people?' Apparently book history has given us answers where other critical approaches did not. 'Reading is not completely invisible and ephemeral [...] it often does generate material traces [...]. Studies of individual readers [...] have helped to restore "actual" historical readers of texts.'[97] Lesser's

---

[96] Levinson, 'What Is New Formalism?', p. 560.

[97] Lesser, *Renaissance Drama*, pp. 4, 5.

book is a self-conscious example of what David Kastan first called 'the New Boredom' in literary studies.[98] His methodology is a part of the New Boredom because it depends first upon 'boring' bibliographical method — the slow accumulation of *Annales* school-type statistical and Genette-type paratextual evidence from editions; and second, upon 'critical interpretations' of the evidence, 'the readings of individual agents [publishers and book sellers]', which are 'boring' by critical measures that value the literary and the canonical.[99] According to Lesser, this methodology solves the problems that formal, aesthetic, poststructuralist, and even New Historicist approaches to literature invariably leave standing. If we are unable to say what 'individual agents' such as Shakespeare intended and thus 'what [...] plays mean', we can substitute other agents — publishers, as a subset of the category of 'actual' historical readers — and recover meaning that way.

Lesser's arguments are persuasive and important; he goes on to gather rich evidence of the place of the book in Renaissance dramatic culture. But here, and throughout much of book history's 'New Boredom', there is a peculiar neo-positivism at work, peculiar because it is less positive about books than the label 'neo-positivism' might suggest. But making books transparent, by making them reliable witnesses to lost pastness, much recent work in book history disregards the presence, in opaque and layered forms, of the book itself. In an early statement of what it meant to return to books in Renaissance literary studies, Peter Stallybrass and Margreta de Grazia argue that close attention to old books is to be preferred to the hermeneutic 'that the standard modern edition encourages, its legibility producing the illusion that Shakespeare can be seen through the text'.[100] In work that follows from this, the preferred mode becomes one in which the surfaces of the page, the results of statistical analysis stand in place of what we, wise critics, know that we *cannot* see: value, genius, intention. Or to put it another way, it is the rare literary scholar who would, at this juncture in critical history, claim to see Shakespeare's 'personal' touch in *Hamlet* (without spending a fair bit of time explaining what she means by 'personal'). But it is not at all unusual to find so distinguished a reader of Shakespeare's texts as Stephen Orgel writing about a copy of the *Mirror for Magistrates* annotated by Lady Anne Clifford and

---

[98] Kastan, *Shakespeare After Theory*, p. 18 (see also Matthew P. Brown, 'Book History'); Kastan does expresses some concern about the way that historicism of all kinds, including the theorized kind he advocates, 'deflects attention from the literary text itself' (p. 41).

[99] Lesser, *Renaissance Drama*, p. 23.

[100] De Grazia and Stallybrass, 'The Materiality of the Shakespearean Text', pp. 279–80.

stating that he has finds 'quite personal moments' in her marginalia.[101] In this way of doing book history, the material evidence supplied by books is not involved in any 'illusion': books, unlike texts, are just true.

But books — those ragged objects in our hands, the 'soil' with which we work — are not just true. The relationship that they bear to us, and to the publishers and readers (as well as authors) of the past *is* illusory, an aspect of the subject's 'Imaginary relationship to his or her Real conditions of existence', to quote Fredric Jameson.[102] We do not find the past simply written in books. As William H. Sherman observes, with characteristic astuteness, the notes in early-modern books actually tell us 'less than we need to do much with them'.[103] By a certainly 'sleight of hand' (McKitterick), the book, even its marginal annotations, has come to seem 'hot' and 'high definition' (McLuhan). Look more closely: you will find that the book is 'less' than this. It is full of gaps and it has few final answers. Perhaps what the field needs, instead of or at least in addition to an approach in which books are the fragmentary pieces of a reality now lost to us, is a more productive history, one that thinks more carefully about the form of books themselves and the ways that we should read these or any traces of the past.

I am proposing a more rigorously theorized history of the book here, perhaps prompted by a swell of critical writing against the routinisation of other historicisms in the field of literary studies, nicely summarized in Marjorie Levinson's 2007 PMLA survey of 'New Formalism'. I do not present a coherent alterative to current bibliographical practice; and I know it is unfair of me to suggest that the histories I have described in this survey are insensitive to the problems I raise. But I would argue that careful theorization of practice is not always characteristic of the field. It is not uncommon for the growth of book history to be described as evidence of 'the pendulum swinging away from theory', in the words of the Oxford University Press editor discussed in the 2006 *Chronicle*. Compare statements made by the editors of the journal *Book History* in their first issue: book history is especially attractive, they suggest, because of the 'exhaustion of literary theory'.[104] This might be an accurate way to describe the field, but it does not represent a helpful way to think about books: book history does not somehow sidestep the variety of dilemmas raised by 'theory'.

---

[101] Orgel, 'Marginal Maternity', p. 269.

[102] Jameson, *Postmodernism*, quoting Althusser quoting Lacan, p. 51.

[103] Sherman, 'What Did Renaissance Readers Write', p. 133.

[104] Rose and Greenspan, 'An Introduction to *Book History*', p. x.

One of the goals of Lerer and Price's 2006 special issue of *PMLA* was to redress the balance: 'What if, instead of asking what book history can do for literary criticism, we asked what literary theory can do for book history?'[105] The most provocative answer to this question comes, in their collection, in Peter D. McDonald's article, 'Ideas of the Book and Histories of Literature: After Theory?' McDonald notes that book history has an easy sort of relationship with the anti-essentialist stance of such cultural and literary theorists as Pierre Bourdieu and Stanley Fish.[106] Their arguments for the social embeddedness of cultural forms — for the socialized invention of the meaning of literature — are akin to the arguments of McGann about texts, to Johns' position on the making of 'print culture', and to the broad thrust of the 'New Boredom'. But the relationship between book history and the more formal, (post-)structuralist anti-essentialism of, say, Jacques Derrida or Maurice Blanchot is awkward. What has book history to say about Derrida's argument that texts make their own law (even as they encounter the law of other texts)?[107] Or, before Derrida, Blanchot's argument that 'poems [...] have their voice which one must hear before thinking one understands them'?[108] And if, as has been suggested lately, there is a neo- or 'New Formalism', a new interest in aesthetics and close reading in literary studies — a concern with literature's 'voice' and literariness, or with the formal dimension of all the materials with which scholars work — where does the book history stand with respect to that?[109]

I have been trying to address that question throughout this section. I argued above for focus on form, the materiality of 'books themselves'. Books have form; this form has the potential to produce meaning; this meaning is not unified or essential or separable from the conditions of its production and utilization, but nor is it exhausted by those conditions. Read closely, books challenge and disrupt the flattened routines of history, and, like literary texts, they do so at the level of their forms. Something like this observation might stand as a corrective to histories of the book that make books secondary to the story of the culture in which they were made or used.

---

[105] Price, 'Introduction: Reading Matter', p. 10.

[106] Bourdieu, *The Field of Cultural Production;* Fish, *Is There a Text in this Class?*

[107] Derrida, *Acts of Literature.*

[108] Blanchot, *A Voice from Elsewhere.*

[109] On 'Form' in medieval literary studies, see Cannon, 'Forms'.

Such an observation would also be a new way to make an old point about book history. The first challenge to Darnton's 1983 definition of the field was that of Thomas R. Adams and Nicolas Barker, who suggest that 'the weakness of Darnton's scheme is that it deals with people, rather than the book'.[110] More recently, David L. Vander Meulen has argued persuasively that in its abandonment of traditional and technical bibliographical method, book history has become a discipline which studies not books, but ideas about those books, for which there is very little bibliographical evidence.[111] Joseph A. Dane makes some comparable observations in *The Myth of Print Culture*. He observes that in the work of Lefebvre and Martin, on which the field is founded, *livre* and more specifically *livre imprimé* are abstractions. 'Livre' refers to no 'material printed book or group of them', which means that its place in the French *histoire du livre* neither real nor assailable, he argues.[112] The rather impoverished bibliographical work associated with *histoire du livre* is exemplified by Lefebvre and Martin's claim that twenty million books were printed in the incunable period. It is a claim that Dane proves as untenable as it is tenacious: what is a 'book' in Lefebvre and Martin's total, he asks? An edition, issue, new impression, *Sammelband*? What evidence is there of the size of print runs or the relative survival of copies of these books? Which catalogue, describing which books in which ways, supply the figures from which it is possible to extrapolate? One argument that follows from Dane's work especially is that book history needs its own 'New Formalism'. It needs a set of procedures that will engage it not in some neo-positivist privileging of material fact over intellectual inquiry; not in the construction of 'feebly digressive book lists' that look no further than the task of description; but in a scholarly endeavour that focuses attention on the book as an object that, as long as it exists, produces everything that we know about it.

It was D. F. McKenzie who leveled the charge of 'feeble' book-listing at descriptive bibliography in 'Bibliography and the Sociology of Texts'.[113] He also, there, gave book history perhaps its most famous maxim: 'forms effect meaning'.[114]

---

[110] Adams and Barker, 'A New Model for the Study of the Book', p. 12.

[111] Vander Meulen, 'How to Read Book History'.

[112] Dane, *The Myth of Print Culture*, pp. 30–31.

[113] One of his 1985 Panizzi lectures, first published in 1986; see McKenzie, *Bibliography and the Sociology of Texts*, p. x.

[114] McKenzie, *Bibliography and the Sociology of Texts*, p. 13.

McKenzie's has been a conspicuous absence in the survey to this point; he is missing because I wish to loosen the connection between his work and the field for which he, along with Darnton, is often assigned some sort of parental responsibility. McKenzie explicitly rejects the term *histoire du livre*. Its remit is 'too limited a field' for the history of books he proposes. The 'sociology of texts' interests him of course; he makes the argument that 'new readers make new texts and their new meanings are a function of their new forms'.[115] But his work cannot simply be conflated with *Annales*-school social history or the 'New Boredom' in literary history; the directions he proposes for the field are several. His 1986 essay on bibliography turns, for instance, on some productive new answers to questions about 'forms' — specifically an eighteenth-century copy of a poem by William Congreve, and the use of the poems by the New Critics W. K. Wimsatt and Monroe Beardsley in their article 'The Intentional Fallacy'. Wimsatt and Beardsley write against the relevance of authorial intention to literary criticism on the grounds that Congreve's (or any author's) intentions for his text are external to it, 'private or idiosyncratic; not a part of the work as a linguistic fact'.[116] Discussion of these intentions thus leads the critic away from the text. By McKenzie's reasoning, Congreve's intentions are internal to textual form; they *are* the words, the very marks that words make on the page (this capital or that use of italics). Forms effect meaning, including authorial meaning, the reader's new meaning, the meaning generated by the work of the print shop, the bookseller, the librarian. Forms — words in their particular order, punctuated like so, printed in this way — must be read, and this reading produces what we know of intention and of the text's past. If we want to write a history of 'human presence' in textual culture, we must, therefore, write a history of the book: a 'physical object put together by craftsmen [...] alive with the human judgments of its makers [...] not even in any sense "finished" until it is read'. And since this book 'is re-creatively read in different ways by different people at different times' what we will find is that 'its so-called objectivity, its simple physicality, is really an illusion'.[117] In this sense, bibliography is one way of accounting for the form and so the life and 'voice' of the texts that we write, and that we read.

---

[115] McKenzie, 'The Sociology of a Text', p. 333; McKenzie, *Bibliography and the Sociology of Texts*, p. x.

[116] Wimsatt and Beardsley, 'The Intentional Fallacy', p. 10.

[117] McKenzie, 'The Sociology of a Text', p. 34.

Much is made, at least in Middle English manuscript studies, of the medieval book's inscrutability, and its difference from all other books. This is probably one of the reasons why it is rare to find a generalizable approach in manuscript studies; the books do not lend themselves to generalizations or articulate their meaning in general terms. Hanna writes that they

> represent defiantly individual impulses — appropriations of works for the use of particular persons in particular situations. [They] may have required no explanation, the private quirks behind their manufacture being abundantly clear; certainly, the medieval disinterest not simply in expressing but even in developing any critical terminology like our own estranges us and renders the objects of our study opaque.[118]

I have just suggested that attention to the particularity of each book's forms might be a fruitful direction for the history of the book. Perhaps manuscript studies is ahead of this argument. If it would be useful to locate medieval codices in a broader cultural history of the book, it might be just as useful to hold close to the slightly disparate procedures and methods that have kept medieval scholars so attentive to matters of form. Students of medieval books are still trained in and still engage in strictly formal tasks — transcription; palaeographical description; provenance work; collation; dialect profiling; and now, thanks largely to Linne R. Mooney, the profiling of scribal hands. It seems to me that, so long as the typically complex and fractured information yielded is not mistaken for 'objectivity', these processes constitute a way to think freshly about the history of the medieval book, and the history of the book as a field.

And it seems to me, as well, that medieval thought about books has something to contribute to a bibliographical history interested in the relationship between forms and meaning. The very word *book* in the Middle Ages recognizes the interesting ways in which the voice of the text and the shape of the object that bears it are involved in the production of meaning. A 'modern' book, the *OED* explains, can be a text (I say that I read a 'book' last night, and so on). But the *OED* also explains that in modern usage this text that is a book is always — or about to be — printed, as if it is knowable only through the technological and social processes that determine its history. Not so in Old and Middle English usage: there, 'books' are always — or about to be — the many and various parts of a rich textual culture. 'Book-land' is *chartered* land; men might make a 'book' of Troilus's life, he realizes 'like a *storie*'; a miracle was wrought 'swa swa boc us *sæʒð*

---

[118] Hanna, 'Miscellaneity and Vernacularity', p. 37.

(my emphasis).[119] Medieval books have shifting shapes; they speak and are spoken; they are rolled, told, crafted, invented, and imagined. A metrical epilogue to Cambridge, Corpus Christi College, MS 41, an early-eleventh-century Old English *Bede* depends on the word's flexible and conflated senses:

> Bidde ic eac   æghwylcne mann,
>
> brego, rices weard,   þe þas boc ræde
>
> and þa bredu befo,   fira aldor,
>
> þæt gefyrðrige þone writre   wynsum cræfte
>
> þe ðas boc awrat   bam handum twam.[120]

(I ask also every person, prince, guardian of the kingdom, leader of men, who may read this book and clasp the boards, that he promote the writer who, with joyful skill, wrote this book with both [of his] two hands.)

The poem is explicitly concerned with the 'boc', which here means the text and the book-as-object, crafted, wrought as well as written, by the hands of the writer. Together, because they cannot be separated, book and text produce all that we know about the writer, 'þe ðas boc awrat', and about the reader, the accusative 'mann [...] þe þas boc ræde'. This poem says that it has been written; that it is meant to be read; that this reading is made possible by the forms of the text-as-book; and that this reading matters. All of that seems to me like a good starting point for any history of the book.

University of Toronto

---

[119] See *MED*, s.v. 'bok'; *Troilus*, in *Riverside Chaucer*, ed. by Benson, V, 585.

[120] Dobbie, *The Anglo-Saxon Minor Poems*, p. 113.

Bibliography

Adams, Thomas R., and Nicolas Barker, 'A New Model for the Study of the Book', in *A Potencie of Life: Books in Society; The Clark Lectures 1986–1987*, ed. by Nicolas Barker (London, 1993), pp. 5–43

Aers, David, 'A Whisper in the Ear of Early Modernists; or, Reflections on Literary Critics Writing the "History of the Subject"', in *Culture and History 1350–1600: Essays on English Communities, Identities, and Writing*, ed. by David Aers (Detroit, 1992), pp. 177–202

Amory, Hugh, and David D. Hall, eds, *Bibliography and the Book Trades: Studies in the Print Culture of Early New England* (Philadelphia, 2004)

Anderson, Benedict, *Imagined Communities*, rev. edn (London, 1991)

Barnard, John, 'Introduction', in *The Cambridge History of the Book in Britain*, IV: *1557–1695*, ed. by John Barnard, D. F. McKenzie, and Maureen Bell (Cambridge, 2002), pp. 1–25

Beal, Peter, *In Praise of Scribes: Manuscripts and Their Makers in Seventeenth Century England* (Oxford, 1998)

Belanger, Terry, 'Descriptive Bibliography', in *Book Collecting: A Modern Guide*, ed. by Jean Peters (New York, 1977), pp. 97–115

Benson, Larry, ed., *The Riverside Chaucer*, 3rd edn (Boston, 1987)

Bishop, Edward L., 'Book History', in *The Johns Hopkins Guide to Literary Theory and Criticism*, ed. by Michael Groden, Martin Kreiswirth, and Imre Szeman, 2nd edn (Baltimore, 2005), <http://litguide.press.jhu.edu>

Blanchot, Maurice, *A Voice from Elsewhere*, trans. by Charlotte Mandell (Albany, NY, 2007)

Blayney, Peter W. M., *The Stationers' Company before the Charter, 1403–1557* (London, 2003)

Boffey, Julia, *Manuscripts of English Courtly Love Lyrics In The Later Middle Ages* (Cambridge, 1985)

——, and A. S. G. Edwards, *A New Index of Middle English Verse* (London, 2005)

Bollème, Geneviève, Marie Boussy, and others, *Livre et société dans la France du XVIIIᵉ siècle*, 2 vols (Paris, 1965, 1970)

Bourdieu, Pierre, *Homo Academicus,* trans. by P. Collier (Stanford, 1988)

——, *The Field of Cultural Production: Essays on Art and Literature*, ed. by Randal Johnson (Cambridge, 1993)

Bowers, Fredson, *The Principles of Bibliographical Description* (Princeton, 1949)

Boyle, Leonard E., *Medieval Latin Palaeography: A Bibliographical Introduction* (Toronto, 1984)

Bringhurst, Robert, *The Elements of Typographic Style*, 2nd edn (Point Roberts, WA, 1996)

Brooks, Dougals, *From Playhouse to Printing House: Drama and Authorship in Early Modern England* (Cambridge, 2000)

——, ed., *Printing and Parenting in Early Modern England* (Aldershot, 2005)

Brown, Cynthia J., *Poets, Patrons, and Printers: Crisis of Authority in Late Medieval France* (Ithaca, 1995)

Brown, Matthew P., 'Book History, Sexy Knowledge, and the Challenge of the New Boredom', *American Literary History*, 16 (2004), 688–706

de Bury, Richard, *The Love of Books: The Philobiblon of Richard de Bury*, ed. and trans. by E. C. Thomas (London, 1913)

Cannon, Christopher, 'Forms', in *Oxford Twenty First-Century Approaches to Literature: Middle English*, ed. by Paul Strohm (Oxford, 2007), pp. 177–90

Cerquiglini, Bernard, *Éloge de la variante: histoire critique de la philology* (Paris, 1989)

Chartier, Roger, 'Frenchness in the History of the Book: From a History of Publishing to a History of Reading', *Proceedings of the American Antiquarian Society*, 97 (1987), 299–329

——, 'The Practical Impact of Writing', in *A History of Private Life*, III: *Passions of the Renaissance*, ed. by Roger Chartier, trans. by Arthur Goldhammer (Cambridge, MA, 1989), pp. 111–59

——, *The Order of Books: Readers, Authors, and Libraries in Europe between the Fourteenth and Eighteenth Centuries,* trans. by Lydia G. Cochrane (Stanford, 1994)

Christianson, C. Paul, *A Directory of London Stationers and Book Artisans, 1300–1500* (New York, 1990)

Clanchy, M. T., *From Memory to Written Record: England 1066–1307,* 2nd edn (Oxford, 1993)

Clegg, Cyndia, 'History of the Book: An Undisciplined Discipline?', *Renaissance Quarterly*, 54 (2001), 221–45

Connolly, Margaret, *John Shirley: Book Production and the Noble Household in Fifteenth-Century England* (Aldershot, 1998)

Da Rold, Orietta, Mary Swan, and Elaine Treharne, 'The Production and Use of English Manuscripts 1060 to 1220', Arts and Humanities Research Council-Funded Project, University of Leicester (2005–), <http://www.le.ac.uk/ee/em1060to1220/index.htm>

Dagenais, John, 'That Bothersome Residue: Toward a Theory of the Physical Text', in *Vox Intexta: Orality and Textuality in the Middle Ages*, ed. by A. N. Doane and Carol Braun Pasternak (Madison, 1991), pp. 246–59

Dane, Joseph A., *The Myth of Print Culture: Essays on Evidence, Textuality and Bibliographical Method* (Toronto, 2003)

Darnton, Robert, 'What Is the History of Books?', in *Books and Society in History*, ed. by Kenneth E. Carpenter (New York, 1983), pp. 3–26

de Certeau, Michel, *The Practice of Everyday Life*, trans. by Steven F. Rendall (Berkeley and Los Angeles, 1984)

de Grazia, Margreta, and Peter Stallybrass, 'The Materiality of the Shakespearean Text', *Shakespeare Quarterly*, 44 (1993), 255–83

De Hamel, Chritopher, *The Book: A History of the Bible* (London, 2001)

Denning, Michael, *Mechanic Accents: Dime Novels and Working-Class Culture in America* (London, 1987)

Derolez, Albert, *The Palaeography of Gothic Manuscript Books from the Twelfth to the Early Sixteenth Century* (Cambridge, 2003)

Derrida, Jacques, *Acts of Literature*, ed. by Derek Attridge (London, 1992)

Dibdin, Thomas Frognall, *The Bibliographical Decameron*, 3 vols (London, 1817)

Dobbie, E. V. K., *The Anglo-Saxon Minor Poems*, Anglo-Saxon Poetic Records, 6 (New York, 1942)

Doyle, A. I. 'A Survey of the Origins and Circulation of Theological Writings in English in the Fourteenth, Fifteenth, and Early Sixteenth Centuries with Special Consideration of the Part of the Clergy Therein', 2 vols (unpublished doctoral dissertation, University of Cambridge, 1953)

——, and Parkes, M. B., 'The Production of Copies of the *Canterbury Tales* and the *Confessio Amantis* in the Early Fifteenth Century', in *Medieval Scribes, Manuscripts and Libraries: Essays Presented to N. R. Ker*, ed. by M. B. Parkes and Andrew Watson (London, 1978), pp. 163–210

Driver, Martha W., *The Image in Print: Book Illustration in Late Medieval England and Its Sources* (London, 2004)

Echard, Siân and Stephen Partridge, eds, *The Book Unbound: Editing and Reading Medieval Manuscripts and Texts* (Toronto, 2004)

Eisenstein, Elizabeth L., *The Printing Press as an Agent of Change: Communications and Cultural Transformations in Early Modern Europe*, 2 vols (Cambridge, 1979)

——, '*AHR Forum*: An Unacknowledged Revolution Revisited', *American Historical Review*, 107.1 (2002), 87–105

——, *The Printing Revolution in Early Modern Europe*, 2nd edn (Cambridge, 2005)

Eliot, Simon, and Jonathan Rose, eds, *A Companion to the History of the Book*, Blackwell Companions to Literature and Culture (London, 2007)

Fein, Susanna, ed., *Studies in the Harley Manuscript: The Scribes, Contents, and Social Contexts of British Library MS. Harley 2253* (Kalamazoo, 2000)

Finkelstein, David, and Alistair McCleery, *An Introduction to Book History* (New York, 2005)

——, and Alistair McCleery, Alistair, eds, *The Book History Reader* (New York, 2002; rev. edn 2006)

Fish, Stanley, *Is There a Text in this Class? The Authority of Interpretive Communities* (Cambridge, MA, 1980)

Flint, Kate, *The Woman Reader, 1837–1914* (Oxford, 1993)

Ford, Margaret Lane, 'Importation of Printed Books into England and Scotland', in *The Cambridge History of the Book in Britain*, III: *1400–1557*, ed. by Lotte Hellinga and J. B. Trapp (Cambridge, 1999), pp. 179–201

Foucault, Michel, 'What Is an Author?', in *Textual Strategies: Perspectives in Post-Structuralist Criticism*, ed. by Josué V. Harari (Ithaca, 1979), pp. 141–60

Foys, Martin K., *Virtually Anglo-Saxon: Old Media, New Media, and Early Medieval Studies in the Late Age of Print* (Gainesville, 2007)

Gardiner, Juliet, 'Recuperating the Author: Consuming Fictions in the 1990s', *Papers of the Bibliographical Society of America*, 94 (2000), 255–74

Gaskell, Philip, *A New Introduction to Bibliography* (Winchester, 1979; repr. with corrections 1995)

Genette, Gérard, *Paratexts: Thresholds of Interpretation*, trans. by Jane E. Lewin (Cambridge, 1997)

Gerson, Carole, and Jacques Michon, eds, *The History of the Book in Canada*, III: *1918–1980* (Toronto, 2007)

Gilissen, Léon, *Prolégomènes à la codicologie* (Ghent, 1977)

Gillespie, Vincent, 'Vernacular Books of Religion', in *Book Production and Publishing*, ed. by Griffiths and Pearsall, pp. 317–44

Gladwell, Malcolm, 'The Coolhunt', in *Life Stories: Profiles from the New Yorker*, ed. by David Remnick (New York, 2001), pp. 468–81

Grafton, Anthony, 'The Humanist as Reader', in *A History of Reading in the West*, ed. by Guglielmo Cavallo and Roger Chartier, trans. by Lydia G. Cochrane (Cambridge, 1999), pp. 179–212

Greetham, D. C., *Textual Scholarship: An Introduction* (New York, 1992)

Greg, W. W., *The Editorial Problem in Shakespeare: A Survey of the Foundations of the Text*, 3rd edn (Oxford, 1954)

Griffiths, Jeremy, and Derek Pearsall, eds, *Book Production and Publishing in England 1375–1475* (Cambridge, 1989)

Habermas, Jürgen, *The Structural Transformation of the Public Sphere* (Cambridge, 1989)

Halasz, Alexandra, *The Marketplace of Print: Pamphlets and the Public Sphere in Early Modern England* (Cambridge, 1997)

Hall, David D., and John B. Hench, eds, *Needs and Opportunities in the History of the Book: America, 1639–1876* (Worcester, 1987)

Hanna, Ralph, III, 'Miscellaneity and Vernacularity: Conditions of Literary Production in Late Medieval England', in *The Whole Book: Cultural Perspectives on the Medieval Miscellany*, ed. by Stephen G. Nichols and Siegfried Wenzel (Ann Arbor, 1996), pp. 37–51

——, *Pursuing History: Middle English Manuscripts and their Texts* (Stanford, 1996)

——, 'Middle English Books and Middle English Literary History', *Modern Philology*, 102 (2004), 157–78

——, 'Middle English Manuscripts and the Study of Literature', *New Medieval Literatures*, 4 (2004), 243–64

Hellinga, Lotte, and J. B. Trapp, eds, *The Cambridge History of the Book in Britain*, III: *1400–1557* (Cambridge, 1999)

Hindman, Sandra L., ed., *Printing the Written Word: The Social History of Books, circa 1450–1520* (Ithaca, 1991)

Horobin, Simon, *The Language of the Chaucer Tradition* (Cambridge, 2003)

Howard, Jennifer, 'At the MLA, Publishers Discuss What's New', *Chronicle of Higher Education* (13 January 2006), <http://chronicle.com/weekly/v52/i19/19a01701.htm>

Howsam, Leslie, *Old Books and New Histories: An Orientation to Studies in Book and Print Culture* (Toronto, 2006)

Hudson, Anne, 'The Variable Text', in *Crux and Controversy in Middle English Textual Criticism*, ed. by A. J. Minnis and Charlotte Brewer (Cambridge, 1992), pp. 49–60

Huglo, Michel, 'Codicologie et musicologie', in *Miscellanea codicologica F. Masai: dicata MCMLXXIX*, ed. by Pierre Cockshaw, Monique-Cécile Garand, and Pierre Jodogne, 2 vols (Ghent, 1979), I, 71–82

Jackson, H. J., *Marginalia: Readers Writing in Books* (New Haven, 2001)

Jameson, Fredric, *Postmodernism, or, the Cultural Logic of Late Capitalism* (Durham, 1991)

Johns, Adrian, *The Nature of the Book: Print and Knowledge in the Making* (Chicago, 1998)

——, '*AHR Forum*: How to Acknowledge a Revolution', *American Historical Review*, 107.1 (2002), 106–25

Kastan, David Scott, *Shakespeare After Theory* (New York, 1999)

Kay, Sarah, 'Analytical Survey 3: The New Philology', *New Medieval Literatures*, 3 (1999), 295–326

Kelly, Stephen, and John J. Thompson, eds, *Imagining the Book*, Medieval Texts and Cultures of Northern Europe, 7 (Turnhout, 2005)

Kerby-Fulton, Kathryn, 'Langland and the Bibliographic Ego', in *Written Work: Langland, Labor, and Authorship*, ed. by Kathryn Kerby-Fulton and Steven Justice (Philadephia, 1997), pp. 67–143

——, *Books Under Suspicion: Censorship and Tolerance of Revelatory Writing in Late Medieval England* (Notre Dame, 2006)

Kwakkel, Erik, 'A New Type of Book for a New Type of Reader: The Emergence of Paper in Vernacular Book Production', *The Library*, ser. 7, 4 (2003), 219–48

Lawton, David, 'Dullness and the Fifteenth Century', *English Literary History*, 54 (1987), 761–99

Lefebvre, Lucien Paul Victor, and Henri-Jean Martin, *L'Apparition du Livre* (Paris, 1958); published in English as *The Coming of the Book: The Impact of Printing 1450–1800*, ed. by Geoffrey Nowell-Smith and David Wootton, trans. by David Gerard (London, 1976)

Lerer, Seth, *Chaucer and His Readers* (Princeton, 1993)

——, 'Epilogue: Falling Asleep over the History of the Book', *PMLA*, 121.1 (2006), 229–34

Lesser, Zachary, *Renaissance Drama and the Politics of Publication: Readings in the English Book Trade* (Cambridge, 2004)

Levinson, Majorie, 'What is New Formalism?', *PMLA*, 122 (2007), 558–69

Loewenstein, Joseph, *The Author's Due: Printing and the Prehistory of Copyright* (Chicago, 2002)

——, *Ben Jonson and Possessive Authorship* (Cambridge, 2002)

Love, Harold, *The Culture and Commerce of Texts: Scribal Publication in Seventeenth-Century England* (Amherst, 1998)

——, 'Early Modern Print Culture: Assessing The Models', *Parergon*, 20 (2003), 45–64

Lucas, Peter J., *From Author to Audience: John Capgrave and Medieval Publication* (Dublin, 1997)

Maguire, Laurie E., 'How Many Children Had Alice Walker?', in *Printing and Parenting in Early Modern England*, ed. by Douglas Brooks (Aldershot, 2005), pp. 327–50

Marotti, Arthur F., *Manuscript, Print, and the English Renaissance Lyric* (Ithaca, 1995)

——, and Michael D. Bristol, eds, *Print, Manuscript, Performance: The Changing Relations of the Media in Early Modern England* (Columbus, 2000)

Masten, Jeffrey, *Textual Intercourse: Collaboration, Authorship, and Sexualities in Renaissance Drama* (Cambridge, 1997)

McDonald, Peter D., 'Ideas of the Book and Histories of Literature: After Theory?', *PMLA*, 121.1 (2006), 214–28

McGann, Jerome J., *A Critique of Modern Textual Criticism* (Chicago, 1983)

——, *The Textual Condition* (Princeton, 1991)

McGill, Meredith L., *American Literature and the Culture of Reprinting, 1834–1853* (Philadelphia, 2002)

McHenry, Elizabeth, *Forgotten Readers: Recovering the Lost History of African American Literary Societies* (Durham, 2002)

McKenzie, D. F., 'The Sociology of a Text: Orality, Literacy and Print in Early New Zealand', *The Library*, ser. 6, 6 (1984), 333–65

——, *Bibliography and the Sociology of Texts* (Cambridge, 1999)

McKerrow, R. B., *An Introduction to Bibliography for Literary Students* (Oxford, 1927)

McKitterick, David, *Print, Manuscript and the Search for Order, 1450–1830* (Cambridge, 2003)

McLeod, Randall, 'UN-Editing Shak-Speare', *Sub-stance*, 33–34 (1982), 26–55

McLuhan, Marshall, *The Gutenberg Galaxy: The Making of the Typographic Man* (Toronto, 1962)

——, *Understanding Media: The Extensions of Man* (New York, 1964)

Minnis, A. J., *Medieval Theory of Authorship: Scholastic Literary Attitudes in the Later Middle Ages*, 2nd edn (London, 1984)

Mooney, Linne R., 'Professional Scribes? Identifying English Scribes Who Had a Hand in More Than One Manuscript', in *New Directions in Later Medieval Manuscript Studies: Essays from the 1998 Harvard Conference*, ed. by Derek Pearsall (Cambridge, 2000), pp. 131–41

——, 'Chaucer's Scribe', *Speculum*, 81 (2006), 97–138

Morgan, Nigel J., and Rodney M. Thomson, eds, *The Cambridge History of the Book in Britain*, II: *1100–1400* (Cambridge, 2007)

Müller, Jan-Dirk, 'The Body of the Book: The Media Transition from Manuscript to Print', in *Materialities of Communication*, ed. by Hans Ulrich Gumbrecht and K. Ludwig Pfeiffer, trans. by William Whobrey (Stanford, 1994), pp. 32–44

Needham, Paul (1999), 'The Customs Rolls and the Printed-Book Trade', in *The Cambridge History of the Book in Britain*, III: *1400–1557*, ed. by Lotte Hellinga and J. B. Trapp (Cambridge, 1999), pp. 148–63

Nichols, Stephen G., 'Introduction: Philology in a Manuscript Culture', *Speculum*, 65 (1990), 1–10

——, 'Philology and its Discontents', in *The Future of the Middle Ages: Medieval Literature in the 1990s*, ed. by William D. Paden (Gainesville, 1994), 113–41

Nolan, Maura, *John Lydgate and the Making of Public Culture* (Cambridge, 2005)

Ong, Walter J., *Orality and Literacy: The Technologizing of the Word* (London, 1982)

Orgel, Stephen, 'Marginal Maternity: Reading Lady Anne Clifford's *A Mirror for Magistrates*', in *Printing and Parenting in Early Modern England*, ed. by Douglas Brooks (Aldershot, 2005), pp. 267–89

Patterson, Lee, 'On the Margin: Postmodernism, Ironic History and Medieval Studies', *Speculum*, 65 (1990), 87–108

Pearsall, Derek, 'The Value/s of Manuscript Study: A Personal Retrospect', *Journal of the Early Book Society*, 3 (2000), 167–81

——, *Studies in the Vernon Manuscript* (Cambridge, 1990)

Petrucci, Armando, *Prima Lezione di Paleografia* (Rome, 2002)

Price, Leah, 'Introduction: Reading Matter', *PMLA*, 121.1 (2006), 9–16

Raven, James, *The Business of Books: Booksellers and the English Book Trade, 1450–1850* (New Haven, 2007)

Richards, Mary P., ed., *Anglo-Saxon Manuscripts: Basic Readings*, Basic Readings in Anglo-Saxon England 2 (New York, 1994)

Roman, Luke, 'The Representation of Literary Materiality in Martial's 'Epigrams'', *Journal of Roman Studies*, 91 (2001), 113–45

Rose, Jonathan, and Ezra Greenspan, 'An Introduction to *Book History*', *Book History*, 1 (1998), ix–xi

——, 'Book History Still Smokin'', message to *Society of the History of Authorship, Reading and Publishing Listserv* (17 July 2006)

Rose, Mark, *Authors and Owners: The Invention of Copyright* (Cambridge, MA, 1993)

Rubin, Jean Shelley, 'What Is the History of the History of Books?', *Journal of American History*, 90 (2003), 555–75

Scase, Wendy, 'Imagining Alternatives to the Book: The Transmission of Political Poetry in Late Medieval England', in *Imagining the Book*, ed. by Kelly and Thompson, pp. 239–51

Secord, James, *Victorian Sensation: The Extraordinary Publication, Reception and Secret Authorship of 'Vestiges of the Natural History of Creation'* (Chicago, 2000)

Sherman, William H., 'What Did Renaissance Readers Write in Their Books?', in *Books and Readers in Early Modern England: Material Studies*, ed. by Jennifer Andersen and Elizabeth Sauer (Philadelphia, 2002), pp. 119–37

Simpson, James, *Reform and Cultural Revolution: The Oxford English Literary History*, II: *1350–1547* (Oxford, 2002)

Stallybrass, Peter, 'Printing and the Invention of the Manuscript,' Toronto Centre for the Book Lecture (Toronto, 4 October 2007)

St Clair, William, *The Reading Nation in the Romantic Period* (Cambridge, 2004)

Stock, Brian, *The Implications of Literacy: Written Language and Models of Interpretation in the Eleventh and Twelfth Centuries* (Princeton, 1983)

Sutherland, Kathryn, ed., *Electronic Text: Investigations in Method and Theory* (Oxford, 1997)

Swanson, R. N., ed., *Promissory Notes on the Treasury of Merits: Indulgences in Late Medieval Europe* (Leiden, 2006)

Tanselle, G. Thomas, *A Rationale of Textual Criticism* (Philadelphia, 1989)

Taylor, Andrew, *Textual Situations: Three Medieval Manuscripts and Their Readers* (Philadelphia, 2002)

Tenner, Edward, 'The Prestigious Inconvenience of Print', *Chronicle of Higher Education*, 9 March 2007, <http://chronicle.com/subscribe/login?url=http%3A%2F%2Fchronicle.com%2F weekly%2Fv53%2Fi27%2F27b00701.htm>

Thompson, John J., *Robert Thornton and the London Thornton Manuscript: British Library MS Additional 31042* (Cambridge, 1987)

Turner, Michael, and Michael Suarez, eds, *The Cambridge History of the Book in Britain*, V: *1695–1830* (Cambridge, forthcoming)

Vander Meulen, David L., 'How to Read Book History', *Studies in Bibliography*, 56 (2003–04), 171–93

Veeser, H. Aram, ed., *The New Historicism* (New York, 1989)

Vincent, Marvin Richardson, *A History of the Textual Criticism of the New Testament* (New York, 1899)

Wall, Wendy, *The Imprint of Gender: Authorship and Publication in the English Renaissance* (Ithaca, 1993)

Walsham, Alexandra, 'Introduction: Script, Print and History', in *The Uses of Script and Print 1300–1700*, ed. by Alexandra Walsham and Julia Crick (Cambridge, 2003), pp. 1–26

Wimsatt, W. K., and Monroe C. Beardsley, 'The Intentional Fallacy', in *The Verbal Icon: Studies in the Meaning of Poetry* (Kentucky, 1954), pp. 3–18

Winkler, Karen J., 'In Electronic Age, Scholars Are Drawn to Study of Print', *Chronicle of Higher Education*, 14 July 1993, <http://chronicle.com/che-data/articles.dir/articles-39.dir/issue-45.dir/45a00101.htm>

Wogan-Browne, Jocelyn, 'Analytical Survey 5: 'Reading is Good Prayer': Recent Research on Female Reading Communities', *New Medieval Literatures*, 5 (2002), 229–97

Woudhuysen, H. R., *Sir Philip Sidney and the Circulation of Manuscripts 1558–1640* (Oxford, 1996)

——, and Michael Suarez, *The Oxford Companion to the Book* (Oxford, forthcoming)